AF906197

International Law in Asia

Series Editor

Eric Yong Joong Lee, YIJUN Institute of International Law, Seoul, Korea (Republic of)

This series aims to provide the latest perspectives on international law in this ever changing region of Asia. Each book of this series will address specific aspect of highly contemporary global issues such as armed conflict, maritime disputes, human rights and refugee crises, sustainable development/climate change, outer space, finance and economy, trade (WTO and FTA), investment, development, technology, intellectual property, international crime, global health, regional questions, etc.

This book series invites leading international law scholars and practitioners in Asia to contribute their expertise in interpreting a wide range of legal questions that arise in relation to the above topics through an Asian lens. This series will serve as useful guide for international lawyers, diplomats, businessmen and students to understand current and future trends of international law in Asia.

Shen Wei
Editor

International Investment Law at the Juncture

An Asian Perspective

Springer

Editor
Shen Wei
KoGuan School of Law
Shanghai Jiao Tong University
Shanghai, China

ISSN 2731-8044 ISSN 2731-8052 (electronic)
International Law in Asia
ISBN 978-981-97-2182-5 ISBN 978-981-97-2183-2 (eBook)
https://doi.org/10.1007/978-981-97-2183-2

© The Editor(s) (if applicable) and The Author(s), under exclusive license to Springer Nature Singapore Pte Ltd. 2024

This work is subject to copyright. All rights are solely and exclusively licensed by the Publisher, whether the whole or part of the material is concerned, specifically the rights of translation, reprinting, reuse of illustrations, recitation, broadcasting, reproduction on microfilms or in any other physical way, and transmission or information storage and retrieval, electronic adaptation, computer software, or by similar or dissimilar methodology now known or hereafter developed.
The use of general descriptive names, registered names, trademarks, service marks, etc. in this publication does not imply, even in the absence of a specific statement, that such names are exempt from the relevant protective laws and regulations and therefore free for general use.
The publisher, the authors and the editors are safe to assume that the advice and information in this book are believed to be true and accurate at the date of publication. Neither the publisher nor the authors or the editors give a warranty, expressed or implied, with respect to the material contained herein or for any errors or omissions that may have been made. The publisher remains neutral with regard to jurisdictional claims in published maps and institutional affiliations.

This Springer imprint is published by the registered company Springer Nature Singapore Pte Ltd.
The registered company address is: 152 Beach Road, #21-01/04 Gateway East, Singapore 189721, Singapore

Paper in this product is recyclable.

Preface

International investment law is at a juncture. Foreign direct investment (FDI) still has not recovered from the global financial crisis but has been badly hit by the COVID-19 pandemic. The rise of developing and transitional economies in outbound FDI is reshaping the FDI landscape leading to more restrictive and conservative regulatory measures toward FDI evidenced by the national security review mechanisms which now have been adopted by most developed countries. The wide spread of the national security review mechanisms toward outbound FDI worsens the neo-liberalism-based international investment law. This book captures this historical moment in the investment arena with a focus on Asia.

Given a more conservative FDI regulatory move and a more intensive geopolitical struggle, it is not a surprise to see a return of the state (which actually started right after the global financial crisis) or a revival of the Calvo Doctrine at least in more South states. It is not merely about more emphasis on police power or the host state's right to regulate in the BIT terms. Rather, not only some developing countries but also more developed countries are now skeptical of international investment law, bilateral investment treaties (BITs) and investor-state dispute settlement (ISDS) system as a whole. As a result, more countries are now abandoning ISDS in free trade agreements (FTAs) or denouncing BITs completely.

Jiang and Li's article first outlines several mainstream lines of arguments analyzing international investment law. Western countries often justify foreign investors' right to arbitrate and right for protection by arguing that BIT terms play as constitutional terms binding host state governments. When Western countries are not shifting their role in the investment arena becoming the major recipient of FDI and more often brought by foreign investors into the investment arbitration cases, they are now arguing for more rights to regulate and claiming that a more balanced approach is desirable. While Shan's article argues that the Calvo Doctrine is not dead, Shen and Feng's article discusses the return of the Calvo Doctrine and explains the background of this return. These three articles rightly draw a picture to the readers and tell the readers the past, the present and the future of international investment law.

Despite the restrictive regulatory move, international investment law, like the WTO law, is now more concerned about human rights including but not limited to environmental protection, labor rights, climate change and corporate social responsibility. Some BITs and FTAs even cover anti-corruption. Qi and Liu's article discusses how carbon neutrality becomes a topic or even a term in BITs.

The next five articles focus on the ISDS's legitimacy crisis and possible reforms. Various reform plans have been proposed and their pros and cons are discussed in some details in these articles. There is no quick action plan in the near future, but some ideas have been put in ink in some new BITs or FTAs. EU is taking a driver's seat, while Asia countries are hesitant waiting for others to move forward first. Li and Shen's article looks at the ISDS reform from a political economy lens. Labin and Soloveva allow us to understand Russia's stance in the ISDS reform. Lee offers a unique picture of Korea's ISDS proceedings in its treaty with the US. Zhao switches from arbitration to mediation which is said to be a valid alternative for future ISDS reform. Zhang's article gives us a sense of China's role in its BIT-making and ISDS reform.

In the last article, Leong gives us a quick update on Macao and its ambition to draw more FDI in its financial sector. Macao is always viewed Asia's Las Vagas and its potential and ambition is worth discussing in a larger picture.

This book has an ambitious agenda to offer more Asian perspectives. This may be a challenging target to meet given the wide span of countries in Asia. It would be interesting to include articles on Japan, ASEAN countries, and central Asian states, among others. This may be the topic of the next book.

Last but not the least, I want to thank all authors for their grateful contribution to this book and the respective publishers' consents (where relevant). I also want to acknowledge and is grateful for the support of the Singapore International Dispute Resolution Academy's BRI program. Professor Eric Lee initiated this project and offered his help throughout the whole publication process. Springer's editing and publishing team is also helpful in making this book happen. I look forward to the readers' comments and criticisms which would make us give more thoughts to the future of international investment law or even globalization as a whole.

Shanghai, China — Shen Wei
The New Year Evening 2024

Contents

Chapter 1
Pluralism, Cosmopolitanism, or International Economic Law Constitutionalism

Tao Li and Zuoli Jiang

Introduction

When discussing scholarship in the area of international economic law ('IEL'), there is a man whose work cannot be ignored. He is Ernst-Ulrich Petersmann, an Emeritus Professor at the European University Institute. Professor Petersmann is well-known for his decades of efforts in developing a monolithic theoretical base for IEL. His writings cover various issues, including the reform of the UN,[1] the future of the world trading system,[2] and the de-fragmentation of international law regimes.[3] However, the instruments he has employed for analyzing those issues are basically unchanged, namely Western constitutionalism theory in conjunction with human rights law. He has thereby developed an IEL constitutionalization theory,[4] which, in his own words, has long been neglected by citizens and governments, to correctly understand the game rules of their participation in the global division of labor.[5]

[1] See, e.g., Petersmann (1997).

[2] See, e.g., Petersmann (2014).

[3] See, e.g., Petersmann (2015).

[4] For a detailed introduction to Petersmann's academic profile, see Marise Cremona et al., *Preface*, *in* Reflections on the constitutionalization of international economic law: liber amicorum for ernst-ulrich petersmann (Marise Cremona et al. eds.), (2014).

[5] Petersmann (2012).

T. Li (✉)
Associate Professor, Law School, Hebei University of Economics and Business, Shijiazhuang, China
e-mail: lawyerlitao@126.com

Z. Jiang
Professor, Law School, Shandong University, Jinan, China

© The Author(s), under exclusive license to Springer Nature Singapore Pte Ltd. 2024
S. Wei (ed.), *International Investment Law at the Juncture*, International Law in Asia,
https://doi.org/10.1007/978-981-97-2183-2_1

The authors believe that Petersmann's theory is paradoxical. On the one hand, he posits that the universal recognition of human rights requires "respect for legitimate 'legal pluralism'" and "respect for the legitimate diversity of 'constitutional pluralism.'"[6] On the other hand, he argues for a cosmopolitan conception of IEL by saying, "Non-hierarchical legal relationships between diverse national and international legal sub-systems must be coordinated and clarified on the basis of 'universalizable' principles of justice, human rights, deliberative democracy, transnational rule of law and other common constitutional principles like judicial comity."[7] Therefore, the question that arises is whether there are such 'universalizable' principles and common constitutional principles that can guarantee the compatibility between 'legal pluralism' and a cosmopolitan conception of IEL. Or, to put it another way, is Petersmann's IEL constitutionalization theory coherent in terms of the interrelationship between 'legal pluralism' and the cosmopolitan conception of IEL? This article aims to inquire into this issue.

The logic and rationality of the development of the above thesis must be explained in a few more words. Professor Petersmann has frequently presented the words 'multilevel governance,' 'multilevel judicial protection,' 'multilevel cooperation,' and 'multilevel constitutionalism' to clarify that his theory covers national, regional, and transnational subsystems of IEL. However, his theoretical sources come primarily from Kant, Rawls, and other Western philosophers, and his empirical support is mainly drawn from European culture.[8] Petersmann has given much less consideration to the thought and practice in non-English speaking countries, including China, as a world member that plays an increasingly important role in global economic development. Hence, inquiry is necessary as to whether the Western-style constitutional conception of IEL is representative of a global understanding and whether the constitutionalization experience in Europe exhibits a world-wide tendency. In addition to the multilevel coverage of his theory, a number of keywords are repeatedly used in Prof. Petersmann's writings, including 'human rights,' 'principles of justice,' 'judicial protection of individual rights,' 'interdependent public goods,' 'participatory democracy,' 'rule of law,' 'cosmopolitan rights,' and 'overlapping consensus.' The authors consider the first three, which constitute the skeleton of Petersmann's IEL constitutionalization theory, the most important. By focusing on the clarification of these three keywords in the context of traditional Chinese thought and China's progressive integration into the world economy, this article will also attempt to make a contribution to improving the discourse on IEL constitutionalism.

---

[6] Id. at 16.

[7] Id.

[8] According to Prof. Petersmann's own words, IEL constitutional elements "are more developed in European law than in other international legal systems." See id. at 3.

Human Rights

A. Human Rights as a Foundation of Petersmann's IEL Constitutionalization Theory

Petersmann regards human rights law as the foundation of the development of IEL in the twenty-first century.[9] Under the premise that human rights were a 'Western invention'[10] and that North America and Europe have different priorities in the protection of human rights,[11] he pays inadequate attention to the interpretation and realization of human rights in China. For the purpose of better clarification and comparison, a recap of Petersmann's articulation in this regard is needed.

Petersmann's understanding of human rights can be epitomized in two words, i.e., individualism and antagonism. Individualism is embedded in his argument for reinterpreting and redesigning IEL by "treating citizens as subjects and 'democratic principals' of international economic regulation of mutually beneficial economic cooperation among citizens."[12] He thinks that the prevailing conception of IEL as "international law among states" to promote national interests cannot be justified in view of its "failures to prevent unnecessary international poverty, banking crises, financial and environmental crises"[13] and that the human rights obligations of all UN member states require an IEL paradigm shift by constitutionalizing IEL to better protect citizen interests. Antagonism is reflected in his repeated comments about "rivalry among individuals, groups and people."[14] Following the Westphalian mode of international economic regulation in which governments and rent-seeking interest groups would often abuse public and private power to the detriment of general consumer welfare, he contends that "human rights and other 'principles of justice' may justify 'struggles for rights' by citizens and parliaments for additional legal, parliamentary and judicial 'checks and balances' of intergovernmental regulation."[15]

Petersmann acknowledges the significance of economic, social, and cultural human rights as well as that of civil and political human rights, which are indivisible in his view. More importantly, in line with the EU tradition but not congruent with human rights specialists in common law states, he attaches greater importance to economic freedoms as fundamental rights.[16] In his earlier work, *Constitutional Functions and Constitutional Problems of International Economic Law*, Petersmann explained the problem of protectionism in domestic foreign trade regulation as a constitutional problem and called for direct application of the GATT rules in domestic courts to

[9] Petersmann (2012).

[10] Petersmann, *supra* note 5, at 240.

[11] Id. at 23.

[12] Id. at 74.

[13] Id. at 4.

[14] Id. at 35.

[15] Id. at 144.

[16] Id. at 173–74.

constitutionalize arbitrary foreign trade policy, thereby protecting individual rights.[17] In view of the fact that market freedoms as fundamental individual rights have gained judicial protection in the EC and played an important role in market integration, he contends that market freedoms "can reinforce and extend the protection of basic human rights."[18] Based on the position that human rights law and economic integration law offer mutually beneficial synergies, he recommends connecting human rights law with the law and practice of intergovernmental organizations.[19] Relying on Kantian and Rawlsian theories of justice to justify the maximum equal liberties in citizen-driven competition and international trade, he argues for legitimizing many state-centered, power-oriented regimes of international economic governance in light of the citizen-oriented principles of human rights law.[20] The authors hold the opinion that this understanding of economic freedoms, notably trade freedom, is the primary impetus behind his entire theory of IEL constitutionalization.

B. Human Rights in Chinese Thought

The Chinese characters 'renquan 人权,' a generally accepted translation of the English term 'human rights,' was never used in the Chinese literature before the late nineteenth century.[21] However, this does not mean that traditional Chinese thought cares less about respect for human dignity. In fact, Chinese philosophy has a particular expression for topics similar to the modern meaning of human rights. Early Confucians provided the basis of Chinese thought on human rights, which can be summarized as regarding the people as the foremost. Confucius said, "If the people have plenty, their prince will not be left to want alone. If the people are in want, their prince cannot enjoy plenty alone."[22] Mencius noted, "Within a state, the people are the foremost, the state comes second, and the ruler is the least important."[23] Xunzi also said, "The monarch is a boat, while the people are water; the water bears the water, but it can also swallows it up."[24] The Confucian thought of regarding the people as the foremost emphasizes that only if the monarch cares for the wellbeing of the people can the monarchy be maintained. However, the key point of this thought

---

[17] See Petersmann (1991).

[18] Petersmann (2002).

[19] Id. at 621. Petersmann's view of economic freedoms as fundamental rights triggered an academic debate on the relationship between trade liberalization and human rights protection in 2002. See P. Alston, *Resisting the Merger and Acquisition of Human Rights by Trade Law: A Reply to Petersmann*, 13 EUR. J. INT'L L. 815, 815–44 (2002); R. Howse, *Human Rights in the WTO: Whose Rights, What Humanity? Comment on Petersmann*, 13 EUR. J. INT'L L. 651, 651–59 (2002); E. U. Petersmann, *Taking Human Dignity, Poverty and Empowerment of Individuals More Seriously: Rejoinder to Alston*, 13 Eur. J. Int'l L. 845, 845–51 (2002).

[20] Petersmann, *supra* note 5, at 139.

[21] Xiangfei (2008).

[22] Confucius, The Analects, Book Xii Yen Yuan, Chap. Ix. See James Legge, The Chinese Classics: With a Translation, Critical and Exegetical Notes, Prolegomena, and Copious Indexes (I & Ii), at 255 (2001).

[23] Mencius, The Works of Mencius, Tsin Sin Part Ii, Chap. Iv. See Id. At 483.

[24] Xunzi, Xunzi (Wang Weiwei Trans. &Annot.), At 63 (2014).

is in the ruler's obligation to the people rather than the positive rights the people may have.[25] Petersmann also properly compares the two boat stories in the works of Xunzi and Plato, saying that the people in the Chinese story are not capable of steering, whereas in the Western story, the people, who are on the same boat with the ruler, own 'constituent power'.[26]

Traditional Chinese thought admits the significance of people's desires for fulfilling lives,[27] which is somewhat akin to Petersmann's emphasis on economic freedoms. Huang Zongxi said, "The people as a whole should benefit," but he did not say to "protect the interests of every individual."[28] Traditional Chinese propriety requires a man to love others with virtues. Therefore, in traditional Chinese thought, people should think of others rather than compete for limited resources. Chinese society is explained as a human community; when people seek to attain what they desire, they have a duty to ensure that others get what they want.[29] Even when the 1890 reformers talked about *minquan* 民权 (people's authority) drawing on the Western concept of 'rights,' they thought of the authority of the people as a group rather than that which can be shared by every individual.[30]

Contemporary Chinese scholars think that cultural traditions have a significant influence on the conception of human rights. As opposed to the individual-centered culture in the West, traditional Chinese culture stresses the indivisibility of individuals, families, and the state, which has fostered a Chinese conception of human rights that prioritizes the rights to subsistence and development and underpins collective rights.[31] All in all, Chinese thought on human rights emphasizes the wellbeing of the people and their utmost significance to the state, but it does not encourage individuals' competition with others and state power. In this sense, Chinese thought on human rights stands in sharp contrast with the individualism and antagonism reflected in Petersmann's human rights understanding.

C. Evolution of Free Trade Right in China as an Illustration of Human Rights Development in China

The Chinese Constitution amended in 2004 declares for the first time that "the state respects and protect human rights."[32] Before then, however, some 'fundamental rights' have been confirmed in it, including voting right,[33] freedom of speech,[34]

---

[25] S. C. Angle, *Human Rights and Chinese Thought: A Cross-Cultural Inquiry* (Cambridge; New York: Cambridge University Press, 2002), at 125.

[26] Petersmann (2016).

[27] ANGLE, *supra* note 25, at 93–98.

[28] Id. at 126.

[29] Id. at 96–97.

[30] Id. at 126.

[31] Xianming (1999).

[32] The Standing Committee of the National People's Congress of the PRC (SCNPC), Zhonghua Renmin Gongheguo Xianfa [The Constitution of the PRC] 2004, art. 33.

[33] Id. art. 34.

[34] Id. art. 35.

personal dignity,[35] and labor right.[36] In the same year, the amended Foreign Trade Law of China also confirms Chinese citizens' foreign trade freedom, though it still has not been recognized as a 'fundamental right' in the Chinese Constitution. Considering that economic freedoms, notably trade freedom, are emphasized in Petersmann's theory, we concentrate on the evolution of Chinese citizens' free trade right in the context of China's progressive liberalization of foreign trade governance, which can be divided into four phases as follows.

1949–1978: State Monopoly

In the beginning, the Chinese Communist Party ('CCP') adopted an economic policy featuring all-around central planning and control as a countermeasure to an economic blockade and embargo imposed by the West. Consequently, a foreign trade policy emphasizing control by the central government came into being. Private foreign trade organizations were gradually eliminated, so all foreign trade transactions were ultimately handled by state corporations under the direct control and supervision of the government pursuant to a master plan. During this period, individuals and private corporations were completely deprived of foreign trade rights.[37]

1978–1992: Tentative Reform

After the Cultural Revolution (1966–76), China entered into a new era accentuating reform and development. As the economy was dragged carefully away from the former stringent planning system, foreign trade policy became less rigid as well. To promote foreign trade growth, a series of tentative reform measures were carried out, including the devolvement of foreign trade operational rights to local branches and the diversification of trade business organs. However, foreign trade was then a privilege of state-owned corporations, which were essentially an arm of the government. Individuals and private corporations were not yet allowed to engage in this industry.[38]

1992–2001: Preliminary Liberalization

During this period, a socialist market economy was confirmed by the CCP as the development goal of China,[39] and the political leaders strongly supported China's

---

[35] Id. art. 38.

[36] Id. art. 42.

[37] The Common Programme (interim Constitution) of the PRC proclaimed on 1 October 1949 make clear that the state implements foreign trade control and adopts protectionist trade policy. See also Ma Fengqin, Zhongguo Duiwa i Maoy i Zhengce Yu Guanli [China's Foreign Trade Policies and Management], at 11–12 (1995).

[38] Shen Muzhu, Zhongguo Duiwai Maoyi Falv [China's Foreign Trade Law], at 8–10 (1989). See also Sally Lord Ellis, *Decentralization of China's Foreign Trade Structures,* 11 Georgia J. Int'l & Comp. L. 283, 284 (1981).

[39] See Zhonggong Zhongyang guanyu Wanshan Shehuizhuyi Shichang Jingji Tizh iRuogan Wenti de Jueding [The Decision of the CCP Central Committee on Relevant Issues concerning Improving the Socialist Market Economy System] (October 2003), http://www.gov.cn/test/2008-08/13/content_1071062.htm.

accession to the GATT-WTO system. To satisfy the accession requirement, preliminary efforts were made to bring its legal system into consistency with the GATT-WTO rules. As a result, the first Foreign Trade Law went into force as of 1 July 1994. This law purported to maintain a fair and liberalized foreign trade order and to safeguard the business autonomy of foreign trade dealers.[40] However, this law also set forth the basic requirements for a foreign trade dealer. In particular, it required permission from the competent authorities.[41] Therefore, foreign trade right was subjected to government license, which, in fact, excluded individuals and most private corporations from this industry.

2001-:Complete Conferral of Foreign Trade Right

After fifteen years of prolonged negotiations, China became the 143rd member of the WTO on December 11, 2001. Additionally, the Foreign Trade Law was amended in April 2004. This amendment clearly stated the protection of the legitimate rights and interests of foreign trade dealers[42] and recognized individuals as subjects of foreign trade dealers.[43] Furthermore, in line with the requirement of China's Protocol of Accession, the amendment changed the previous licensing requirement to the current registration requirement for obtaining foreign trade rights.[44] In this sense, free trade right has been completely conferred to Chinese citizens from that time.

From the above overview of the evolution of foreign trade rights in China, the CCP policymakers significantly pushed forward this historical process according to the international and domestic environment. Although those reform policies, notably the conferral of foreign trade freedom, have sometimes been reflected in laws, the legislator approving those laws is essentially an extended branch of the CCP bureaucracy,[45] meaning the laws are hardly an outcome of participatory democracy. To put it another way, this is not a process of 'struggles for rights' as advocated by Petersmann.[46] Even without such 'struggles for rights,' however, the Chinese people are largely better off, along with China's progressive integration into the world. The Chinese people were not unhappy, even with the government's overall decision-making in a less democratic mode during the past four decades. In contrast, by purporting to "represent…the fundamental interests of the overwhelming majority

---

[40] SCNPC, Zhonghua Renmin Gongheguo Duiwai Maoyi Fa [Foreign Trade Law of the PRC] 1994, art. 4.

[41] Id. art. 9.

[42] SCNPC, Zhonghua Renmin Gongheguo Duiwa i Maoy i Fa [Foreign Trade Law of the PRC] 2004, art. 1.

[43] Id. art. 8.

[44] Id. art. 9.

[45] For example, among the 175 members of the 10thCNPC, which is also the legislator of the 2004 Amendment of the Foreign Trade Law, 118 were from the CCP, making the CCP the predominant component. See Zhang Tao, *Dishijie Quanguo Renda Changweihui Zuchengrenyuan Jiegou Fenxi: Zhuyao Tedianyu Jiegou Fenxi [An Analysis of the Constituent Structure of the 10th SCNPC: Main Characteristics and Development Tendency]*, 7 Dangdai Zhongguo Zhengzhi Yanjiu Baogao [Contemporary Chinese Politics Review] 78, 80(2009).

[46] E. U. Petersmann, *supra* note 5, at 144.

of the Chinese people,"[47] the CCP obtained external legitimacy for its ruling. As the Three-Step Development Strategy has illustrated,[48] the people's lives are always the primary concern, which is bound up with state development. In short, the evolution of foreign trade freedom in China is a modern embodiment of traditional Chinese thought on human rights, which is characterized by regarding the people as the foremost, while abating individualism and antagonism.

Principles of Justice

A. Petersmann's Theory of Justice for IEL

Petersmann's elaboration on justice for IEL is a mixture of Kantian and Rawlsian theories on justice and human rights law, as illustrated in the three principles of justice he suggested.[49] Inspired by Kant's extension of the constitutional conception of law to international law,[50] Petersmann asserts that "maximum equal freedoms as a first principle of justice ...... has become a matter of positive national and international law"[51] In particular, he implies that worldwide 'market freedoms' may be defined as cosmopolitan expansions of Rawls' first principle of justice.[52] In contrast to Rawls' refusal to extend his 'difference principle' from liberal nations to the international level, Petersmann opines that deepening globalization and modern human rights law may provide convincing reasons for a cosmopolitan 'second principle of justice.'[53] Borrowing Kant's phrase the 'moral imperative,' Petersmann recommends "multi-level constitutional protection of a just cosmopolitan order" as the third principle of justice, given that citizens agree on the constitutional principles of justice.[54] In toto,

[47] See NPC, Zhonghua Renmin GongheguoXianfa [Constitution of the PRC] 2004, Preamble.

[48] The Three-Step Development Strategy is China's overall economic development objective from 1980s to the middle of the twenty-first century: step one is to double the 1980 GNP and ensure that the people have enough food and clothing; step two is to quadruple the 1980 GNP by the end of the twentieth century and ensure the Chinese people a well-off life; step three is to increase per-capita GNP to the level of the medium-developed countries by the mid-twenty-first century and to ensure the Chinese people a wealthy life. See ZHAO Ziyang, Yanzhe You ZhongguoTese de Shehuizhuyi Daolu Qianjin: Zai Zhongguo Gongchan Dang Dishisanci Quanguo Daibiao Dahuishang de Baogao [Walk on the Road to Socialism with Chinese Characteristics: Report Delivered at the 13th National Congress of the CCP] (1987), http://cpc.people.com.cn/GB/64162/64168/64566/65447/4526368.html.

[49] See PETERSMANN, *supra note 5, at 355–371.*

[50] See Petersmann, *supra* note 5, at 164.

[51] Petersmann (2003).

[52] Petersmann, *supra* note 9, at 307.

[53] Petersmann, *supra* note 5, at 361.

[54] However, the inevitable nature of certain normative disagreements is the major concern in Rawls' later work. See John Rawls, *The Idea of Public Reason Revisited*, 64 U. CHI. L. REV. 765, 798–805 (1997).

economic freedoms, equality, and human rights are the three major components of Petersmann's theory of justice for IEL.

It seems that Petersmann has not provided fully convincing reasoning on how to institutionalize the 'cosmopolitan public reason' in multilevel economic governance by endorsing the three principles of justice; in other words, there might be an internal tension in his arguments for 'economic freedoms' and for 'a just cosmopolitan order.' In line with the Kantian acknowledgement of man's selfish tendencies purportedly contributing to a law-governed social order,[55] Petersmann stresses the importance of citizens' transnational market competition free of abuses of public and private power. However, in a transnational market where wide-ranging disagreements among billions of people should be respected when they compete for their own interests, how can the 'overlapping consensus' on a constitutionally justified 'cosmopolitan order' be attained? Brexit shows that there are certain people who are antagonistic to the idea of a single European market. With the new Trump administration, which has successfully echoed the voices of low-income people (rather than some protectionist groups) to suspend trade liberalization, the US is likely to take a more conservative view on economic globalization. Although Petersmann mentioned the 'Arab spring' to demonstrate poor people's 'struggle for justice' for the purpose of establishing a justified national and international legal system, its consequence was multiple wars, political instability, and economic decline in the Arab region, with little freedom seen. All these landscapes would imply that it is difficult to arrive at an 'overlapping consensus' on the constitutionalization of IEL from Petersmann's advocating of economic freedoms.

B. Social Justice in Chinese Thought

Petersmann is congruent with Rawls insofar as they favor 'reasonable rules and institutions' over natural resources.[56] According to traditional Chinese thought, however, all institutional arrangements are subject to the feelings and assessment of mankind, and social justice and its realization are no exception. That is, regardless of whether social justice is to be realized by putting the Rawlsian, utilitarian, or any other theory of justice into practice, a good development of the moral sense of mankind is the most important thing. According to this idea, no matter how reasonable and justified a social institutional arrangement is, a man without a righteous heart can always maximize his own interests by craftily seizing advantages. In contrast, even in an authoritarian society, a controller of the public power with good moral sense can do justice to the society by carrying out social governance that can promote social development while benefitting the least advantaged. Consequently, traditional Chinese thought is more concerned with the issue of men's hearts than institutional problems; it believes that justice emanates from an innate disposition rather than from external rules. Only when the people have self-conscience in social justice

[55] I. Kant, *Idea for a Universal History with a Cosmopolitan Purpose, in* Kant, Political Writings *(Hans Reiss ed.) (1970).*

[56] Petersmann, *supra* note 5, at 156.

can the rules and institutions play a concrete role in maintaining social justice more effectively. A Confucian classic states,

> The ancients, who wished to illustrate illustrious virtue throughout the kingdom, first ordered well their own States. Wishing to order well their States, they first regulated their families. Wishing to regulate their families, they first cultivate their persons. Wishing to cultivate their persons, they first rectified their hearts. Wishing to rectify their hearts, they first sought to be sincere in their thoughts ...... From the Son of Heaven down to the mass of the people, all must consider the cultivation of the person the root of everything besides.[57]

Confucian philosophers believed in oneness between the natural world and the human world. Xunzi said, "The nature has its own intrinsic rules, which is not subject to meritocracy or tyranny of a monarch."[58] Therefore, people were taught to regard themselves as an integral part of nature and to accord themselves with nature by acting in conformity with the rules of nature. Confucian thought regards harmony as fundamental in interpersonal relationships[59]; in terms of the interactions between people and the state, a collective sense of promoting stability and solidarity is emphasized. Nevertheless, harmony does not mean the denial of diversity and difference. As reflected in the saying that "harmony gives birth to all things while being the same leads to no development,"[60] harmony is based on pluralistic coexistence, whereas justice is not tantamount to egalitarianism. As a reflection of this harmonious worldview and the emphasis on self-cultivation, Chinese thought has constantly emphasized keeping *yi* 義 in mind when looking for benefits.[61] Confucius said, "Riches and honours acquired by unrighteousness, are to me as a floating cloud."[62] Hence, if there is a clash between *yi* and 利 benefits, it is suggested to practice *yi* and to ignore benefits.

C. Social Justice Practiced in China

The whole process of China's opening-up and progressive integration into the world economic system is also a way to realize social justice. In the late 1970s, China began to open its doors to the outside world by putting forward preferential policies to draw in foreign investment.[63] Its subsequent arduous efforts in entering into the WTO system revealed a strong will to "develop equal and mutually beneficial

---

[57] The Great Learning *in* The Book of Rites. See LEGGE, *supra* note 22, at 357–59.

[58] Xunzi, *supra* note 24, at 166.

[59] Confucius, The Analects, Book I Hsio R, Chap. XII (saying that application of the rites is for harmony. See LEGGE, *supra* note 22, at 143.

[60] ZuoQiuming, Guoyu [Discourses Of The States] (Zhang Yongxiang trans. &annot.), at 322 (2015).

[61] Yi is a Confucian virtue roughly equivalent to righteousness or justice in English.

[62] Confucius, The Analects, Book VII Shu R, Chap. XV. See LEGGE, *supra* note 22, at 200.

[63] The preferential policies have been reflected in several Chinese laws, including Zhonghua Renmin Gongheguo Zhongwa iHeziJingying Qiye Fa [Law of the PRC on Chinese-Foreign Equity Joint Ventures], Zhonghua Renmin Gongheguo Zhongwai Hezuo Jingying Qiye Fa [Law of the PRC on Chinese-Foreign Contractual Joint Ventures], and Zhonghua Renmin Gongheguo Waizi Qiye Fa [Law of the PRC on Wholly Foreign-owned Enterprises]. The former two were adopted in July 1979, and the third was adopted in April 1986.

economic cooperation with various countries."[64] The results following these efforts are splendid: China has risen onto the world stage; hundreds of millions of Chinese people come out of impoverishment; and China has made a positive contribution to world development.[65] This process strongly proves the correctness of China's belief in the oneness and harmonious nature of the world.

Some might think, as expressed by Petersmann,[66] that it is the WTO system that plays a major role in helping China alleviate poverty. However, insofar as the social justice it has brought about is concerned, this process complies with an indigenous Chinese tradition rather than a Western-fashioned liberal way. In the early stage of modern China's economic reform, China faced a large population, a weak economic foundation, and unbalanced development. China has since strived to find its own way to development by "feeling the stones before crossing the river"[67] instead of completely adopting some kind of "reasonable rules and institutions." This way is an exact exemplification of the traditional Chinese holism concept in terms of its consistent stress on collective flourishing, namely not merely the prosperity of the state but also the richness of the people.[68]

Following China's accession into the WTO, the 2004 Chinese Constitution clarified that the state protects the lawful rights and interests of the individual[69] and that the lawful private property of citizens may not be encroached upon.[70] In this regard, the Chinese socialist market economy has not been developed by predominantly relying on citizens' struggles for economic freedom.[71] Instead, it has always been directed by a master plan, as illustrated by the periodically updated Five-year Guidelines for Development.[72] Undoubtedly, this is not a way to realize social justice as

---

[64] See Zhongguo Gongchan Dang Dishiyijie Zhongyang Weiyuanhui Disanci Quanti Huiy iGongbao [Gazette of the 3rd Plenary Session of the 11th Central Committee of the CCP] (2009), http://www.gov.cn/test/2009-10/13/content_1437683.htm.

[65] It is estimated that China will still contribute to global economic growth in future years. See OECD, *Looking to 2060: A Global Vision of Long-Term Growth' OECD Economics Department Policy Notes, No 15*, (November 2012), https://www.oecd.org/eco/outlook/2060policynote.pdf.

[66] Petersmann (2011).

[67] See Chen Yun, Chen Yun Wen Xuan [Selected Essays of Chen Yun], Vol. 3, at 279 (1986) (stating that reforms must be carried out on the basis of careful initiative and the instant summarization of experience).

[68] See Xijinping, Zai Dishierjie Quanguo Renmin Daibiao Dahui Diyic iHuiyishang de Jianghua [Speech on the First Session of the 12th National People's Congress] (March 17, 2013), http://news.xinhuanet.com/2013lh/2013-03/17/c_115055434.htm.

[69] SCNPC, Zhonghua Renmin Gongheguo Xianfa [The Constitution of the PRC] 2004, art. 11.

[70] Id. art. 13.

[71] The distinctiveness of the Chinese market economy can be indirectly perceived by the continuing denial of a market economy status by the EU and the US even after a15-year period expired after China's accession to the WTO. See Request for Consultations by China, *United States—Measures Related to Price Comparison Methodologies*, WT/DS515/1 (December 12, 2016); Request for Consultations by China, *European Union—Measures Related to Price Comparison Methodologies*, WT/DS516/1 (December 12, 2016).

[72] Five-year Guidelines (Plans) are formulated by the CCP through the plenary sessions of the Central Committee and passed by national congresses. The ongoing 13th Five-year Guideline runs from 2016 to 2020 and includes such goals as fostering green industry, bridge the

perceived by Rawls or Petersmann, especially given that China allowed some people to get rich 'first'.[73] However, due to China's well-designed development plan, 1.1 billion people have gone out of poverty,[74] which would be seen as a great achievement for global justice.[75] In addition, as China attaches more importance to 'rule of virtue'[76] and pays more attention to the problem of wealth inequality, traditional Chinese thought on *yi* will play a more important role in achieving social justice.

At the global level, the "Belt and Road" Initiative is a China-promoted public good for regional cooperation and development. It has been inspired by the ancient Chinese Silk Road spirit: "peace and cooperation, openness and inclusiveness, mutual learning and mutual benefit."[77] As discerned from its commitment to cooperation, harmony, inclusiveness, and mutual benefit,[78] the "Belt and Road" Initiative is another exemplification of the traditional Chinese view of a harmoniously co-progressing world. With regard to the implementation of this strategy, cooperation priority is given to facilities' connectivity, i.e., to "jointly push forward the construction of international trunk passageways, and form an infrastructure network connecting all sub-regions in Asia, and between Asia, Europe and Africa step by step."[79] China will share with other countries its experience in infrastructure construction and related investment as an engine for economic development. In this sense, the "Belt and Road" Initiative is much like an extension of Chinese 'virtues' based on China's 'self-cultivation.' This is an exact illustration of Confucius' saying, "The man of perfect virtue, wishing to be established himself, seeks also to establish others; wishing to be enlarged himself, he seeks also to enlarge others."[80]

---

existing welfare gaps, and deep participation in global economic governance. See Zhonghua Renmin GongheguoDishisangeGuominJingji he ShehuiFazhanDishisangeWunianGuihuaGangyao [The 13th Five-year Guidelines for Economic and Social Development of the PRC], http://news.xinhuanet.com/politics/2016lh/2016-03/17/c_1118366322.htm.

[73] See Deng Xiaoping, Deng Xiaoping Wen Xuan [Selected Essays Of Deng Xiaoping], VOL. 3, at 155 (2001) (stating that subject to the principle of common prosperity, a part of the people and regions are allowed to get rich first to prompt other people and other regions to get rich).

[74] Xinhua, President Xi Jinping's UN speech in 6 key words (September 28, 2015), http://www.xinhuanet.com/english/china/2015-09/29/c_134672436.htm.

[75] For poverty and inequality as a major issue in global justice, see Frank J. Garcia, *Trade and Inequality: Economic Justice and the Developing World*, 21 Mich. J. Int'l L. 975, 975–1049 (2000).

[76] See Xinhua, *Xi Stresses Integrating Law, Virtue in State Governance* (December 10, 2016), http://news.xinhuanet.com/english/2016-12/10/c_135895641.htm.

[77] See National Development and Reform Commission of the PRC, Vision and Actions on Jointly Building Silk Road Economic Belt and 21st-Century Maritime Silk Road (Mar. 28, 2015), http://en.ndrc.gov.cn/newsrelease/201503/t20150330_669367.html.

[78] See id.

[79] See id.

[80] Confucius, The Analects, Book Vi Yung Yey, Chap. Xviii. See Legge, *supra* note 22, at 194.

Judicial Protection of Individual Rights

A. Multilevel Judicial Protection of Individual Rights in IEL as Designed by Prof. Petersmann

Judicial protection of individual rights is another facet of Petersmann's IEL constitutionalization theory. Within a nation state, the legislature, the executive, and the judiciary are all important branches for safeguarding constitutionalization in light of the original meaning of the word 'constitution.' Within the global community, however, there is not yet a world government. How will citizens' constitutional rights be protected at the global level? To resolve this issue, Petersmann attaches significance to courts of justice, which he considers "the most independent guardians of the constitutional rights of citizens."[81]

Drawing on the experience of European courts in interpreting IEL for individual interests, Petersmann calls for extending this methodology to other parts of the world.[82] Although it is difficult to understand Petersmann's articulation of this point, the authors would address rough clues in his writings as follows. First, the universal recognition of human rights provides constitutional justification for the connection and coordination between national and international legal systems and judicial procedures for peaceful dispute settlement on the basis of judicial clarification of 'principles of justice.'[83] Second, constitutional nationalism must be complemented by multilevel constitutionalism by empowering individuals adversely affected by international economic regulation with 'access to justice' in national and international judicial procedures.[84] Third, judicial interpretation of IEL in compliance with human rights law has the potential to enhance legal coherence in worldwide governance institutions and to decrease legal fragmentation among national and transnational legal regimes.[85]

B. A Comparison from the Perspective of Chinese Judicial Thought and Practice

Historically, China has no tradition of separation of powers between the executive and the judiciary, mainly because there was little inherent calling for such separation due to the country's stress on social harmony. Additionally, a precondition for Petersmann's vision of multilevel judicial protection of individual rights in IEL is the independence of courts of justice and arbitral tribunals at the national and international levels. Without a strong force calling for judicial independence in the current anarchic world, it is difficult to assure adjudication of cases in strict compliance with the so-called 'principles of justice,' including respect for human rights.

[81] Petersmann, *supra* note 9, at 291.

[82] Petersmann, *supra* note 5, at 456.

[83] Petersmann, *supra* note 5, at 438–39.

[84] Petersmann, *supra* note 5, at 445.

[85] Petersmann, *supra* note 9, at 313.

"Rule of virtues" is an important teaching of Confucianism. By advocating "government exercises by means of virtue,"[86] Confucius attached greater importance to moral sense than man-made rules in adjusting the relationship between people, with a view toward "causing the people to have no litigations."[87] This approach fits with the Confucian thought of regarding the people as the foremost, in terms of its respect for the people as a whole and its reliance on human nature. The prioritized pursuance of harmony in Confucian thought entails a prevalent anti-ligation mindset among Chinese people. In the Protocol on China's WTO accession, China provides a guarantee for all specific administrative cases to be reviewed by an impartial and independent judicial body.[88] In conformity with this undertaking, the Supreme People's Court makes clear that the adjudication of administrative cases relating to antidumping and countervailing investigations shall be handled by at least an intermediate court.[89] Subsequent to the promulgation of these judicial interpretations, however, no relevant cases have yet been brought to these courts, indicating a persistent anti-litigation mindset regarding China's foreign trade regulation today.[90] In contrast, mediation, as an alternative dispute-settlement mechanism focusing on conciliation based on the disputants' own will, plays an important role in Chinese judicial practice. Compared to litigation, mediation has its advantages in saving cost and time. Due to the voluntary acceptance by the disputants, furthermore, the mediation result can be easily implemented without any negative effect on later cooperation between the disputants.[91]

Until now, a target of "comprehensively advancing rule of law" has been confirmed in China. Because of a "socialist rule of law with Chinese characteristics,"[92] there must be some aspects of traditional ideas in the Chinese judiciary that fundamentally differentiate China's practices from those of Western countries. On one hand, the mission of "comprehensively advancing the rule of law" falls under the leadership of the CCP,[93] which implies that rule of law is still an instrument to fulfill the overall goal

[86] Confucius, The Analects, Book II Wei Chang, Chap. I. See LEGGE *supra* note 22, at 145.

[87] Confucius, The Analects, Book XII Yen Yuan, Chap. XIII. See LEGGE *supra* note 22, at 257.

[88] Protocol on the Accession of the PRC, 23 November 2001, WT/L/432, art. 2(D)(1).

[89] Zuigao Renmin Fayuanguanyu Shenli Fanqingxiao Xingzheng Anjian Yingyong Falv Ruogan Wenti de Guiding [The Supreme People's Court's Interpretation Concerning Several Questions about Adjudication of Administrative Cases Relating to Antidumping Investigation] 2003, art. 5; Zuigao Renmin Fayuanguanyu Shenli Fanbutie Xingzheng Anjian Yingyong Falv Ruogan Wenti de Guiding [The Supreme People's Court's Interpretation Concerning Several Questions about Adjudication of Administrative Cases Relating to Countervailing Investigation] 2003, art. 5.

[90] This conclusion is based on case searching in major online case databases in China, including China Judgment on Line (www.wenshu.court.gov.cn), PKULAW (www.pkulaw.cn), Jufa Cases (www.jufaanli.com), and www.wenshu.court.gov.cn.

[91] For a detailed analysis of China's mediation system, see Wang Liming, *Characteristics of China's Judicial Mediation System*, 17 ASIA PAC. L. REV. 67, 67–74 (2009).

[92] See Zhonggong Zhongyang guanyu QuanmianTuijin Yifa Zhiguo Ruogan Zhongda Wenti de Jueding [The Decision of the CCP Central Committee Concerning Important Issues on Comprehensively Advancing the Rule of Law (October 23, 2014), http://news.xinhuanet.com/politics/2014-10/28/c_1113015330.htm].

[93] See id.

of economic and social development in China. On the other hand, diverse forms of dispute settlement mechanisms, including consultation and mediation, have always been promoted in the Chinese judicial system, with a view toward boosting social justice and maintaining social harmony.[94] Interpretation of the law in specific cases is generally subject to uniform interpretation by the Supreme People's Court,[95] which is unlike the human rights-oriented method advocated by Petersmann. In addition to the pursuit of justice in individual cases, the Chinese judiciary has a broader concern for social harmony and national development, exemplifying traditional Chinese holism thought.

Value Divergence: Evaluation of Petersmann's Theory from a Chinese Perspective

The above sections demonstrate that there is both similarity and disparity between Petersmann's theory and Chinese thought insofar as the conceptions of human rights, justice, and judicial review are concerned. The similarity can be found in their common emphasis on respect for all human beings. Petersmann prioritizes human dignity in his words, whereas Chinese thought regards the people as the foremost concern. The disparity is perceptible in their distinctive methodologies for attaining the respect for all human beings: the former features bottom-up individual struggles, whereas the latter is characterized by top-down overall consideration. The implications of 'human rights', 'justice,' and 'judicial review' as related concepts are intimately shaped by the philosophical ideas, culture, and even natural conditions in a specific society. Traditional Chinese dialectics considers that all things are composed of two poles, namely Yin 陰 (darkness) and Yang 陽 (light), which stresses heavily the complementarity between the two poles.[96] Western dialectics, as expounded by Hegel, also refers to the principle of polarity, but means the coexistence of opposites.[97] The divergent values exemplified in the different dialectics engender the friction between Petersmann's theory and Chinese thought.

Since "all the sciences are related, more or less, to human nature",[98] the friction between Petersmann's theory and Chinese thought can be explained from the perspective of their different views of human nature. Petersmann's elaboration on

[94] See Guanyu Renmin Fayuan Jinyibu Shenhua Duoyuanhua Jiufen Jiejue Ji hi Gaige de Yijian [The Opinions on Further Promotion of Plural Dispute Settlement Mechanisms in People's Courts] (June 2016), http://www.court.gov.cn/fabu-xiangqing-22742.html.

[95] SCNPC, Zhonghua Renmin GongheguoLifa Fa [The Legislation Law of the PRC] 2015, art. 104 (prescribing that the interpretations on specific application of law in trial work as developed by the Supreme People's Court shall conform to the objectives, principles, and original meaning of legislation).

[96] Monroe (1927).

[97] Bodenheimer (1990).

[98] Hume (2007).

his theory proceeds from the "'animal spirits' and rational egoism of individuals,"[99] which somehow resonates with the evil human nature presumed by many Western philosophers. They would thus call for limiting the power of the government as 'a necessary evil' by constitutional arrangement to more effectively protect the equal human rights of citizens. Hume stated that "every man ought to be supposed a knave and to have no other end, in all his actions, than private interest."[100] Madison, the founding father of the US Constitution, also stated, "If men were angels, no government would be necessary."[101] In contrast, mainstream traditional Chinese thought is based on the goodness of human nature. Mencius observed that all men are created good, just as water flows downstream forever.[102] San Zi Jing, a traditional Chinese classic summarizing Confucianism, starts by saying that "man's nature at birth is good."

Both Chinese and Western views of human nature have their pros and cons. By focusing on moral self-cultivation and self-restraint instead of rigid legal rules, controllers of power can improve themselves as role models for the entire society so that abuses of power may be forestalled. Confucius asserted, "When a prince's personal conduct is correct, his government is effective without the issuing of orders. If his personal conduct is not correct, he may issue orders, but they will not be followed."[103] However, due to the mutability and unreliability of human nature, evilness cannot be absolutely prevented merely by moral self-cultivation and self-restraint. In contrast, Western constitutional theory, based on the evilness of human nature, underlines a mechanism of rights protection by power limitation. It is significant in terms of its emphasis on a principle of 'checks and balances' for the prevention of the abuse of power. If the laws for limiting private and government powers are extremely rigid, however, some beneficial attempts and endeavors will be smothered.[104] Further, the presumption that a power controller is unreliable due to the evilness of political power is likely to cause moral degradation of the power controller without moral restriction himself. A historical lesson should not be neglected: the Weimar Constitution was once considered the most representational constitution among democratic nations, but from this constitutional system emerged the Nazi government, which brought enormous disasters to the world. In short, the opposing presumptions of human nature between Petersmann's theory and Chinese thought lead to an irresolvable theoretical discord.

[99] Petersmann, *supra* note 5, at 6.
[100] Hume (1882).
[101] Hamilton (1898).
[102] Mencius, The Works Of Mencius, Book VI, Kao Tsze. See LEGGE, *supra* note 22, at 395–96.
[103] Confucius, The Analects, Book XIII Tsze-lu, Chap. VI. See LEGGE, supra note 22, at 266.
[104] Bodenheimer (1999).

Conclusion

Three centuries ago, Montesquieu stated, "Laws should be so appropriate to the people for whom they are made that it is very unlikely that the laws of one nation can suit another."[105] Today's globalization has brought humankind closer together than in the era of Montesquieu. However, people still tend to devote their loyalty to and value commonality with families, intimates, and groups of the same identity rather than abstractive and void cosmopolites. Although such keywords as 'human rights', 'social justice', and 'judicial review' used by Petersmann in his theory are known to people all around the world, they may be interpreted in different ways due to different values implanted in different lands. Petersmann draws a theoretical foundation one-sidedly from Western liberal thought and acquires empirical support mainly from European practice. Hence, he may, as heralded in Montesquieu's expression, have difficulty in developing a widely acceptable cosmopolitan constitutionalization theory for IEL. Even though Petersmann also makes allowances for 'constitutional pluralism', the legal conception is so pluralistic that it gives rise to failure in attaining 'universalizable' principles of human rights, justice, and judicial review. As illustrated by the friction between Petersmann's theory and Chinese thought due to the divergent values, 'legal pluralism' becomes an insurmountable obstacle to a cosmopolitan conception of IEL.

Petersmann has foreseen the potential objection to the philosophical and constitutional premises of his theory from other perspectives,[106] just as presented in this article. The authors respect Petersmann for his persistent development of theory from the foundation of human dignity. However, he has taken little consideration of Chinese philosophy and thought, which is likely to provide new valuable insights on supplying transnational public goods. On the same global plane, we compete for limited resources but also rely on each other to ensure a better flight. By the same token, for the theorization of IEL, both Western and Chinese thought should be incorporated.

References

Bodenheimer E (1990) Hegel's politico-legal philosophy: a Reevaluation, 35 AM. J JURIS 217:242–243

Bodenheimer E (1999) Bodenheimer, Jurisprudence: the philosophy and method of the law (Deng Zhenglai trans.), at 404

Hamilton, Madison J, Jay J (1989) The federalist papers: a commentary on the constitution of the united states (Paul Leicester Ford ed.) No 51, at 344

Hume D (1882) On the interdependence of parliament. In: Essays: Moral, Political, And Literary(T. H. Green and T. H. Grose eds.), at 117–18

Hume D (2007) A treatise of human nature (David Fate Norton & Mary J. Norton eds.), at 4

[105] Montesquieu (1989).

[106] See Petersmann, *supra* note 5, at 41.

Monroe P (1927) China: a nation in evolution, at 78–79
Montesquieu CS (1989) The spirit of the laws (A. M. Cohler, B. C. Miller & H. Samuel eds. & trans.), at 8
Petersmann EU (2002) Time for a united nations 'Global compact' for integrating human rights into the law of worldwide organizations: lessons from european integration, 13 Eur. J Int'l l 621:628–629
Petersmann EU (2003) Theories of Justice, Human Rights, and the constitution of international markets, 37 LOY. L a l R 407:416–417
Petersmann EU (2014) Multilevel governance problems of the world trading system beyond the WTO conference at Bali 2013, 17. J INT'L Econ l 233:233–270
Petersmann EU (1991) Constitutional functions and constitutional problems of international economic law
Petersmann EU (1997) How to reform the UN system? constitutionalism, international law and international organizations, 10 LEIDEN J INT'L L 421:421–74
Petersmann EU (2011) International economic law in the 21st century: need for stronger "democratic ownership" and cosmopolitan reforms, 31 Polish Y.B. Int'l L 9:32
Petersmann EU (2012) International economic law in the 21st century: constitutional pluralism and multilevel governance of interdependent public goods, at 4
Petersmann EU (2012) Human rights and international economic law, 4 Trade L Dev 283:284
Petersmann EU (2015) How to reconcile health law and economic law with human rights—administration of justice in Tobacco control disputes, 10 Asian J WTO Int'l Health L Pol'y 27:27–78
Petersmann EU (2016) EUI Working Papers: Methodology problems in international economic law and adjudication, http://cadmus.eui.eu/bitstream/handle/1814/40467/EUI_LAW_2016_12.pdf?sequence=1&isAllowed=y
Xiangfei Q (2008) The words 'Renquan' used in China in the late 19th early 20th centuries, 4 Fa Xu Jia [The Jurist] 19, 20
Xianming X (1999) An analysis on the human rights universality and human rights culture, 6 FaxuePinglun [Law Review] 16, At 20

Chapter 2
Is Calvo Dead?

Wenhua Shan

The "death" of the Calvo Doctrine is not at all a new topic. As early as 1955, Shea had pronounced its death because the Doctrine "failed to receive recognition as a principle of international law," by which he meant recognition by Western Countries.[1] In the mid-1990s, the "imminent death" of this doctrine was again declared due to changing attitudes in Latin American states toward foreign investment as witnessed in their international and domestic law making practice.[2] Now that ten years have passed, have the predictions of "imminent death" come true? This study shows that Calvo is not completely dead, even though it has been, by and large, deactivated.

The article has four Parts. Part I explores the essence and elements of the doctrine, thus setting forth the criteria for assessment; Part II introduces the broader background of the attitude changes in Latin America toward foreign investment and arbitration since the 1980s. Parts III and IV examine international treaty practices and domestic legislation, with a view toward assessing whether and to what extent the Calvo Doctrine is dead. Part V summarizes and concludes the article.

[1] Shea (1955).

[2] Manning-Cabrol (1995).

W. Shan (✉)
School of Law, Xi′an Jiaotong University, 28 Xianning West Road, Beilin DIstrict, Xi′an 710049, Shaanxi, China
e-mail: shan@mail.xjtu.edu.cn

© The Author(s), under exclusive license to Springer Nature Singapore Pte Ltd. 2024

S. Wei (ed.), *International Investment Law at the Juncture*, International Law in Asia,
https://doi.org/10.1007/978-981-97-2183-2_2

Calvo Doctrine: Essence and Elements

The Essence of the Calvo Doctrine

It is often said that the essence of the Calvo Doctrine is "equal treatment/national treatment" or "equality." For example, Donald Shea, probably the most eminent researcher on this theory, has asserted that "these two concepts of non-intervention and absolute equality of foreigners with nationals are the essence of the Calvo Doctrine."[3] Manning-Cabrol, a more recent writer on this principle, has also maintained that "equality is the central tenet of the Calvo Doctrine."[4] Yet while "equality of states," in conjunction with state sovereignty, has provided the legal foundation of the Calvo Doctrine, it in itself does not fundamentally characterize Calvo. Instead of emphasizing "absolute equality" between states or between nationals and foreigners, the Calvo Doctrine actually emphasizes the rejection of superiority or imperial prerogatives of powerful states and their nationals. In other words, the Calvo Doctrine is essentially "anti-superstate" or "anti-super-national-treatment," focusing on the opposition and rejection of any discriminatory treatment by Western powers against weak, developing host states and their nationals, as compared to the treatment those Western powers accord each other and demand for their citizens in these host states. Unlike "equal/national treatment," "anti-super-national-treatment" does not deny or reject the special privileges that host countries often grant or reserve to their own nationals. A close reading of Calvo's writing supports this distinction: though he did use equality of states and individuals as the legal basis of his arguments, what he specifically rejected was special privileges enjoyed by foreign states and their nationals, not the privileges that a national might enjoy in his or her home state based on citizenship. For instance, he wrote,

> The rule that in more than one case it has been attempted to impose on American states is that foreigners merit *more regard and privileges more marked and extended* than those accorded even to the nationals of the country where they reside. This principle is intrinsically contrary to the law of equality of nations. To admit that in the pre sent case governmental responsibility, that is the principle of an indemnity, is to create *an exorbitant and fatal privilege, essentially favorable to the powerful states and injurious to the weaker nations,* establishing an unjustifiable inequality between nationals and foreigners.[5]

He then concluded that "the responsibility of governments towards foreigners cannot be *greater* than that which these governments have towards their own citizens."[6]

Calvo's "anti-super-state" or "anti-super-national-treatment" approach is reified in the widely used "Calvo Clauses" in domestic constitutions and laws, and in bilateral

---

[3] Shea, *supra* note 1, at 19–20.

[4] It is noted that the doctrine embraced two levels of equality, namely "equality of nation-states or the equal treatment of nationals and foreigners." *See* Manning-Cabrol, *supra* note 2, at 1172.

[5] Shea, *supra* note 1, at 18.

[6] *Id.* at 19.

and regional treaties; such clauses often highlight that the treatment of foreigners and foreign investors should be "no more favorable than" that accorded to national and national investors, as we will see below in Section I.C. The "anti-super-national-treatment" approach of Calvo can be explained by the specific background against which this theory was developed. *As* Shea pointed out, the Calvo Doctrine was born at a time when "strong logical, moral and legal defenses" were badly needed in Latin American countries, which then were facing "real or imagined abuses of either diplomatic protection of aliens living within their territories or armed intervention in behalf of their foreign creditors" and which were unable to resist by force.[7]

Characterizing the Calvo Doctrine as supportive of "anti-superstate" and "anti-super-national-treatment" rather than of "equality" or "national treatment" not only more accurately reveals the focus of this theory, but also distinguishes Calvo from the "national treatment" standard frequently used in Bilateral Investment Treaties (BITs). Indeed, although both standards highlight the value of "equality" and therefore are often confused by commentators,[8] the "anti-super-national-treatment" under the Calvo Doctrine and the "national treatment" under BITs actually represent the two extremes of the spectrum of "equality": while the former focuses on the elimination of discrimination against host states and their nationals, the latter emphasizes the abandonment of discrimination against foreigners.[9] The distinct character of the "national treatment" principle in BITs is evidenced by the use of the expression "treatment *no less favorable than* that accorded to national investors" in most BITs, provisions which might better be characterized as "anti-inferior-national-treatment." Nevertheless, these two distinctive principles might converge and unite as one principle under the umbrella of the principle of "equality" or "national treatment." This is particularly the case when the phrase "the same treatment" is used; as will be discussed below, this appears to be what happened in the 1990s in Latin America.

Key Elements of the Calvo Doctrine

The essence of the Calvo Doctrine may be broken down into two key elements: a substantive sense and a procedural sense.[10] In the substantive sense, the Calvo Doctrine emphasizes that host states shall not grant foreigners any rights or benefits

---

[7] *Id.* at 14.

[8] For example, Manning-Cabrol considers national treatment in international investment treaties to be the same as the "equal/national treatment" principle enshrined in the Calvo Doctrine, and argues that Calvo found new life in such treaties (as well as in domestic legislation). *See* Manning-Cabrol, *supra* note 2, at 1195.

[9] Zamora also noted such a distinction between the two principles and has pointed out that, "[U]nlike concepts of national treatment, however, the Calvo Doctrine was created to address the perceived favoritism granted to foreigners, rather than discrimination against them. In other words, the purpose of the Calvo Doctrine is to bring foreigners down to the level of nationals, while the purpose of national treatment is to raise them up to the level of nationals." *See* Zamora (1997).

[10] Vandevelde (1998).

greater than those they accord to their own nationals. This carries both specific and abstract implications: on a specific or practical level, it prohibits the provision of any special privileges or incentives to foreigners and foreign investors by a host state; on an abstract or theoretical level, it rejects the so-called "international minimum standard" as a standard of law applicable to the treatment of foreigners including foreign investors. In the procedural sense, the Calvo Doctrine emphasizes that foreigners shall not be entitled to any remedies other than those available to nationals of a host state. It therefore implies a rejection of both non-local remedies (i.e., foreign or international remedies including diplomatic protection or military intervention) and non-local laws (i.e., foreign or international law) as applicable laws. *As* a procedural requirement, the rejection of non-local laws echoes and coincides with the substantive law requirement of rejection of an "international minimum standard." The two requirements may therefore be regarded as one element. It can thus be seen that the Calvo Doctrine indeed takes a very classic, state-centric view of international law, based on an absolutist view of state sovereignty and equality of states.

In short, the Calvo Doctrine effectively means, on the one hand, a rejection of special substantive privileges to foreigners and foreign investors ("no super-national treatment"), including specific incentives and benefits and in an abstract sense the "international minimum standard" of treatment they allegedly may enjoy; and, on the other hand, a rejection of any special procedural privileges to foreigners, including recourse to non-local remedies and the applicability of non-local laws. More specifically, the rejection of special substantive and procedural privileges for foreigners may be described in three basic elements, namely the "anti-super-national-treatment" standard, exclusive local jurisdiction, and exclusion of diplomatic protection,[11] with the first being the substantive requirement, and the latter two the procedural requirements. As the substantive standard for the doctrine, the "anti-super-national-treatment" standard may thus be regarded as the body of the norm, while "exclusive local jurisdiction" and "exclusion of diplomatic protection" may be regarded as the legs on which the body stand, or the arms without which the body could not effectively operate. In a sense, the procedural aspects of the Calvo Doctrine, namely "exclusive local jurisdiction" and "exclusion of diplomatic protection," are actually more important than the substantive aspect, the "anti-super-national-treatment" standard.

[11] Such factors are also the three key elements of the Calvo Clause; see Manning-Cabrol, *supra* note 2, at 1173. However, according to Lipstein, the Calvo Clause has five elements: "submission to local jurisdiction, free choice of law, sphere of application, waiver of protection by home state and surrender of rights under international law." *See* Lipstein (1945). Wesley likewise observes that there are five common provisions in the clause: "(1) Submission to local jurisdiction; (2) application of local law; (3) assimilation of foreigners for purposes of local contractual arrangements; (4) waiver of diplomatic protection by the foreigner's home state; and (5) surrender of rights arising under international law." Wesley (1975).

The Calvo Doctrine and Calvo Clause

The Calvo Doctrine understandably did not win acceptance by European and U.S. governments and lawyers, as it not only eliminates the possibility of abusing diplomatic protection, but also "[e]liminate[s] the institution itself, without substituting an acceptable alternative."[12] Latin American states, on the other hand, "enthusiastically received" this doctrine and, as a countermeasure to the rejection of the doctrine by Western powers, they resorted to "Calvo Clauses" to enforce it.[13] Calvo Clauses typically can be found in constitutions, domestic legislation, international treaties, and contracts signed between foreign investors and Latin American governments.[14] The 1933 constitution of Peru, for example, included the following article:

> Article 31. Property, whoever may be the owner, is governed exclusively by the laws of the Republic and is subject to the taxes, charges, and limitations established in the laws themselves.
>
> The same provision regarding property applies to aliens as well as Peruvians, except that in no case may the said aliens make use of their exceptional position or resort to diplomatic appeals.[15]

A piece of Ecuadorian legislation from 1938 likewise stipulated that:

> [f]oreigners, by the act of coming to the country, subject themselves to the Ecuadorian laws without any exception. They are consequently subject to the Constitution, laws, jurisdiction and police of the Republic, and may in no case, nor for any reason, avail themselves of their status as foreigners against the said conditions, jurisdiction, and police.[16]

As an example of a "Calvo Clause" implemented by contract, the contract between Mexico and the North American Dredging Company of Texas contained the following provision:

> Article 18: The Contractor and all persons, who as employees or in any capacity may be engaged in the execution of the work under this contract either directly or indirectly, shall be considered as Mexicans in all matters, within the Republic of Mexico, concerning the execution of such work and the fulfillment of this contract. *They shall not claim, nor shall they have, wither regard to the interests and the business connected with this contract, any other rights or means to enforce the same than those granted by the laws of the Republic of Mexicans, nor shall they enjoy any other rights than those established in favor of Mexicans. They are consequently deprived of any rights as aliens, and under no conditions shall the intervention of foreign diplomatic agents be permitted, in any matter related to this contract.*[17]

---

[12] Shea, *supra* note 1, at 20.

[13] *Id.* at 21.

[14] *Id.* at 21–32.

[15] *Constitution of 9 April 1933, in* Constitutions of the Americas 670–71 (Russell H. Fitzgibbon ed., 1948), as cited in *id.* at 24.

[16] Shea, *supra* note 1, at 26 and n. 56 (with sources for further examples of such constitutional provisions).

[17] Shea, *supra* note 1, at 29 (emphasis added).

The Calvo Doctrine was also fully embodied in international treaties,[18] particularly in regional integration arrangements within Latin America. For example, Decision 24, the first foreign investment code of the Andean Pact countries, forbade Andean Community member countries from "granting to foreign investors any treatment more favorable than that granted to national investors"[19] and required that "in no instrument relating to investments or the transfer of technology shall there be clauses that remove possible conflicts or controversies from the national jurisdiction and competence of the recipient country or allow the subrogation by States to the rights and actions of their national investors."[20]

The Calvo Doctrine was first embraced in Latin America, but its influence has gone well beyond that quarter of the world, particularly after World War II when a number of new states emerged in Asia and Africa as the result of the decolonization process. These newly independent states, like Latin American states, were more than ready to embrace this state-centric or absolutist international law theory that they believed would help safeguard their state interest, particularly by taking back control over natural resources within their territories that were previously controlled by developed Western powers. Meanwhile, communist governments that formed the Soviet Bloc also found this theory appealing, as it would help them expel and exclude the presence and influence of Western capitalists. As a result, "Calvo Clauses" have been embedded in the domestic laws of developing states beyond Latin America, especially in Asian and African states. For example, Chinese law dealing with foreign related contracts, since 1986 and as stands today, has a "Calvo Clause," which provides that all Sino-foreign equity joint venture contracts, Sino-foreign cooperative joint venture contracts, and Sino-foreign contracts for the joint exploration and development of natural resources shall be governed by Chinese law and subject to the exclusive jurisdiction of Chinese courts.[21] Furthermore, a Calvo Clause was also included in United Nations General Assembly (UNGA) resolutions when the New International Economic Order (NIEO) movement reached its summit, when the aforementioned two forces, namely the newly emerged states and the Soviet Bloc, formed a united front in the 1960s with a vast majority in the U.N.[22] Article 2(2) of UNGA Resolution 3281confirms, on the one hand, states' rights to regulate foreign investment in accordance with their respective laws and regulations and to reject the granting of preferential treatment to foreign investment. On the other hand, it stipulates that in case of expropriation, compensation should be paid by the state adopting such measures, "taking into account its relevant laws." Resolution 3281 might therefore

---

[18] For an extensive list of such treaties, see *id.* at 23 and n. 44.

[19] Article 50, Decision 24. Andean Commission: Decision 24, Common Regime of Treatment of Foreign Capital and of Trademarks, Patents, Licenses, and Royalties, Article 50, Nov. 30, 1976, 16 I. L.M. 138, at 153 (1977) [hereinafter Decision 24).

[20] Article 51, Decision 24.

[21] See Article 126 of the Contract Law of the People's Republic of China (stating that such contracts should be governed only by Chinese law) and Article 246 of the Civil Procedural Law of the People's Republic of China (stating that any disputes arising out of such contracts should only be subject to the jurisdiction of Chinese courts).

[22] Vandevelde, *supra* note 10, at 384.

be regarded as a global version of a "Calvo Clause."[23] The Calvo Doctrine thus reached its historical high in this Resolution.

However, the acceptance by an overwhelming majority of U.N. members in Resolution 3281 did seem to have secured a permanent international footing for this principle. Not long after the Resolution was adopted, the world was swept by the tides of economic liberalization and globalization. The Calvo Doctrine faced severe challenges ahead, which brought it to the brink of death.

Investment Liberalization and Latin American States

Investment liberalization, as a manifestation of economic liberalization and globalization, started to sweep the developing world in the 1980s and reached its peak in the 1990s. A number of factors contributed to this phenomenon, the most important among which were believed to be the debt crises of developing states since the early 1980s (hence a further hunger for foreign direct investment, or "FDI"), the collapse of the Soviet Bloc in the 1990s (hence a further boost of market-oriented economic reform in the former USSR and Eastern European countries), and the success stories of "Asian Tigers" characterized by private investment and export trade.[24]

One of the most important elements of investment liberalization is the liberalization of regulatory regimes of foreign investment. According to the World Investment Report 2005, since 1991, an average of 64 states per year made changes to their FDI laws and regulations. Among the 2,156 changes during that period, 2,006 were changes for more liberal investment regimes, accounting for 93% of the total changes.[25] (Table 2.1). Another element of investment liberalization has been the sharp rise of BITs. UNCTAD statistics show that by the end of 2004, the number of BITs worldwide had reached 2,392, of which 2,010 were concluded in the 1990s, with 1996 being the peak year in terms of the number of new BITs[26] (Figs. 2.1 and 2.2). Meanwhile, states have been very active in entering into bilateral, regional, and trans-regional preferential trade and investment agreements (PTIAs). By April 2005, 212 such agreements had also been concluded, of which about 87% were signed in the 1990s.[27] These PTIAs differ from BITs in their coverage, yet they resemble the latter in their content on investment protection and liberalization. They almost invariably guarantee national and most favored nation (MFN) treatment, free transfer

---

[23] Lillich noted that Latin American efforts on the Charter were "no more than a thinly-disguised attempt to endow the Calvo Doctrine." *See* Lillich (1975). Schneiderman considers that the Calvo Doctrine was "a central plank of the new International Economic Order (UNGA 3171 of 1973) and the UN Charter of Economic Rights and Duties of States (1974)"; Schneiderman (2000a).

[24] Vandevelde, *supra* note 10, at 386–91.

[25] UNCTAD, *World Investment Report* 2005, UNCTAD/WIR/2005, at 26.

[26] UNCTAD, *World Investment Report* 2005, UNCTAD/WIR/2005, at 28.

[27] *Id.*

Table 2.1 Changes in domestic legislations (1991–2004)

Year	Number of countries changed FDI laws	Number of changes made to FDI laws	Changes in favor of foreign investors	Changes detrimental to foreign investors
1991	35	82	80	2
1992	43	79	79	0
1993	57	102	101	1
1994	49	110	108	2
1995	64	112	106	6
1996	65	114	98	16
1997	76	151	135	16
1998	60	145	136	9
1999	63	140	131	9
2000	69	150	147	3
2001	71	208	194	14
2002	70	248	236	12
2003	82	244	220	24
2004	102	271	235	36

Source UNCTAD World Investment Report 2005, p. 26

of funds and profits, compensation for expropriation, and resort to international arbitration tribunals in case of disputes between a foreign investor and the host state. In other words, these bilateral, regional, and multilateral treaties aim to set standards at the international level and to guarantee access to international dispute settlement platforms, both of which run in the opposite direction of the Calvo Doctrine.

It is not a surprise that Latin American states had initially resisted investment liberalization and such treaties. However, economic events in the 1980s, principally the Latin American debt crisis, forced many Latin American countries to shift their attention from commercial loans back to foreign direct investment (FDI). The debt crisis caused "drastic reductions in net voluntary commercial bank lending to LDCs."[28,29] These reductions forced the LDCs to correct their external balances and seek alternative forms of external financing, most notably FDI.[30] Meanwhile, the worldwide trend of investment liberalization rendered the Latin American state no choice but to open up their markets and adopt higher standards of treatment for foreign investors

[28] LDC here stands for Less Developed Countries.

[29] *See* Claessens (1991).

[30] The term "alternative finance" refers to "all forms of external financing outside the public sector. [Alternative finance] thus includes FDI, project lending, portfolio investment, closed end equity funds, private non-guaranteed debt, licensing, joint ventures, quasi-equity contracts, and other forms of private-to-private lending." *Id.*

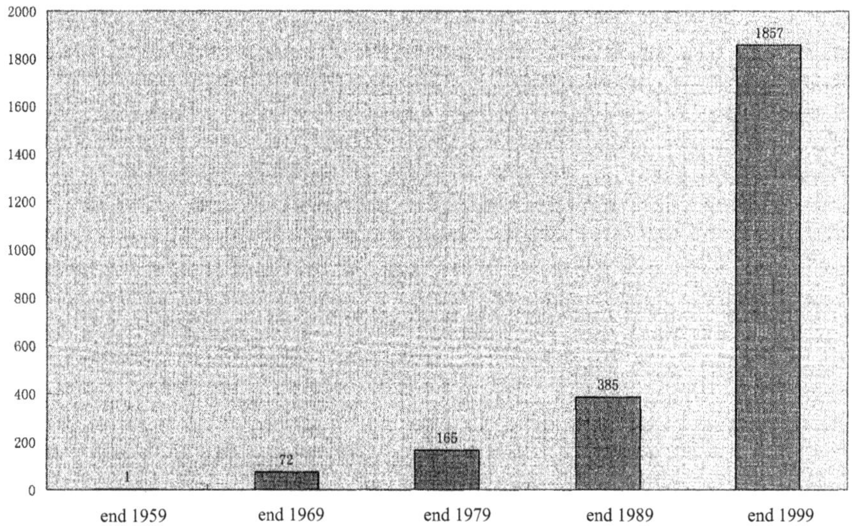

Fig. 2.1 Increase in BITs (1959–1999). *Source* UNCTAD: Bilateral Investment Treaties (1959–1999), UNCTAD/ITE/IW2 (2000), p. 1

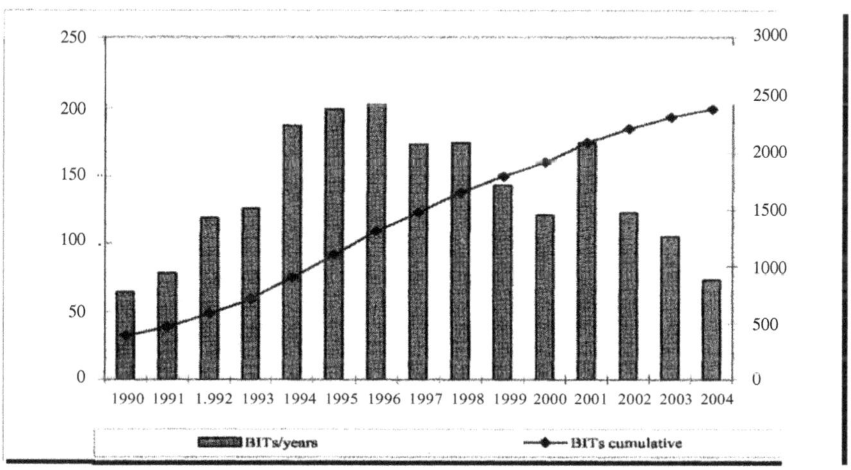

Fig. 2.2 BITs (1990–2004). *Source* World Investment Report 2005, p. 27

to attract foreign investment.[31] Consequently, many Latin American countries began to conclude international investment treaties in the late 1980s, while modifying their

[31] Some economists considered that such a change marked a rejection of the import substitution model of the 1950s, 1960s, and 1970s, and the emergence of a development model. *See generally,* The Macroeconomics of Populism in Latin America (Rudiger Dornbusch & Sebastian Edwards eds., 1991), and Bulmer-Thomas (1994).

domestic legislation to accommodate international arbitration and international standards of treatment for foreign investment. A close look follows in the next two parts, examining these international treaties and domestic laws, respectively.

International Investment Treaties by Latin American States

In the last couple of decades, Latin American states have been active in entering into international investment treaties at all levels: bilateral, regional, and global. The following explores the three levels of treaties in turn and assesses how far they have deviated from the Calvo Doctrine.

Bilateral Investment Treaties (BITs)

UNCTAD Statistics show that Latin American states did not engage in BITs until the late 1980s.[32] By the end of the 1990s, Latin American states had entered into a total of 300 BITs, of which 93% were signed in the 1990s.[33] With the exception of Brazil and Colombia, all Latin American states have ratified some BITs; Argentina leads the field with 43 ratified BITs, followed by Peru with 24 BITs, Chile (22), Cuba (19), Ecuador (18), Venezuela (17), Bolivia (15), Paraguay (15), Uruguay (13), and El Salvador (10).[34] The remaining states have also ratified BITs, including Panama (9), Mexico (3), Honduras (3), Nicaragua (3), Belize (2), Costa Rica (3), Guiana (2), and Dominica Republic (1).[35] Like all other BITs, BITs by Latin American states contain two categories of provisions: substantively, they accept general standards of

[32] UNCTAD, *Bilateral Investment Treaties 1959–1999*, UNCTAD/ITE/IIA/2, at 15 (2000). According to UNCTAD, however, the total number of BITs concluded by Latin American and Caribbean States reached 451 by the end of 2004. *See* UNCTAD: *Recent Developments in International Investment Agreements,* IIA MONITOR No. 2 (Aug. 30, 2005) UNCTAD/WEB/ITE/IIT/2005/1, at 2.

[33] UNCTAD, *Bilateral Investment Treaties 1959–1999*, UNCTAD/ITE/IIA/2, at 15 (2000).

[34] UNCTAD, *Bilateral Investment Treaties 1959–1999, supra* note 32, at 7–14.

[35] Some countries have signed some BITs without ratifying any of them. For example, Brazil and Colombia have signed 14 and 6 BITs respectively, but neither of them has ratified any of them. UNCTAD, *Country-specific Lists of BITs, available at* http://www.unctad.orgfl'emplates/Page.asp?intltemlD=2344&lang=l (last visited June 14, 2006). For an analysis on the legal effects of such un-ratified BITs, see UNCTAD: *Recent Developments in International Investment Agreements, supra* note 32, at 8. For a more elaborate discussion on its implication on the consent to international arbitration, see Ceskoslovenska Obchodni Banka, A.S. v. The Slovak Republic (ICSID Case No. ARB/97/4), Decision on the Further and Partial Objection to Jurisdiction (Dec. 1, 2000), paras. 33–59. The text of this Decision is published online as it appears in Vol. 15, No. 2 issue of ICSID Review Foreign Investment Law Journal (2000): http://www.worldbank.org/icsid/cases/csob.pdf (last visited Feb. 5, 2007). In this case, the relevant BIT was signed but not ratified, and the Arbitration Tribunal held that state consent to submission to ICSID arbitration could not be established on the basis of the BIT. The Tribunal nevertheless found such consent was given by

treatment such as fair and equitable treatment, national treatment and MFN treatment, free transfer of funds and guarantee of compensation in case of expropriation; procedurally, they accept the jurisdiction of international arbitration tribunals.[36]

It has been observed that the early BITs by Latin American states still had elements influenced by Calvo, requiring certain conditions to be fulfilled before recourse to international arbitration.[37] For example, earlier Argentine BITs required that submission to international arbitration might not be initiated until the issue had been submitted to a local court, and either the local court decided the issue, or the issue did not receive a verdict from the local court after the lapse of a certain period of time.[38] In other words, resorting to local remedies was the prerequisite for launching international arbitration. Such local remedy requirements, however, were abandoned in later BIT practice. The Argentina-U.S.A. BIT of 1991, for example, does not require exhaustion of local remedies as a prerequisite.[39] One commentator concluded, therefore, that this BIT signaled "the abandonment, by Argentina, of the Calvo Doctrine which has governed for more than a century investments from abroad."[40]

In the other 11 BITs entered into between the U.S. and the Latin American states, including Bolivia, Ecuador, El Salvador, Grenada, Haiti, Honduras, Jamaica, Nicaragua, Panama, Trinidad and Tobago, and Uruguay (see Table 2.2), submission to international arbitration is not conditioned on prior recourse to local remedies.[41] With regard to applicable law, although most of these BITs do not refer to specific applicable laws, they generally require the BITs not prejudicing legal effects of domestic laws of the host state, any investment agreement, or investment licenses, as well as any "international legal obligations."[42] The Uruguay-U.S.A. BIT signed in 2004 (the first U.S. BIT since its 2004 model was released) went further, stipulating in Articles 3 to 10 that the current BIT itself, as well as applicable rules of international law, will be the applicable law in case of alleged violation of the substantive obligations contained in the BIT; if the claim involves violation of an investment agreement or investment authorization, then the applicable law will be the "rules of law" specified in the pertinent investment agreement or investment authorization, or the rules of law to which the disputing parties may otherwise agree. If such rules of law have not been specified or otherwise agreed, then the applicable law will be "(i) the law of the respondent, including its rules on the conflict of laws; and (ii) such rules

---

the Czech Government by way of the Consolidation Agreement entered into between the parties expressing that the Agreement should be governed by domestic laws and the BIT.

36 Salacuse (1990).

37 In a recent article, Scheurer called this one of "Calvo's grandchildren." Scheurer (2005).

38 Cremades (2004).

39 Article 7, Argentina-U.S. BIT.

40 Golsong (1991).

41 See Article 9, Bolivia-U.S. BIT; Article 6, Ecuador-U.S. BIT; Article 9, El Salvador-U.S. BIT; Article 6, Grenada-U.S. BIT; Article 7, Haiti-U.S. BIT; Article 9, Honduras-U.S. BIT; Article 6, Jamaica-U.S. BIT; Article 7, Nicaragua-U.S. BIT; Article 1, 2000 Amending Protocol to Paraguay-U.S. BIT; Article 9, Trinidad and Tobago-U.S. BIT; and Article 24, Uruguay-U.S. BIT.

42 See, e.g., Article 10, Argentina-U.S. BIT.

Table 2.2 U.S. BITs with Latin American states

Partner	Date of signature	Date of entry into force
Argentina	14-Nov-91	28-0ct-94
Bolivia	17-Apr-98	6-Jun-01
Ecuador	27-Aug-93	11-May-97
El Salvador	10-Mar-99	
Grenada	2-May-86	3-Mar-89
Haiti	13-Dec-83	
Honduras	1-Jul-95	11-Jul-01
Jamaica	4-Feb-94	7-Mar-97
Nicaragua	1-Jul-95	
Panama	27-0ct-82	30-May-91
Trinidad and Tobago	26-Sep-94	26-Dec-96
Uruguay	4-Nov-05	

Source UNCTAD: Total number of Bilateral Investment Agreements concluded by United States, June 1, 2005, available at: http://www.unctad.org/Templates/Page.asp?intltemID=2344&lang= last visited May 27, 2006)

of international law as may be applicable."[43] In other words, applicable international law is one of the default rules of law to be applied, unless the dispute involves an investment agreement or investment authorization, in which case the rules of law are otherwise specified or agreed upon.

The previous survey of BITs concluded by Latin American states shows that, while earlier BITs were somewhat influenced by the Calvo principle (requiring resort to local remedies as a prerequisite to international arbitration), recent BITs have generally accepted nonlocal remedies and general international law as the governing norms, departing significantly from the Calvo principle. Indeed, a "silent revolution" has taken place, particularly in the sense that some BITs accept international arbitration for state-investor disputes.[44]

Regional Arrangements

Regional integration in Latin America dates back to the 1960s when some Latin American states entered into the Andean Pact.[45] However, the liberalization movement in Latin American states has resulted in some changes to the Andean Pact since

[43] Article 30, Uruguay-US BIT.

[44] Blackaby et al. (2002).

[45] The recent wave of regional integration within that region, however, demonstrated a marked difference from the original Andean Pact movement, in that it no longer sticks to the nationalistic approach and import substitution policies but places the emphasis on market forces. Edwards (1993).

the late 1980s. Decision 24, the original FDI code of the Andean Pact, as mentioned above, had two distinctive "Calvo Clauses" (Articles 50 and 51) prohibiting the provision of "super-national treatment" to foreign investors and recourse to remedies of foreign jurisdiction. However, these two clauses were gradually changed in the late 1980s and early 1990s. In 1987, the Andean Group modified its FDI code and replaced it with Decision 220, which maintained the "anti-super-nationaltreatment" provision[46] but loosened the strict national jurisdiction requirement. Article 34 of Decision 220 provided that, "[flor the settlement of disputes or conflicts deriving from direct foreign investments or from the transfer of foreign technology, Member Countries shall apply the provisions established in their local legislation."[47] It thus left member states discretion to stick to or derogate from the Calvo Doctrine. This, nevertheless, leaves doubt as to whether investors in the Andean Pact countries are still limited to taking recourse in national law and tribunals, given that "anti-super-national-treatment" provision survived.[48]

The Andean Group's alleged shift in attitude toward foreign investment occurred in 1991 when Decision 291,[49] the latest and most liberal FDI code, was adopted. In an attempt to stimulate foreign capital and technology flows into sub-regions of the Andean Community (ANCOM), the Andean Group relaxed the "anti-super-national-treatment" provision in the previous FDI codes.[50] Article 2 of Decision 291 provides that "foreign investors shall have the same rights and obligations as pertain to national investors, except as otherwise provided in the legislation of each Member Country."[51] Apart from allowing member countries discretion in deciding the treatment of foreign investors, this provision also marked a subtle change of emphasis from "anti-super-national-treatment" toward "equal treatment" or "national treatment," which are closer to the national treatment standards embedded in most BITs. Hence, it might be an example of the said "convergence" of the two originally distinct standards of "equal" and "national" treatment. Decision 220 and Decision 291 thus opened the possibility for ANCOM member countries to accept international

46 Article 33 of Decision 220 provided that "member countries could not grant foreign investors more favorable treatment than that granted to national investors." It is noted that although Article 33's text differed slightly from that of Article 50, the effects were identical: foreign investors were not to be granted rights greater than those granted to nationals. *See* Wiesner (1993).

47 Article 34, the Common Foreign Investment and Technology Licensing Code, Decision 220 of May 11, 1987, Commission of the Cartagena Agreement, *reprinted in* 27 I.L.M. 974 (1988) [hereinafter Decision 220].

48 One commentator argued that, while Decision 220 did not completely denounce the Calvo principle, it nevertheless denied "an ANCOM passport to roam the Andes at will." However, another commentator argued that, "[l]f, as this article argues, national laws only permit the settlement of disputes before local courts and under local laws, then Calvo's other principle that there is no right to diplomatic protection must also survive." *See* Murphy Jr (1990); and Wiesner, *supra* note 46, at 448–49.

49 Commission of the Cartagena Agreement: Decision 291, Common Code for the Treatment of Foreign Capital and Trademarks, Patents, Licenses, and Royalties, Mar. 21, 1991, *reprinted in* 30 I.L.M. 1283 (1991) [hereinafter Decision 291].

50 Article 2, Decision 291.

51 *Id.*

standards of treatment and the jurisdiction of international arbitration tribunals. It is therefore essential to look into the domestic legislation of member states to ascertain the extent of such a change of attitude, which will follow in Part IV.

Another example of regional integration is MERCOSUR, the Common Market of the South created in 1991 by four countries in Latin America: Argentina, Brazil, Paraguay, and Uruguay.[52] MERCOSUR adopted two Protocols that use more or less the same language, regulating investment between member states and from non-member states: respectively, the Buenos Aires Protocol (extrabloc) and the Colonia Protocol (intrabloc). The Protocol regulating investments from non-member states (the Buenos Aires Protocol)[53] provides in Article 2(c) for national treatment MFN treatment and "just and equitable treatment" for foreign investment. The terms "national treatment" and "MFN treatment" are typical BIT language, meaning, respectively, treatment "no less favorable" than that granted to national investors or investors from other non-member states.[54] With regard to state-investor dispute resolution, Article 2(h) of the Protocol provides a "fork in the road" clause, which avails investors of choosing between two options: either competent courts of the host state, or an international arbitration tribunal, which may be either an ad hoc or an institutional tribunal.[55] Since the Protocol uses local remedies only as a conclusive alternative to international arbitration, it differs significantly from the Calvo principle of "exclusive local remedies." The Protocol goes on to stipulate that the governing law of such disputes must include the terms of the present Protocol, the laws of the host state including its rules on conflicts of law, the terms of any agreements between the investor and the host state, and "principles of international law."[56] Clearly this Protocol, although yet to take effect, generally follows a liberal BIT approach rather than the Calvo principle.

Finally, although the negotiation of the Free Trade Agreement of the Americas has been suspended, the latest negotiation draft suggests acceptance of international standards of treatment and the jurisdiction of international arbitration tribunals.[57] It therefore might be regarded as another attempted departure from the Calvo Doctrine in the form of regional integration instruments.

---

[52] For the basic treaty of Mercosur, see Treaty Establishing a Common Market between the Argentine Republic, the Federal Republic of Brazil, the Republic of Paraguay, and the Eastern Republic of Uruguay, *available at* http://www.sice.oas.org/trade/mrcsr/mrcsrtoc.aspercosur&hl=zh-CN&ct=clnk&cd=7 (last visited June 16, 2006).

[53] Protocol on Promotion and Protection of Investment Proceeding from NonMember Countries of the MERCOSUL, *available at* http://www.cvm.gov.br/ingl/inter/mercosul/buenos-e.asp (last visited June 15, 2006).

[54] *Id.* Article 2(c).

[55] *Id.* Article 2(h).

[56] *Id.* Article 2(h)(4).

[57] Subsection C.2.b, Chapter XVII Investment, of the Free Trade Area of the Americas (Draft Agreement) (Derestricted, FTAA.TNC/w/133/Rev.3, Nov. 21, 2003), particularly Articles 29 & 41.

Global Conventions

Although so far there is no comprehensive global agreement on investment protection, there are a few global conventions that bear significant implications for international investment. Most important among these global conventions are two World Bank initiatives: the Convention on the Settlement of Investment Disputes between States and Nationals of Other States (ICSID Convention),[58] and the Convention Establishing the Multilateral Investment Guarantee Agency (MIGA Convention).[59] The New York Convention on the Recognition and Enforcement of Foreign Awards[60] is also important in the context of investment dispute settlement.

As an important companion to BITs, the ICSID Convention aims at providing an international mechanism for the settlement of stateinvestor disputes, particularly by facilitating international arbitration and conciliation. This mechanism appears to go against the Calvo Doctrine, which advocates exclusive national jurisdiction and local remedies. It is therefore unsurprising that Latin American states boycotted this convention in 1964 even after the drafters made efforts to revise some of the provisions to address Latin American states' concerns.[61] Before 1980, only a few small Latin American and Caribbean states (Jamaica and Trinidad and Tobago) had joined the convention. But now most Latin American states have become members of the Convention (with the notable exceptions of Brazil and Mexico), and most of these states realized their membership in the 1990s (Table 2.3). This again confirms that the investment liberalization took place most dramatically in the 1990s.

Meanwhile, Latin American states also dropped their rejection of the New York Convention facilitating the enforcement of arbitration awards made in other states.[62] Now almost all Latin American states, even Brazil and Mexico, have become members of the Convention. This demonstrates that Latin American states have made a Uturn in their attitudes toward international arbitration, from utter rejection to general acceptance and recognition.

Latin American states have finally also accepted the MIGA Convention, aimed at providing guarantees for international investment.[63] Since the MIGA mechanism is based on host states' recognition of the subrogation of rights of investors by the

---

[58] The Convention is *available at* http://www.worldbank.org/icsid/basicdodbasicdoc.htm (last visited June 15, 2006).

[59] The Convention is *available at* http://www.miga.org/sitelevel2/level2.cfm?id=1107 (last visited June 15, 2006).

[60] The full text of the Convention is *available at* http://www.jus.uio.no/lm/un.arbitration.recognition.and.enforcement.convention.new.york.1958/doc (last visited June 16, 2006).

[61] Biggs (2004).

[62] Latin American states had long been hostile to the New York Convention, and were, in general, among the last countries to accept it. For example, Brazil did not accept it until 2002. *See* Gonzalo Biggs, *id.* at 63.

[63] According to the MIGA website, MIGA members from Latin America and the Caribbean include Antigua and Barbuda, Argentina, Bahamas, Barbados, Belize, Bolivia, Brazil, Chile, Colombia, Costa Rica, Dominica, Dominican Republic, Ecuador, El Salvador, Grenada, Guatemala, Guyana, Haiti, Honduras, Jamaica, Nicaragua, Paraguay, Panama, Peru, St. Kitts & Nevis, St. Lucia, St.

Table 2.3 Latin American members of the ICSID convention (as of January 25, 2006)

Contracting state	Date of signature	Date of ratification	Date of entry into force
Argentina	21/05/1991	19/10/1994	18/11/1994
Bahamas	19/10/1995	19/10/1995	18/11/1995
Bolivia	03/05/1991	23/06/1995	23/07/1995
Colombia	18/05/1993	15/07/1997	14/08/1997
Costa Rica	29/09/1981	27/04/1993	27/05/1993
Dominican Republic	20/05/2000		
Ecuador	15/01/1986	15/01/1986	14/02/1986
El Salvador	09/06/1982	06/03/1984	05/04/1984
Grenada	24/05/1991	24/05/1991	23/06/1991
Guatemala	09/1111995	21101/2003	20/02/2003
Haiti	30/01/1985		
Honduras	28/05/1986	14/02/1989	16/03/1989
Jamaica	23/06/1965	09/09/1966	14/10/1966
Nicaragua	04/02/1994	20/03/1995	19/04/1995
Panama	22/11/1995	08/04/1996	08/05/1996
Paraguay	27/07/1981	07/01/1983	06/02/1983
Peru	04/09/1991	09/08/1993	08/09/1993
Trinidad and Tobago	05/10/1966	03/0111967	02/02/1967
Uruguay	28/05/1992	09/08/2000	08/09/2000
Venezuela	18/08/1993	02/05/1995	01106/1995

Source ICSID: List of Contracting States and other Signatories of the Convention (as of Jan. 25, 2006), available at http://www.worldbank.org/Iicsid/Iconstatel/c-states-en.htm last visited May 19, 2006)

MIGA, the states' acceptance again evidences derogation from the Calvo Doctrine by Latin American states.

Observations

The preceding survey suggests that since the 1980s, Latin American states have generally deviated from the Calvo Doctrine in their international investment treaty practice, as most of them have entered into BITs that guarantee international standards of treatment and access to international arbitration. At the regional level, MERCOSUR follows the BIT approach, and the Andean Pack has been revised to accommodate

Vincent, Suriname, Trinidad & Tobago, Uruguay, and Venezuela. See MIGA: *MIGA Member Countries* (Last updated: Oct. 27, 2005), *available at* http://www.miga.org/sitelevel2/level2.cfm?id=1152 (last visited May 28, 2006).

the member states' need for flexibility in departing from the Calvo Clause. Most of the Latin American states have also accepted the ICSID Convention providing an international platform for arbitration of state-investor disputes, the MIGA Convention recognizing rights of subrogation, and the New York Convention facilitating worldwide enforcement of arbitration awards.

It may still, however, be a step too far to conclude that all Latin American states have completely abandoned Calvo in their treaty practice. There are three main reasons supporting this argument. First of all, there are significant exceptions to such general treaty practice. For instance, Brazil, the largest state and FDI recipient[64] in the region, has not yet ratified any BITs (although has concluded a few of them) or the MERCOSUR Protocols,[65] nor has it accepted the ICSID regime. Furthermore, it seems unlikely that Brazil will change its approach in the near future, as it is doing enormously well as a magnet for foreign investment.[66] Colombia also has not ratified any BITs despite the fact that it has signed six of them.[67] Moreover, Mexico, another important state in the region, also has not signed the ICSID Convention, although it joined the North America Free Trade Agreement (NAFTA) and concluded a number of BITs. Second, some investment treaties contain significant reservations to the acceptance of international standards and international arbitration. Using Schuruer's language, some of the treaty provisions are actually "Calvo's Grandchildren." Early BITs by Latin American states, for example, often make local remedies a prerequisite for international arbitration. Given the uncertainty about the applicability of MFN to procedural aspects following recent arbitration cases such as *Salini* vs. *Jordan*[68] and *Plama* vs. *Bulgaria*[69] cases, such reservations should not be ignored. Also, the Andean FDI code still, as a general principle, requires "equal treatment" between domestic and foreign investors and leaves member states the discretion to adopt higher standards of treatment or access to international arbitration, not "requiring" them to do so. It is therefore essential to look into domestic legislation in the region to establish whether the Calvo Doctrine has actually been abandoned in the Andean Community. Third, it has been argued and has increasingly been recognized that developing countries including Latin American states enter into BITs and other

64 UNCTAD Press Release, UNCTAD Doc. UNCTAD/PRESS/EB/2004/007 (Mar. 5, 2004).

65 Inter-American Development Bank (IADB), *Legislation for Foreign Investment Statutes in Countries in the Americas, Comparative Study—Brazil* (2006), http://alca-ftaa.iadb.org/eng/invest/BRA-1.HTM (May 16, 2006).

66 Cremades, *supra* note 38, at 81.

67 UNCTAD, *Country-specific Lists of* BITs, *supra* note 35.

68 Salini Construttori S.p.A. and Italstrade S.p.A. v. the Hashemite Kingdom of Jordan (Case No. ARB/02/13), Decision of the Tribunal on Jurisdiction, Nov. 29, 2004. This case and the following case, Plama v. Bulgaria, basically decided that MFN clauses in BITs do not generally extend privileges under procedural provisions, which marks a reversal of the view as held in earlier cases, notably the Emilio Agustin Maffezini v. Kingdom of Spain (Case No. ARB/9717), Decision on Objections to Jurisdiction, Jan. 25, 2000 (Maffezini v. Spain), and Siemens A.G. v. Argentine Republic (Case No. ARB/02/8), Decision on Jurisdiction of Aug. 3, 2004 (Siemens v. Argentina), para. 103.

69 Plama Consortium Limited v. Republic of Bulgaria (Case No. ARB/03/24), Decision on Jurisdiction of Feb. 8, 2005.

investment treaties mainly for economic considerations,[70] rather than because of a genuine belief in the norms embedded therein. In other words, the departure from or even rejection of the Calvo Doctrine represents only a change in technique, not a change in principle. This is supported by the following examination of the domestic constitutions and laws.

Domestic Legislations in Latin American States

Compared with international treaties, domestic legislation better reveals the real attitude of Latin American states toward the Calvo Doctrine, as domestic legislation more accurately reflects the unilateral wills of the host states, unlike international treaties, in which the host state must compromise with other states. Also, the Andean Pack FDI code refers to domestic laws to determine the treatment and methods of dispute settlement for foreign investment. It is therefore crucial to look into domestic laws and regulations to ascertain whether Latin American states have shifted their attitudes toward foreign investment. This section intends to do so by exploring and comparing domestic legislation, particularly the rules on standards of treatment and the investment dispute settlement, in nine major Latin American states, namely Argentina, Bolivia, Brazil, Chile, Colombia, Ecuador, Mexico, Peru, and Venezuela.

Argentina

Argentina has been lauded as having "probably the most probusiness" FDI legislation in the world.[71] The general standard of treatment of foreigners and foreign investors is

[70] *See*, e.g., Dolzer (1981), Schachter (1984), Guzman (1997).

[71] One Argentine website highlights the main aspects of investment liberalization as follows: (1) Foreign investments are warmly welcomed and virtually unrestricted, with no sector restrictions—investments are allowed even in sensitive areas such as oil, mass media (broadcasting, cable, newspapers, and magazines), nuclear power generation, and nuclear mineral mining; (2) No approvals or paperwork of any kind are required to materialize foreign investments—there is absolutely no red tape; (3) No registration of investments is ever required: complete confidentiality assured; (4) Foreign investors are entitled, without approvals or formalities, to repatriate capital and remit profits abroad at any time—no waiting periods whatsoever; (5) Unrestricted access to foreign exchange markets—absolutely no approvals or formalities for making transfers abroad; (6) No discrimination against foreign investors: foreign and domestic companies are treated equally under the law, including access to domestic or foreign currency financing in the local market and full eligibility for economic development incentive programs; (7) No performance requirements to be met by foreign investors; and (8) International law protection: most capital exporting countries covered by a valid bilateral investment treaty. *See* Hacienda Virtual Realty Argentina—HVRA, Legal Reforms and the Foreign Investor, *available at* http://www.hvra.com.ar/enforinv.htm (May 20, 2006).

laid down in the national constitution and laws.[72] Article 20 of the Argentine Constitution establishes the principle of "equal treatment" of foreigners and nationals, stating that:

> [f]oreigners enjoy in the territory of the Nation all the civil rights of a citizen; they may engage in their industry, commerce or profession; own real property, purchase it and alienate it[73]

Accordingly, the Foreign Investment Law of 1993 (No. 21,382) grants foreign investors rights equal to those of local investors in all fields, while liberalizing the entry and outflow of capital.[74] The legal and tax treatment is virtually the same for Argentine citizens and foreigners.[75] Decree 1853/93 of September 1993, which combines in one piece of legislation the liberalization measures contained in the Economic Emergency and State Reform Acts of 1989 and the above-mentioned Foreign Investment Law,[76] confirms in Article 2 that "foreign investors may invest in the country without any prior approval, on the same terms as investors domiciled in the country." Thus, it is clear that Argentina enshrines national treatment as the cardinal principle of treatment for foreign investors.

On the settlement of state-investor disputes, Argentina also insists on the equal treatment principle. Foreign investors are therefore entitled to "exactly the same recourse" available to local investors.[77]

It can thus be concluded that, within its domestic legislation, Argentina loyally adheres to the cardinal Calvo principle of equal/national treatment for foreign investors. Such national treatment, however, seems to subtly differ from Calvo, as it emphasizes absolute equality between foreigners and nationals, and does not have the classical "Calvo stress" emphasizing the non-discrimination against nationals, i.e., the prohibition of special favor to foreigners.

On the other hand, it must be noted that Argentina has been very active in entering into investment promotion and protection treaties. So far it has signed the ICSID Convention, the MIGA Convention,[78] the New York Convention, the Inter-American Convention on International Commercial Arbitration (the Panama Convention),[79] and at least 58 BITs, of which 53 have entered into force.[80] So it has also signed on to some regional treaties, including the two MERCOSUR Protocols on investment

---

[72] IADB: *Legislation for Foreign Investment Statutes in Countries in the Americas, Comparative Study-Argentina* (2006), http://alca-ftaa.iadb.org/eng/invest/ARG-1.htm (May 16, 2006) [hereinafter IADB: *Argentina*], Section 2.1.

[73] Article 20, Argentine Constitution.

[74] IADB: *Argentina, supra* note 72, at Section 1.2.

[75] *Id.*

[76] HVRA, Legal Reforms and the Foreign Investor, *supra* note 71.

[77] IADB: *Argentina, supra* note 72, at Section 5.1.

[78] Alessandro Spinillo & Emilio Vogelius, *Argentina, in* International Arbitration in Latin America, *supra* note 44, at 19.

[79] *Id.* at 439.

[80] UNCTAD, *Country-specific Lists of BITs, supra* note 35.

protection (namely the Colonia Protocol and the Buenos Aires Protocol) and a few arbitration conventions.[81]

Such treaties have effectively raised the standards of treatment for foreign investors well beyond the standards of treatment for national investors, most notably by allowing foreign investors to resort to international arbitration mechanisms such as the ICSID, and by accepting the applicability of general principles of international law. These treaties thus raise a question of constitutionality: since international treaties are subordinate to the Constitution in Argentina,[82] does it constitute a breach of the constitutional requirement of absolute equality of treatment between national and foreign investors to grant foreign investors higher treatment than that given to domestic investors? Such an unconstitutional challenge has already been raised by the Argentine government in the proceedings of some of the investment arbitration cases against the country.[83] The Argentine prosecutor, for example, argued in a hearing in the *CMS Gas Transmission Company v. Republica Argentina* case[84] that bilateral treaties do not supersede the National Constitution and that a company therefore cannot invoke such a treaty to avoid trying the case in Argentina before local courts.[85] The Argentine judiciary has also recently echoed the government's position by deciding in a landmark case (*Jose Cartellone Construcciones v. Hid roelectrica Norpatagonica S.A.*) that, as far as matters of public policy are involved, the Argentine courts may review the reasonability, fairness, and constitutionality (i.e., the merits) of an arbitration award.[86] Further developments down this line include a new decree passed in 2003 to terminate a decision made in 1996 authorizing the submission of disputes between Argentine Government and a foreign investor, Bulgheroni Group, to international arbitration tribunals,[87] and a reportedly proposed bill aimed at limiting the intervention of national or international arbitral tribunals in cases involving the State, State agencies, or enterprises.[88] Indeed, such anti-BIT

[81] For details of such regional arbitration conventions, see Spinillo & Vogelius, *supra* note 78, at 20, 25–26.

[82] IADB: *Argentina, supra* note 72, at Section 5.4.

[83] Alfaro and Lorenti (2005).

[84] ICSID: CMS Gas Transmission Company v. The Republic of Argentina (Case No. ARB/01/8) Decision of the Tribunal on Objections to Jurisdiction, July 17, 2003, *reprinted as* 42 ILM 788 (2003).

[85] Alfaro (2004a).

[86] Alfaro (2004b).

[87] Laurence Norman, Government Reopens 7-Year-Old Case Vs Oil Group, Dow JoNEs Newswires, Oct. 28, 2003, 15–16.

[88] The proposed bill prohibits access to international arbitration in such cases unless (a) an appeal of their decision before Argentine federal courts is provided, or (b) the State's counterparty in the dispute is a foreign State (State-State disputes); or (c) the Congress has provided for an exception in the case through a specific statute. The bill also requests the Executive to inform the appropriate authorities of Argentina's repeal of any treaty by means of which Argentina has accepted such jurisdiction; and, meanwhile, demands the Executive, its agencies, and enterprises to issue necessary orders or decisions in order to annul prior agreements or decisions contrary to such provisions. Since the bill generally requires all state-investor arbitration cases to be subject to the ultimate control of national courts, it would effectively abolish the finality, and hence the autonomy, of arbitration. In

and investment arbitration moves in Argentina, together with similar moves in other Latin American states, have been regarded as signals of the "resurgence of the Calvo Doctrine."[89]

The constitutionality of BITs and treaty-based investment arbitration, as we will see below, is an issue existing in many Latin American countries that has already been tested before local courts in these countries, notably in Colombia.

Bolivia

The standard of treatment for foreign investors in Bolivia is governed by Bolivian Foreign Investment Law (Law No. 1182).[90] Article 2 of the law expressly adopts the national treatment standard by providing that:

> [e]xcept where otherwise established by law, foreign investors and the entities or companies in which they take part, have the same rights, duties and guarantees that the laws and regulations give to national investors.[91]

With regard to investment dispute settlement, Article 24 of the Constitution of Bolivia expressly denies foreigners the right to diplomatic protection by stating:

> [f]oreign subjects and enterprises are subject to Bolivian laws, and in no case may they invoke exceptional positions or have recourse to diplomatic claims.[92]

Article 10 of the Foreign Investment Law of Bolivia nevertheless permits investors to agree to settle their disputes in courts of arbitration.[93] Accordingly, cases involving technical disputes may be referred to international arbitration panels governed by

this sense, it can be said that it will mean that the Calvo Doctrine finally returns to its birthplace. It remains to be seen, however, whether this is mere rhetoric or will lead to concrete steps toward its adoption. For details of the proposed bill, see Tawil (2005).

[89] Similar recent events in other Latin American States include Brazil's 2004 Private Public Partnership Act prohibiting international arbitration, and Venezuela's constitutionality challenge against international arbitration, which will be discussed below. Indeed, a seminar was organized in order to look into the issue of the resurgence of Calvo and its implications on international arbitration. *See* D.C. Bar Lunch eon Program: The Resurgence of the Calvo Doctrine? *available at* http://www.bgconsulting.com/docs/calvo_program.jpg (last visited July 11, 2006). *See also* Cremades, *supra* note 38, esp. 81–82. For further details of such events in and beyond Latin America and their implications in international investment law, see Shan (2007).

[90] *Ley de Sept. 17, 1990, Inversiones No. 1182, Gaceta Oficial de Bolivia, Sept. 26, 1990. See also* IADB (2006): *Legislation for Foreign Investment Statutes in Countries in the Americas, Comparative Study-Bolivia,* http://alca-ftaa.iadb.org/eng/invest/BOL-1.HTM (05/16/06) [hereinafter IADB: *Bolivia],* Section 1.2.

[91] *Article 2, Ley de Sept. 17, 1990, Inversiones No. 1182, Gaceta Oficial de Bolivia, Sept. 26, 1990.*

[92] Article 24, The Constitution of Bolivia (as amended by No. 2410, Aug. 8, 2002), *in* Constitutions of the Countries of the World (Albert P. Blaustein & Gisbert H. Flanz eds.) Doose-leaf], (20 Vols., Oceana Publications, 1971) [hereinafter World Constitutions).

[93] IADB: *Bolivia, supra* note 90, Section 5.

international arbitration rules.[94] In 1997, Bolivia passed Law No. 1770, a legal framework for dispute settlement and arbitration to which the parties may resort before bringing their disputes before the courts.[95] In this context, it is noted that Bolivia has entered into 22 BITs[96] and is a member of the ICSID Convention, the MIGA Convention, the New York Convention, and the Inter-American Convention on International Commercial Arbitration.[97]

Like Argentina, Bolivia enshrines equal/national treatment as the cardinal standard of treatment for foreign investors. Bolivia appears, however, to be more loyal to the Calvo Doctrine than Argentina, in that Bolivia's Constitution still explicitly renounces diplomatic protection. Nevertheless, technical disputes are allowed to be submitted to international arbitration.

Brazil

Brazilian laws also embrace equal/national treatment for foreign investors. Article 5 of Brazilian Constitution (as amended) states:

> [A]ll persons are equal before the law, without any distinction whatsoever, Brazilians and foreigners residing in the country being ensured of inviolability of the right to life, to liberty, to equality, to security and to property.[98]

This marks a significant change from the 1988 Constitution, which differentiated "Brazilian Company of National Capital" and "Brazilian Company of Foreign Capital" and treated them differently.[99] Law No. 4131 stipulates in Article 2 that "the same legal treatment dispensed to national capital shall, under the same circumstances, be dispensed to the foreign capital invested in the country, any and all forms of discrimination not foreseen in this present law being prohibited."[100] This article is repeated in Article 2 of the Decree No. 55762 that sets down implementing regulations with regard to Law No. 4131 (as amended).[101]

---

94 Wiesner, *supra* note 46, at 460.

95 WTO, *Trade Policy Review-Bolivia: Secretariat's Report* 18, WT/TPR/154/ Rev.l (2005).

96 UNCTAD, *Country-specific Lists of BITs, supra* note 35.

97 IADB: *Bolivia, supra* note 90, Section 5.2.

98 The Constitution of Brazil (including amendments until Constitutional Amendment 52, enacted on Mar. 8, 2006), *available at* http://www.v-brazil.com/governmentllaws/constitution.html (last visited June 16, 2006).

99 Veiga (2004).

100 Law No. 4131, Sept. 3, 1962, which regulates the investment of foreign capital and remittance of funds abroad, *in* ICSID: Investment Laws of the World, [loose leaf] [hereinafter Investment Laws of the World]; *see also* IADB: *Legislation for Foreign Investment Statutes in Countries in the Americas, Comparative Study-Brazil,* http://alca-ftaa.iadb.org/eng/invest/BRA-1.HTM (May 16, 2006) [hereinafter IADB: *Brazil]*, Section 3.1.b.

101 Decree No. 55,762 of Feb. 17, 1965, which sets out regulations for implementation of Law No. 4131, Sept. 3, 1962, as amended, in Investment Laws of the World, *supra* note 100.

With regard to settlement of investment disputes, Brazil also adheres to the aforementioned national treatment principle. Foreign investors are therefore able to resort to the same procedures as the national investors do and there is no special form of recourse for foreign investors.[102] It is important to note, however, that Brazil did not accept arbitration until the Arbitration Act was passed in 1996. Yet the constitutionality of the Act was immediately challenged in the case *MBV u. Resil* before the Brazilian Federal Supreme Court soon after it was promulgated.[103] Although the Act was declared constitutional in the end, the lengthy deliberation on the case (more than five years) and the substantial portion of dissenting judges (four out of eleven including the reporting judge) has clearly demonstrated the country's hesitation and substantial resistance to arbitration, particularly to international arbitration.[104] A year later, on December 30, 2004, Brazil adopted Federal Law No. 11079, establishing a legal framework for Brazilian public–private partnerships (the PPP Law).[105] The PPP Law permits parties to choose arbitration as a means to settle any disputes arising from PPP contracts,[106] but requires that the seat of the arbitration be in Brazil and the proceedings be conducted in the Portuguese language.[107] Also, it only accepts domestic arbitration and expressly prohibits international arbitration. It thus demonstrates the reluctance of the Brazilian government to subject cases involving public entities, such as state-investor disputes, to international arbitration.[108]

This is confirmed by the fact that although Brazil has signed 14 BITs[109] and two MERCOSUR Protocols, it has ratified none of these agreements and protocols.[110] Indeed, the government decided to withdraw these agreements from the consideration of the Brazilian Parliament, because some elements of their texts were considered by members of Parliament to be incompatible with the Brazilian Constitution.[111]

---

[102] IADB: *Brazil, supra* note 100, Section 5.

[103] For details of the case, see Joao Bosco Lee, *Brazil, in* International Arbitration in Latin America, *supra* note 44, at 63–66; Tawil (2006).

[104] Tawil, *supra* note 103.

[105] The law is posted at the Brazilian Ministry of Planning, Budget and Management website, https://www.planalto.gov.br/ccivil_03/_Ato2004-2006/2004/Lei/L11079.htm (last visited June 22, 2006). An English version is also *available at* http://www.planejamento.gov.br/arquivos_down/ppp/legislacao/lei_11079_301204_eng.pdf (last visited June 22, 2006).

[106] Article 11 III, THE PPP LAw, *id.*

[107] *Id.*

[108] As noted by Rubins, the only path toward international arbitration recognized in Brazil is the carefully drafted arbitration clause in contracts between a foreign investor and the Brazilian Government, as "Brazil lacks the legal infrastructure that [exists] in many other countries in Latin America give[ing] foreign investors explicit guarantees of equitable treatment and access to international arbitration." *See* Rubins (2003).

[109] Namely, BITs with Belgium, Chile, Cuba, Denmark, Finland, France, Germany, Italy, the Republic of Korea, the Netherlands, Portugal, Switzerland, the United Kingdom and Venezuela. *See* UNCTAD, *Country-specific Lists of BITs, supra* note 35. *See also* Rubins, *supra* note 108, at 1979, 1088–90.

[110] WTO: *Trade Policy Review-Brazil: Secretariat's Report* 24, WTtrPR/S/140 (Nov. 1, 2004).

[111] *Id.*

Brazil can therefore be regarded as a country that unreservedly upholds the absolute "national/equal treatment" principle in dealing with foreign investors. It does so not only through its domestic laws, but also by rejecting international treaties that would have the effect of granting more favorable treatment to foreign investors.

Chile

The Chilean Constitution establishes national treatment for both national and foreign investors.[112] Article 9 of the Foreign Investment Statute establishes that foreign investment and the enterprises participating in it shall also be subject to the regular legal regime that applies to national investment, and may not be discriminated against either directly or indirectly.[113] The law further clarifies that any legal or regulatory provisions applicable to most of a particular productive activity and that exclude foreign investment shall be deemed discriminatory.[114] Similarly, rules that establish sectoral or zonal exception regimes are discriminatory if foreign investment does not have access to them.[115]

According to Chilean law, foreign investors have the same procedural recourse as local investors.[116] Article 10 of the Statute, furthermore, prescribes that in the event that legal provisions are issued which foreign investors or enterprises with foreign capital may consider to be discriminatory, the investors or enterprises may request the Foreign Investment Committee to eliminate the discrimination, provided that no more than one year has lapsed since the provision was issued.[117] Besides its purely domestic law, Chile is an ICSID signatory, as well as a signatory to the MIGA Convention, the New York Convention, and the Panama Convention.[118] Chile has also signed at least 51 BITs, 15 of which were yet to enter into force.[119]

---

[112] IADB: *Legislation for Foreign Investment Statutes in Countries in the Americas, Comparative Study-Chile*, http://alca-ftaa.iadb.org/eng/invesUCHI-1.HTM (May 16, 2006) [hereinafter IADB: *Chile]*, Section 4.1.

[113] Article 9, Foreign Investment Statute, *in* Investment Laws of the World, *supra* note 100. *See also* IADB: *Chile, supra* note 112, Section 4.1.

[114] *Id.*

[115] *Id.*

[116] IADB: *Chile, supra* note 112, Section 5.1.

[117] Article 10, Foreign Investment Statute, *in* Investment Laws of the World, *supra* note 100. *See also* IADB: *Chile, supra* note 112, Section 5.1.

[118] Carlos E. Jorquiera et al., *Chile, in* International Arbitration in Latin America, *supra* note 44, at 91–92.

[119] Chile has effective BITs with Argentina, Australia, Austria, Belgium, Bolivia, China, Costa Rica, Croatia, Cuba, the Czech Republic, Denmark, Ecuador, El Salvador, Finland, France, Germany, Greece, Guatemala, Honduras, Italy, Indonesia, Lebanon, Malaysia, Nicaragua, Norway, Panama, Paraguay, Peru, the Philippines, Poland, Portugal, Romania, Spain, Sweden, Switzerland, Ukraine, the United Kingdom, Uruguay and Venezuela. Further bilateral investment agreements have been, or are being, negotiated with Brazil, Colombia, the Dominican Republic, Egypt, Greece, Hungary, the Netherlands, New Zealand, South Africa, Tunisia, Turkey, and Viet Nam; those were not yet

It can thus be said that Chile seriously upholds the national treatment principle, with an emphasis on the elimination of discriminatory measures against foreign investors. Meanwhile, Chile is active in signing investment treaties that have the effect of upgrading the standard of treatment and protection afforded to foreign investors, well beyond those accorded to national investors; this may, in turn, result in the "constitutionality" issue elaborated above in Argentina's case. The general attitude of the country seems to be moving away from the Calvo Doctrine toward a more liberal investment regime.

Colombia

The Colombian Constitution generally grants national treatment to foreigners in Colombia, subject to exceptions maintained by the Constitution and the laws.[120] Accordingly, Article 3 of Resolution 51 (issued by the National Economic and Social Policy Council of Colombia (CONPES) pursuant to Law No. 9 of 1991 regulating foreign investment and foreign exchange in Colombia[121]) further elaborates the national treatment standard for foreign investment:

> Subject to Article 100 of the Constitution of Columbia, and to Article 15 of Law 9 of 1991, and except for those matters relating to the transfer of funds abroad, the investment in Colombia of foreign capital will be treated, for all effects and purposes, *in the same way* as are the investments of residents in Colombia. Consequently, and without prejudice to the provisions set forth in special regulations or regimes, *no discriminatory conditions or treatments may be imposed on those who invest foreign capital vis-a-vis national private resident investors, nor may investors of foreign capital be given a more favorable treatment than that granted to national private resident investors.* (emphasis added).[122]

Thus, Colombian law unambiguously states its absolute equal/national treatment principle, which means a prohibition of any sort of discrimination between foreign and domestic investors, subject to express exceptions. Columbian law distinguishes itself from other Latin American legislation in that it still explicitly declares its

in force in May 2003. WTO, *Trade Policy Review-Chile: Secretariat's Report* 18, WT/TPR/S/124 (2003). For more updated information, see UNCTAD, *Country-specific Lists of BITs, supra* note 35.

[120] Article 100 of the Colombian Constitution stipulates that, "[F]oreigners in Colombia enjoy the same civil rights that are granted to the Colombians. Nevertheless, for reasons of public order, the law may subject foreigners to special conditions or deny their exercise of certain civil rights. Also, foreigners enjoy, in the territory of the Republic, the guarantees granted to the nationals, save the limitations established by the Constitution or the law." *See Constituci6n de 1991 con reformas hasta 2005* [Political Constitution of 1991 through 2005 reforms], *available at* http://pdba.georgetown.edu/Constitutions/Colombia/col91.html (June 16, 2006).

[121] IADB: *Legislation for Foreign Investment Statutes in Countries in the Americas, Comparative Study-Colombia*, http://alca-ftaa.iadb.org/eng/invest/COL-1.HTM (May 16, 2006) [hereinafter IADB: *Colombia]*, Sections 3.1 and 4.1.

[122] Article 3 of Statute of Foreign Investment (Resolution 51 as amended), *in* The Investment Laws of the World, *supra* note 100. *See also* IADB: *Colombia, supra* note 121, Section 3.1b.

prohibition of discrimination against domestic investors, i.e., special privileges for foreign investors.

The most important provision related to investment dispute resolution is Article 23 of Resolution 51, which states:

> Except as provided by in international treaties and conventions in force, the provisions set forth in Colombian law shall be applied to the resolution of controversies or conflicts derived from the application of the Regime of Investments of Foreign Capital [the Statute]. International arbitration will be subject to the provisions of Decree 2279 of 1989 as well as the norms and regulations that amend or supplement it.
>
> With the same exception established in the preceding paragraph and without prejudice to actions that may be brought before foreign jurisdictions, all matters pertaining to the investment of capital from abroad will also be subject to the jurisdiction of Colombian courts as well as to Colombian arbitration rules.[123]

Article 23 thus establishes that, as a general principle, foreign investment disputes are subject to the jurisdiction of Colombian courts and tribunals applying local laws, including local arbitration rules. However, if an effective international treaty or convention to which Colombia is a party gives foreign investors the right to submit investment-related disputes to the jurisdiction of a non-Colombian court and/or to apply non-Colombian laws, then the above-quoted local jurisdiction and local law requirements may be waived. Paragraph 2 of Article 23 also suggests that in certain cases it is possible to bring a suit in a foreign jurisdiction, in which case the parties are not required to subject the dispute to Colombian jurisdiction and Colombian arbitration rules. Article 23 therefore opened the door for Colombia to enter into international treaties that accept international arbitration and international law. In this vein, it should be noted that, although Colombia has joined the ICSID Convention, MIGA Convention and the New York Convention, it has so far, like Brazil, not ratified any BITs even though it has signed six of them.[124]

Two constitutionality challenges might have contributed to such a conservative approach toward BIT ratification. The first was a 1995 case against the 1994 BIT with the U.K. The 1994 ColombianU.K. BIT contains such normal BIT provisions as national treatment, MFN treatment, and expropriations, and their compensation. In particular, expropriation is prohibited unless it is for a public purpose, non-discriminatory, and accompanied by the payment of "prompt, adequate, and effective compensation."[125] As required by the Constitution,[126] the BIT (as enacted by Law 246/95) was presented to the Colombian Constitutional Court for its certification. The Court ruled by a six to three majority that the BIT was contrary to the Colombian

[123] Article 23 of Statute of Foreign Investment (Resolution 51 as amended), *in* Investment Laws of the World, *supra* note 100. *See also* IADB: *Colombia, supra* note 121, Section 5.1.

[124] UNCTAD, *Country-specific Lists of BITs, supra* note 35.

[125] Schneiderman (2000b).

[126] Article 241, Colombian Constitution of 1994.

Constitution, particularly in two respects.[127] First, the BIT would effectively deactivate such provisions of the Colombian Constitution as the provision on expropriation without the payment of compensation in the interests of equity.[128] It was held that the government could not waive the exercise of a power delegated to it by the Constitution by conceding the payment of prompt, adequate, and effective compensation in case of all expropriation. Second, the investment treaty runs against the equal/national treatment provisions of the Constitution by granting British investors more favorable treatment with respect to expropriations than that available to Colombian nationals. The Constitutional Court rendered a similar decision in a later case with regard to a Cuba-Colombia BIT.[129] It is notable that despite the removal of the expropriation without compensation in case of equity provision after the 1999 amendment to the Constitution, the Colombian government still has not ratified any BITs.

It can thus be concluded that, on the one hand, Colombian laws uphold the Calvo Doctrine by adhering to the principle of equal/national treatment for foreign investment in an absolute sense, prohibiting discrimination against either foreign or domestic investors. On the other hand, Colombian laws deviate from the Doctrine in that they opened the door through domestic legislation to accept non-national jurisdiction and the application of non-national law based on international treaties. However, the constitutionality challenge to and the non-ratification of the signed BITs suggest that strong resistance still exists in Columbia toward such deviation from Calvo principles.

Ecuador

Ecuador also sets forth national treatment as the cardinal standard for foreign investment. This stems from Article 13 of the Ecuadorian Constitution, which stipulates that, with the exception of limitations established in the Constitution and by law, foreigners generally enjoy the same rights as do Ecuadorians.[130] Under the Constitution, the Law on Investment Promotion and Guarantees and its implementing regulations and the Foreign Trade and Investment Law are the key instruments governing foreign investments in Ecuador.[131] Article 13 of the Law on Investment Promotion and Guarantees confirms that foreign investments enjoy the same conditions as those provided for investments by Ecuadorian natural and legal persons.[132] However,

[127] Colombian Constitutional Court Decision No. C-358/96, *as cited in* Schneiderman, *supra* note 125, at 107 and n. 176.

[128] Article 58, Colombian Constitution as of 1994.

[129] Colombian Constitutional Court Decision No. C-379/96, *as cited in* Schneiderman, *supra* note 125, at 107 and n. 178.

[130] It was Article 14 in the 1979 Constitution. In the current Constitution, the Constitution of 1998, it is retained but renumbered as Article 13.

[131] WTO: Trade Policy Review-Ecuador: Secretariat's Report 18, WTtrPR/S/rev.1 (2005).

[132] *Id.*

the Law on Investment Promotion and Guarantees allows discriminatory treatment between domestic and foreign investors in "strategic" areas, including fisheries, mining, and hydrocarbons.[133] The Constitution restricts the purchase, for economic purposes, of land or concessions in national security areas by foreigners.[134] Thus, the national treatment principle is provided to foreign investors but with important reservations.

With regard to settlement of disputes, the Ecuadorian Constitution used to reject diplomatic protection and foreign jurisdiction in foreign investment contract disputes.[135] The current Constitution modifies this provision, establishing an exception to the exclusive local jurisdiction requirement in cases where foreign jurisdiction was established in accordance with an international treaty. Article 14 of the 1998 Constitution reads:

> [C]ontracts executed between the Government, or between Public Entities and natural or legal foreign persons, will implicitly entail the waiver of any diplomatic protection;
>
> it is not allowed to agree to submit the aforementioned contracts to a foreign jurisdiction if they are executed in the territory of the Republic of Ecuador, unless it is provided for in an international agreement.[136]

Accordingly, the Law on Investment Promotion and Guarantees affirms, "[B]oth the State and foreign investors shall be able to submit any dispute arising from the application of this law to any Arbitration Court constituted under the terms of international treaties of which Ecuador is a member, as well as to the procedures specifically agreed upon or set forth in bilateral or multilateral agreement executed and ratified by Ecuador."[137] In this context, Ecuador has signed 29 and ratified 22 BITs, mostly in the 1990s.[138] Ecuador also accepted ICSID Convention, MIGA Convention and New York Convention.[139]

Ecuador thus serves as another example of a Latin American state that generally still insists on the Calvo Doctrine but has modified it so as to allow the flexibility provided for in international treaties.

Mexico

In general, Mexico grants national treatment to foreigners and foreign investors. This stems from Article 33 of the Mexican Constitution, which entitles them the

---

[133] *Id.*

[134] Article 15, The Political Constitution of the Republic of Ecuador 1998.

[135] Article 16, The Political Constitution of the Republic of Ecuador 1979.

[136] Article 14, The Political Constitution of the Republic of Ecuador 1998.

[137] Article 32, The Law on Investment Promotion and Guarantees, *in* Investment Laws of the World, *supra* note 100.

[138] UNCTAD, *Country-specific Lists of BITs*, *supra* note 35.

[139] Ramiro S. Cordero, *Ecuador, in* International Arbitration in Latin America, *supra* note 44, at 135.

guarantees granted by Chapter I Title I of the Constitution. In terms of property rights, Article 27 contains a well-known Calvo provision:

> Only Mexicans by birth or naturalization and Mexican companies have the right to acquire ownership of lands, waters, and their appurtenances or to obtain concessions for the exploitation of mines or waters. The State may grant the same right to foreigners, provided they agree before the Ministry of Foreign Affairs to consider themselves as nationals in respect to such property, and bind themselves not to invoke the protection of their governments in matters relating thereto; under penalty, in case of non-compliance with this agreement, of forfeiture of the acquired property to the Nation.[140]

This provision clearly upholds the national treatment principle and at the same time denounces diplomatic protection. It was reiterated and implemented in Mexico's previous FDI law and regulations, namely the Foreign Investment Law of 1973[141] and Foreign Investment Regulations of 1989.[142] It was, however, deleted from the current FDI legal regime, which consisted mainly of the Foreign Investment Law of 1993 and the Foreign Investment Regulations 1998, a sign of a more liberal approach taken by the authorities. Despite such deletions, however, Mexico's general adherence to the Calvo principle elaborated above remains valid, as the constitutional provision remains unchanged.

With regard to dispute settlement, foreign investors generally have the same procedural recourse as national investors.[143] In this regard, it is notable that relevant local

140 Article 27, Mexican Constitution.

141 *1973 Law to Promote Mexican Investment and to Regulate Foreign Investment,* Official Gazetie, Mar. 9, 1973. Article 3 of this law provided:

> Foreigners who acquire properties of any kind in the Mexican Republic agree, because of such action, to consider themselves as Mexican nationals with regard to these properties and not to invoke the protection of their governments with respect to such properties, under penalty, in case of violations, of forfeiting to the Mexican Government the properties thus acquired.

142 Regulations of the Law to Promote Mexican Investment and to Regulate Foreign Investment (as amendments), *Diario Oficial de la Federaci6n* (Mexico), May 16, 1989. It stipulated in Article 31:

> When the "foreigners exclusion clause" is not in the company by-laws, the express agreement or covenant, which is an integral part of the company bylaws, whereby the present or future foreign partners of the companies in question shall be obligated to formally agree with the Secretary of Foreign Relations to be considered as nationals with respect to shares of said companies which they acquire or of which they are holders, as well as of the assets, rights, concessions, participation or interest which they hold in such companies, or else of the rights and obligations which they derive from the contracts in which the same companies are party to with the Mexican authorities, and to not invoke, for that purpose, the protection of their Governments, under the penalty, otherwise, of losing their equity interests in favor of the Nation.

143 IADB: *Legislation for Foreign Investment Statutes in Countries in the Americas, Comparative Study-Mexico*, http://alca-ftaa.iadb.org/eng/invest/MEX-1.HTM (May 16, 2006) [hereinafter IADB: *Mexico*], Section 5.1.

laws, such as the Federal Code of Civil Procedure and the Code of Civil Procedure of the Federal District, have established the exclusive competence of the national courts on certain matters, including matters relating to land and water, resources of exclusive economic zones, acts of authorities, criminal liability, most family matters, tax matters, employment matters, and certain agricultural matters.[144]

Special recourse for foreign investors, however, is envisaged only in the dispute settlement sections of free trade treaties or BITs to which Mexico is a party.[145] In this context, it must be noted that in 1992 Mexico ratified the North America Free Trade Agreement (NAFTA), the Chapter 11 of which contains a very liberal investment regime. Since NAFTA, Mexico has concluded several BITs, of which 12 have entered into force.[146] Mexico is a member of the New York Contention and the Inter-America Convention for Commercial Arbitration, but notably has not joined with ICSID Convention or MIGA Convention.

Here again, it appears to be an issue of the constitutionality of these international treaties because Mexican nationals are not entitled to such standards and access to international remedies as are provided for in these treaties. In an effort to address this issue, the Mexican government passed the Law Regarding the Making of Treaties in 1992,[147] which authorizes the state to negotiate international treaties with enforceable dispute settlement mechanisms.[148] Some commentators believe that this law has cleared "any doubts about the scope of the Calvo Clause in the Constitution."[149] However, given that the Law Regarding the Making of Treaties is law subordinate to the Constitution, one has to doubt whether such a statement is overoptimistic. Besides, the Law also requires such dispute settlement mechanisms to render equal treatment to Mexicans and foreigners.[150]

Peru

The Peruvian Constitution of 1993 (as amended) established the principle of equal treatment for foreign and national investment with an exception to ensure reciprocity.[151] Article 63 of the Constitution states:

---

[144] Claus von Wobeser, *Mexico, in* International Arbitration in Latin America, *supra* note 44, at 160–62.

[145] *Id.*

[146] UNCTAD, *Country-specific Lists of BITs, supra* note 35.

[147] Law Regarding the Making of Treaties, Dec. 21, 1991, Mex., 31 I.L.M. 390 (1992). The official text of the law appears in CDLX *Diario Oficial de la Federaci6n*, Jan. 2, 1992 at 2.

[148] Canovas (1992).

[149] *See id.* at 391. *See also* Daly (1994); Schneiderman, *supra* note 23.

[150] Garza Canovas, *supra* note 148, at 391.

[151] WTO: *Trade Policy Review-Peru: Secretariat's Report* 17, WTtrPR/S/69 (2000).

> Domestic and foreign investments are subject to the same conditions. If another country or countries adopt protectionist or discriminatory measures that prejudice the national interest, the State may, in defense of the latter, adopt similar measure.[152]

This national treatment standard is reflected in Legislative Decree No. 662 of August 29, 1991, on foreign investment promotion.[153] Decree 662 sets as its objective the removal of "[o]bstacles and restraints to foreign investors in order to guarantee the equality of rights and duties applicable to foreign and national investors."[154] and establishes in Article 2 the national treatment standard by providing that, except for constitutional and decree limitations, foreign investors and their companies have "the same rights and obligations as those of national investors and companies." It goes further by requiring, in absolute terms, that "the national laws shall, in no event, discriminate against investors or companies on the basis of national or foreign investors participating therein."[155] In particular, Decree 662 announces that "all laws limiting or restricting in any manner foreign investments in any economic activity are hereby revoked as from the effective date thereof."[156] It is therefore clear that the national treatment standard established in Peruvian law emphasizes the prohibition of discrimination against foreign investors in an attempt to attract FDI.

With regard to dispute settlement, Peruvian Constitution contains the following provision:

> In all State contracts and those of public officials with resident aliens, submission of latter to the laws and competent authorities of the Republic and their renunciation to all diplomatic claims are in order. Contracts of financial nature may be exempted from the national jurisdiction.
>
> The State and other persona of public law may submit disagreements stemming from contractual relations to courts established by virtue of treaties in force. They may also submit to domestic or international arbitration in the form provided by law.[157]

This constitutional provision might be regarded as a moderated "Calvo Clause." It is essentially a Calvo Clause in that it absolutely denounces diplomatic protection and generally upholds the exclusive use of domestic law and domestic jurisdiction. It is moderated by allowing two exceptions: one is for contracts of a financial nature, which are allowed to resort to non-national jurisdiction; the other is for treaty-based arrangements on jurisdiction and applicable law. One commentator maintains that there is a presumption in favor of investment-dispute settlement before Peruvian courts and under Peruvian law, since although Article 16 of Decree 662 permits

---

[152] Article 63, paras. 1–2, The Political Constitution of the Republic of Peru 1993 (as amended to 2005), *in* World Constitutions, *supra* note 92.

[153] *Supra* note 151.

[154] Preamble and Article 2 respectively, Legislative Decree No. 662 of 29 Aug. 1991, *as in* Investment Laws of the World, *supra* note 100.

[155] *Id.* Article 2.

[156] *Id.* Article 31.

[157] Article 63, The Political Constitution of the Republic of Peru 1993 (as amended to 2005), *in* World Constitutions, *supra* note 92.

the State to submit disputes to arbitration tribunals based on international treaties, foreign investors can never be certain if the Peruvian government will actually agree to do so.[158] Nevertheless, this exception at least makes it constitutionally possible for the government to enter into international agreements on the solution of investment disputes. Indeed, Peru has signed 29 and ratified 26 BITs.[159] Peru is also a member of ICSID Convention, MIGA Convention, New York Convention and the Panama Arbitration.[160]

Venezuela

In accordance with the 1999 Venezuelan Constitution, foreigners and foreign investors enjoy national treatment. Article 301 of the Constitution states:

> [B]usiness enterprises, organs or persons of foreign nationality shall not be granted with regimes more advantageous than those established for Venezuelan nationals. Foreign investment is subject to the same conditions as domestic investment.[161]

The Investment Protection and Promotion Law of 1999[162] affirms such a principle by stating in Article 7 that, in similar circumstances, foreign investors and their investments are subject to the same rights and obligation as national investors and their investments, except for measures provided for in special laws and the limitations contained in the present law.[163] The law also provides in Article 6 "fair and equitable treatment" for foreign investment in accordance with international law, and guarantees that foreign investors will not be subject to "arbitrary or discriminatory measures affecting the maintaining, management, use, enjoyment, expansion, sale or liquidation" of their investment.[164] Article 9 goes further, allowing foreign investors to enjoy the more favorable of the two treatment standards established by Articles 6 and 7, i.e., between national treatment and fair and equitable treatment.[165] Article 8 establishes MFN treatment for foreign investment.[166] While the preceding four articles seem to have, distinctively, adopted BIT language guaranteeing the best

[158] Wiesner, *supra* note 46, at 463.

[159] UNCTAD, *Country-specific Lists of BITs, supra* note 35.

[160] Pelipe 0. Parodi, *Peru and Annex 1: Table of Adherence to the New York Convention, Panama Convention and Washington Convention, in* International Arbitration in Latin America, *supra* note 44, at 194 and 439.

[161] Article 301, The Constitution of the Bolivarian Republic of Venezuela (adopted at the referendum of Dec. 15, 1999), *as in* World Constitutions, *supra* note 92.

[162] *Ley de Promoci6n y Protecci6n de Inversiones (Decreto N° 356, 3 de octubre de 1999), Gaceta Oficial N° 5.390 Extraordinario de fecha 22 de octubre de 1999* [hereinafter Investment Protection and Promotion Law].

[163] *Id.* Article 7.

[164] *Id.* Article 6.

[165] *Id.* Article 9.

[166] *Id.* Article 8.

standards of treatment for foreign investors, Article 10 turns the attention to national investors and assures that, in similar circumstances, they will be not be treated in a way that is "less favorable" than the treatment accorded to foreign investors.[167] Thus, the Investment Protection and Promotion Law establishes high standards of treatment for all investors and their investments.

On dispute settlement, the 1999 Venezuelan Constitution includes an unambiguous "Calvo Clause" that says:

> Article 151: In the public interest contracts, unless inapplicable by reason of the nature of such contracts, a clause shall be deemed included even if not expressed, whereby any doubts and controversies which may raise concerning such contracts and which cannot be resolved amicably by the contracting parties, shall be decided by the competent courts of the Republic, in accordance with its laws and shall not on any grounds or for any reason give rise to foreign claims.[168]

The Constitution thus not only renounces diplomatic protection, but also unreservedly upholds the exclusive jurisdiction of national courts and national law on public interest contracts. In this regard, it appears that Article 155 of the Constitution would not be of relevance, as it seems to cover treaties between state parties, but not contracts made by the state as governed in Article 151. Article 155 essentially establishes that if there is any international agreement entered into by the Venezuelan government and a foreign party, any disputes arising between the parties in connection with the interpretation or implementation of the agreement should be resolved by "peaceful means recognized under international law or agreed upon between them in advance."[169]

Such a Calvo position does not, however, seem to have been taken in the Investment Protection and Promotion Law, which effectively adopts a very liberal, BIT-style approach toward the settlement of international investment disputes.[170] Articles 21 through to 23 of the Law deal with such issues. Article 23 sets forth the rule for the resolution of disputes relating to the application of the present law. It provides that investors (presumably national or foreign) may choose to submit the dispute to a local court or a local arbitration tribunal after having exhausted all administrative remedies.[171] If a dispute involves an "international investor," special channels will apply as provided for in Articles 21 and 22. Article 22 deals with situations where a dispute arises between Venezuela and an international investor whose home state has an investment treaty arrangement with Venezuela, or where provisions of the ICSID Convention or MIGA Convention are applicable to the dispute.[172] In such cases,

---

[167] *Id.* Article 10.

[168] Article 151, The Constitution of the Bolivarian Republic of Venezuela (adopted at the referendum of Dec. 15, 1999), *as in* World Constitutions, *supra* note 92.

[169] *Id.* Article 155.

[170] Articles 21–23, Investment Promotion and Protection Law, *supra* note 161.

[171] *Id.* Article 23.

[172] *Id.* Article 22.

arbitration under the terms of the relevant treaty or agreement would apply.[173] Alternatively, the international investor may opt to institute proceedings in Venezuela.[174] Related to these policies, Venezuela has signed 25 and ratified 21 BITs[175] and is a member of the ICSID Convention, MIGA Convention, New York Convention, and the Panama Convention.[176]

In such disputes, where the disputant international investor is a national of a state with which Venezuela does not have an investment treaty and the dispute is related to "the interpretation and application of the rules provided for in the present Law," then the international investor may assign the dispute to its home state, which may then submit the case to international arbitration once diplomatic channels are exhausted.[177] In that case, the composition, method of selection, procedure, and treatment of costs of the arbitration are to be determined by mutual agreement of the investor's home state and Venezuela.[178] Alternatively, the international investor may opt to take the domestic remedies established in Article 23.[179]

Two major conflicts between the Constitution and the FDI Law may be observed here. First, the diplomatic protection envisaged in Article 21 conflicts with the denunciation of diplomatic claims stipulated in Article 151 of the Constitution, as it could well the case that the dispute also involves a public interest contract. Second, for the same reason, the international remedies for disputes involving international investors provided for in Articles 21 and 22 also seem to breach the exclusive national jurisdiction requirement in the same constitutional provision.

In this regard, it would be useful to recall that the Venezuelan government had already been challenged by local citizens for violation of Article 151 on its agreement to submit disputes arising out of oil concession agreements to international arbitration. In the socalled "Exploration Round Case," a group of Venezuelan citizens filed a petition in December 1995 with the Venezuelan Supreme Court asking for a ruling on the constitutionality of arbitration provisions in the Congressional Accord approving the 1995 Exploration Bidding Round, which included a provision (Condition 17) requiring all disputes arising from Association Agreements (i.e., oil exploration agreements with investors concluded following the bid) be resolved by binding arbitration.[180] Although the case was resolved in favor of arbitration and foreign investors, the uncertainty of the constitutionality of arbitration has not

---

173 *Id.*

174 *Id.*

175 UNCTAD, *Country-specific Lists of BITs, supra* note 35.

176 Bernardo Weininger & David M. Lindsey, *Venezuela and Annex 1: Table of Adherence to the New York Convention, Panama Convention and the Washington Convention, supra* note 44, *in* International Arbitration in Latin America, at 227 and 439.

177 Article 21, Investment Promotion and Protection Law, *supra* note 161.

178 *Id.*

179 *Id.*

180 Elisabeth E. Elijuri, *Oil Opening: A Constitutional Challenge, available at* http://www.natlaw.com/pubs/spveenl.htm (last visited Feb. 12, 2006).

been eradicated because the Supreme Court did not do much to clarify the ambiguity surrounding the "nature of the contract" exception. This ambiguity was not helped by the new Constitution adopted in 1999 after the case was settled, which kept the contested provision (Article 127 in the previous Constitution but merely renumbered it as Article 151). Further, in March 2001 the President of Venezuela issued Instructive Order No. 4 "[t]o regulate the internal review mechanisms for public interest contracts to be executed by the Republic, particularly, in connection with the inclusion of international arbitration clauses."[181] According to the Order, contracts concerning public interests must be submitted to the Attorney General of the Republic for an opinion on the legality of the arbitration clause in light of the Article 151 of the new Constitution.[182] In a more recent case, the *Minera las Cristinas, C.A. (MINCA) v. Corporacion Venezuelana de Guyana (CVG) case* (the *MINCA Case*),[183] the Supreme Court dismissed MINCA's petition on the ground that the subject matter concerned state assets and therefore could not be subject to arbitration.[184] The Court founded its decision on, *inter alia,* the aforementioned Article 151 of the Constitution, which generally subjects public interests contracts to the exclusive jurisdiction of local courts.[185] It thus re-started the uncertainty of Venezuela's position toward international arbitration.

Venezuelan law is therefore characterized by, on the one hand, the rather traditional provisions in the Constitution that adopt a Calvo approach, and, on the other hand, the very liberal provisions in the FDI law that adopt BIT-style standards of treatment and dispute settlement methods. Venezuelan law thus displays significant disparities between the two levels of laws, particularly on dispute settlement. The constitutionality of governmental actions has already been challenged again and again before Venezuelan courts.

Observations

Despite differences in detail, four general observations might be extracted from the preceding survey on the domestic laws in the nine major Latin American states.

First of all, all the countries considered subscribe to the national/equal treatment standard. In most of the countries, the national/equal treatment standard is guaranteed in the national constitutions and reaffirmed in relevant FDI laws. Though this generally demonstrates the continued existence and validity of the Calvo principle, it must be noted that there has been a shift of emphasis, from non-discrimination against nationals and national investors, toward a general requirement of non-discrimination

---

[181] Werninger & Lindsey, *Venezuela, supra* note 176, at 235.

[182] *Id.*

[183] Decision No. 0083 of the Political Administrative Chamber of the Supreme Court of July 15, 2004.

[184] *Id.*

[185] *Id.*

based on nationality. Thus, in the constitutions of most countries, foreigners and foreign investors are guaranteed the "same rights and obligation" as nationals and national investors. In some countries, such as Colombia and Venezuela, emphasis has been explicitly placed on both ends of the national treatment standard: the non-discrimination against foreign investors on one end and non-discrimination against national investors on the other. Clearly such legislation reflects the influence of BITs; the recent Venezuelan FDI law effectively copies BIT standards. It might be said that Calvo and BIT approaches, the two traditionally distinct and opposing approaches toward national treatment, have both been transformed and have converged here to formulate a standard of national treatment that pursues genuine equality: equality of treatment regardless of nationality. Nevertheless, such transformation and convergence may still be regarded as changes within the Calvo paradigm of national treatment, a paradigm based on the equality of states and the equality of individuals.

Second, apart from Brazil (and, to a lesser degree, Colombia,) all countries have accepted international investment treaty-based arbitration, by explicit domestic provisions and/or by actively entering into investment treaties. However, the degree of such acceptance varies. Thus in Bolivia only "technical disputes" might be referred to international arbitration, while in Venezuela, foreign investment disputes can be submitted for international arbitration even though there is no treaty obligation specifically providing for such submissions. Needless to say, international investment treaty-based arbitration is simply inaccessible to foreign investors in Brazil. The access of different foreign investors to international arbitration varies, depending on whether there is a valid BIT between their home states and the host country, and on the specific provisions on dispute settlement contained in such BITs. Nonetheless, despite the potential issue of constitutionality in some countries and apart from Brazil, it is clear that Latin American states have generally moved away from absolute exclusive national jurisdiction and have accepted general international law as applicable law. In this sense, one may say that Calvo has been substantially eroded and generally discarded, albeit with certain important exceptions and reservations highlighted in the end of Part III.

Third, diplomatic protection is still expressly denounced in the constitutions of most countries, namely Bolivia, Colombia, Ecuador, Mexico, Peru, and Venezuela, particularly in relation to public interest contracts. In this regard, it might be said that Calvo is still very much alive.

Finally, recent years seem to have seen a "resurgence" of Calvo, witnessed most notably by constitutionality challenges in Argentina, Colombia, and Venezuela against BITs and investment arbitration, and Brazil's PPP Law prohibiting international arbitration.

Conclusion: Calvo Is Not Dead but Deactivated

The preceding survey of domestic laws and international treaties by Latin American States shows that Calvo is still alive with regard to diplomatic protection, alive but transformed and melded with BITs on the national treatment standard, and greatly eroded and largely discarded on the exclusive national jurisdiction and national law requirement. Admittedly, the last element, the exclusive national jurisdiction and national law requirement, constitutes the core of the whole doctrine. Even on this point, as discussed above, Calvo is not completely dead, as there are still important exceptions and reservations. It would therefore only be fair to conclude that Calvo has been significantly changed, or substantially "disfigured," or generally "deactivated," but not yet completely "dead." When political and economic climates are "right," it could be re-activated again and "resurge," as what seems to be happening.

References

Alfaro CE, Lorenti PM (2005) The growing opposition of Argentina to ICSID arbitral tribunals: a conflict between international and domestic law? J World Invest Trade 6:426–427, 428–430

Alfaro CE (2004a) The battle of the century: Argentina against the ICSID arbitration and the BITs. World Law Group E-News 31. http://www.imakenews.com/bcastro/e_Art000332318.cfm?x=Bl,O,w (last visited July 9, 2006).

Alfaro CE (2004b) ICSID arbitration and BITs challenged by the argentine government. http://www.alfarolaw.com/ima/tapa/alfaro3.htm (last visited July 9, 2006)

Biggs G (2004) The Latin American treatment of international arbitration and foreign investments and the Chile-U.S. free trade agreement. ICSID Rev-Foreign Invest Law J 19.68

Blackaby N et al (2002) Overview of regional developments. In: Blackaby N et al (eds) International arbitration in Latin America, at 10

Bulmer-Thomas V (1994) The economic history of Latin America since independence

Canovas AG (1992) Introductory note to the law regarding the making of treaties. ILM 31:390, 391

Claessens S (1991) Alternative forms of external finance. World Bank, Working Paper No. 812

Cremades BM (2004) Disputes arising out of foreign direct investment in Latin America: a new look at the Calvo doctrine and other jurisdictional issues. Disput Resolut J 59:78, 80

Daly J (1994) Has Mexico crossed the border on state responsibility for economic injury to aliens?-Foreign investment and the Calvo Clause in Mexico after NAFTA. St. Mary's L J 25:1147, at 1189 (1994)

Dolzer R (1981) New foundations of the law of expropriation of alien property. Am J Int Law 75:553, 583–589

Edwards S (1993) Latin American economic integration: a new perspective on an old dream. World Economy 16:317

Golsong H (1991) Introduction to treaty concerning the reciprocal encouragement and protection of investment between Argentina and the USA. ILM 31:124

Guzman AT (1997) Explaining the popularity of bilateral investment treaties: why LDCs sign treaties that hurt them? Harvard, Jean Monnet Working Paper No.12/97, at 72

Lillich R (1975) The diplomatic protection of nationals Abroad: an elementary principle of international law under attack. Am J Int Law 69:359, 361

Lipstein K (1945) The place of the Calvo clause in international law. In: British yearbook of international law, vol 22, pp 130, 131–33

Manning-Cabrol D (1995) The imminent death of the Calvo clause and the rebirth of the Calvo principle: equality of foreign and national investors. Law Poly Int Bus 26:1169
Murphy EE Jr (1990) The Andean decisions on foreign investment: an international matrix of national law. Int Law 24:643, 653
Rubins ND (2003) Investment arbitration in Brazil. J World Invest Trade 4, at 1080–1081, 1091
Salacuse JW (1990) BIT by BIT: the growth of bilateral investment treaties and their impact on foreign investment in developing countries. Int Law 24:655, 664–673
Schachter O (1984) Compensation for expropriation, editorial comment. Am J Int Law 78:121, 127
Scheurer C (2005) Calvo's grandchildren: the return of local remedies in investment arbitration. Law Pract Int Courts Trib 4:1, at 3–5
Schneiderman D (2000a) Investment rules and the new constitutionalism. Law Soc Inquiry 25:757, 766
Schneiderman D (2000b) Constitutional approaches to privatization: an inquiry into the magnitude of neo-liberal constitutionalism. Law Contemp Pross 63:83, at 107
Shan W (2007) From "north-south divide" to "private-public debate": revival of Calvo Doctrine and the changing land scape in international investment law. Northwest J Int Law Bus (Spring, forthcoming) 27(3)
Shea D (1955) The Calvo clause: a problem of inter-American and international law and diplomacy 20
Tawil GS (2005) Is Calvo finally back? Trans Disput Manag 3. http://www.transnational-dispute-management.com/news/tdm2-2005_5.htm (last visited Feb. 18, 2006)
Tawil GS (2006) The role of arbitration and international, regional, subregional and bilateral treaties in Latin America. http://66.249.93.104/search?q::cache:xjw8Vj40l7wJ:www.bomchilgroup.org/argdec02.html+Brazilratifiedcolonialprotocolercosur&hl=zhCN&ct=clnk&cd==9 (May 22, 2006)
Vandevelde KJ (1998) Sustainable liberalism and the international investment regime. Mrch J Int Law 19:373, 379 (1998)
Veiga PDM (2004) Foreign direct investment in Brazil: regulation, flows and contribution to development 3–4 (2004). http://www.iisd.org/pdf72004/investment_country_report_brazil.pdf (last visited May 20, 2006)
Wesley RC (1975) The procedural Malaise of foreign investment disputes in Latin America: from local tribunals to fact-finding. Law Poly Int Bus 7:813, 818
Wiesner EA (1993) ANCOM: a new attitude toward foreign investment? Unvi Miami Inter-Am Law Rev 435, 447
Zamora S (1997) Allocating legislative competence in the Americas: the early experience under NAFTA and the challenge of hemispheric integration. Haus J Int Law 19:615, 622

Wenhua Shan Professor of Law, Dean of the School of Humanities and Social Sciences, Xi'an Jiaotong University, and University Chair Professor of Law, Xiamen University, China; Reader in International Economic Law, Oxford Brookes University, England. Ph.D. (Cambridge), Ph.D. (Xiamen). Senior Consultant, Haoliwen PRC Attorneys, Shanghai. This article is based on a paper presented at the Society of Legal Scholars Symposium 2006, entitled *Redefining Sovereignty: An International Debate on Sovereignty and International Economic Law*, held at Oxford Brookes University, May 2006. The author would like to thank the conference participants, particularly Professor James Crawford, Professor M. Sornarajah and Dr. Joachim Karl, for their invaluable comments, and Mr. Zhang Sheng for assistance on the footnotes.

Chapter 3
Calvo is Back! Changing Sovereignty and Evolutionary Investment Law in a Leaving and Return of the State Paradigm

Shen Wei and Feng Shuo

Introduction

Following the structural transformation of the global economic development model along with global economic liberalization, transnational investment has turned into a vital driving force accelerating the pace of economic globalization. As the trend of de-globalization unfolds, however, the modern international investment law regime is currently undergoing structural changes and has increasingly drawn global attention. Unlike other transnational economic activities such as international trade, international investment not merely concerns the private interests of investors but relates to the economic interests of capital importing and exporting states. Hence, the modern international investment law regime premised on international investment agreements (IIAs) has its main content developed and evolving on the basis of the triangular relationship among host states, home states, and investors and the dual dimensions of public–private. The institutional development and structural constraints of the entire

---

The author acknowledges and is grateful for the support of the Singapore International Dispute Resolution Academy's BRI program.

W. Shen (✉)
Shanghai Jiao Tong University Law School, 1954 Huashan Road, Xuhui District, Shanghai 200230, China
e-mail: shenwei@sjtu.edu.cn

S. Feng
International Law School, Shanghai University of Political Science and Law, No. 7989 Waiqingsong Road, Qingpu District, Shanghai 201701, China

© The Author(s), under exclusive license to Springer Nature Singapore Pte Ltd. 2024
S. Wei (ed.), *International Investment Law at the Juncture*, International Law in Asia,
https://doi.org/10.1007/978-981-97-2183-2_3

investment governance regime essentially cannot be separated from the dynamic balance among the interests of the three players and the private–public dimensions.[1]

In recent years, there has been a new movement in international investment law along with the transformative changes in global economic growth.[2] In the article titled, *The Return of the State*, José E. Alvarez investigated the institutional changes in the field of international investment *vis-à-vis* some key states represented and led by the United States (US).[3] Some states are increasingly emphasizing the protection of a host state's sovereignty (in the form of its sovereign right or power to regulate foreign investment activities) in the context of reshaping the modern international investment law regime, labeled as the "return" of the state.[4] Opposite to this movement was the leaving of the state where the host state imposes various constraints on its sovereignty in exchange for better investor protection with the aim of attracting more foreign investment and promoting economic development.[5]

This research is composed of five parts including Introduction and Conclusion. Part two, through the lens of the Calvo Doctrine, will review the construction process of the modern international investment law regime. This part first illustrates the limitations of customary international law in coordinating international investment interests. With the development of international investment, maximizing the benefits of capital flows needs the "leaving" of the state in investment substantive rules. Meanwhile, the "leaving" of the state also promotes investor–state dispute settlement (ISDS). Part three will address the "return" of the state, a recent change to the course of international investment law. First, states' "return" has become the most vital feature of the ISDS reform in recent years. Second, after the global financial crisis, the anti-liberalization transformation of foreign investment law shows a more pronounced tendency to the "return" of the states. Finally, the goal of the international investment law regime also shifts from investor protection to the right to regulate, indicating the rise of sovereignty and the return of the Calvo Doctrine. Part four will preliminarily assess the evolutionary process of the modern international investment law regime under the "leaving" and "return" of the state and make predictions as to the development trend as a whole.

---

[1] Shan (2007).

[2] Sornarajah (2015).

[3] Alvarez (2011).

[4] *Id.*

[5] *See generally* Strange (1996).

The State's "Leaving" and the Construction of the Modern International Investment Law Regime

A. Limitations of Customary International Law and the Coordination of Interests in International Investment Law

States are not immune from the international law discourse when they partake in international investment activities. Sovereignty constitutes the core element of international law and is always the crown of a nation-state.[6] As early as the eighteenth century, Emer de Vattel, from the standpoint of natural law and by analogy between the state and the individual, pointed out:

> Since men are naturally equal, and a perfect equality prevails in their rights and obligations, as equally proceeding from nature - nations composed of men, and considered as so many free persons living together in the state of nature, are naturally equal, and inherit from nature the same obligations and rights. Power or weakness does not in this respect produce any difference.[7]

Therefore, the principle of sovereign equality of states, as a fundamental principle of modern international law, is the basic principle followed by sovereign states in transacting relevant international activities, including investment.

Different from other transnational economic activities, international investment activities are substantially a process in which foreign investors make capital contributions to and participate in the economic construction of the host state. Investment activities are deeply rooted in the host state's existing governance and regulatory regime, touching upon all aspects of the host state's legal and governance regimes. Foreign investors making capital investments in a host state should unquestionably comply with the host state's law while respecting its sovereignty. Thus, where foreign investors invest, how they invest, how investment income is protected, and what remedial measures are taken for the damages they may have suffered in this model, all depend on the demands of the host state.

Since customary international law principally coordinates the relations between sovereign states, investors as private actors are not eligible subjects under customary international law.[8] Early theories of international law highlighted the importance of eligible subjects in international law. The so-called protection of aliens was once a defining feature of international law. It involved mostly Western powers demanding respect for certain minimum standards toward their nationals abroad. It gave rise to a variety of mixed claims commissions notably between the US and Latin American states. It was deeply embedded in imperialist practices and shaped the international law of state responsibility.[9]

---

[6] A. Cassese, *State: Rise and Decline of the Primary Subjects of the International Law*, *in* The Oxford Handbook of The History of International Law 51 (B. Fassbender & A. Peters, eds., 2012).

[7] de Vattel (2008).

[8] Roxburgh (2005).

[9] Sucharitku (1996).

Carlos Calvo contended that: "Domestic courts shall be entitled to exclusive jurisdiction over disputes between foreigners and sovereign states, and foreigners should not seek non-local remedies such as diplomatic protection."[10] Once put forward, this view was recognized and welcomed by Latin American states that had just gained independence and existed as weak states with colonial trauma in the world order and gradually developed into a regional pattern in this region. Latin American countries were heavily exposed to abuses of diplomatic protection as well as armed intervention and occupation by domestic forces of foreign investors.[11] Some scholars state: "two concepts of non-intervention and absolute equality of foreigners with nationals are the essence of the Calvo Doctrine."[12] It rejects the imperialist privileges and super-national treatment formerly sought and enjoyed by Western powers and their nationals.

Although the investment disputes settlement via diplomatic protection has eased and changed the host state's absolute control over investment activities under the Calvo Doctrine, economic disputes have in essence risen to the political level for the settlement. As a result, such a highly politicized way of resolving investment disputes not merely increases the costs of dispute settlement, but also fails to meet the requirements of investors. As a resultof the continuous development of international investment law, diplomatic protection, as an important legal rule in customary international law, is weakened in the foreign investment protection regime.[13] In other words, diplomatic protection is left to supplement relevant institutional arrangements that fail to grant investors access to direct action. It is therefore no surprise to see the ultimate disappearance of the Calvo Doctrine.

B. Maximizing the Benefits of Capital Flows and the "Leaving" of the State

After the two world wars, states have gradually come to realize that wanton exercise of sovereignty and sovereign interests by resorting to wars or other violent means causes more harm than good. Since the signing of the UN Charter, states have restricted sovereignty to achieve a balance of interests in concluding international treaties, in a bid to achieve sustainable peace and development, which has become the starting point of the "leaving" of states.

The postwar economic recovery required a great deal of financial resources for international investment. On the one hand, developed states, represented by the US, wish to export capital to acquire more revenue, while on the other hand, a large number of developing states are eager to drive their own economic development by attracting foreign capital. However, investors from developed economies are not willing to rashly make capital investments in areas without strong legal protection.

[10] Carbonneau and Mourra (2008).

[11] Shihata (1986a).

[12] Shea (1955).

[13] CMS Gas Transmission Company v. Republic of Argentina, ICSID Case No. ARB/01/8, Decision on Jurisdiction, 45 (July 17, 2003), 7 ICSID Rep.17 (2007).

The walls of sovereignty are no longer effective protection against the capital movement in a much more integrated global market.[14] Developed and developing states, albeit divergent in interests and agenda, should make a compromise and have gradually reached a consensus in pursuit of common interests. Consequently, the capital-importing states (host states) have to make promises to give foreign investors various economic benefits and comprehensive protection through bilateral investment treaties (BITs). Meanwhile, the host state has also assigned part of its judicial sovereignty, allowing investors to submit disputes to relevant international agencies instead of local courts or tribunals for settlement when their investment rights are infringed upon and disputes arise, thereby avoiding the risk of being arbitrarily infringed upon in the host state. Since then, the protection of investors' interests has transitioned from a customary law one to a treaty-based one.[15]

After taking the first step of urging the "leaving" of states through treaties, along with increasingly active international investment, developed economies, represented and led by the US, have attached more importance to the role of investment treaties and made compromises in giving consent to arbitration instead of relying upon diplomatic protection in the field of international investment. It has led to a rapid increase in the number of IIAs since the 1980s, and subsequently, an explosive growth of IIA-based investment arbitration cases. There was once a trend that Latin American countries would belong to the ICSID Convention. Ecuador, Paraguay, and El Salvador were Contracting States to the ICSID Convention and had entered into several BITs with developed countries. Apart from increasing numbers, the content of the IIAs also indicates and confirms a trend of the "leaving" of states in both substantive and procedural protection of international investment. Domestically, both developed and developing states liberalized their foreign investment regulations; they instead relied upon the ICSID Convention and ISDS to upgrade and stabilize investment and economic policies.[16]

With respect to substantive rules, for the sake of protecting the interests of the host states, especially the right to regulate, the host state often restricts foreign investment premised on its sovereignty, which, as a result, has increased the political risk of investment. Hence, in the treaty model, various states have gradually changed their positions of diplomatic protection and state intervention based on state sovereignty under customary international law.[17] Rather, they established national treatment and most-favored-nation (MFN) treatment and extended these non-discriminatory standards to the pre-entry stage of investment through BITs to protect foreign investors provided that the status and standards accorded by the host state to investors are not lower than those of their own nationals and other third-state nationals.[18] Apart from the host state's macro commitment to grant national treatment and MFN treatment to foreign investors, BITs have also established standards for protecting the substantive

[14] Higgins (1999).

[15] El-Hosseny (2017).

[16] Puig (2013).

[17] Sornarajah (2010).

[18] *Id.*

and procedural rights of foreign investors, of which the compensation clause lies at the core.[19]

In the postwar period, foreign investors were most afraid of the expropriation or nationalization of investors' property by the host government. This was the main source of investment disputes between the investors and the host states. Early in 1938, the then US Secretary of State Cordell Hull put forward the "Hull Formula" concerning the compensation standard for the expropriation of foreign investors' property when the US investor's property in Mexico was expropriated by the Mexican government.[20] The Hull Formula required the host state to "timely, fully and effectively" compensate the losses suffered by the foreign investor from the expropriation.[21] In this case, the host state should compensate the foreign investor promptly, or within a reasonable period of time, and fully for the losses caused by the expropriation, while the compensation must be made in "hard currency" that can be allowed to flow out of the expropriating state freely.[22]

Against this background, the Hull standards have gradually been referred to by or included in more BITs. As José E. Alvarez points out, in establishing the international investment treaty regime in the 1980s, the US gradually raised the protection standards for investors. The 1984 and 1987 US Model BITs not only emphasized the Hull standard on the issue of expropriation and compensation, but extended the standard as a core principle to other aspects of BITs, which has severely restricted the sovereignty of the host state and substantially encouraged the "leaving" of states.[23]

C. "Leaving" of the States and the ISDS

The ISDS regime has, to a certain extent, achieved a new equilibrium between the jurisdiction of domestic courts and the settlement mechanism for international investment disputes given the fact that it has selectively ensured the minimum level of respect for state sovereignty and the minimum protection for the interests of foreign investors in a balanced manner within a limited boundary. States that are part of this IIA regime also recognize and share the mutual benefits of this regime.[24] The traditional investment dispute settlement mechanism premised on state sovereignty and diplomatic protection is too often tainted by strong political intervention by home states in defense of their investors, rendering it difficult to directly and effectively resolve disputes, and impossible to satisfy investors' demands for better and effective rights protection.[25]

The Calvo Doctrine has also proved to be an inadequate response to the needs of developing countries whose primary policy target is to attract foreign investment and promote economic growth and social development. Therefore, the modernization

---

[19] Alvarez, *supra* note 3, at 231–2.

[20] Del Duca (2003).

[21] Hackworth (1942).

[22] *Id.*

[23] Alvarez, *supra* note 3, at 231–2.

[24] Popova (2007).

[25] J. Salacuse, The Law of Investment TREATIES 358–9 (2010).

and liberalization of the settlement mechanism for international investment disputes is a neo-liberalist process of depoliticization and de-centralization of the states in the dispute settlement process.[26]

From the perspective of depoliticization, the settlement of investment disputes has been transformed from politically appealing but counterproductive diplomatic protection to a treaty-based and non-domestic judiciary-centered regime by both: directly prescribing the settlement of investment disputes in treaties and subjecting the sovereignty of the host state to non-political fora. Considering the content, granting foreign investors the right to directly sue the host state has essentially limited or even deprived the host state of its jurisdiction over disputes. ICSID has taken over the sovereignty assigned by the host states and formed a set of multilateral regimes covering dispute settlement and enforcement of investment arbitration awards.[27]

The investment dispute settlement mechanism established on the basis of BITs and more recent Free Trade Agreements (FTAs), a type of new international legal instrument, does not abandon the other dispute settlement methods in customary international law. For instance, the host state's courts have not been completely excluded from the settlement of investment disputes[28] since BITs also grant the host state the right to limit disputes that can be submitted to the ICSID for arbitration. Accordingly, the host state is allowed to require investors to resolve investment disputes before local courts, a partial exhaustion of local remedies as well as constraining the home state from exercising their rights of diplomatic protection. Given the opt-in nature of the ISDS system as *lex fori*, Latin American countries gradually changed their reluctant attitudes and started to join the ICSID in the 1980s, which coincided with efforts by developing countries to promote their interests through a proposal for a new agenda covering a wide range of trade, investment, finance, natural resources issues under the auspices of so-called New International Economic Order in the 1980s.[29]

There are two ways of defining the nature of the ICSID Convention in the context of the leaving or return of sovereign states. It is an institutional structure placed in the middle of a spectrum, as indicated in Chart 3.1 below, with the Calvo Doctrine on the one extreme representing the maximum protection of the host state's interest, and diplomatic protection on the other extreme, maximizing the sovereignty and interest of the home state of foreign investors. In between these two extremes is a compromise of the sovereignty and interests of both home and host states of foreign investment.[30] The ICSID system pays considerable attention to the Calvo Doctrine by allowing for the exhaustion of local remedies in the host state (as a condition to

[26] Shihata (1986b).

[27] Gilbert (2018).

[28] Alvarez (2009).

[29] Declaration on the Establishment of a New International Economic Order, G.A. Res. 3201, (VI) U.N. GAOR, 29th Sess., Supp. No.1, U.N. Doc. A/Res/3201(VI) (May 1, 1974).

[30] Barker (2006).

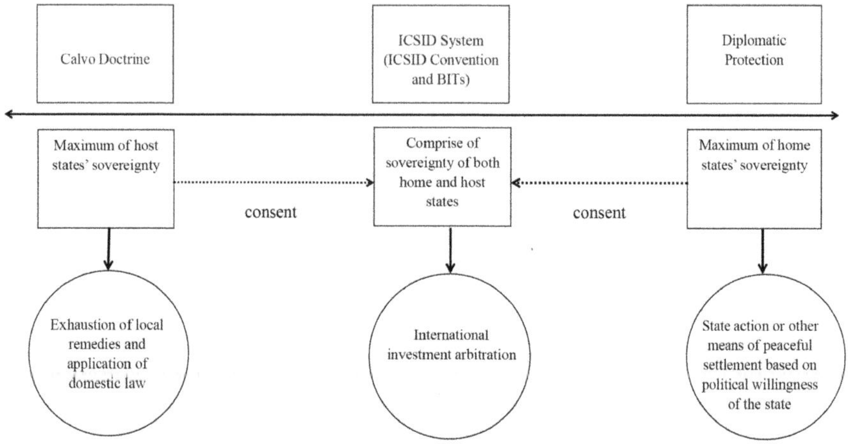

Chart 3.1 Spectrum of Sovereignty in ISDS. *Compiled by the authors

its consent to ICSID arbitration)[31] and for the application of the domestic law of the host state,[32] which can be agreed upon by the host state and codified in its BITs.

Meanwhile, the exclusivity of the ICSID system, as an alternative mechanism built upon the ICSID Convention and BITs, disallows the investor from asking their home state to espouse their case and prohibits the home state from giving diplomatic protection or bringing an international claim with respect to a dispute because its national and the host state have consented to submit to the ICSID arbitration. Therefore, the host state's consent (showing its own agreement to dilute sovereignty) under the BIT guarantees the foreign investor access to a neutral international forum for enforcing the host state's treaty obligations and precludes the home state from intervening in the dispute via diplomatic protection. Essentially, the ISDS system, as *lex fori* for investment disputes, sidestepped clashes between developing and developed states over the limits or excesses of sovereignty as competing frameworks to resolve conflicts involving foreign investors.[33]

The second layer of significance attached to the ICSID system, in brief, is its representation of the "leaving" of both home and host states in the investment dispute settlement mechanism. ICSID and its affiliated ISDS system, as a means of de-politicizing investment disputes, have been gradually accepted by Latin American countries previously indifferent or opposed to ICSID.[34] Framing the ICSID as a minimalistic enterprise of the World Bank and an investment dispute settlement

[31] ICSID Convention art. 26.

[32] *Id.* art. 42.

[33] Thaliath (2016).

[34] Gomez (2011).

forum served to limit power abuses traditionally observed with the practice of diplomatic protection and reluctance or even hostility toward international rule of law for stronger rights protection to foreign investors.[35]

Although closing a gap between developed and developing states, there still exist differences in the degree of "leaving" due to discrepancies in the interests of countries and the level of the rule of law. Hence, the investment dispute settlement provisions in BITs are not merely a vital indicator that could be relied upon for the evaluation of a state's level/degree of "leaving" and "return," but also a mechanism choice of governance regime—either politicized diplomatic protection or rule-based ISDS. Given the dynamic equilibrium between the home and host states as well as between the Calvo Doctrine and diplomatic protection in terms of their popularity and utility in the global governance system, the state's "return" is destined to come back at a certain point.[36]

The "Return" of the States and the Path of International Investment Law

A. Imbalanced Interests and the Host States' Dissatisfaction with the ICSID Arbitration

1. ICSID's Efficient Operations

The ICSID arbitration regime based on the ICSID Convention is a vital component for maintaining the operation of the modern international investment law regime. ICSID has become operationally inefficient, triggering a wide range of criticisms and suspicions. Judging from the recent development of the ICSID arbitration, a large number of cases illustrate that the arbitral tribunals restrict the power of the host state and protect investors excessively when they are called upon to interpret and apply treaty terms. As pointed out by commentators, investment arbitration awards accorded greater protection to foreign investment than many realized was possible.[37]

For instance, with regard to the application of the host state's law by the arbitration tribunal, Article 42, Paragraph 1 of the ICSID Convention stipulates that: "The Tribunal *shall* decide a dispute in accordance with such rules of law as *may be agreed* by the parties. In the absence of such agreement, the Tribunal *shall* apply the law of the Contracting State party to the dispute (including its rules on the conflict of laws) and such rules of international law as *may be applicable*." [Emphasis added] In accordance with this provision, the applicable law can be determined in two scenarios. First, in the case that the parties have chosen the applicable law, the arbitration tribunal shall apply the law as chosen by the parties. Second, when the parties do not

[35] Franck (2011).

[36] Cu (2020).

[37] Lowe (2002).

choose the applicable law, the arbitration tribunal shall apply the laws of one of the contracting states and the rules of international law to the dispute.[38]

A closer examination shows the following points worth discussing in the interpretation and application of this provision. In the first case, the so-called "possible consent" essentially gives the arbitration tribunal a greater presumption right. Since the "legal rules" are too abstract, they provide the arbitration tribunal with more discretion in exercising the presumption right, and the arbitration tribunal can infer the above-implied agreement from various events and specific cases associated with the parties.[39] In the second case, since the ICSID Convention does not prioritize the choices of applicable law, the arbitration tribunal can choose the applicable law at will. As the compulsory application of the host state's law is not required, it creates the possibilities for the alternative application of law by arbitration tribunals.[40]

The main methods adopted in these analyses are as follows. First, international law is used to exclude the application of the host state's domestic law. In the case of *Wena Hotels v. Egypt*, the arbitration tribunal once pointed out that the ICSID Convention does not limit the scope of application of the host state's law and international law (including BITs), so that the arbitration tribunal is entitled to decide on the specific applicable law.[41] In the case of *ADC Affiliate v. Hungary*, facing the BIT's explicit agreement to apply the host state's law to the calculation of compensation for expropriation, the arbitration tribunal directly excluded the application of the host state's law to other disputed matters, emphasizing its position that international law shall be applied preferentially except for special agreements in the BIT.[42] Second, the influence of the host state's law is diluted by its combination with international law. In the case of *Antoine v. Burundi*, the arbitration tribunal recognized that excessive restrictions on the host state's law would lead to an imbalance of interests in the investment arbitration regime.[43] Therefore, when settling disputes, the host state's law and international law are often combined to be used to deal with the cases. In this process, in applying the host state's domestic law at the parties' choice, the arbitration tribunal emphasized the supplementary, corrective and even restrictive function of international law.[44]

This tendency to exclude and restrict the application of the host state's law has occurred frequently in the ICSID arbitration practices in recent years. In the case of *Kim and others v. Uzbekistan*, when the host state interpreted the BIT in accordance with the Vienna Convention on the Law of Treaties (VCLT) to prove that

---

[38] Reisman and Arsanjani (2015).

[39] ICSID, Documents concerning the Origin and Formulation of the Convention 1968, 39.

[40] Gaillard and Banifatem (2003).

[41] Wena Hotels Ltd. (2002).

[42] ADC Affiliate Limited and ADC & ADMC Management Limited v. The Republic of Hungary, ICSID Case No. ARB/03/16, Award, Oct. 2, 2006, 288–293, https://www.italaw.com/sites/default/files/case-documents/ita0006.pdf.

[43] Antoine Goetz and others v. Republic of Burundi, ICSID Case No. ARB/95/3, Award, Feb. 10, 1999, 98, https://www.italaw.com/sites/default/files/case-documents/ita0380.pdf.

[44] Chen (2010).

when investors violate the laws of that state and raised objections to jurisdiction, the arbitration tribunal, while demonstrating the applicability of VCLT,[45] still rejected the host state's defense on the vague ground that investors had conducted investment activities in accordance with the host state's law and did not seriously damage the interests of the host state, deliberately avoiding the application of the host state's law.[46] Although Philippe Sands, the arbitrator in this case, held in a dissenting opinion that the host state's law should be considered and applied in combination with relevant international laws[47] based on the opinions of the arbitration tribunal in the case of *Urbaser v. Argentina*,[48] this view was not supported or adopted by other arbitrators finally. In the case of *Bear Creek Mining v. Peru*, the host state proposed that the host state's local law should be treated differently from international law. However, the arbitration tribunal rejected this view.[49] Therefore, in ICSID arbitrations, even if the ICSID Convention and BITs both stipulate that the host state's law can be applied, the arbitration tribunal could possibly evade the application of the host state's law. Even if the host state's law has to be applied, other methods have often been employed to control the influence of the host state's law to a minimum level.[50]

As a result of vague substantive terms in a large number of BITs, the inconsistent interpretative techniques applied by a large number of arbitration tribunals probably with the pre-set objective of offering better rights protection to foreign investors as well as the lack of independence of ISDS owing to a close-knit community of party-appointed international arbitrators,[51] the ISDS system left varying negative impressions to the users and commentators. Some cases may have indicated a tendency that investors from wealthy states were equipped with more power over the governments of less wealthy host states, while other cases may have justified the existence and utility of ISDS as a tool for protecting foreign investors from opportunistic actions like expropriations in host states without strong rule of law and legal institutions.[52]

Consequently, both accusations may be in existence simultaneously. In this regard, weak or poor host states are fighting large multinational companies, while private

[45] The Vienna Convention on the Law of Treaties, adopted and opened for signature on May 23, 1969, entered into force January 27, 1980 (1155 U.N.T.S. 331) was acceded to by Kazakhstan on January 5, 1994 and by Uzbekistan on July 12, 1995.

[46] Pavel Borissov, Aibar Burkitbayev, Almas Chukin and others v. Republic of Uzbekistan, ICSID Case No. ARB/13/6, Decision on Jurisdiction, Mar. 8, 2017, 413, 541, https://www.italaw.com/sites/default/files/case-documents/italaw8549.pdf.

[47] Pavel Borissov, Aibar Burkitbayev, Almas Chukin and others v. Republic of Uzbekistan, ICSID Case No.ARB/13/6, Partial Dissenting Opinion Professor Philippe Sands, Mar. 8, 2017, 10, https://www.italaw.com/sites/default/files/case-documents/italaw8549.pdf.

[48] Urbaser S.A. and Consorcio de Aguas Bilbao Bizkaia, Bilbao Biskaia Ur Partuergoa v. The Argentine Republic, ICSID Case No. ARB/07/26, Award, Dec. 8, 2016, 1199, https://www.italaw.com/sites/default/files/case-documents/italaw8136_1.pdf.

[49] Bear Creek Mining Corporation v. Republic of Peru, ICSID Case No. ARB/14/21, Award, Nov. 30, 2017, 267–269, https://www.italaw.com/sites/default/files/case-documents/italaw9381.pdf.

[50] Elombi (1994).

[51] Karamanian (2011).

[52] Kahale (2018).

entities are fighting arbitrary actions taken by developing states. Increasing public disapproval has shaken public confidence in ISDS and caused outcry.

2. Developing States' Withdrawal from the ICSID

It is precisely the excessive investor protection in the ICSID arbitration that causes more states' dissatisfaction with this regime. In light of relevant statistics, over the past thirty years, Latin American states, represented by Argentina have been among the top respondent states in the ICSID arbitration cases.[53] The large amount of compensation arising from investment arbitration cases became a vital factor affecting these countries' economic development. Since 2007, Bolivia, Ecuador, Venezuela, and other states have announced their decisions to withdraw from the ICSID Convention. Argentina was to reconsider its participation in the regime because more than sixty arbitration cases have dragged down its economic development.[54]

There has been a domino effect in Latin America. After having entered 23 BITs, Bolivia denounced the ICSID Convention in 2007. After the new Constitution of Bolivia was enacted in 2009, the government announced its plan to denounce and renegotiate the existing BITs as they were deemed to be contrary to the new Constitution. Ecuador's denunciation was notified in July 2009 and came into effect in January 2010.[55]

Venezuela announced its withdrawal in January 2012 which became effective in July 2012. The Foreign Ministry's 2012 press release points out that the country acceded to the ICSID Convention in 1993 by "a decision of a provisional and weak government, devoid of popular legitimacy, and under the pressure of transnational economic sectors involved in the dismantling of Venezuela's national sovereignty."[56]

As of May 2013, Latin American countries were parties in 81 out of 262 cases concluded (approximately 31%). Of the 167 cases still pending, 73 of them were against Latin American countries (approximately 44%).[57] Argentina alone had 25 cases before ICSID, passed a draft bill dated March 21, 2012, and then indicated its plan to exit.[58]

Withdrawals from ICSID by Bolivia, Ecuador, Venezuela and Argentina, and their termination of BITs[59] are not only a radical expression of these countries' dissatisfaction with the ICSID Convention's regime, but also a dramatic portrayal of a broader

---

[53] UNCTAD statistics show that Argentina has been indicted 62 times in ICSID, ranking first in ICSID, https://investmentpolicy.unctad.org/investment-dispute-settlement?id=8&name=argentina&role=respondent.

[54] Goodman (2007).

[55] Fiezzonil (2011).

[56] Ripinsky (2012).

[57] Beoglin (2013).

[58] Bill of Argentina Congress dates April 21, 2012. Text of the draft of that bill, http://www1.hcdn.gov.ar/proyxml/expediente.asp?fundamentos=si&numexp=1311-D-2012.

[59] In 2008, Ecuador terminated nine BITs—with Cuba, the Dominican Republic, El Salvador, Guatemala, Honduras, Nicaragua, Paraguay, Romania and Uruguay, https://www.iisd.org/itn/2017/06/12/ecuador-denounces-its-remaining-16-bits-and-publishes-caitisa-audit-report.

trend to revisit key aspects of international investment law. The exit from the ICSID Convention and the global forum for the settlement of investment disputes signals these countries' loss of faith in the ISDS system. Although the withdrawal from the ICSID Convention does not entirely block the future international investment arbitration against these countries, denouncing the ICSID Convention does send a political message to show the state refusal of future cooperation in the regime, and more realistically, the lack of likelihood of the collection of damages ordered by ICSID tribunals against these countries.[60]

Some scholars therefore pointed out that the Calvo Doctrine, which was once popular in Latin American states, has not died out and is possible to revive to be used as resistance in a mildly radical way.[61] In this sense, the Calvo Doctrine still has value in contemporary international law even though ICSID is said to be a superior solution to the Calvo Doctrine. While the ICSID in its operation indicated its mechanical or even institutional defects as an arbitration machinery and an instrument of international public policy,[62] the Calvo Doctrine has emerged as a vital institutional source and theoretical basis for the "return" of developing states in the field of international investment.[63]

Apart from the revival of the Calvo Doctrine and the withdrawal of many Latin American states from the ICSID regime, emerging economies as non-parties of ICSID such as India, Brazil, and South Africa,[64] which have become increasingly crucial in the field of international investment in recent years, also restrict or even exclude the use of the ISDS regime by updating their model BITs and amending their domestic laws.[65] The decline or rise of the Calvo Doctrine suggests the "leaving" or "return" of the state when it comes to settling its disputes with foreign investors. The changing role of the Calvo Doctrine indicates the uncertainty of its application which is likely related to the host state's view over its sovereignty. Nevertheless, the principle of diplomatic protection remains part of the realities of international life.[66]

For example, India's model BIT published in 2016 contains full restrictions on the ISDS mechanism. On the one hand, the model BIT highly emphasizes the local remedies such as administrative and judicial tribunals that foreign investors have to resort to in resolving investment disputes with the Indian Government after their rights are damaged.[67] Meanwhile, India believes that the international arbitration tribunal has

---

[60] Kownacki (2010).

[61] Shan (2007).

[62] ICSID, Annual Report (1984), at 5, https://icsid.worldbank.org/sites/default/files/publications/annual-report/en/1984-ar-final-en.pdf.

[63] Cremades (2006).

[64] By the end of January 2019, India, Brazil and South Africa had not joined ICSID. *See* ICSID, About ICSID: Member States, https://icsid.worldbank.org/en/Pages/about/Member-States.aspx.

[65] Rolland (2017a).

[66] Shihata (1986c).

[67] 2016 Model Text for the Indian Bilateral Investment Treaty, art. 15.1, 15.2, 15.4 & 15.5.

no right to review the judicial decisions of sovereign states, thus denying international agencies the right to review the decisions of their own courts.[68] For another example, Brazil signed a number of BITs as early as the 1990s. However, its legislative authority did not approve these BITs in order to safeguard its right to regulate foreign capital. Brazil showed no interest in ratifying the ICSID or any BIT despite having signed some BITs and even though Brazil named the ICSID Secretary-General the "appointing authority" of arbitrators in some guarantee agreements executed by Brazil in favor of foreign lenders to Brazilian public entities.[69]

3. Developed States' Rising Opposition to the ISDS

Apart from the challenges raised by developing states toward ISDS, developed states represented by the US and the member states of the European Union (EU) have also joined the ranks of opposing the current ISDS regime. As the world's major capital exporting state, the US has long played the role of the largest home state of claimants in the ICSID arbitration.[70] Nevertheless, the US has also come to recognize the legal risks of ISDS. In March 2018, US Trade Representative Robert Lighthizer testified before US Congress and highlighted the reasons why the US Government opposes the inclusion of the mandatory ISDS clauses in the NAFTA renegotiation. He addressed that it would severely damage the American national sovereignty and put the US at great legal risk.[71] In the meantime, ISDS has also been criticized by many parties, and the US does not have to continue to cheer for the regime.[72] Similarly, in the Comprehensive and Progressive Agreement for Trans-Pacific Partnership (CPTPP) reached by eleven Pacific states including Canada, Japan, Australia, and others in February 2018, New Zealand, Canada, and Chile explicitly excluded the settlement of investment disputes with investors from specific states through ISDS by way of having explicit appendices.

After the Treaty of Lisbon was passed, the power of the EU member states to sign BITs was exclusively possessed and controlled by the European Commission, which also began to reassess the ISDS system and responded to the reform of the modern international investment law regime.[73]

The EU has been calling for the reform of ISDS in recent years, especially in the relevant discussions organized by the United Nations Commission on International Trade and Law (UNCITRAL), clearly pointing out the main problems of the ISDS regime as follows. First, there is a lack of consistency in the interpretation and application of a series of provisions. Second, arbitration tribunals have consistently shown selective contempt for the sovereign matters of the host states in their long-term investment arbitration practice and have failed to effectively grasp the scale of

[68] *Id.* art. 13.5.

[69] Delaume (1983).

[70] UNCTAD, World Investment Report 2018, at 93, https://unctad.org/en/PublicationsLibrary/wir2018_en.pdf.

[71] *See Brady-Lighthizer ISDS Exchange*, International Economic Law and Policy Blog, Mar. 21, 2018, https://worldtradelaw.typepad.com/ielpblog/2018/03/brady-lighthizer-isds-exchange.html.

[72] *Id.*

[73] Roberts (2013).

protection. Third, the lack of a necessary appeal regime makes ISDS lose its ability to self-correct. Even with the annulment mechanism under the ICSID Convention, its practical functionality is rather limited. Fourth, the appointment of arbitrators under this regime is often made ex-post the dispute. When appointing arbitrators, the host state also takes its own interests into account and ignores its public law functions as a sovereign state, which makes the arbitration tribunal lack neutrality in interpreting and applying treaties. Fifth, as the investment arbitration tribunal is not a permanent international organization, huge costs have been involved in maintaining the operation of the whole system.[74] Sixth, the current ISDS is derived from commercial arbitration which mainly deals with commercial disputes. As a result, the ISDS system does not have appropriate institutional arrangements for the checks and balances of public power so as to ensure transparency and fairness.[75]

Apart from voicing support for the reform of ISDS, the EU believes that the defects exposed by ISDS are no longer suitable for the twenty-first century.[76] It then proposes to establish an investment court premised on sovereign states as a feasible regime for settling investment disputes. The EU's idea of an investment court directly points to the disadvantages of the current ISDS. First of all, in the scope of actionable disputes, the EU hopes to grant the contracting parties comprehensive rights to regulate in the fields of public safety, environmental protection, consumer rights protection, among others, emphasizing that disputes in these fields can only be resolved through the contracting parties' own judicial channels.[77] Moreover, the EU wishes to prevent the arbitration tribunals from interpreting the treaty arbitrarily under the ISDS regime by establishing a political body authorized by the contracting parties to interpret the investment treaties in a uniform manner.[78] Further, the EU hopes to change the regime of appointing arbitrators by both disputing parties to disputes under ISDS to tenured judges publicly appointed by the investment court so as to strengthen the legitimacy of the dispute settlement mechanism and the effectiveness and consistency of the rulings thereof.[79] Finally, the EU proposes to change the status quo of the finality of arbitral awards under the ISDS system and to enhance the self-corrective capability of the investment dispute settlement mechanism by setting up a feasible appeal regime.[80]

---

[74] Gaukrodger and Gordon (2012).

[75] UNCITRAL, Possible Reform of Investor-State Dispute Settlement (ISDS) Submission from the EU, U.N. Doc. A/CN.9/WG.III/WP.145 (Dec. 12, 2017) at 7–12, https://documents-dds-ny.un.org/doc/UNDOC/LTD/V17/088/32/PDF/V1708832.pdf?OpenElement.

[76] Malmstrom (2015).

[77] EU Parliament, TTIP: Ease Access to US Market, Protect EU Standards, Reform Dispute Settlement, July 8, 2015, http://documents.nam.org/IEA/EU%20Parliament%20Press%20release%20July%202015.pdf.

[78] *Id.*

[79] *Id.*

[80] *Id.*

4. South-North Divide in the ISDS Reform

The core design features of BITs and international investment arbitration were to mitigate imbalances between foreign investors and host states, a typical South and North divide, which can destabilize power balances between capital importing and exporting states that the ICSID attempted to achieve.[81] The ICSID arbitration nevertheless maintains a restrictive policy toward the diplomatic espousal of investment claims by more powerful states, the unexpected consequence of which was to empower foreign investors and create new power imbalances between foreign investors and host states. The side effect of the ISDS system is the over-privatization of ISDS, which can be corrected and rebalanced toward a constructive relationship between foreign investors and host states.[82]

Given this Private–Public divide in nature,[83] such a rebalancing trend is mainly reflected and evidenced by the return of the state movement in which host states, either developed or developing ones, are trying to liberate or restore their autonomy, authority, or state sovereignty by taking these back from the private parties in the ISDS proceedings at least in the field of regulating foreign investment in conformity with their internal police power and public interests. Influenced by this Public–Private tension, a pragmatic shift from the ICSID system to domestic courts may be an alternative solution, or a technical response, to the public dissatisfaction with the ISDS (including the ICSID) which has been seen as a sacrifice for more corporate sovereignty. The rebalancing or re-politicization in the spectrum of sovereignty in the ISDS system appears to be for the general good of the world even though it may be labeled as conservative or nationalistic in nature.[84]

In short, facing restrictions on the host state's power exposed in the ICSID arbitration in recent years, whether developing economies withdraw from and evade the ISDS regime or developed economies attempt to reshape the investment dispute settlement mechanism, they all emphasize the due respect for national sovereignty in shaping the investment dispute settlement mechanism. This series of measures is rooted in the sovereignty of all states while nurturing and strengthening sovereignty simultaneously. The trend of the "return" of states at the procedural level of international investment law has already taken shape.[85] In contrast to the depoliticization process in which the states were leaving their sovereignty with the aim of mitigating the tensions between the North and the South,[86] the re-politicization movement is

[81] Matveev (2015).

[82] Puig and Strezhnev (2017).

[83] Trakman (2013).

[84] Shan, *Supra* note 1, at 632.

[85] Odumosu (2007).

[86] *ID.*

an effort to address the distorted tensions between the private and public spheres in international investment.

B. Anti-liberalization Transformation of Foreign Investment Law in the Post-Financial Crisis Era

1. Changing Patterns of FDI and FDI Regulation

The international investment law regime formed on the basis of the "leaving" of states has effectively facilitated the liberalization of global investment and stimulated the economic takeoff of developing states in the 1980s and 1990s. However, along with the in-depth development of international investment in recent years, especially the economic recession in developed states since the latest global financial crisis, the economic gap between the North and the South has been continuously narrowing. Especially, the developing states represented by emerging states are catching up with or even competing with the developed states in FDI, making developed states begin to be on guard.[87]

From a global point of view, the rise of developing or emerging states in the field of international investment has deprived developed states of their original dominant position, which leads to a policy transformation of various states tightening up the regulation over foreign capital or investment.[88] The global financial crisis and the emerging states' rise to be the more important players in FDI have resulted in a sweeping change to investment-related policies and measures. It has been gradually shifting from the liberalization stance in the 1990s evidenced by deregulation over-investment in the context of major liberalization processes, to a restrictive or nationalistic position connecting the dispute settlement back to politics instead of law. Especially before and after the 2008 financial crisis, this policy-tightening trend became more obvious, and the policy was not relaxed until 2014. Nevertheless, the position of intervention and restriction of foreign investment has not yet returned to the level of the 1990s.

The general trend of anti-liberalization in the field of international investment is embodied in the specific changes in the domestic laws of various states regarding foreign investment supervision policies and the turn of international investment agreements in the direction of treaties. The mode of interaction among stakeholders in investment dispute settlement faces new challenges.[89]

2. Developed States' Conservative Policy Shift

Developed states have played a vital role in tightening international investment law in this new anti-globalization or anti-liberalization movement due to the increased regulatory restrictions they imposed on foreign investment. Structural changes in the international investment pattern have made developed states more aware of or

---

[87] UNCTAD, World Investment Report 2019, at 92–3, https://unctad.org/en/PublicationsLibrary/wir2019_en.pdf.

[88] Sauvant et al. (2009).

[89] UNCTAD, World Investment Report 2010, at 76, https://unctad.org/en/docs/wir2010_en.pdf; World Investment Report 2019, at 84, https://unctad.org/en/PublicationsLibrary/wir2019_en.pdf.

even cautious about potential risks that foreign investors may bring into their countries in the fields of science and technology, information, finance, and others. These risks and potential regulatory failures, to a certain extent, forced these states to tackle and resolve the corresponding risks by raising the market access threshold and strengthening regulation over and monitoring of foreign investment activities.[90]

Judging from these regulatory movements, relevant states pay more attention to the supervision of mergers and acquisitions involving foreign investment. In light of the UNCTAD's observation, in the past few years, quite a number of host governments have frequently opposed the sales of key or strategic domestic assets by domestic enterprises to foreign investors on the grounds of national security. In 2017 alone, at least ten transactions in high-tech manufacturing, financial services, or telecommunications industries were canceled for regulatory or political reasons.[91] Among these transactions, the US and New Zealand are the top two host states of investment, while China is the main home state of investment. According to the data in the first four months of 2018, for a total of seven times, merger and acquisition transactions were put off for national security concerns, primarily in the US.[92]

Since the Trump Administration came into power, it has taken stricter regulatory measures against emerging economies represented by China. The Trump Administration modernized the Committee on Foreign Investment in the United States (CFIUS) review process by passing the Foreign Investment Risk Review Modernization Act (FIRRMA), which was the first update to the CFIUS statute in more than a decade.[93] The FIRRMA, which came into effect in 2018, comprehensively strengthens the state's right to regulate the field of foreign investment by expanding the review scope of national security and controlling the sharing of key technologies with emerging economies. The effect of FIRRMA includes potentially longer timelines, the disclosure of more material agreements related to the transaction under review in the notice, and mandatory declarations made over whether a transaction is covered or foreign government controlled.[94]

Likely, additional types of Chinese investment would be subject to CFIUS review. The FIRRMA impacts both investments directly by Chinese entities and investments by non-Chinese entities that might have significant ties to China. FIRRMA's key concerns include proximity to sensitive US government facilities, sensitive personal data, critical infrastructure, critical technology, and technology transfer to China.[95]

[90] UNCTAD, National Security-related Screening Mechanisms for Foreign Investment an Analysis of Recent Policy Developments, Investment Policy Monitor (Dec. 2019), https://unctad.org/en/PublicationsLibrary/diaepcbinf2019d7_en.pdf.

[91] UNCTAD, World Investment Report 2018, at 85, https://unctad.org/en/PublicationsLibrary/wir2018_en.pdf.

[92] *Id.* at 83–5.

[93] Jalinous et al. (2017).

[94] Remarks by President Trump at a Roundtable on the Foreign Investment Risk Review Modernization Act (FIRRMA), Aug. 23, 2018, https://www.whitehouse.gov/briefings-statements/remarks-president-trump-roundtable-foreign-investment-risk-review-modernization-act-firrma.

[95] J. Shields, *Smart Machines and Smarter Policy: Foreign Investment Regulation, National Security, and Technology Transfer in the Age of Artificial Intelligence*, 51 J. Marshall L. Rev. 286–7 (2018).

State-directed and state-funded investment in these areas will be highly scrutinized in particular.

The FIRRMA does allow for greater information sharing with the US state and local governments and foreign allied governments. CFIUS's formal process for information sharing reflects a broader US government initiative to assist and incentivize partner countries to strengthen their own investment review mechanisms and pursue reviews of transactions of interest to the US government.[96] Reforms have recently been enacted, or are being actively considered, in the EU, the UK, Canada, Australia, and Japan, among others, and there is growing awareness and interest in investment-security issues worldwide. The US, EU, and Japan have already agreed to engage in investment security formally with an aim for cooperation, information exchange, and potential coordination.[97] With respect to specific transactions, the increasingly close collaboration on investment-security matters among governments means that certain transactions could face (somewhat) coordinated review across multiple jurisdictions in the future. The potential harmonization of investment security review processes is an area to watch.[98]

The EU has also stressed the importance of foreign investment monitoring in recent years. Specifically, the EU emphasizes the effective implementation of the existing investment laws in Europe. In the field of energy such as electricity and natural gas, for example, it should strengthen the maintenance of the safety of relevant infrastructure and attach great importance to the integrity of property rights, so as to prevent possible operational risks.

Take another example. In the aviation sector, the legal requirement is that the EU citizens possess absolute control over the equity of such enterprises (over 50%), and the EU is entitled to terminate this transaction when investment activities lead to the control of aviation enterprises falling into the hands of non-EU citizens.[99] Similarly, in the exploration and production of hydroxides, the EU also allows member states to refuse citizens of a third state to control related enterprises for reasons of national security.[100] Moreover, while strengthening law enforcement, the EU hopes to establish effective Foreign Direct Investment Screening Mechanisms (FDISM).[101]

From a policy-oriented perspective, the mechanism will examine direct investment into the EU while taking into consideration public safety. Also, it hopes to provide a non-exhaustive list to determine which direct investments will affect the EU's public

---

96 Jalinous et al., *Supra* note 93.

97 Rand and Tankel (2015).

98 Jalinous et al., *Supra* note 93.

99 Directive (EU) 2016/1148 of the European Parliament and of the Council of 6 July 2016 concerning measures for a high common level of security of network and information systems across the Union, https://eur-lex.europa.eu/legal-content/EN/TXT/PDF/?uri=CELEX:32016L1148&rid=1.

100 Directive 94/22/EC of 30 May 1994 on the conditions for granting and using authorization for the prospection, exploration and production of hydrocarbons, https://eur-lex.europa.eu/legal-content/EN/TXT/PDF/?uri=CELEX:31994L0022&from=EN.

101 EU Commission, Screening of Foreign Direct Investment, https://trade.ec.europa.eu/doclib/press/index.cfm?id=2006.

security. This will emphatically prevent foreign State-owned enterprises (SOEs), economic entities that are playing an increasingly vital role in current international investment,[102] by interfering in the EU's key technologies and information security.

From the perspective of follow-up measures, on the one hand, the EU will formulate more detailed foreign investment supervision rules under FDISM for important strategic areas (such as energy, space, transportation) or assets (technologies and inputs linked with strategic departments, key infrastructure across departments, sensitive data) that may cause problems in areas such as safety and public order, and strengthen data analysis and case screening in evaluation.[103]

On the other hand, the EU will also set up an investment policy coordination group composed of the president of the European Commission and representatives of the member states to discuss and formulate policies on such issues as public safety, environmental protection, and fair competition to ensure the effective operation of FDISM.[104]

C. Shifting Focus from Investor Protection to the Right to Regulate

Apart from the trend of anti-liberalization evidenced by the legislative and administrative measures of various states, IIAs, as legal instruments directly regulating and promoting foreign investment, have also taken on some new features in recent years. Compared with IIAs signed in the 1990s, those signed or revised in recent years placed more emphasis on the host state's right to regulate, and weakened the constraints of ISDS on the host state's sovereignty.[105] In terms of the definition of investment, certain specific assets are excluded so as to limit the scope of application of the treaty. The obligations of the host state government are further clarified concerning expropriation and compensation clauses, and the investors' rights are further clarified with respect to the currency exchange and other issues.[106] With respect to a specific direction, recent IIAs have changed the past mode of focusing solely on the protection of the private interests of investors to pay more attention to non-traditional government's right to regulate such as labor treatment, environmental protection, and public safety, highlighting the interests of sovereign states.[107]

The ISDS system has been on a trajectory of re-politicization.[108] This is the case due to a variety of inherent features of the ISDS system. Although a dispute submitted to the ICSID for arbitration is supposed to be an investment case, the tribunal is often called upon to examine the legality of the host state's policies and regulations,

[102] UNCTAD, World Investment Report 2017, at 30, https://unctad.org/en/PublicationsLibrary/wir2017_en.pdf.

[103] EU Commission, Welcoming Foreign Direct Investment while Protecting Essential Interests, COM (2017) 494 final, at 5, https://eur-lex.europa.eu/legal-content/EN/TXT/?uri=CELEX%3A52017DC0494.

[104] *Id.*

[105] Fei and Li (2020).

[106] UNCTAD, World Investment Report 2018, at 95–6, https://unctad.org/en/PublicationsLibrary/wir2018_en.pdf.

[107] *Id.* at 107–15.

[108] Titi (2015).

which, by their nature, are political. The adjudication of investment disputes has a great regulatory chill on future policy-making and legislative activities involving the host state's public interest.[109]

As a leading country in making the "leaving" gesture and pushing forward the liberalization of international investment, the US shows a conceptual transformation in drafting a treaty when facing changes in foreign investment patterns since the beginning of the twenty-first century. As early as 2004, the US model BIT underwent a shift from emphasizing the protection of investors to more respect of the right to regulate of sovereign states in terms of public safety and labor treatment.[110] Generally speaking, the model includes the protection of the right to regulate of contracting parties in terms of public safety, environment and labor treatment in the BIT's objectives, while in specific provisions, it emphasizes the power of the host state with regard to environment and labor treatment,[111] allowing the host state to levy taxes due to the above factors and limiting the scope of application of national treatment and MFN treatment. At the same time, it values the role of local relief measures in the host state in settling investment disputes and further restricts the discretion of the investment arbitration tribunal in the legal interpretation linked to the above factors.[112]

When a financial crisis or security interest is at stake, the host state is likely to interfere into so-called internal affairs, in which protection takes precedence over investment obligations. As a result, these countries also have deep suspicion about global investment rules that are increasingly stacked against their interests. Their skepticism is further complicated by the growing strategic competition for economic dominance by emerging states, typically China and some BRICS states. Following the economic recession in developed states due to the 2008 global financial crisis and the rapid economic growth in emerging states the economic gap has been narrowed between the North and the South once again, thereby arousing the vigilance of developed states and intensifying their sovereign supervision over foreign investment, including investment originating from emerging economies.[113]

Although Trump announced the US's withdrawal from TPP after taking office, the consensus reached by Pacific Rim states under the TPP framework still exerts an impact on reshaping the current international economic governance regime. For instance, CPTPP stipulates the non-traditional right to regulate the contracting parties while inheriting TPP. On the one hand, the investment chapter of the CPTPP emphasizes that the investment activities carried out by investors in contracting parties shall conform to the laws and regulations of the host state in the fields of public health, safety, and environment, allowing the host state to exercise right to regulate, such as applying expropriation for the above reasons.[114] On the other hand,

[109] *Id.*

[110] Kantor (2004).

[111] 2004 Model BIT, arts. 12 & 13.

[112] Gagné and Morin (2006).

[113] Shen (2018).

[114] CPTPP arts. 9.2, 9.10, 9.16 & annex 9-B.

the CPTPP also provides for investment-related matters in the status of SOEs, labor treatment, environmental protection, non-market economy, and competition policies through special chapters. It further ensures the consistency of the protection standards of contracting parties in the above-mentioned fields, thereby facilitating the upgrade to higher standards in relevant international economic activities including investment.[115]

Considering the development of investment supervision policies in states represented by the US and the EU, the protection of investors' rights in developed economies is increasingly giving way to expanding the host state's right to regulate, while the government has taken increasing initiative in investment supervision.[116] Those developed states who used to rely on the "leaving" of the state to push forward the shaping of the modern international investment law regime have "rebelled" and further affected the formulation of investment policies of developing states. Here, the "return" of the state has turned into a reality in neo-international investment law. In this round of "return" of states, the governments of various states have also paid more attention to the protection of the right to regulate in the fields of, *inter alia*, labor treatment, environmental and health protection, the status of SOEs, and industrial policies. As a matter of fact, the scope of the modern international investment law regime focusing on the protection of investors' interests has been expanded further, highlighting the status of the overall interests of states in the entire governance regime. There emerged a new trend of re-politicization, a novel movement in international investment law when disputes come to some sensitive public policy issues.[117]

The re-politicization movement is harder to define or characterize than the past politicization in the sense that the state is engaged in diplomatic protection through some legal means but clearly with political intentions or agendas.[118] The "return" of the state in ISDS and the international investment law re-introduces politics, if not nationalistic centralism, and re-expands regulatory space in a politically-charged legal order. Due to the "return" of the state trend, the protection of aliens may be witnessing a resurgence. This is in large part because a number of Global South powers, reconnecting with old patterns, are increasingly wrestling with ideas about how to best protect their diasporas, in a context where territorial human rights remedies may not always be available or adequate.[119] It is also a reflection of the old Arendtian intuition that having the backing of a sovereign is a key to protecting one's rights.[120] Finally, it is a result of the influence of human rights themselves, which increasingly encourage people to expect a certain level of protection from the

[115] Desierto (2018).

[116] UNCTAD, World Investment Report 2020, at 115, https://unctad.org/system/files/official-document/wir2020_en.pdf..

[117] Tita (2010).

[118] Titi (2015).

[119] Rolland (2017b).

[120] See generally Arendt (1973).

state in relation to their harm suffered from aboard. International investment law still concerns with how to protect a state's nationals abroad.[121]

Conclusion

This article has attempted to reveal some of the patterns of difference, dominance and disruption that belie state sovereignty and international investment law's proclaimed universality. International investment law suffers from a type of legal schizophrenia. On the one hand, the US, the EU, and other developed states have sought since the mid-twentieth century to liberalize global investment law. The resulting BIT-based and ISDS-centered international investment law regime and a plethora of BIT networks have successfully broken down barriers to investment and lifted investor protection standards.[122] On the other hand, alongside those moves, international investment law also has allowed, created or even maintained exceptions to depart from those primary rules in case of national security or other criteria that pose a risk to host states' economic security. Taken together, these two legal categories seem benign. Currently, the former is being overtaken by the latter. As a result, the world is facing de-globalization as well as legal crises like uncertainty.[123]

In the leaving-and-return-of-the-state paradigm, the evolution of international investment law has followed a pattern. Following the rapid development of global investment, customary international law, primarily premised upon sovereignty, no longer sufficiently served the interests of states.

Against this background, a number of states have recognized the detrimental effect of over-emphasizing sovereignty in an international investment law regime which hardly maximized the best interests of these states in terms of attracting foreign investment and boosting economic growth. Developed states then were decreasing their adherence to the concept of sovereignty, thereby pushing forward the shaping of the contemporary international investment law regime, focusing more on foreign investment protection.[124]

However, considering the new changing trend in international investment primarily evidenced by the rise of developing and emerging states, the" leaving" of the state (sovereignty), to a certain extent, damages the interest of the capital importing states and casts doubt over the benefits of the states' leaving away from sovereignty. On the one hand, the excessive restrictions imposed by the ISDS system on the host states break the balance between the states and foreign investors. On the other hand, a policy shift to more restrictive regulation after the global financial crisis also turned the regulatory framework of foreign investment to a less liberal

[121] Subedi (2008).

[122] Salacuse (1990).

[123] Dongxiao and Yu (2017).

[124] Bjorklund (2004).

one.[125] Judging from the regulatory movements toward foreign investment in the US, the EU, and other developed countries, there has been a definite return of the state to paying more attention to national security, environmental protection, public health, and other concerns with public interests. The "leaving" or "return" of the state paradigm informs and transforms our understanding of sovereignty and the role of the state in the context of international investment law.

References

Alvarez (2009) A BIT on custom, 42 N.Y.U. J Int'l L Pol 72
Alvarez J (2011) The return of the state. 20 Minn J Int'l L, 230–31
Arendt H (1973) The origins of totalitarianism
Barker (2006) The protection of diplomatic personnel, 64–5
Beoglin (2013) ICSID and Latin America: criticisms. Withdrawals and Regional Alternatives, July 4, 2013, http://www.cadtm.org/ICSID-and-Latin-America-criticisms.
Bjorklund (2004) Reconciling state sovereignty and investor protection in denial of justice claims, 45 Va. J Int'l L, 836–7
Carbonneau T, Mourra M (2008) Latin american investment treaty arbitration: the controversies and conflicts, 8
Chen H (2010) The application of host state's law in international investment arbitration: the acceptability of Article 30 of US Model BIT [论东道国法律在国际投资仲裁中的适用-兼评2004年美国BIT范本第30条的可接受性], J. Int'l Econ. L. [国际经济法学刊], 162–7
Cremades B (2006) Resurgence of the Calvo Doctrine in Latin America, 7 Bus L Int'l, 57
Cui J (2020) Global investment governance: a call for greater system diversity and rule uniformity. 11 Beijing L Rev, 621
de Vattel E (2008) 75. Liberty Fund Inc., T. Nugent trans
Delaume F (1983) ICSID and the banker, 2 Int'l Fin L Rev, 13
Desierto D (2018) ASEAN investment treaties, RCEP, and CPTPP: regional strategies, norms, institutions, and politics, 27 Wash Int'l L J, 405–6
Del Duca P (2003) The rule of law: Mexico's approach to expropriation disputes in the face of investment globalization, 51 UCLA L Rev 118
Dongxiao C, Yu Ye (2017) Global economic governance: new challenges and China's approaches. 63 China Int'l Stud, 7–9
El-Hosseny F (2017) Civil society in investment treaty arbitration: status and prospects, 293–6
Elombi G (1994) ICSID awards and the denial of host state laws. 11 J Int'l Arb, 67–8
Fei X, Li Z (2020) Host States' logic of balance in applying the right to regulate foreign investment admission, 17 US-China L Rev, 65
Franck S (2011) The ICSID effect? Considering potential variations in arbitration awards, 51 Va J Int'l L, 837
Fiezzoni1 S (2011) The challenge of UNASUR member countries to replace ICSID arbitration, 2 Beijing L Rev, 135–6
Gagné G, Morin J (2006) The evolving american policy on investment protection: evidence from recent FTAs and the 2004 Model BIT, 9 J Int'l L Arb, 381–2
Gaillard E, Banifatemi Y (2003) The meaning of "and" in Article 42(1), second sentence of the ICSID convention: the role of international law in the ICSID choice of law process. 18 ICSID Rev, 399–411

[125] J. Commission, *The Global Financial Crisis and International Investment Regimes* 104 Am. Soc'y Int''l L. Proc. 444 (2010).

Gaukrodger D, Gordon K (2012) Investor-state dispute settlement: a scoping paper for the investment policy community 19 (OECD Working Papers on International Investment)
Gilbert P (2018) Sovereignty and tragedy in contemporary critiques of investor state dispute settlement, 6 London Rev Int'l L, 211–6
Gomez (2011) Latin America and ICSID: david versus Goliath. L Bus Rev Am, 213–21
Goodman C (2007) Uncharted waters: financial crisis and enforcement of ICSID awards in Argentina, 28 U Pa J Int'l Econ L, 483
Hackworth G (1942) US Department of State, Pub. No. 1708, (1942) 3 Digest of United States Practice in International Law, at 655
Higgins R (1999) International law in a changing international system. 58 Cambridge L J 82
Jalinous F, Mildorf K, Schomig K (2017) FIRRMA: proposed CFIUS legislation would bring significant changes, white & case: Publicationa & Events (Nov. 7, 2017), https://www.whitecase.com/publications/alert/firrma-proposed-cfius-legislation-would-bring-significant-changes
Kahale G II (2018) Rethinking ISDS, 44 Brook. J Int'l L, 12–20
Kantor (2004) The new draft model U.S. BIT: Noteworthy Developments, 21 J Int'l L Arb, 383
Karamanian S (2011) International decision, Compania de Aguas del Aconquija S.A. & Vivendi Universal S.A. v Argentine Republic, 105 Am J Int'l L, 555
Kownacki (2010) Prospects for ICSID arbitration in post-denunciation countries: an updated approach, 15 UCLA J Int'l L Foreign Aff, 559–60
Lowe V (2002) Regulation or expropriation?. 55 Curr Legal Prob, 456
Malmstrom C (2015) Investments in TTIP and beyond-towards an International Investment Court (May 5, 2015), http://trade.ec.europa.eu/doclib/docs/2015/may/tradoc_153408.PDF
Matveev (2015) Investor-state dispute settlement: the evolving balance between Investor Protection and State Sovereignty, 40 U.W. Austl L Rev, 386
Odumosu (2007) The law and politics of engaging resistance in investment dispute settlement, 26 Pa. State Int'l L Rev, 257
Popova R (2007) Sarei v. Rio Tinto and the exhaustion of local remedies rule in the context of the alien tort claims act: short-term justice, but at What Cost 28 Hamline J Pub L & Pol'y 529
Puig S, Strezhnev A (2017) The david effect and ISDS, 28 Eur J Int'l L, 739–42
Puig S (2013) Emergence & dynamism in international organizations: ICSID. Investor-state arbitration & international investment law, 44 Geo J Int'l L, 570–1
Rand D, Tankel S (2015) Security cooperation & assistance: rethinking the return on investment, p 6, Aug. 5, 2015, Center for a New American Security (Aug. 2015), https://www.files.ethz.ch/isn/192879/CNAS%20Report_Security%20Cooperation_FINAL.pdf
Reisman W, Arsanjani M (2015) Applicable law under the ICSID convention: the tortured history of the interpretation of Article 42. In: Kinnear M et al (eds), Building international investment law: the first 50 Years of ICSID, 10–1
Ripinsky S (2012) Venezuela's Withdrawal from ICSID: What it Does and Does Not Achieve, Apr. 13, 2012, https://www.iisd.org/itn/2012/04/13/venezuelas-withdrawal-from-icsid-what-it-does-and-does-not-achieve/#_ftn2
Roberts (2013) Clash of paradigms: actors and analogies shaping the investment treaty system, 107 Am J Int'l L, 45–7
Rolland S (2017a) The return of state remedies in investor-state dispute settlement: trends in developing countries, 49 Loy. U Chi L J, 395–9
Rolland S (2017b) The return of state remedies in investor-state dispute settlement: trends in developing countries, 49 Loy U Chi LJ, 403
Roxburgh R (ed) Oppenheim international law: a treatise (Vol. I: Peace) 17–8 (reproduced by The Lawbook Exchange, 2005)
Salacuse (1990) BIT by BIT: the growth of bilateral investment treaties and their impact on foreign investment in developing countries, 24 Int'l Law, 660
Sauvant, Maschek W, McAllister G (2009) Foreign direct investment by emerging market multinational enterprises, the impact of the financial crisis and recession and challenges ahead, at 18,

OECD Global Forum on International Investment (Dec. 8, 2009), http://www.oecd.org/investment/globalforum/44246197.pdf
Shan W (2007) From North-South divide to private-public debate: revival of the Calvo doctrine and the changing landscape in international investment law, 27 Nw J Int'l L & Bus, 664
Shan W (2007) Is Calvo Dead?, 55 Am J Comp L, 163
Shea D (1955) The Calvo clause: a problem of inter-American and international law and diplomacy, 19–20
Shen W (2018) Recent evolution of international financial governance system and international economic order under the background of anti-globalization: the new institutionalism represented by the g20 and the B&R [逆全球化背景下的国际金融治理体系和国际经济秩序新近演化-以二十国集团和"一带一路"为代表的新制度主义], 187 Contemp. L. Rev. [当代法学] 44
Shihata (1986a) Towards a greater Depoliticization of investment disputes: the roles of ICSID and MIGA, 1 ICSID Rev 1
Shihata (1986b) Towards a greater Depoliticization of investment disputes: the roles of ICSID and MIGA, 1 ICSID Rev, 24–5
Shihata (1986c) Towards a Greater Depoliticization of investment disputes: the roles of ICSID and MIGA, 1 ICSID Rev, 3
Sornarajah M (2010) The international law on foreign investment, 358–60
Sornarajah M (2015) Resistance and change in the international law on foreign investment, 4–10
Strange S (1996) The retreat of the state: the diffusion of power in the world economy, 16
Subedi S (2008) International investment law: reconciling policy and principle, 158
Sucharitkul S (1996) State responsibility and international liability under international law 18 Loy. L.A. Int'l & Comp L, 828–31. https://digitalcommons.law.ggu.edu/cgi/viewcontent.cgi?article=1225&context=pubs
Thaliath (2016) Bilateral investment treaties and sovereignty: an analysis with respect to international investment law. 5 Christ U. L J, 3–5
Tita (2010) Investment insurance in international law: a restatement on the regime of foreign investment, 11 J W Inv Trade, 655–6
Titi C (2015) Are investment tribunals adjudicating political disputes? Some reflections on the Repoliticization of investment disputes and (New) forms of diplomatic protection, 32 J Int'l L Arb, 262
Titi (2015) Are investment tribunals adjudicating political disputes? some reflections on the repoliticization of investment disputes and (New) forms of diplomatic protection, 32 J Int'l L Arb, 286–7
Trakman (2013) The ICSID under Siege, 45 Cornell Int'l L J, 649
Wena Hotels Ltd. v. Arab Republic of Egypt, ICSID Case No. ARB/98/4, Decision, (Dec. 8, 2000), 6 ICSID Rep. 939 (2002)

Chapter 4
Carbon Neutrality, Economic Transformation, and Foreign Investment Protection: A China's Perspective

Tong Qi and Diwan Liu

Background

As climate change has arisen as a momentous global concern and even the most pressing global challenge[1] here and now, carbon neutrality has become a new global fashion in dealing with it, which in turn leads to a profound transformation in the pattern of the world economic development. Climate change is not only the result of long-term environmental pollution under the old economic development model but also the motivation for environmental protection in the current world economic transformation. It is the natural disasters caused by climate change in recent years that have seriously threatened the human living environment that has prompted the international community to attach importance to environmental protection in transnational economic activities. Environmental protection has brought about an irreversible "green revolution," a non-negligible independent variable of current economic development, and even an all-important factor for evaluating the quality of future economic growth. Countries, no matter developed or developing, strive to contribute to tackling climate change. In this atmosphere, the economy of globality is undergoing a profound revolution.

Amid this round of world economic transformation, China is not immune from the changes. In addition to being the largest capital outflow country, China, which attracted an estimated $163 billion in inflows in 2020, has overtaken the US as the

[1] Asteriti (2016).

T. Qi (✉) · D. Liu
School of Law, Wuhan University, 299 Bayi Road, Wuchang District, Wuhan 430072, Hubei, China
e-mail: fxyqt@whu.edu.cn

© The Author(s), under exclusive license to Springer Nature Singapore Pte Ltd. 2024

S. Wei (ed.), *International Investment Law at the Juncture*, International Law in Asia,
https://doi.org/10.1007/978-981-97-2183-2_4

world's largest recipient of foreign investment,[2] occupying an increasingly important position in international investment. After more than 40 years since the reform and opening-up of extensive development, China's economy is facing transformation, from profit to sustainability oriented and from industrial to ecological civilization,[3] with the idea that "a sound ecological environment is the most basic public good and the most universally beneficial well-being of the people"[4] being gradually accepted and recognized, and then to be propagated more broadly. China's economy has currently stepped into a phase of medium–high growth from the high-speed growth of the past 40 years, and the economic development pattern is changing from scale and speed to quality and efficiency. According to the "Environmental Kuznets Curve" hypothesis[5] put forward by American economists Grossman and Krueger, it can be said that the relationship between China's economic development and ecological environment will soon usher in the so-called "inflection point" and is moving toward the era of the green economy. At this critical moment, it is necessary to scientifically understand the mechanism between economic development and ecological environmental protection to actively promote the positive interaction between the two.

However, rationally realizing that the turning point is about to come is far from enough; the top priority in the transitional period is to deal with the value conflicts between environmental protection and investment protection. The value conflict between environmental protection and investment protection is an indisputable and

[2] UNATCD, Global Investment Trend Monitor, No. 38, <https://unctad.org/system/files/official-document/diaeiainf2021d1_en.pdf> accessed 16 April 2022.

[3] Western countries have achieved great theoretical achievements and made significant theoretical contributions in the process of exploring the "ecological civilization" theory. The development of interdisciplines in the name of ecology and the emergence of Green Politics together further consolidate these studies. In Chinese context, on the basis of drawing on the lesson of "treatment after pollution" and reasonably referencing the advanced experience of environmental rule of law in Western countries, China's current "ecological civilization" theory is mainly based on the series discussions made by President Xi, from which four core ideas can be extracted as follows: (1) A civilization may thrive if its natural surroundings thrive, and will suffer if its natural surroundings suffer; (2) Lucid waters and lush mountains are invaluable assets; (3) The mountains, rivers, forests, farmlands, lakes, grasslands, and deserts are part of the community of life; (4) The environment is people's livelihood. In general, the ecological civilization rule of law theory of Xi Jinping is a theoretical innovation of the Marxist theory of the rule of law combining with China's national conditions, and also new findings of the development of world civilizations and international sustainable development researches. More discussions can be found in the articles made by Prof. Zhongmei Lv.

[4] "Pursuing Sustainable Development in a Concerted Effort, To Build an Asia–Pacific Community with a Shared Future: Keynote Speech by H. E. Xi Jinping President of the People's Republic of China at the APEC CEO Summit (11 November 2021)" <http://m.cnr.cn/news/20211111/t20211111_525658010.html> accessed 12 November 2021.

[5] The environmental Kuznets curve (EKC) is a hypothesized relationship between various indicators of environmental degradation and per capita income. In the early stages of economic growth, pollution emissions increase and environmental quality declines, but beyond some level of per capita income (which will vary for different indicators) the trend reverses, so that at high income levels, economic growth leads to environmental improvement. This implies that environmental impacts or emissions per capita are an inverted U-shaped function of per capita income. See Stern (2008).

inevitable fact, as the former has only been taken seriously by the international investment community in recent years, but the latter has remained an eternal topic of the investment rule of law. Environmental protection is closely associated with the right of regulation and the right to the development of host states. However, investment protection relates to the legitimate rights of investors under international law. The throes of transition are inevitable, but there is no making without breaking. The emerging environmental concerns and their interactions with traditional investment issues deserve our attention since they are propositions with the practical significance of the new era.

Precisely, the ever-closer relationship between environment and investment embodies mainly in two aspects: the practice of concluding treaties and environment-related investment disputes. Some recent bilateral investment treaties (BITs) or treaties with investment provisions (TIPs) include simple terms of environment-related measures[6] or particular articles dealing with investment and the environment,[7] some even providing a whole chapter just for the environment[8] while others make environmental exceptions.[9] Regarding investment-environment disputes, the *Chemtura v. Canada* tribunal reiterates the standpoint that environmental regulations, even when justified under the host's domestic laws, can still be challenged by foreign investors through investment arbitration.[10] However, even with arbitrability, the existing arbitration opinions are inconsistent on the issue of which benefit overwhelms, investment, or environment. Tribunals like *Methanex v. USA*,[11] *Plama v. Bulgaria*,[12] *Glamis Gold v. USA*,[13] *Al Tamimi v. Oman*,[14] and *Allard v. Barbados*[15] are in favor of the host states' taking environmental measures, while tribunals like

[6] For example, the China-Hong Kong CEPA Investment Agreement (2017) and the Israel-Japan BIT (2017).

[7] For example, the China-EU Comprehensive Agreement on Investment (CECAI) and the Austria-Kazakhstan BIT (2010).

[8] For example, the Comprehensive and Progressive Agreement for Trans-Pacific Partnership (CPTPP) and the Agreement between the United States of America, the United Mexican States, and Canada (USMCA).

[9] For example, the Cambodia-Turkey BIT (2018), the ASEAN-Hong Kong, China SAR Investment Agreement (2017), the Colombia-United Arab Emirates BIT (2017), the China-Hong Kong CEPA Investment Agreement (2017), and the Israel-Japan BIT (2017).

[10] Crompton (Chemtura) Corp. v. Government of Canada, Award dated 2 August 2010, para. 123.

[11] Methanex Corporation v. United States of America, Final Award of the Tribunal on Jurisdiction and Merits dated 3 August 2005, Part IV-Chapter B-Page 5. Methanex put forward a 4-criteria standard of proof for the USA to justify the validity of its environmental measure: (1) necessity; (2) proportionality; (3) the least restrictive of foreign investment; and (4) not constitute a disguised restriction on foreign investments.

[12] Plama Consortium Limited v. Republic of Bulgaria, ICSID Case No. ARB/03/24, Award dated 27 August 2008, para. 218.

[13] Glamis Gold Ltd. v. United States of America, Award dated 8 June 2009.

[14] Adel A Hamadi Al Tamimi v. Sultanate of Oman, ICSID Case No. ARB/11/33, Award dated 3 November 2015, para. 368.

[15] Peter A. Allard v. The Government of Barbados, PCA Case No. 2012–06, Award dated 27 June 2016, para. 249.

Metalclad v. Mexico,[16] *Myers v. Canada,*[17] and *Tecmed v. Mexico*[18] are in favor of investors' benefit. Besides, there are also cases where particular environmental concerns are involved but not decided. Although the jury is still out, it has been assumed that environmental considerations were "normalized" or "mainstreamed" in the reasoning of investment tribunals.[19]

On China side, China is faced with the dilemma and challenge of continuing its rapid economic development and doubling the efforts in improving environmental protection. The sustained and rapid development of China's economy in the past 40 years has mainly been driven by massive energy consumption; however, such output growth, which is at the cost of environmental pollution and resource abuse, is neither conducive to the adjustment and optimization of industrial structure nor the sustainable and healthy development of the national economy. With a profound evolution of China's development philosophy and the Scientific Outlook on Development proposal, economic development has been revised from "fast and well" to "well and fast." Henceforth, China has gradually optimized and upgraded its industrial structure from "secondary-tertiary-primary" to "secondary-primary-tertiary," and to "tertiary-secondary-primary," attempting to minimize the environmental pressure caused by the secondary industry. As socialism with Chinese characteristics entered a new era, the principal contradiction facing Chinese society has evolved into the one between the unbalanced and inadequate development and the people's ever-growing needs for a better life. Along with the imbalance of economic growth comes another imbalance: a highly asymmetrical environment, resources, and energy location. Neither is the government's fiscal input in ecological and environmental protection adequate nor is the distribution structure perfect.[20]

Apart from the internal obstacles in the process of deepening structural reform, China also faces practical challenges from external factors. The latest *AsiaPhos* case vividly shows the strained relations between implementing investment protection and pursuing environmental value. Establishing natural reserves is one of the systematic strategic measures to achieve China's carbon neutrality goal; however, in this case,

---

[16] Metalclad Corporation v. The United Mexican States, ICSID Case No. ARB(AF)/97/1, Award dated 30 August 2000, para. 111.

[17] S. D. Myers, Inc. v. Government of Canada, Partial Award dated 13 November 2000 (Merits), para. 221.

[18] Técnicas Medioambientales Tecmed v. United Mexican States, ICSID Case No. ARB(AF)/00/2, Award dated 29 May 2003, paras. 121–122.

[19] Viñuales (2019).

[20] See The National People's Congress of the People's Republic of China, "Comments and Suggestions on the Report on the Allocation and Use of Fiscal Funds for Ecological and Environmental Protection" <http://www.npc.gov.cn/npc/c30834/202001/7ed4c12ed52b4750b55092caddf1888b.shtml> accessed 16 April 2022; Ministry of Finance of the People's Republic of China, "Report of The State Council on the Allocation and Use of Fiscal Funds for Ecological and Environmental Protection" <http://www.mof.gov.cn/zhengwuxinxi/caizhengxinwen/201912/t20191226_3450288.htm> accessed 16 April 2022.

the local authority refused, based on "public interest considerations,"[21] to renew the exploration rights of AsiaPhos, whose mines were partly located inside the area of a planned panda reserve which was later officially classified as one of China's first national parks,[22] but led to the alleged "unlawful expropriation."[23]

The realization of the goal of carbon neutrality will undoubtedly affect foreign investments more or less, especially the ones active in environment-related fields. However, is it always in the public interest that host countries adopt a one-size-fits-all approach to environmental issues? Aren't there any mitigation measures investors are permitted to take? On the other side, is it the price that host states are destined to pay to achieve their environmental goals? Should all bets be on host states? Shouldn't investors, or multinational corporations[24] (MNCs), make any sacrifices in realizing such a global goal as carbon neutrality?

This article is to explore, from the perspective of China, which is acting simultaneously as both host country and home country: (1) how and to what extent the increasing global environmental concerns would affect China's practices in the field of international investment law and (2) the subtle impact the environmental concerns would have on the course of the China's negotiation and conclusion of prospective investment treaties as well as its foreign investment management system, and, in turn, on foreign investments that have already existed and are about to establish therein. Specifically, Part II is to give an overview of China's practices on investment-related environmental protection; Part III is to analyze the conflicts between these relatively new environmental protection measures and the traditional protection objectives of international investment law; Part IV is first to review the investment-related environmental measures mentioned above, and then to look into the future of China's IIAs, and, finally, to express expectation on ISDS reform. For all that purpose, interdisciplinary perspectives, normative analysis, and case analysis will be used herein as the primary research methods.

[21] Jarrod Hepburn and Luke Eric Peterson, "China warned of possible investment treaty arbitration" (Investment Arbitration Reporter (IA Reporter), 06 March 2018) <https://www.iareporter.com/articles/china-warned-of-possible-investment-treaty-arbitration/> accessed 29 August 2021.

[22] "Keynote Speech by Xi Jinping at the 15th Summit of the Conference of the Parties to the Convention on Biological Diversity" <http://news.cctv.com/2021/10/12/ARTIZ3sdwy5gtJJeS3fOYPJW211012.shtml> accessed 13 October 2021.

[23] Damien Charlotin, "Creation of Giant Panda Park prompts treaty-based arbitration against China" (IA Reporter, 15 January 2021) <https://www.iareporter.com/articles/china-faces-treaty-based-arbitration-claim-prompted-by-wildlife-conservation-measures/> accessed 29 August 2021.

[24] To avoid ambiguity, no matter what the specific differences might exist between "corporation" and "enterprise," the term "corporation" is chosen in this article to refer to the kind of legal persons with transnational elements.

China's Domestic and International Practices on Investment-Related Environmental Protection

The "1 + N" Policy Framework for Achieving Carbon Neutrality

In 2012, the 18th CPC National Congress (CPCNC) incorporated the construction of ecological civilization into its Five-Sphere Integrated Plan for building socialism with Chinese characteristics, putting ecology together with economy, politics, culture, and society on an equal footing. In 2015, strengthening the progression of ecological civilization was written into, for the first time, the national Five-Year Plan by the 5th Plenary Session of the 18th CPCNC. From then on, China's economic transformation goes hand in hand with its ecological construction. In 2018, ecologic construction was even written into the preamble of China's constitution for the first time in the newly adopted amendment.

After laying a solid policy foundation, in September 2020, President Xi Jinping formally put forward China's "30·60 Dual Carbon" goal—to achieve the peak of carbon dioxide emissions by 2030 and neutralization by 2060.[25] However, the time China has pledged to bring it from peak to neutral is only 30 years, which is much less than what some major developed countries would have spent,[26] meaning less time and heavier tasks. In October 2021, President Xi called on all humankind's endeavors at the 2020 UN Biodiversity Conference to make green transformation a driving force for sustainable global development. Hereupon, President Xi declared China's firm determination to release, successively, implementation plans and a series of supporting measures in critical sectors and industries, building a "1 + N" policy system for the "30·60" goal. Furthermore, it was also clearly indicated that China would continue to adjust its industrial and energy structures and vigorously develop renewable energy.[27] Besides, the State Council released the Action Plan for Carbon Dioxide Peaking Before 2030, reaffirming the commitment to promoting the Green Belt and Road Initiative and further proposing to improve the environmental sustainability of overseas projects.[28]

The above macro-strategic guiding ideology as a whole fully reveals the transformation of China's value proposition—from efficiency to high quality oriented,

---

[25] "Statement by Xi Jinping at the Leaders' Summit on Climate" <http://www.gov.cn/xinwen/2021-04/22/content_5601526.htm> accessed 12 August 2021.

[26] For example, the United States has pledged to realize net-zero emissions by 2050, however, its emissions had already peaked as early as in 2007. See Center for Climate and Energy Solutions, "U.S. Emissions" <https://www.c2es.org/content/u-s-emissions/> accessed 12 August 2021. Japan has also made it in 2013.

[27] "Keynote Speech by Xi Jinping at the 15th Leaders' Summit of the Conference of the Parties to the Convention on Biological Diversity" <http://www.gov.cn/xinwen/2021-10/12/content_5642048.htm> accessed 20 October 2021.

[28] Notice by the State Council of the Action Plan for Carbon Dioxide Peaking Before 2030, No. 23 [2021] of the State Council, Part IV (3).

which in a manner represents the "1" of the so-proposed "1 + N" policy system. The "1" means not only a guiding principle of the overall policy system but can also be interpreted to mean that the desired policy system is taking the environment as its starting point and the ultimate foothold—under the framework of the "1," China is to unveil successively a series of supporting policies, with the environment at the core, as its implementation mechanism. The "N," correspondingly, could have twofold meanings: First, all the implementation plans and supporting measures of key fields and industries,[29] both the already enacted ones and the ones to be introduced, and second, dimensions closely related to the environment, such as the focus of this article, the investment side. Thus, the "1 + N" policy system can be read as both "general principle + supporting measures" and "environment + investment." Henceforth, the development of environment-related investment measures in China is expected to be from unitary to pluralistic and from piecemeal to systematic.

Domestic Laws and Regulations on Ecological and Environmental Protection

An Overview of the Legislation, Justice, and Supervision of Environmental Protection in China

China has attached increasing importance to the environment, mainly reflected in its legislation, enforcement, justice, and supervision of ecological and environmental protection. China's legislation on environmental protection could date back to the very late 1970s. The first environmental protection law was issued in 1979, and after a 10-year implementation trial, an Environmental Protection Law in the true sense was formally issued and immediately enacted.[30] The law was later revised only once in 2014 and remains in force today. The 18th CPCNC is an essential milestone for China's environmental protection legislation. Since then, China has at least newly enacted five laws,[31] comprehensively revised four laws,[32] and partly

---

[29] Such as energy, transportation, industry, and circular economy. See "Pursuing Sustainable Development in a Concerted Effort, To Build an Asia–Pacific Community with a Shared Future: Keynote Speech by H.E. Xi Jinping President of the People's Republic of China at the APEC CEO Summit (11 November 2021)" <http://m.cnr.cn/news/20211111/t20211111_525658010.html> accessed 12 November 2021.

[30] Chinese scholar Danni Liang believes that the first major environmental protection legislation in China was enacted in 1989. See Danni Liang, "Environmental concerns and China's international investment agreements" in Kate Miles (ed) *Research Handbook on Environment and Investment Law* (Edward Elgar 2019) 366.

[31] They are Nuclear Safety Law, Soil Pollution Prevention and Control Law, Environmental Protection Tax Law, Biosecurity Law, and Yangtze River Protection Law.

[32] They are Marine Environment Protection Law (Amendment 2017), Water Pollution Prevention and Control Law (2017 Revision), Atmospheric Pollution Prevention and Control Law (2018

amended five laws,[33] to implement the ecological civilization strategy. It could be said that it is from that time China's system of laws and regulations on ecology and environment has taken shape. Regarding the judicial work on environmental protection, the Supreme People's Court releases typical cases of judicial protection of the ecological environment, covering three types of environmental litigation in China: civil as well as administrative public interest litigation, and ecological environment compensation litigation. In the aspect of the supervision of environmental protection, since 2021, the ecological and environmental protection inspectors of the Central Committee of the CPC have been kept reporting on typical cases.[34]

Specific Measures for Investment-Related Environmental Protection

With the formation, refinement, and continuous improvement of the environmental protection law system, relevant measures in the field of international investment have also been gradually developing in China. In 2013, the Ministry of Commerce (MoC) and the Ministry of Environmental Protection (MoEP, dissolved in 2018, now, the Ministry of Ecology and Environment, MoEE) released the Guidelines for Environmental Protection in Foreign Investment and Cooperation.[35] The 2013 Guideline directs Chinese enterprises to regularize their environmental protection behaviors in foreign investment and cooperation activities, timely identifying and preventing environmental risks. Furthermore, it guides Chinese enterprises to actively perform their social responsibilities of environmental protection, supporting the sustainable development of the host country while setting up good international images for all Chinese enterprises. Later in 2021, MoC and MoEE, again, jointly released the Guidelines for Green Development of Outbound Investment and International Cooperation, integrating the environment into foreign trade and economy, thus making it more comprehensive than the 2013 Guideline. The 2021 Guideline makes general requirements and critical tasks to (1) pursue the vision of green development; (2) promote green production and operations, green technical innovation, and green transformation of enterprises; (3) build green infrastructure as well as green overseas economic and trade cooperation zones; (4) guard against ecological and environmental risks; (5) follow international rules for green development; (6) improve green regulatory services; and (7) enhance the credibility of green development.

Amendment), and Law on the Prevention and Control of Environment Pollution Caused by Solid Wastes (2020 Revision).

[33] They are Cleaner Production Promotion Law (2012 Amendment), Marine Environment Protection Law (Amendment 2017), Law on Environmental Impact Assessment (2018 Amendment), Circular Economy Promotion Law (2018 Amendment), and Law on Prevention and Control of Pollution from Environmental Noise (2018 Amendment).

[34] See MoEE, <https://www.mee.gov.cn/ywgz/zysthjbhdc/dcjl/202105/t20210506_831813.shtml> accessed 8 April 2022

[35] The 2013 guideline is a departmental normative document, belonging to the category of comprehensive regulation for environmental protection.

To optimize the business environment, efforts have also been made from the perspective of encouraging environmental protection. Article 20 of MoC's Measure for the Administration of Overseas Investment (2014) stipulates that Chinese enterprises shall require their overseas enterprises to honor social responsibilities and effectively conduct environmental protection. In 2017, the National Development and Reform Commission (NDRC) released the Measures for the Administration of Overseas Investment of Enterprises, where Article 41 encourages Chinese investors to fulfill essential social responsibilities and pay attention to environmental protection.

Hereto, the above-mentioned investment-related environmental measures (IREMs), from the very soft "guideline" to a little bit harder "measure," are all at a broad international level. However, the year 2017 was a turning point that witnessed a shift of the focus of IREMs to a narrower multilateral level, the Belt and Road. In 2017, four ministries and commissions—MoEP, the Ministry of Foreign Affairs, NDRC, and MoC—jointly released a departmental working paper, the Guiding Opinion on Promoting Green Belt and Road Initiative, piloting more new policies on a smaller international scope. With the guidance of the concept "green development" has been strengthened, the four bodies once again, in March 2022, issued the Opinion on Promoting Green Development under the Belt and Road Initiative, coordinating and advancing the cooperation of green development in critical areas[36] and the green development of overseas projects through the encouragement of corporations.

It is not hard to see that all the IREMs, whether applicable to the large or small multilateral level, are targeted at Chinese outbound investment corporations. In the wake of the transition from being a capital import country to a capital export country, as well as of the move to actively cultivate the image of a significant responsible power, China is increasingly focusing on the responsible environmental behavior of its overseas corporations. Corporate social responsibility (CSR) is by no means a brand-new issue in various contexts, especially in the management sector. Still, it does win a place for itself in the intersection of environment and investment in recent years. Be that as it may, when the old concept of CSR is incorporated into IREMs, it is faced with new challenges, whether in the international dimension or at China's domestic level. A growing number of international legal instruments are actively promoting responsible business conduct.[37] As for China, early in 2008, the State-Owned Assets Supervision and Administration Commission of the State Council released the Instruction on Central Enterprises' Fulfilling the Social Responsibilities. Ten years later, the Company Law (2018 Amendment) added a new rule that a company shall bear social responsibilities.[38] It can be seen that CSR is no longer just a freewill commitment made by companies but one of the formal legal requirements for them to meet to survive and compete in the Chinese market.

---

[36] Nine areas have been enumerated: infrastructure, energy, transportation, industry, trade, finance, technology, standard, and climate change.

[37] The most frequently mentioned ones are the OECD Guidelines for Multinational Enterprises, the ILO Tripartite Declaration of Principles concerning Multinational Enterprises and Social Policy, the UN Global Compact, and the UN Guiding Principles on Business and Human Rights.

[38] Company Law of the People's Republic of China (2018 Amendment), Article 5.

Summing up the above, the governance logic of environment-related investment issues (ERIIs) in China can be summarized as follows: unilateral adjustment aiming at overseas investment corporations comes first, and then two-way adjustment for all companies that are subject to Chinese company law—internalized, comprehensive, and balanced, step by step. Specifically, the first batch of IREMs focuses on the standardization of the behavior of outbound corporations by imposing soft social responsibility, which is later written into domestic law. In other words, environmental protection, one of the essential pillars of CSR, is initially introduced to encourage our domestic "going out" corporations to better respect the environment of destination countries rather than their own home country. Regarding domestic legislation, the existing legal documents dealing with ERIIs are almost at a low legal hierarchy. Moreover, it is also a pity that the Foreign Investment Law issued in 2019 is silent on environmental protection, let alone the later released Regulation for Implementing the Foreign Investment Law.

Environmental Protection Commitments in China's International Investment Agreement Practices

China's growing awareness of environmental protection is also reflected in international treaties. Among the many international investment agreements (IIAs) China has ever concluded, some, but only a tiny part, involve environmental clause(s). Generally, such provisions usually appear in the following treaty elements: preamble, expropriation, general exceptions, and environmental measures. Some appear in only one part of the IIAs, either as a tiny fraction briefly mentioned or as a whole module, others in two or three pieces.

"Lonely Planet"

If the environment-related language only appears in one part of the treaty, such a situation is likely to happen in the first generation of China's IIAs. However, it does not rule out the new generation of IIAs doing the same. China-Mauritius BIT (1996), which is the very first BIT where China made its environmental commitment, writes in the "Prohibitions and Restrictions" part that the treaty provisions "shall not in any way limit the right of either Contracting Party to apply prohibitions or restrictions of any kind or take any other action which is directed to … the protection of its environment."[39]

Expressing environmental concerns through preambular paragraphs is common in China's IIAs. Both China-Trinidad and Tobago BIT (2002) and China-Guyana BIT (2003) make the same agreement in their preamble that the treaty objectives "can be achieved without relaxing … environmental measures of general application"

[39] China-Mauritius BIT (1996), Article 11.

(hereinafter referred to as "without relaxing" clause). In China-Pakistan FTA (2006) and China-Peru FTA (2009), the parties recognized that considering sustainable development, environmental protection, and conservation should be a proper manner of implementing the agreement.[40] Analogously, in China-Iceland FTA (2013), the parties are mindful that environmental protection, as well as economic development and social development, "are interdependent and mutually reinforcing components of sustainable development, and that closer economic partnership can play an important role in promoting sustainable development."[41]

In addition to making it a programmatic prologue, China generally places its environmental concerns under either exception or expropriation clause. China-Australia FTA (2015) puts necessary environmental measures into "General Exceptions" for the purpose of its investment chapter.[42] In the Regional Comprehensive Economic Partnership (RCEP) (2020), China directly confirms that discriminatory regulatory actions designed and applied to achieve environmental objectives do not constitute certain types of expropriation.[43]

Dualistic Arrangement

With the enhancement of the awareness of environmental problems and the corresponding emergence of environment-related ISDS cases, languages addressing environmental concerns have doubled in China's subsequent IIAs. This form of treaty arrangement comes at least 10 years later than the declarative commitments described above.

The dual regulation of environmental issues mostly appears in the form of "preamble + X." The "X" can be one of the general exceptions. Aspiring to achieve an appropriate balance between the economic, social, and environmental components of sustainable development,[44] China-Costa Rica FTA (2010) incorporates Article XIV (b) of GATS into the agreement, making necessary environmental measures the general exceptions for arbitrary or unjustifiable discrimination or a disguised restriction on investment.[45] However, the much more common case is that the "X" is a specific article or an entire chapter adjusting the intersection of environment and investment. Japan-Korea-China Trilateral Investment Agreement (2012) matches

---

[40] The same statement also appears in Chile-China FTA (2005) and China-Switzerland FTA (2013).

[41] Such consensus also appears in China-New Zealand FTA (2008), China-Switzerland FTA (2013), China-Korea FTA (2015), etc.

[42] Australia-China FTA (2015), Article 9.8.

[43] RCEP, Chap. 10, Annex 10B (Expropriation), 4.

[44] China-Costa Rica FTA (2010), Article 2 (1) (f).

[45] *Id.*, Article 159 (2).

a "without relaxing" clause with Article 23, "Environmental Measures." China-Switzerland FTA (2013) gives a whole chapter on "Environmental Issues,"[46] not only reiterating the importance of environmental protection but taking the cooperation of environmental issues "part of a global approach to sustainable development." The parties commit to "strive to further improve the level of environmental protection by all means," especially by attaching importance to the scientificity, technicality, and effectiveness of domestic laws and regulations when preparing and implementing measures related to the environment. It is a huge step forward for China in balancing environmental protection under FTA.

The "expropriation + Y" combination is another typical model. China-Turkey BIT (2015) makes it clear in "Expropriation and Compensation" that non-discriminatory legal measures for the purpose of legitimate public welfare, including environmental protection, do not constitute indirect expropriation,[47] and also in "General Exceptions" that non-discriminatory and necessary measures for the protection of the environment cannot be prevented from adopting, maintaining, or enforcing.[48] Completely different from the 1996 BIT, China-Mauritius FTA (2019) pragmatically puts its environmental concerns in the "Expropriation" and "Performance Requirements" sections, turning the expression of "not limit" into something more concrete.

Ternary or More Diversified

In China-New Zealand FTA (2008), the parties take notice of the inseparable relationship between economic development, social development, and environmental protection,[49] thus they commit to enhancing communication and cooperation on labor and environmental matters[50] and making governmental environmental measures the exception to indirect expropriation.[51] Along with "exception + expropriation" sections, China-Canada BIT (2012) also puts the parties' environmental commitments into "Consultations," whose content is similar to the "without relaxing" clause.[52]

---

[46] Chapter 12 (Environmental Issues) contains the following articles: Context and Objectives, Multilateral Environmental Agreements and Environmental Principles, Promotion of the Dissemination of Goods and Services Favouring the Environment, Cooperation in International Fora, Bilateral Cooperation, Resources and Financial Arrangements, Implementation and Consultations, and Review.

[47] *Id.*, Article 5.3.

[48] China-Turkey BIT (2015), Article 4.1.

[49] China-New Zealand FTA (2008), Preamble.

[50] *Id.*, Chapter 14 (Cooperation), Article 177.

[51] *Id.*, Annex 13 (Expropriation), 5.

[52] "The Contracting Parties recognize that it is inappropriate to encourage investment by waiving, relaxing, or otherwise derogating from domestic health, safety or environmental measures." See Canada-China BIT (2012), Article 18.3.

China-EU Comprehensive Agreement on Investment[53] sets aside an independent section named "Investment and sustainable development," under which Sect. 4.2, "Investment and Environment," is entirely devoted to ERIIs with six articles.[54] Article 1 plays a chapeau role since it recognizes the parties' right to regulate, specifically, the right "to determine its sustainable development policies and priorities, to establish its levels of domestic labor and environmental protection, and to adopt or modify its relevant laws and policies," provided that doing so is consistent with their multilateral commitments in the fields of labor and environment. Article 2 sets the levels of protection that consist of a "shall strive to" clause (Article 2.1), a "without relaxing" clause (Article 2.2), three obligation clauses—the non-derogation clause (Article 2.3), the non-enforcement clause (Article 2.4), and the non-restrictive and non-discriminatory application clause (Article 2.6)—relating to domestic legislation, and an innovative exemption clause (Article 2.5) for resource allocation decisions out of good faith. Besides, the Comprehensive and Progressive Agreement for Trans-Pacific Partnership, which China has applied to join, also provides a whole chapter just for the environment, integrating environmental concerns systematically into the free trade agreement. Among others, Article 20.2 (Objectives), Article 20.3 (General Commitments), Article 20.9 (Public Submissions), Article 20.12 (Cooperation Frameworks), and Article 20.18 (Environmental Goods and Services) have something to do with investment.

China's environmental commitments in IIAs develop from nothing, from less to more, and from fragmentation to integration, accompanied by an increasing emphasis on cooperation. However, compared with the total number of investment treaties signed by China,[55] only a handful cover environmental protection issues. Despite such quantitative characteristics, in terms of the specific content of current environmental protection clauses, Chinese treaty practice is consistent with the general international situation—that is, environmental issues are not only buried in a sea of investment protection clauses but written in a declarative language, expressed by a soft tone, and demonstrated with weak execution. Beyond that, China's existing environmental clauses also present some distinct characteristics—some obvious deficiencies: the lack of proper pre-contractual planning, full theoretical argument, and unified treaty expression; the lack of necessary consideration in how to reflect environment-related contents in the treaty context, thus leading to the lack of stable components of forming a standard configuration for IIAs; and the lack of a systematic summary of international good practices, neither reflecting China's actual needs nor interacting or echoing between the clauses.[56]

[53] The agreement has not been ratified yet due to the dissension over some sensitive issues between China and the EU.

[54] The six articles are, in order: Right to regulate, Levels of protection, Dialogue and cooperation on investment-related environmental issues, Multilateral environmental agreements, Investment favoring green growth, as well as Investment and Climate Change.

[55] China has signed 148 IIAs in total, including 124 (107 in force) BITs and 24 (19 in force) TIPs. See UNCTAD, Investment Policy Hub, <https://investmentpolicy.unctad.org/international-investment-agreements/by-economy> accessed 3 December 2021.

[56] See Feng (2017).

The Examination of the Conflicts Between China's IREMs and Its Commitments to Investment Protection Under IIAs

China's IREMs could indeed attract foreign capital and advanced technology for its environmental governance, where the positive influence is needless to say; however, as every coin has two sides, IREMs also have a negative effect in that they might conflict with China's commitment to protecting foreign investors and their investments. Investment protection is a package of international law commitments made by the host country; accordingly, IREMs should also comply with relevant obligations under IIAs. Even so, China recognizes that these investment protection commitments should be considered in conjunction with relevant public interests,[57] where environmental benefits are included, of course. Nevertheless, there is an inherent tension between environmental regulation and investment protection. The conflicts thereof are divided into normative and legitimacy in terms of their nature.[58] With the diversified development of modern international law, its legal branches become more specialized, each law merely autonomously[59] stipulating particular matters within its domain—investment law emphasizes investment protection, while environmental law focuses on environmental protection. On this ground, the conflicts can ascribe to the non-interaction or fragmented interaction of two value pursuits. Previous scholars have identified and systematically studied such conflicts from different perspectives, such as the state's right to regulate for a public purpose, the practice of lowering environmental standards to attract FDI which is recognized as competition distortion, and the possibility of making environmental screening a mechanism to select green FDI at the stage of admission.[60] In this part, this article will make a specific analysis, from China's perspective, of the underlying contradiction between the two protecting objectives.

Environment Access

There is no special environmental scrutiny under the framework of investment law; moreover, neither environmental commitment nor environmental contribution is a prerequisite for investors to enter the Chinese market. Since the Foreign Investment Law along with its implementation regulation were promulgated in 2019 and came into effect in 2020, the management system of pre-establishment national treatment plus a negative list has been formally established at China's national level; thus, the previous foreign investment examination and approval system has officially retired from the stage of history. After reviewing relevant laws and regulations, China has

[57] Liang (2019).

[58] See Viñuales (2009).

[59] See Fischer-Lescano and Teubner (2004).

[60] See Joubin-Bret (2016).

abolished at least 56 normative documents,[61] including those related to the environment. Meanwhile, the negative list has also been slimmed year by year, and more environmentally friendly industries and sectors are opening up in an orderly manner. In reality, in 2007, China started to restrict or prohibit foreign investment projects with high material consumption, high energy consumption, or high environmental pollution.[62] Since 2019, Hainan Province has completely banned the development of all "3 high" industries.[63] In years to come, China is to continue to revise and expand the Catalogue of Industries to Encourage Foreign Investment to guide more foreign investments into the field of energy conservation and environmental protection, especially in the mid-west and northeast.[64]

Though lacking explicit stipulations under the framework of investment law, China sets environmental thresholds for the admission of foreign investment through the framework of environmental law. In terms of environmental access, China has put into practice the concept of differentiated environmental governance. Instead of imposing uniform restrictions on environmental access at a national level, the central government has delegated authority to each local government to develop individual implementation plans that are better tailored to specific local conditions. Early in 2008, Chinese scholars once proposed establishing an "environmental access" system, which requires investment projects to comply with environmental standards and policies, and, in the meantime, authorizes the government to comprehensively consider environmental pressure and the impact brought by foreign investments.[65] By the end of 2021, all Chinese provincial-level administrative regions—24 provinces, 5 autonomous regions, 4 municipalities, and 2 special administrative regions—as well as municipal and prefectural cities, have published their own "three lines, one list,"[66] demarcating more than 40,000 environmental control units. A nationwide

---

61 Announcement No. 59 [2019] of MoC, Announcement of the Ministry of Commerce on Repealing Certain Regulatory Documents <http://www.mofcom.gov.cn/article/b/f/201912/20191202925578.shtml> accessed 15 April 2022.

62 See MoC, Catalogue of Industries for Guiding Foreign Investment (2007 Revision), <http://www.mofcom.gov.cn/aarticle/b/f/200711/20071105248462.html> accessed 18 April 2022.

63 See Development and Reform Commission of Hainan Province, The Industry Access Prohibition and Restriction Catalog of Hainan Province (2019), <http://plan.hainan.gov.cn/sfgw/0400/201909/92e94bc2d2324268bd5bf23c797ed6db.shtml> accessed 18 April 2022; Department of Ecology and Environment of Hainan Province, The Ecological Environment Access List of Hainan Province (2021), <http://hnsthb.hainan.gov.cn/xxgk/0200/0202/hjywgl/hjyxpj/202110/t20211027_3081935.html> accessed 18 April 2022.

64 "Keynote Speech by Xi Jinping at the Opening Ceremony of the Fourth China International Import Expo" <http://www.gov.cn/xinwen/2021-11/04/content_5648892.htm> accessed 12 November 2021.

65 See Jiang (2008).

66 I.e., ecological conservation red line, environmental quality bottom line, resource utilization upper limit line, and ecological environment access list.

ecological and environmental zoning management and control system has thus been established.[67]

The admission of foreign investment is one of the most sensitive issues in the field of international investment. In theory, the continued market liberalization is good news for foreign investors looking to enter the Chinese market. However, a measure that, on its face, looks more advantageous, may not be so if evaluated in the light of some other realistic considerations. In practice, there are numerous intangible obstacles to be wrestled with. One of these difficulties is the remarkably increased cost of establishing and operating in increasingly environmentally demanding investment destinations. Such additional cost can be either the cost of meeting local environment access standards or adjusting its original investment plan, and also the cost of either technical or human resources. Higher cost of investment can lead to China being accused of disguised investment protection, which is contrary to investment liberalization. Apart from concerns about cost, whether an assessment of ecological impact or sustainability would fall into the category of national security review could be investors' other worry. Environmental issues are not merely natural but also economic issues, and even social and political issues. As non-traditional national security, ecological security has been brought into China's national security system and is as essential as the other 15 of the Holistic View of National Security.[68] Thus, at least in the era of carbon neutrality, the uncertainty brought about by environmental protection measures is both an opportunity and a challenge for the establishment of foreign investment. Neither will China be the reproached "pollution haven" nor environmental protection be the bottomland of cost for foreign investment. Environmental factors are indispensable pre-investment considerations that deserve careful pondering.

Non-discriminatory Treatment

Investment protection is one of the cornerstones of international investment law, and treatment standard is the most essential basis for evaluating the degree of investment protection. Like most host countries, China has committed itself to providing non-discrimination treatment to foreign investors, with both relative treatment standards—most favored nation treatment (MFN) and national treatment (NT), and absolute treatment standard—fair and equitable treatment (FET). Under the commitment of MFN, China should apply the same set of standards to foreign investors and their investments who are from the countries with which it has signed investment agreements, while under the commitment of NT, China should treat these foreign investors and their investments like its own nationals, even at the stage of pre-establishment.

---

[67] Central People's Government of China, "A Nationwide Ecological and Environmental Zoning Management and Control System Has Been Basically Established" <http://www.gov.cn/xinwen/2021-12/24/content_5664332.htm> accessed 18 April 2022.

[68] For example, the traditional ones like political security, military security, and economic security.

FET is much more broadly interpreted as an international minimum standard or needs further interpretation under the principle of good faith.

As relative treatment standards, when environmental protection becomes one of the factors used for comparison, the challenges facing MFN and NT may come mainly from the type and source of inter-comparable foreign investment. The emphasis on environmental protection would virtually and automatically divide investment projects into two camps, environmentally friendly and non-environmentally friendly. Traditionally, when analyzing "like circumstance" or "similar situation," factors to be considered are usually whether the comparators are in the same market and whether they are in competition. However, the new classification of investment projects appears to bring a result-oriented approach, which kind of deviates from the traditional criteria. On the other hand, as foreign investors and their investments would come from countries with different types of development whose environmental commitments and capabilities vary, applying different environmental standards may lead to inequality among foreigners.[69]

Discrimination may occur under the guise of ecological and environmental protection. In the Ecological Environment Access List of Xiamen, there seem to be some provisions that could probably cause a violation of the principle of NT. In the planning for the Caicuo area, the access requirements for commerce and trade service might be problematic. Of the seven requirements, only two investment restrictions apply to both domestic and foreign capitals; as for the remaining five, one limits the form of the distribution of audiovisual products to cooperation only, three impose restrictions on foreign investment in related businesses, and one prohibits foreign investment in salt wholesale.[70] However, among the restrained businesses, only the retail tobacco trade is indeed forbidden by the Special Administrative Measures (Negative List) for the Access of Foreign Investment (2021), and the salt industry is not on the Negative List at all. Such a list is not only contrary to the provisions of its superior "law" but also likely to violate China's commitment to investment liberalization and, further, constitute a breach of the principle of NT. Is there any obvious or direct relationship between the restricted fields of foreign investment and ecological and environmental protection? For example, what impact on earth will salt wholesale have on environmental protection so that foreign investments are not allowed to operate? The grounds for discrimination should be more precise, more scientific, and more reasonable.

In investment arbitration practice, to decide whether the host state violates MFN and/or NT, tribunals usually consider three interrelated factors: likeness, favorableness, and justification.[71] Environmental factors would affect, to some extent, the assessment process of these elements. In the "likeness" test, the tribunal of *S. D. Myers v. Canada* takes into account twofold, general principles emerging from the

[69] See Li and Zhao (2019).

[70] Bureau of Ecology and Environment of Xiamen, Ecological Environment Access List of Xiamen (2021), p. 127, <http://sthjj.xm.gov.cn/zwgk/zhengce/gfxwj/202112/W020211224393074441511.pdf> accessed 18 April 2022.

[71] See Viñuales (2012).

applicable law and public interest.[72] Moreover, the tribunal of *Parkerings v. Lithuania* takes a step forward to consider the environmental impact.[73] Despite the two cases together suggesting the necessity of examining the environmental context,[74] among all other elements, whether the environmental considerations are decisive or complementary is undefined. In the "favorableness" test, IREMs would indeed increase the cost of doing business, thus leading to less favorable treatment. Still, it might not be so if evaluated from the long-term policy dividend effect and the analysis of other assessments. A distinction may need to be made between a tolerable "less favorable" and an intolerable one, thus making it a combination of investment protection and environmental protection principles—common but differentiated non-discrimination treatment. As for the "justification" test, though IREMs can be justified by several defense arguments, such as the police power doctrine, the margin of appreciation doctrine, and the emergency and necessity clauses,[75] the proportionality of the IREMs is still facing challenges. It is worth further discussion whether environmental considerations should be injected into the analysis of each factor or be made as a fourth separate factor to compare.

Lastly, when China's IREMs meet the principle of FET, procedural and detailed matters are of great importance. While carbon neutrality is a pressing priority, the formulation and enforcement of IREMs should follow due process and be as open and transparent as possible, thus leaving room for investors' reasonable expectations. Environment polluters are subjected to Chinese civil, administrative, or even criminal punishment; in turn, it is also necessary to ensure that the channels for foreign investors to seek relief are open, unimpeded, and as diversified as possible, to avoid arbitrary decisions brought about by information asymmetry. Platforms of complaints of foreign-invested enterprises at both central and local levels set a good example. Just as the principle of FET should not be the shield of unreasonable investment protection claims, nor should the host country exercise regulatory power arbitrarily in the name of pan-environmental protection.

Indirect Expropriation

The expropriation issue is the most prominent manifestation of the conflict between the public interests of the host country and the individual interests of investors. At a time of economic transition, the government's directly depriving of private property and nationalizing to develop the national economy are no longer common. Instead, the new normal is that regulatory measures in the public interests are increasingly

[72] S. D. Myers, Inc. v. Government of Canada, Partial Award dated 13 November 2000 (Merits), para. 250.

[73] Parkerings-Compagniet AS v. Republic of Lithuania, ICSID Case No. ARB/05/8, Award dated 11 September 2007, para. 392.

[74] See Viñuales (2012).

[75] See Viñuales (2012).

accused of indirect expropriation, more specifically, "regulatory expropriation"[76] or "taking." Generally, a legal expropriation needs to meet four requirements: for a public purpose, following due process of law, in a non-discriminatory manner, and on compensation. Specifically, in deciding whether environmental measures constitute indirect expropriation, tribunals would further consider the effect and objective of the measures, whether the measures are proportionate, and whether the measures are supported by scientific evidence.[77] However, the practical application of these analytical methods does not yield consistent results. There is no accepted precedent, but it is generally accepted by tribunals that case analysis should be adopted to determine this kind of issue.

As briefly mentioned above, *AsiaPhos v. China* is an ongoing ICSID case that is to explore whether the actions of the Chinese local government—noticing AsiaPhos halt part of its mining operations, further requiring it to vacate and rehabilitate the mines lying in the environment-threatening location, and finally rejecting the company's application for the extension of mining rights[78]—constitute illegal indirect expropriation. Similar facts can be found in *Metalclad v. Mexico*. In that case, the Mexican government refused to renew the permit for Metalclad to build a landfill as the land was reclassified as an ecological preserve. The tribunal found that "the construction permit was denied without any consideration of or specific reference to" the construction itself, but merely for ecologic concerns.[79] However, the tribunal held that, concerning the identification of expropriation, there was no need to explore "the motivation or intent" of law based on ecological considerations.[80] It is the first case to hold environmental measures as expropriation by a tribunal that adopted an "effect-only" approach, regardless of any other policy considerations. Nevertheless, more recent cases suggest that tribunals are looking for better-balanced approaches to non-investment issues such as environmental protection.[81] In *Glamis Gold v. USA*, the tribunal was asked to assess the purpose and character of the alleged governmental actions.[82] In *Methanex v. USA*, the tribunal upheld the application of the police power doctrine to justify environmental regulations.[83] In *Plama v. Bulgaria*,[84] the tribunal found no evidence that the modification of Bulgaria's environmental law was aimed directly against Plama, nor did the tribunal believe that the applicable law could be

---

[76] See Viñuales (2012).

[77] See Zhang (2016).

[78] Jarrod Hepburn and Luke Eric Peterson, "China warned of possible investment treaty arbitration" (Investment Arbitration Reporter (IA Reporter), 06 March 2018) <https://www.iareporter.com/articles/china-warned-of-possible-investment-treaty-arbitration/> accessed 29 August 2021.

[79] Metalclad Corporation v. The United Mexican States, ICSID Case No. ARB(AF)/97/1, Award dated 30 August 2000, paras. 92–93.

[80] *Id.*, at para. 111.

[81] See Viñuales (2021).

[82] Glamis Gold Ltd. v. United States of America, Award dated 8 June 2009, para. 356.

[83] Methanex Corporation v. United States of America, Final Award of the Tribunal on Jurisdiction and Merits dated 3 August 2005, Part IV-Chapter D, para. 7.

[84] Mr. Albert Jan van den Berg was appointed as arbitrator in both *Plama v. Bulgaria* and *AsiaPhos v. China*.

interpreted as protecting investors "against any and all changes in the host country's laws."[85]

According to the applicable law in *AsiaPhos v. China*, herein the 1985 China-Singapore BIT, which is also the very first IIA where environmental language occurs,[86] the scope of exceptions to expropriation is very vague, broadly allowing measures that are taken for any purpose authorized by law. Taking it literally, on the condition that the other requirements are met, as long as the environmental measures have a legal basis, it does not constitute indirect expropriation. Furthermore, the legality of the alleged expropriation-like measures may be reviewed by the competent court of the Contracting Party taking those measures,[87] herein the Chinese court. Under the circumstances, the court will likely come to a negative conclusion, as the applicable law here to review the measures is Chinese law, which can justify the claimed IREMs. Besides, it might be interesting that, in addition to being parties to the 1985 BIT, China and Singapore, the countries involved in this case, are also parties to ASEAN-China Investment Agreement and RCEP. Unlike the 1985 BIT, ASEAN-China Investment Agreement constricts the scope of exceptions to expropriation to allowing only measures taken for a public purpose.[88] Similarly but also further, RCEP, which has already officially entered into force on 1 January 2022, makes it clear that a Party's regulatory actions, if they are designed and applied to achieve legitimate public welfare objectives, such as protecting the environment, and if they are made without discrimination, do not constitute indirect expropriation.[89]

From another angle, China's shift toward green development does not happen overnight; instead, it is progressive and can be traced. As in this case, the People's Government of Sichuan Province issued a public notice for the environmental evaluation of the ecological restoration project in its local nature reserve early in October 2011,[90] and later, the Department of Ecology and Environment of Sichuan Province made it public the adjustment of nature reserves in March 2014.[91] It's making firm policy choices regarding environmental protection and is sending clear and positive signs, which is enough to provide strong predictability for the existing and incoming investors. In other words, a sophisticated policy-sensitive investor can and should be alert to such no small changes in the overall investment climate, as scholar Jorge E.

---

[85] Plama Consortium Limited v. Republic of Bulgaria, ICSID Case No. ARB/03/24, Award dated 27 August 2008, paras. 218–219.

[86] Kathryn Gordon and Joachim Pohl, "Environmental Concerns in International Investment Agreements: A Survey" (OECD Working Papers on International Investment 2011/01) 5 <https://www.oecd-ilibrary.org/finance-and-investment/environmental-concerns-in-international-investment-agreements_5kg9mq7scrjh-en> accessed 4 April 2022.

[87] China-Singapore BIT (1985), Article 6.2.

[88] ASEAN-China Investment Agreement, Article 8 (1) (a).

[89] RCEP, Annex 10B (4).

[90] "Notice for the Environmental Evaluation of Ecological Restoration Project of Jiudingshan Provincial Nature Reserve, Sichuan Provinces" <https://www.sc.gov.cn/10462/10464/10727/10712/2011/10/24/10185553.shtml> accessed 9 February 2022.

[91] "Notice of Nature Reserve" <http://sthjt.sc.gov.cn/sthjt/c104114/2014/3/21/14bd1f4954064155b97e24f30a5d81e1.shtml> accessed 9 February 2022.

Viñuales regards environmental protection as "a basic component of the commercial risk of foreign investment ventures,"[92] not a political one.

Conclusions and Prospects

International investment law is not and should by no means be "international investment protection law,"[93] on the contrary, it is in a second transition[94] from a narrow protection law to a more inclusive one. This inclusive international investment law system focuses not only on investment protection but also on the balance of investment-related interests, such as environmental concerns. Investment law should act as an incentive, not an obstacle,[95] in the process of the transition toward the green economy that we pursue. The conflict between investment protection and environmental protection is only a tiny fraction of the multilayered relationship[96] between foreign investment and the environment. According to materialistic dialectics,[97] contradictions can be transformed into each other under certain conditions. By the same token, though, in a sense, environmental protection and investment protection are opposite and fighting each other, they can transform in opposite directions in a mutually reinforcing way. Only by constantly negating each other can this pair of contradictions promote mutual development. In this process, the purpose of environmental protection should be de-disguised, while the content of investment protection should be de-generalized.

As the wheel of sustainable development rolls on, international investment has an evolving relationship with environmental protection, which is reflected in the growing space left for environmental considerations both in the literature of international investment law and in the practice of investment arbitration. However, not all these increased interactions result in affirmative synergies thus mutually promoted; instead, they would collide with each other either in theory or in practice. Because fundamentally speaking, the two systems speak for two interests—one is the public, and the other is the private, and as long as there are public and private, conflicts

[92] See Viñuales (2012).

[93] See Nowrot (2014).

[94] The first transition could be roughly boil down to be from the initial Friendship, Commerce and Navigation Treaties, or what have been labeled "the first generation" BITs, to "the second generation" BITs that have greatly strengthened investment protection.

[95] Jorge E. Viñuales, 'The environmental regulation of foreign investment schemes under international law' in Pierre-Marie Dupuy and Jorge E. Viñuales (eds), *Harnessing Foreign Investment to Promote Environmental Protection: Incentives and Safeguards* (CUP 2013) 273.

[96] Kate Miles, '44. Investment' in Lavanya Rajamani and Jacqueline Peel (eds), *The Oxford Handbook of International Environmental Law* (2nd edn, Oxford University Press 2021) 768.

[97] The methodology states that the world is universally connected and the world is eternally developing. It contains three basic laws: the law of unity of opposites, the law of interchange of quality and quantity and the law of negation of negation. The law of unity of opposites indicates that the conflicting sides are both opposed and united, thus all together promoting the development of things.

can always exist. For the public, proper IREMs should not only encourage or, even in a stricter manner, require investors to fulfill their environmental obligations, but also protect the reasonably expected investment interests from suffering or at least minimize such damages. And for private, legitimate investment rights and interests should be pursued, but meanwhile, the new international situation also calls for their appropriate contributions to national or, more broadly, common environmental goals.

Formally, taking environmental protection measures is the embodiment of the state's exercising the right of regulation, which aligns with the trend of current international investment reform. The unbalanced relationship between the protection of foreign investment and the protection of the host state's regulatory right has long been a much-maligned problem, as all the full and equitable protections required by investors or ruled by tribunals have all the time been largely taken for granted. The consequence is that these bottomless protection demands inhibit some justifiable regulations in the host country. With the opportunity of carbon neutrality and driven by economic transformation, taking steps toward environmental protection under the framework of international investment law is an essential practice that could release the regulatory chill and conform to the reforming trend. Technically speaking, it is also in line with the international trend to put environmental protection, a policy objective usually achieved through international soft law, into the hard law framework of international investment. Compared with investment protection, environmental protection used to be promoted through voluntary commitments with no adverse consequences, but now, the situation changes with the insertion of environmental policy into the international investment law system. Environmental protection is given a more robust legal status while still put on the back burner.

Theoretically, China's aggressive adoption of domestic environmental measures is justified in achieving the sustainable development goals (SDGs) and is consistent with international law. Chinese IREMs are far away from realizing all of the 17 SDGs set out by the UN, especially those specific goals on a personal level, such as no poverty and zero hunger. Still, they are making a difference, at least partly, in improving or promoting the general aims of the whole society, by taking the goals of "industry, innovation, and infrastructure" and "responsible consumption and production," for instance. SDGs themselves are inherently forward-looking and therefore call for some ground-breaking actions. The breakthrough at the rule level implies incorporating new value elements into existing ones, in which process conflicts are inevitable but seasonable and legitimate. In other words, though there are conflicts of goal and value between environmental protection and investment protection, they are positive, beneficial, and solvable conflicts with legitimacy. It is such conflicts that are driving SDGs, slowly but effectively.

Procedurally, however, in the process of formulating and implementing IREMs, special attention must be paid, either in transparency or in due process, to abide by the rule of law. Procedural justice usually plays a vital role in conflict resolution. Besides, procedural justice should be an inherent part of environmental justice. The consideration of the legitimacy of the substantive IREMs taken is to ensure the legitimacy of the procedural. When a country obtains more rights of investment regulation for itself through environmental means, it should accordingly assume more obligations. Imperative attention must be paid to the rule of law; namely, it is to be ensured that the exercise of the environmental regulation right is open and transparent, and corresponding remedies available to investors should also be guaranteed. On the other hand, as it is the embodiment of the precautionary principle of international environmental law to take IREMs, such preventive measures require a much more rigorous procedure to justify their necessity than other average measures do. *Quoad hoc*, the tribunal in *Aven and others v. Costa Rica* made a good statement by adopting a dichotomy in emphasizing the decisive importance of procedural justice in holding the balance. There, the tribunal held that, on the one hand, the rights of investors are subordinate to the right of States to ensure that investments are carried out "in a matter sensitive to environmental concerns," but, on the other hand, such subordination is not absolute in that the basic principle of international law—to act in good faith—remains the prerequisite for its legality judgment, that is, it requires that the adoption and enforcement of environmental laws should be done "in a fair, non-discriminatory fashion," "following principles of due process."[98]

From a methodological perspective, this article considers that investment protection and environmental protection should be linked but also decoupled. The essence of ERIIs is another typical example of the classical international investment law dilemma in a new field: the balance between the right to regulate of host countries and investment protection for investors. It is hard to say that either IIAs or ISDS is an appropriate forum to deal with public policy concerns like environmental protection. Such as it is, these two methods do offer a channel and provide the possibility of conflict resolution, at least. The international investment law framework could be more inclusive, as public policy issues such as environmental protection can better balance the relationship between investors and the host country. As a whole, the factors for identifying investment protection should be diversified, but different considerations should be decomposed when analyzing specific issues. Hopefully, one day, a quantifiable evaluation index will be established between investment protection and environmental protection.

As already discussed above, investment protection and environmental protection are not in actual conflict. On this basis, the innovation of China's future IIAs and its position on the coming round of ISDS reform could be considered from the following perspectives.

The Negotiation and Conclusion of Future IIAs: Toward a More Systematic IIA

In the first place, China's future IIAs should pay more attention to the interaction of national law and international law. As a reference for domestic legislative reform to interact with the development of international law, Chile's approach to establishing

[98] David R. Aven, Samuel D. Aven, Giacomo A. Buscemi and others v. Republic of Costa Rica, ICSID Case No. UNCT/15/3, Final Award dated 18 September 2018, para. 412–413.

a specific legal hierarchy between treaties as well as between treaties and national laws is worth learning. Taking Chile's amending its constitution as an example, the revised constitution makes it clear that "international human rights treaties have legal supremacy to other treaties and preeminence to sub-constitutional legislation, and value equivalent to the rights established by the constitution."[99] That is, China could emphasize the legal status of environmental protection and environment-related rights in its constitution, or specify the relationship between environmental protection and investment protection. International investment treaties of the old generation sometimes do prevent a state from formulating policies that are more conducive to public interests. Given the time-consuming, inefficient, and inflexible characteristics of treaty renegotiation, especially in the context of a large number of fragmented IIAs and of China being faced with the practical urgency to achieve its commitment to the "30·60" goals in a short time, it would be of great help to deal with the hard nut if the interaction between environment and investment increases either under the constitutional framework or within foreign investment law.

In the second place, China's future IIAs should focus on system integration and reform to better frame the terms of environmental protection clauses, making it a circular argument system. The de-conflict or re-balance of environmental protection and investment protection is not limited to the hedging of the conflict between the two value objectives but contains complex tradeoffs of multiple interests, including but not limited to public and private interest, long-term and immediate interest, rights and obligations of host state and investor. Subtle changes in treaty language can have profound effects on the practical application of the treaty, which makes it all the more necessary for environmental provisions to be considered in the wider context of the text, which in turn requires far-reaching considerations and self-consistent arrangements as a whole. To do so could not only provide supplementary but crucial justification or, say, "establish by persuasive evidence sufficient justification,"[100] for the legitimacy of domestic environmental measures taken by either central and/or local governments, but could also form a more complete and responsive environmental protection system within the investment framework. Furthermore, given China's dual role as both home and host country, it is necessary for China, from the perspective of combining the interests of capital-importing and capital-exporting countries, to explore a middle way of interests balancing by its current national conditions and investment conditions. China is making efforts to offer a solution, for itself and the whole world, to the longstanding universal difficulty of finding common ground[101] on such a fundamental question: how to secure intact investment protection while also maintaining maximum policy space in the same investment treaty. In this respect, the Model Green Investment Treaty[102] might offer use for reference.

[99] "Let's Ensure the Sovereignty of the Peoples in Free Trade Agreements!" <https://plataforma.chileconvencion.cl/m/iniciativa_popular/detalle?id=33622> accessed 2 February 2022.

[100] Antoine Biloune and Marine Drive Complex Ltd. v. Ghana Investments Centre and the Government of Ghana, Award on Jurisdiction and Liability of 27 October 1989, para. 81.

[101] See Walter (2011).

[102] See Magraw (2019).

Last but not least, China's future IIAs should clarify investors' environmental obligations. The responsibility of environmental protection lies not only with the government but also, and more importantly, with corporations. Seeing it from the perspective of rights and obligations, the conflict between environmental protection and investment protection can be rooted in the absence of investor obligations under the framework of IIAs. Under the framework of IIA, which is inherently more investor-friendly, the deficiency of investors' environmental protection obligation has indirectly impaired the value of environmental protection. What is worse, such structural deficiency has unfortunately become a common phenomenon in the overall system of IIA rather than an individual problem in the IIAs concluded by China. Although there are a few CSR clauses, these provisions are far from legally binding on corporations, let alone considerable limitations in practice. IIAs should not be reduced to a single value pursuit and evaluation system but should adequately reflect the balance between capital's profit-pursuing and socially sustainable development. Thus, China's future IIAs should continue following up on relevant CSR clauses, with particular emphasis on the trend of international hard law regulation thereof.

It seems that China's existing environmental guidelines are tailored for "going out" corporations; however, looking at it from another angle, it can be seen as a roundabout way to achieve the regulation of foreign investment in China through the basic principle of national treatment. Under such an approach, NT serves as the bridge leveling the institutional treatment. The further question to consider should be how to translate those encouraging these good policies into more enforceable laws and regulations.

Position on Future ISDS Reform: Toward an Environmentally Friendly Investment Arbitration

The international investment tribunal is one of the many "borrowed" and "ill-suited" forums[103] for the adjudication of environmental disputes. Though still lacking an ideal solution for environment-related disputes at the international level, the existing investment arbitration mechanism should set specific limits on such non-investment issues. For, in reality, investors do not have to win the case, the mere willingness, as a corporate strategy, to initiate arbitration, as well as the inevitable fact of lengthy proceedings, are enough to hinder the host country's taking measures that it should have taken.[104]

In dealing with investment-environment arbitration, host states could consider making "environment-friendly" a prerequisite as the consent to arbitrate. Besides, to better link investment protection with environmental protection, it could be done by host states to integrate environmental protection into the definition of "investment," making it a dispensable factor that contributes to the development of its economy.

---

[103] Viñuales (2009).

[104] See Tienhaara (2018).

On the other side, the proposal for future reform of arbitral institutions would be to "green" arbitration rules. Establishing a link with environmental protection in investment arbitration rules could help arbitral institutions provide specific guidance for adjudicators of their adjudicator pool on the balance of interests between investment and the environment. Adjudicators have relatively broad discretion in deciding whether or not to integrate the different value objectives under the two branches of international law and also in determining which one trumps. Thus, as a matter of fact, it is up to the adjudicators themselves to draw the boundaries between the state's environmental regulatory measures and investment protection measures.[105] Therefore, concerning the appointment of adjudicators and the establishment of the tribunal of an environment-related case, relevant arbitral institutions could absorb specific provisions requiring environmental competence and expertise in their arbitration rules. In this case, the host country's environmental defense could be appropriately considered by a more just tribunal through amended due process. There should be certain openness to the investment tribunal's use of international environmental law either to interpret relevant investment rules or to delimit the boundaries between vague rules and State's right to regulate.[106] We can see from the existing precedent that the previous arbitral tribunals seem to have presupposed a competitive relationship between investment protection and environmental protection, thus forming a stereotype that an "either/or" decision must be made. Therefore, future adjudicators need to possess the capacity to break the mental inertia and establish a dynamic balance between the two equally essential values. Moreover, third-party participation in environmental protection should be encouraged, and *amicus curiae* submissions should also be allowed. Furthermore, whether the binding and enforceable award should be subject to an additional environmental review could also be further discussed in the future reform of ISDS rules. In a word, through a series of well-designed procedural devices,[107] environmental protection should be able to obtain at least procedural justice in investment arbitration.

Further on, it might be a possible way out to "freeze" ERIDs, that is, to press the pause button on ERIDs somehow, to give priority to climate goal—the upper goal of environmental protection. Earlier in May 2020, in the face of Covid-19, Columbia Center on Sustainable Investment (CCSI) once called for the ISDS moratorium during such an extraordinary time.[108] Although climate change issues, or more broadly speaking, environmental protection issues, are not as urgent as the epidemic, which can have an immediate and direct effect on foreign investment, its structural policy adjustment is bound to exert a creeping but profound influence on traditional

---

[105] See Climate Change Counsel, "ECT, climate change and clean energy transition: A Study of the Jurisprudence," p. 74.

[106] See Viñuales (2009).

[107] Such as resort to experts, counterclaims and *res judicata*. See Laurence Boisson de Chazournes, "Environmental Protection and Investment Arbitration: Yin and Yang" (2017) 10 Anuario Colombiano de Derecho Internacional (Colombian Yearbook of International Law) 371, 389–395.

[108] CCSI, "Call for ISDS Moratorium During COVID-19 Crisis and Response" <https://ccsi.columbia.edu/content/call-isds-moratorium-during-covid-19-crisis-and-response> accessed 13 March 2022.

investment protection. With the strengthening of environmental protection and the promotion of relevant measures, ERIDs are inevitable, at least before achieving the climate goals. It could be an open-ended question of whether future investment protection should be claimed under the premise of realizing or at least contributing to climate or environmental justice. It might be more advisable to take a wait-and-see hindsight attitude toward the country's environmental measures—making a deferred but possibly more comprehensive response.

References

Asteriti A (2016) Climate change policies and foreign investment: some salient legal issues. In: Levashova Y, Lambooy T, Dekker I (eds), Bridging the gap between international investment law and the environment. Eleven International Publishing

Feng G (2017) Creativity of environment clause in TPP and its inspiration for Chinese IIAs' design. J Central South Univ (Soc Sci) 79:83–84 23(3)

Fischer-Lescano A, Teubner G (2004) Regime-collisions: the vain search for legal unity in the fragmentation of global law. J Int'l L 999

Jiang H (2008) International investment and environmental protection legal mechanisms 4. Academics 170, 172

Joubin-Bret A (2016) Protecting the investor and protecting the environment: conflicting objectives in international investment agreements. In: Levashova Y, Lambooy T, Dekker I (eds), Bridging the gap between international investment law and the environment. Eleven International Publishing, p 134

Li J, Zhao J (2019) Approach for solving the conflicts between international investment agreements and international climate change treaties. In: The perspective of substantive rules of international investment agreements. 37 Hebei Law Science 130

Liang D (2019) Environmental concerns and China's international investment agreements. In: Miles K (ed) Research handbook on environment and investment law. Edward Elgar 2019, 368

Magraw D, others (2019) Model green investment treaty: International investment and climate change. 36 J Int Arbitration, 95–134

Nowrot K (2014) How to include environmental protection, human rights and sustainability in international investment law. 15 J World Investment Trade 612:618–624

Stern DI (2008) The rise and fall of the environmental Kuznets Curve (2004) 32 world development 1419–1439; Van Alstine J, Neumayer E (2008) The environmental Kuznets curve. In: Gallagher KP (ed), Handbook on trade and the environment. Edward Elgar, 49–59

Tienhaara K (2018) Regulatory chill in a warming world: the threat to climate policy posed by investor-state dispute settlement. 7 Trans Environ Law, 229

Viñuales JE (2009) Foreign investment and the environment in international law: an ambiguous relationship. 80 British Year Book Inte Law 244:331

Viñuales JE (2009) Foreign investment and the environment in international law: an ambiguous relationship. 80 British Year Book Int Law 244:332

Viñuales JE (2009) Foreign Investment and the Environment in International Law. Cambridge University Press; Viñuales JE (2009) Foreign investment and the environment in international law: an ambiguous relationship. 80 British Year Book of International Law 244, 253–254

Viñuales JE (2012) Foreign investment and the environment in international law. Cambridge University Press, p 318–319

Viñuales JE (2012) Foreign investment and the environment in international law. Cambridge University Press, p 329

Viñuales JE (2012) Foreign investment and the environment in international law. Cambridge University Press, p 366–390
Viñuales JE (2012) Foreign investment and the environment in international law. Cambridge University Press, p 295, 305–315
Viñuales JE (2012) Foreign investment and the environment in international law. Cambridge University Press, p 393
Viñuales JE (2019) Foreign investment and the environment in international law: current trends. In: Miles K (ed) Research handbook on environment and investment law. Edward Elgar 2019, 37
Viñuales J (2019) Foreign investment and the environment in international law: current trends. In: Miles K (ed), Research handbook on environment and investment. Edward Elgar, 12–37; Miles K (2021) 44. Investment. In: Rajamani L, Peel J (eds), The Oxford handbook of international environmental law, 2nd edn, Oxford University Press, 774–777
von Walter A (2011) Balancing investors' and host states' rights—what alternatives for treaty-makers?. In: Herrmann C, Philipp Terhechte J (eds), International investment law and EU law. Springer, p. 141
Zhang G (2016) On environmental measures of host countries and indirect expropriation—based on several international investment arbitration cases. 31 Legal Forum 61, 64–66

Chapter 5
Legitimacy Crisis and the ISDS Reform in a Political Economy Context

Shuping Li and Shen Wei

Introduction

ISDS is a mechanism that allows an investor from one country to initiate arbitral proceedings directly against another country in which it has invested.[1] The mechanism is typically set out in bilateral investment treaties (BITs), free trade agreements (FTAs), and national foreign investment laws. It seeks to promote foreign investment by giving investors coherent expectations and fair processes for dispute resolution. The ISDS system includes binding rules (treaties and conventions), non-binding rules (international documents, arbitral practices) and participants (investors, states, relevant third parties, arbitrators).

[1] Thomson Reuters Practical Law, Investor-State Dispute Settlement (ISDS) (2021). https://uk.practicallaw.thomsonreuters.com/0-624-6147?Transitiontype=Default&contextdata=(sc.Default)&firstpage=true, accessed 28 December 2021.

S. Li
University of Hong Kong, 425 Cheng Yu Tung Tower, Hong Kong, China

W. Shen (✉)
Shanghai Jiao Tong University Law School, 1954 Huashan Road, Shanghai 200230, Xuhui District, China
e-mail: shenwei@sjtu.edu.cn

© The Author(s), under exclusive license to Springer Nature Singapore Pte Ltd. 2024

S. Wei (ed.), *International Investment Law at the Juncture*, International Law in Asia,
https://doi.org/10.1007/978-981-97-2183-2_5

In recent years, intense debates on the legitimacy of the ISDS regime have called for fundamental reform. Marked-out deficiencies in the ISDS regime include inconsistency of arbitral awards,[2] partial and self-interested arbitrators,[3] lack of transparency,[4] long durations and high costs.[5] Growing discontent arising from these deficiencies has made countries such as Ecuador, Indonesia and Venezuela decide on terminating many of their investment treaties that include ISDS provisions.[6] Brazil, India and South Africa separate the existing ISDS model in the new BIT text. The European Union (EU) initiated the multilateral investment court (MIC)[7] as a new forum for arbitration. Countries advocating the current regime submitted different reform proposals. There are discussions at the UNCITRAL Working Group III[8] and Proposed Amendment to the ICSID Rules.[9]

As the ISDS regime becomes more institutionalised and deeply entrenched in the global economic system, its reform is bogged down with changing interests and considerations. The ISDS regime was initially designed to protect the interests of foreign investors.[10] This inherent bias may threaten the host state's right to regulate and policy autonomy. Previously ignored stakeholders in the ISDS regime, such as the affected communities by foreign investment, indigenous peoples and civilian populations, are calling for the protection of their interests in the rule-making and arbitration practice. These interests are reciprocal and dynamic in the pursuit of wealth and power by countries. Governments increasingly find that no method of dispute settlement is permanent or perfect, nor can one solution satisfy the needs of all stakeholders. The ultimate question then becomes how the states are keen to cooperate in the field of foreign investment.

Sovereign states are created to achieve certain political-economic functions in domestic and international spheres. As the subject of rationality, states act with a meaningful purpose, and their behaviours can be interpreted in sociology for a

[2] Yu (2017).

[3] UNCITRAL, Report of Working Group III: Investor-State Dispute Settlement Reform, *Status of Work as of August 2021*, https://uncitral.un.org/en/working_groups/3/investor-state, accessed 14 December 2021.

[4] Klett (2016).

[5] UNCITRAL Working Group III, Possible Reform of Investor-State Dispute Settlement (ISDS)—Cost and Duration, U.N. Doc. A/CN.9/WG.III/WP.153, at 8, 17–18 & 21, *available at* https://undocs.org/en/A/CN.9/WG.III/WP.153, accessed 28 December 2021.

[6] Nicolas Boeglin, ICSID and Latin America: Criticisms, Withdrawals and Regional Alternatives, June 2013; Caio Cesar Soares, Investor-State Dispute Settlement: An Analysis of the Reform Proposals on Its Institutional Structure (May 11, 2017). https://ssrn.com/abstract=2984581, accessed 14 December 2021.

[7] Council of the EU, *Multilateral Investment Court: Council Gives Mandate to the Commission to Open Negotiations*(2018), https://www.consilium.europa.eu/en/press/press-releases/2018/03/20/multilateral-investment-court-council-gives-mandate-to-the-commission-to-open-negotiations/, accessed 14 November 2021.

[8] UNCITRAL, Report of Working Group IIIReform.14 December 2021.

[9] ICSID Secretariat, *ICSID Rules and Regulations Amendment-Working Papers*(2021), *available at* https://icsid.worldbank.org/resources/rules-amendments, accessed 14 December 2021.

[10] Vandevelde (2005).

causal explanation of their courses and consequences. Action is 'social' insofar as the acting entity attaches a subjective meaning to its behaviour—be it overt or covert, omission or acquiescence—and its subjective meaning takes into account the behaviours of others.[11] States have both instrumental rationality (the means used to achieve ends) and value rationality (legitimate ends in themselves) to create or join an institution.[12] The former implies the motivation from the outside world to achieve specific goals. For states, the objective of the ISDS regime used to involve investment promotion and economic collaboration for mutual development as part of the efforts towards market integration and globalisation. Economic globalisation is marked by mobilising goods, services, capital and information across borders. Parallel to this trend, policy discretion and regulatory autonomy concerning domestic issues, such as public health, environmental protection, labour protection, industrial policies and human rights protection, are often left unattended. Integrating these interests into a dispute resolution mechanism, a legitimate ISDS regime is founded on the consent of states after their careful political-economic considerations on participating in the ISDS regime.

This article uses this political economy narrative to examine the legitimacy crisis and illustrate the difficulties in ISDS reform. It shifts the focus of discussion from the regime itself to state participants. Section 5.2 discusses how the external variation leads to considerable resistance to the current ISDS due to its procedural and substantive drawbacks. Section 5.3 examines the source of legitimacy of the ISDS regime, namely the consent of states and the political-economic benefits of the regime. Section 5.4 reflects on current ISDS reform proposals, including incremental ISDS reform and alternatives, such as an investment court. It also advocates top-town and bottom-up efforts to issue guiding cases and interpretation notes to align key standards and concepts. Section V concludes that fixing the complex ISDS regime entails systemic work, whether in terms of the jurisdiction given to the tribunal or the substantial protection standards agreed by the state parties. ISDS reformers should respect spatial and temporal discrepancies of public policies and leave room for manoeuvring by national governments. Meanwhile, soft laws can play a role in shaping new and solidifying previous consensus on protection standards and other institutional designs.

Legitimacy Crisis of the ISDS Regime

A. Inconsistency of Arbitral Awards

The inconsistency of arbitral processes and outcomes challenge the predictability and, thus, legitimacy of the ISDS regime. Divergence interpretations occur based on

[11] Weber (1978).

[12] Rutgers and Schreurs (2006).

the recognition of jurisdiction and admissibility, as well as procedural and substantive standards. This inconsistency is most unjustifiable when tribunals interpret the same provision in the same treaty in two different ways,[13] such as *BG Group v. the Argentine Republic,*[14] limiting full protection and security in the UK–Argentina BIT to physical security, and *National Grid v. the Argentine Republic,*[15] which found no reason to limit protection to physical assets. The problem could also occur where two tribunals apply the same or similar provisions differently to the identical facts. For instance, there are different interpretations of whether the treatment of most favoured nations (MFNs) can be imported from treaties with third countries. Some opened this possibility (such as *White Industries v. India*[16]), while others did not (such as *Içkale v. Turkmenistan*[17]). Inconsistency discourages states from adopting legitimate regulatory measures, either through the internalisation of the treaty constraints or the threat of investors of investment arbitration. For investors, arbitral inconsistency also imposes uncertainty regarding the legality of state regulatory measures.

This phenomenon arises from the inherent characteristics of the current decentralised ISDS regime. First, unlike common law systems, there are no binding requirements for arbitrators to follow previous cases as precedents. Investment arbitral decisions do not have a *stare decisis* effect, and arbitral awards are binding only on the parties of the dispute.[18] Arbitrators are not obligated to promote coherent investment legal norms, focusing on the specific context of a case. Moreover, granting arbitrators power and discretion that is too broad to consider other international law sources opposes the privity nature of the arbitration.

Secondly, the interpretation and application of treaty provisions are at the discretion of selected arbitrators. The substantive law that the tribunals are shaping through precedents is fragmented—there are over three thousand investment treaties that are similar in content but formally distinct. The broad and variant wording of investment treaties generates divergent interpretations. For instance, the term 'any dispute' in an umbrella clause may cover *any* dispute or only the engagement of states in a sovereign capacity. The procedural 'after six months…may…consent to the submission' in Article VI(3)(a) of the US–Czechoslovakia BIT is different from the mandatory 'provided that six months have elapsed' in Article 1120 of the North American Free Trade Agreement (NAFTA), thereby resulting in divergence in *Lauder v. Czech*[19] and *Mesa Power v. Canada.*[20] Each arbitral award is conditioned upon the specific context of the case. 'Like circumstances' in national treatment provisions often means a combination of several factors. What an investor may legitimately

[13] Dolzer (2012).

[14] BG Group Plc. v. The Republic of Argentina, UNCITRAL (2007).

[15] National Grid plc v. The Argentine Republic, UNCITRAL (2008).

[16] White Industries Australia Limited v. The Republic of India, UNCITRAL (2011).

[17] İçkale İnşaat Limited Şirketi v. Turkmenistan, ICSID Case No. ARB/10/24 (2016).

[18] ICSID Convention, Article 53(1).

[19] Ronald S. Lauder v. The Czech Republic, UNCITRAL (2001).

[20] Mesa Power Group, LLC v. Government of Canada, UNCITRAL, PCA Case No. 2012-17.

expect in a jurisdiction active in environmental matters can differ from a less pro-environment country.[21] Further, arbitrators can have different interpretations based on their understandings and experience. For example, as far as the MFN provisions are concerned, some awards favoured permitting the MFN clause to modify or override conditions on access to ISDS and expand the jurisdiction of tribunals (*Maffezini v. Spain*,[22] *Siemens v. the Argentine Republic*[23] and *RosInvestCo UK v. Russian Federation*[24]). In contrast, others disallow such access (*Salini v. Jordan*,[25] *Plama v. Bulgaria*[26] and *ICS v. the Argentine Republic*[27]). If arbitrators do not give specific reasons for adopting a particular standard or interpretation, this will leave even more uncertainties in future cases.

The third is a lack of a framework to govern how precedent is used or a control mechanism to guarantee arbitral consistency. The arbitration tribunal is constituted to resolve a single dispute. There is no recourse for a country or investor to challenge the misapplication of the law or rulings that are substantively flawed. According to Article 52 of ICSID, the ad hoc Committee merely has the power to annul awards with procedural injustice, that is, to determine whether a tribunal manifestly exceeded its powers or failed to apply the applicable law. It does not have the power to overturn an award for errors of fact or law.[28] This conforms to the desire of the Washington Convention drafters to ensure the finality and binding effect of awards, which is an expression of customary law based on the concepts of *pacta sun servanda* and *res judicata* and is in line with the objective and purpose of the Convention.

As ISDS reformers seek consistency and coherence in treaty interpretation and arbitral awards, the problem is whether inconsistency itself is legitimate and brings more benefits than without. Binding consistency would imply that earlier rulings could impose persuasive effects of their interpretation of the rules on future cases and drive the system towards judicialisation and centralised institutions, such as the domestic courts and the World Trade Organization (WTO). However, this can hardly be suitable for an international investment regime. FDIs and investors vary in policy and political significance. Fairness in investment arbitration thus does not have a fixed meaning and may vary in different contexts.

---

[21] Glamis Gold, Ltd. v. United States of America, UNCITRAL; Metalclad Corporation v. United Mexican States, ICSID Case No. ARB(AF)/97/1.

[22] Emilio Agustín Maffezini v. The Kingdom of Spain, ICSID Case No. ARB/97/7 (2000).

[23] Siemens A.G. v. The Argentine Republic, ICSID Case No. ARB/02/8 (2007).

[24] RosInvestCo UK Ltd. v. The Russian Federation, SCC Case No. V079/2005.

[25] Salini Costruttori S.p.A. and Italstrade S.p.A. v. The Hashemite Kingdom of Jordan, ICSID Case No. ARB/02/13.

[26] Plama Consortium Limited v. Republic of Bulgaria, ICSID Case No. ARB/03/24.

[27] ICS Inspection and Control Services Limited (United Kingdom) v. The Republic of Argentina, UNCITRAL, PCA Case No. 2010-9.

[28] ICSID Convention, Article 52(1).

B. Selection of Arbitrators

Another problem regarding the ISDS regime is the lack of diversity, independence and impartiality of arbitrators. Concerns about the qualification and conduct of arbitrators include the following issues: (i) insufficiently precise codes of independence and impartiality of arbitrators[29]; (ii) potential conflicts of interest, such as double hatting and the prejudgment of issues[30]; (iii) the limited number of individuals repeatedly appointed as arbitrators, and the lack of diversity in gender, age, ethnicity and geographical distribution of appointed arbitrators representing different levels of interests[31]; and (iv) the challenge mechanism to disqualify an arbitrator based on actual or perceived lack of independence and impartiality.[32] To begin with, legitimate arbitration needs qualifications and experience. Raising the standards of arbitrator selection effectively enhances fairness, credibility, and impartiality. Progress has been made in the revised rules of the selection and appointment of tribunal members under ICSID and UNCITRAL arbitration rules.

The widespread criticism also calls for the diversity of arbitrators to enhance the legitimacy of dispute settlements. Diverse adjudicators are more likely to avoid cognitive biases and group-thinking in decision making.[33] Empirical evidence also showed that selected arbitrators are primarily men from either North America or Europe.[34] Participants from developing countries will benefit if arbitral institutions make diversity and heterogeneity a required standard of arbitrator selection. Diversity requirements would encompass more arbitrators from developing countries. Nationals from developing countries are more likely to understand and determine the nature of the dispute involving domestic law and the public policy of similar countries. Moreover, arbitration needs democracy and respect for the will of the parties to depoliticise the ISDS regime. Arbitration bias can be inherent and subtle due to the nationality of arbitrators, gender, age, ethnicity and other identities.

A still controversial issue is how far tribunals could scrutinise decisions of fact or law made at the domestic level. When the treaty or contract remains silent or obscure on a topic, arbitrators face a challenging situation to decide the appropriateness and legality of public policy. It is an open question whether arbitrators should accommodate the social needs that might affect their decisions, irrespective of whether those involved were the litigants before them. Unlike domestic public officials, current arbitrators only have limited obligation and power to consider economic forces, scientific reports and stated public opinions. The answer may lie in the intention of states in signing BITs and building the ISDS regime. Arbitrators cannot decide on the real purpose and objectives of BITs on behalf of the state. It can be challenging to empower arbitrators to decide on these issues unless there are clear political wills of cooperation (similar to the EU and its trading partners).

---

[29] Giorgetti et al. (2020).

[30] van Harten (2010).

[31] UNCITRAL Working Group III, A/CN.9/WG.III/WP.152.

[32] Laborde (2010).

[33] Kidane (2017).

[34] Langford et al. (2017).

C. **Transparency**

The ISDS regime has been criticised for lacking transparency[35] and giving insufficient opportunities for third parties to participate in the proceedings.[36] These transparency issues have been addressed in conventions, such as the Mauritius Convention adopted within UNCITRAL. Amendments to the ICSID Convention Arbitration Rules include strengthened disclosure requirements for arbitrators,[37] a provision on the possibility to hold open hearings,[38] expanded transparency provisions into publishing awards as soon as possible[39] and the opportunity for non-disputing parties to file submissions (*amicus curiae* briefs).[40] By allowing the participation of non-party stakeholders, tribunals are pressured to raise the quality of awards and ensure fairness with pertinent information from all stakeholders. The efficiency and fairness of procedures have also been improved by updating rules on the appointment of arbitrators and third-party funding.

Compared to enhancing transparency, unresolved ISDS legitimacy challenges are complex and indicate no single answer. Primarily, states now cast doubt on the scope of consent they gave when signing the investment treaties. Early BITs were designed to constrain capricious autocrats to prevent arbitrary treatment by the host state and political interference with dispute settlement. However, these initial intentions gradually evolved into a situation where ISDS awards tend to overcompensate investors and override the right of states to regulate.[41] This is probably because arbitrators have incentives to favour the interests of those who have the power to invoke the use of the system.[42] It is either that the states have not given consent to such compromise of their regulatory authority at the beginning or the scope of the consent of states has changed during the operation of the ISDS regime, or both. It is necessary to re-examine the source to re-establish the legitimacy of the ISDS regime.

Political Economy of the ISDS Regime

To a more or less degree, the legitimacy of an international regime comes from the consensus of parties, the beneficial consequences the regime brings about, and public reasons or democratic approval given by the specific community. In a state-centred international investment regime, the attitudes of states towards foreign investment evolve with changing circumstances in international and domestic societies.

---

[35] Duval (2020).

[36] Jesse Coleman, et al., Third-Party Rights in Investor–State Dispute Settlement: Options for Reform (2019).

[37] Arbitration Rule 6(2), Article 13(2) of the Arbitration (Additional Facility) Rules.

[38] Arbitration Rule 32(2), Article 39(2) of the Arbitration (Additional Facility) Rules.

[39] Arbitration Rule 48(4), Article 53(3) of the Arbitration (Additional Facility) Rules.

[40] Arbitration Rule 37(2), Article 41(3) of the Arbitration (Additional Facility) Rules.

[41] Henckels (2016).

[42] Van Harten (2012).

A. **Interests of States in Foreign Investment**

The interests of states in the ISDS regime is a series of complex adaptive decisions. Before BITs were conceived of, foreign investment was protected by customary international law,[43] under which a state can vindicate injury caused to its citizen by the host state through diplomatic protection, such as reprisals or even force.[44] Developed countries imposed Western minimum standards on developing countries through diplomatic protection and imperial legal enclaves, moving foreign investment law 'from a base of reciprocity, to one of imposition'.[45] The nations forming these rules were primarily wealthy European countries, whose nationals were engaged in investment abroad. In response to the minimum standard of treatment, some states endorsed a national treatment or equality of treatment standard, particularly in Latin America.[46] The Calvo Doctrine was created with three key arguments: foreign nationals are entitled to no better treatment than host state nationals, the rights of foreign nationals are governed by host state law, and host state courts have exclusive jurisdiction over disputes involving foreign nationals.[47] The Hull Rule, put forward by the then US Secretary of State Cordell Hull in his exchanges with Mexico in the 1930s in defending the rights of US investors in Mexico, set out the principle of 'prompt, adequate, and effective' compensation for expropriation.[48]

In the 1990s, along with the spread of market liberalism and neoliberal capitalism, most states joined the trend of signing BITs to embrace the profits of global free markets. Therefore, international investment arbitration became an efficient way of resolving disputes independent from host state politics.[49] The binding ISDS provisions in more than 3000 BITs and FTAs[50] allow foreign investors to rely upon international arbitration for rights protection, rebalancing the asymmetric relations between sovereign states and investors. States hoped that the ISDS system could contribute to a more investor-friendly environment, expand economic and political cooperation between contracting states and enhance the stability and predictability of the policy framework. BITs reduce asymmetric information costs, increase economies of scale and strengthen the enforcement of contracts. Even if not protected by the BIT, investors may see it as a signal of the engagement of the host state in the protection of FDIs and its willingness to formally and legally commit to it.[51]

---

[43] Newcombe and Paradell (2009).

[44] Johnson and Gimblett (2011).

[45] Miles (2013).

[46] Garcia-Mora (1949).

[47] Bernardo Cremades, Resurgence of the Calvo Doctrine in Latin America, 5 Transnationall Dispute Management (2005), in Investor-State Disputes-International Investment Law. https://www.transnational-dispute-management.com/article.asp?key=592, accessed 14 December 2021.

[48] Id.

[49] Salacuse and Sullivan (2005).

[50] UNCTAD, World Investment Report 2018: Investment and New Industrial Policies, p. 88.

[51] Liesbeth Colen and Andrea Guariso, What Type of FDI Is Attracted by Bilateral Investment Treaties?, LICOS Discussion Paper 346/2014.

Despite the presumed benefits of signing BITs, there is no clear evidence showing the correlation between monetary value (in the form of inbound investment) and an ISDS regime.[52] Early econometric studies revealed a positive correlation between the signing of BITs and economic growth.[53] However, the investment increase may be too slight to affect the total economic growth of the host state significantly. Policies can affect other determinants of FDI flows, which usually takes time to materialise the change.[54] The quality of domestic institutions is another pivotal factor,[55] as BITs are crucial complements to sound local legal systems.

As the economic benefits of the ISDS regime remain dubious, an alternative explanation is that states may want to strengthen their political and diplomatic ties through bilateral and regional trade agreements. Law is the link binding centres and peripheries to one another, as well as the vernacular through which power and wealth justify their exercise and shroud their authority. States cooperate for a complex set of reasons, such as national security, specialisation, less policy externality, collective decision-making, dispute resolution, the credibility of policy commitments and lock-in by creating policy bias.[56] Therefore, it is sensible to regard international law as a terrain for political and economic struggle rather than a normative or technical substitute for political choice.[57] The states do not seek involvement in dispute resolution or any financial burdens resulting from arbitration.

The case of China offered a representative illustration of the compound motivations of states. Promoting FDI, together with stimulating consumption and export, has been one of the strategies China adopted for future economic development. Meanwhile, the change in the Chinese identity from a capital-importing state to a capital-exporting state raises new issues about how to protect the interests of its outbound investments. Along the Belt and Road Initiative, Chinese enterprises are likely to encounter political, economic, legal and financial risks in their overseas operations. The need for efficient settlement of investment disputes becomes even more pressing. Additionally, the need for a reliable investment regime is driven by the US–China political economy disputes, the growing tension with countries like Australia and corresponding policy adjustments and the 'poison pill' provision in the United States-Mexico-Canada Agreement,[58] which are all intended to prevent the active participation of China in the global economy.

---

[52] UNCTAD, The Role of International Investment Agreements in Attracting Foreign Direct Investment to Developing Countries xiii (UN, 2009). https://unctad.org/system/files/official-document/diaeia20095_en.pdf, accessed 28 December 2021.

[53] Neumayer and Spess (2005); Büthe and Milner (2008).

[54] Colen et al. (2016).

[55] ENeumayer & Spess, World Development (2005).

[56] Powell (1999).

[57] Kennedy (2013).

[58] USMCA, Article 32.10; Vidigal (2020).

Given this matrix of challenges and opportunities, China and the EU reached a consensus on the EU–China Comprehensive Agreement on Investment (CAI).[59] The CAI is expected to promote sustainable, balanced and inclusive growth of both economies and elevate the economic relationship into a genuine strategic partnership. Similar to the Regional Comprehensive Economic Partnership that China signed in 2020 with member states of the Association of Southeast Asian Nations and other five states in the Asia–Pacific region, CAI creates sufficient space for future negotiations on investment protection and investment dispute settlement. Participation in these treaties is part of the diplomatic strategies that China utilises as bargaining chips in the negotiation from one to another to achieve its political-economic goals. It is crucial to understand the relationship of the ISDS regime with domestic public policies in a systemic way.

B. Globalisation, Democracy, and Sovereignty

The neoliberal ideology states that free trade and investment promote market efficiency at the international level, and capitalist expansion is embedded in the current ISDS regime. In signing BITs, states 'legalise' their target interests in inward and outward FDIs, such as funds and capitals, technologies, management skills, natural resources and the creation of employment opportunities.

The efficiency-oriented ISDS regime is challenged by other social values, including democracy and sustainable development. To have democratic legitimacy, international agreements must offer broad benefits with democratic participation and public involvement. Democracy has various meanings with the core of safeguarding the autonomy and participation of people in collective decision-making. Democracy should not be imposed on people who endorse a different set of values.[60] The formation of public opinion depends on baseline consensus and various views on institutional design.[61] Previous negotiations and signature of investment treaties paid little attention to this as capital-exporting countries seek market expansion with gunboat diplomacy. Meanwhile, democracy sometimes conflicts with FDI due to the misalignment of the interests of governments with their citizens. Democratic institutions—such as the institutions and procedures of changing policies and leaders, checks and balances of the executive power, and civil liberties of political participation—may hinder FDI inflows by prioritising the protection of indigenous businesses over foreign investors.[62] In the ISDS regime, democracy and markets should not be put antithetical. A social welfare-oriented market shall mark a higher level of development than unlimited capital expansion.

The legitimacy crisis of the ISDS regime also comes from the idea of sustainable development, which incorporates broader social goals, such as climate change, clean energy, reduced inequalities, good health and well-being and peaceful and inclusive

[59] CAI: Milestones and Documents. https://trade.ec.europa.eu/doclib/press/index.cfm?Id=2115, accessed 28 December 2021.

[60] Valentini (2014.

[61] Habermas (1989).

[62] Li and Resnick (2003).

societies. Governments are now required to adopt various policies to create a better environment for developing manufacturing industries, in some cases through targeted industrial policies to support high-end manufacturing industries. As the US re-joined the Paris Agreement[63] and China restricted Australian coal,[64] potential ISDS claims may arise, and tribunals will adapt to address new political-economic concerns. Tribunals may adopt high thresholds of a breach of fair and equitable treatment, as was held in *Al Tamimi v. Oman* that the breach required a 'gross or flagrant disregard for the principles of fairness'.[65] Investors should prepare to see more robust climate policies implemented by the host state under high carbon-emission reduction targets and observe environmental protection along with other international obligations. The transition towards cleaner energy sources while shutting down existing power plants involves a series of policy adjustments and compensation. The conflict is reflected in the reform of the Energy Charter Treaty (ECT) used by foreign investors to challenge the regulation of a coal-fired power plant in Germany[66] and the Dutch decision to phase out coal power.[67] Since the EU sees climate change as a fundamental and continuous task to work on, minor revisions to the existing investment treaties may not be enough to handle the complexity of this transformation.

States are often faced with the choice between sovereignty, economic integration and democracy, which involves a two-level game (negotiations and politics) in international and domestic societies.[68] In the rise and fall of globalisation, interactions initially at the economic level engender complex interdependence in inter-state relations that change the governance of FDI.A legitimate public institution needs to accommodate different stages of national development and various economic, political, social, cultural and legal systems. If there is a need to tie the interests of countries and power together towards some common goals, the regime designer, or the ISDS reformer, has to hear all voices, disciplines, perspectives, interests and ideologies. This coordination and integration will be a tedious task, given the 'slow haste' and numerous configurations of political interests and the preference of states of foreign investment and use of capital at a specific period, including the pandemic. Instead of directly resolving unsettled ISDS problems, institutional efforts should be placed to present all factors in the choice set and let states weigh their own decisions.

---

[63] Antony J. Blinken, The United States Officially Rejoins the Paris Agreement (2021).

[64] Cave, (2021).

[65] Adel A Hamadi Al Tamimi v. Sultanate of Oman, ICSID Case No. ARB/11/33.

[66] Vattenfall AB and others v. Federal Republic of Germany, ICSID Case No. ARB/12/12.

[67] RWE AG and RWE Eemshaven Holding II BV v. Kingdom of the Netherlands (ICSID Case No. ARB/21/4).

[68] Putnam (1988).

Rethink ISDS Reform Options

Disparities in the ISDS reform proposals reflect different strategies and considerations in establishing the ISDS regime. As a rational entity, the state may adapt the rules to its interests and needs. The ISDS reform offers an opportunity for states to reconsider the legal and consent bases of international investment arbitration.

A. Consent Base

1. Multilateral or Bilateral

The numbers and members of regime participants certainly affect the scope and difficulty of state cooperation. A multilateral institution provides rules for the game in the management of FDIs, trying to incorporate universal values, reducing transaction costs and uncertainties in domestic policies.[69] It influences domestic policies mainly by changing the costs and benefits of alternatives. The notion of reciprocity and the desire to depend on the observance of rules of other nations leads many countries to observe rules to which they do not want.[70] In response to domestic political pressures, national administrative entities may choose to internationalise domestic issues, politicise economic and trade issues, and blame other states for their problems. This has created the breeding ground for political populism and isolationism, which will cause as much damage to the state itself as to others. An effective ISDS regime should eliminate the role of power and politics in protecting FDIs and reducing arbitrary interventions by host states.

The current multilateral investment regime led by the ICSID Convention offers an appropriate prototype to which incremental reform can be made. Multilateralism means that the designing of BIT and ISDS regimes are not purely driven by competitive forces that put countries seeking FDI in a weak bargaining status but a holistic evaluation of the political-economic effects of the regime. Compared with bilateral arrangements, multilateralism enhances the indivisibility of interests. It diffuses reciprocity between countries, particularly if it is guaranteed by a dispute settlement mechanism through which redress can be sought. A multilateral regime will help build a more harmonised, open, stable, transparent and enforceable legal regime to govern how foreign investors are treated. Such preference for multilateral institutions, such as the WTO and Permanent Court of Arbitration, is shown in Article 19.11 of the Regional Comprehensive Economic Partnership Agreement by fifteen Asia–Pacific countries. Compared to domestic litigation and state-state arbitration, a multilateral ISDS regime empowers investors with stronger capabilities to file claims, enables more neutrality of arbitral awards without interference from domestic power and diplomacy, imposes binding obligations on states and grants more certainty in the operation of FDI.

---

[69] Young (1991).

[70] Jackson (2000).

The multilateral reform led by UNCITRAL provides a wide range of possible solutions for ISDS reform.[71] The multilateral system is expected to incorporate extensive reform recommendations from governments and other stakeholders. These include, but are not limited to: terminating investment treaties or withdrawing consent to ISDS procedures; allowing states to bring counter-claims based on international human rights obligations and environmental duties; protecting the right and duty of states to regulate by dismissing claims against legitimate, non-discriminatory, and lawful decisions to protect the public interest; denying access to ISDS for investors that violate domestic or international obligations; allowing affected third parties to join a case with full rights on equal grounds with the main parties to the dispute; setting up a permanent appellate mechanism; and imposing higher qualification standards of arbitrators.[72] Previous ISDS cases have accumulated diverse experience and knowledge of reform options. It is a systemic work that party states decide whether to give more or less arbitration power and discretion to the tribunal. For instance, if procedural fairness and transparency are enhanced, states may be willing to have a broader interpretation of jurisdictional concepts and allow for a wider scope of decisions made by the tribunal. Once contentious issues are settled, the multilateral reform can reduce uncertainties in arbitration through straightforward clarification and discussions among participating states.

Multilateralism is imperfect and may involve various drawbacks and dysfunctions in its operation. As legal foundations of arbitration, multilateral agreements have to avoid political manipulation and try to coordinate consensus among different parties. In some ways, the problem experienced by investment communities is similar to the situation of the trading system, the impasse of the WTO Dispute Settlement Body (DSB). There is now vociferous criticism against the WTO DSB, such as the abuse of the appellate mechanism,[73] the long duration of the proceedings under appeal,[74] the quasi-automatic approval of the expert report under the principle of negative consensus,[75] the excessive use of narrow textualist argument,[76] the exertion of trade-restrictive measures in the violating country[77] and the interference with sensitive democratic processes in sovereign nations.[78] Among these, an imperative problem for the WTO is the deadlock over the reappointment of members of the appellate

[71] UNCTAD High-level IIA Conference 2017, Reforming the International Investment Regime: Phases 1 and 2, Introductory Statement by James Zhan, Director Investment and Enterprise, UNCTAD Oct 9, 2017.

[72] Reform Options for ISDS, UNCITRAL Working Group III. https://www.somo.nl/nl/wp-content/uploads/sites/2/2018/04/UNCITRAL-recs-and-justification-final.pdf, accessed 14 November 2021.

[73] Ala'i (1998).

[74] Ehlermann (2017).

[75] Ehlermann (2003).

[76] Ortino (2006).

[77] See, e.g., Appellate Body Report, European Communities–Measures Concerning Meat and Meat Products, WT/DS26/AB/R, WT/DS48/AB/R, January 16, 1998; Appellate Body Report, Brazil-Measures Affecting Imports of Retreaded Tyres, WT/DS332/AB/R, December 3, 2007.

[78] Walker (1998).

body,[79] which brought significant challenges to the powers and competencies of the Dispute Settlement Understanding mechanism. The jurisprudence of WTO used to be understood as resistance to constitutionalisation in international trade law[80] to build a law-based, depoliticised global trading system. In order to facilitate dispute resolution before the appellate body resumes, nearly twenty WTO member states approved an alternative dispute resolution system called multi-party interim appeal arbitration arrangement (MPIA),[81] acting under Article 25 of the DSU. The MPIA system uses arbitration to provide binding resolutions for trade disputes in placing an appellate body and conduct independent and impartial reviews in the place of panel reports. The experience of the WTO DSU system provides an essential lesson to the ISDS reformmultilateral disciplines should be reflected in the ISDS rules to avoid hegemony in future operations and abuses of the mechanism by superpowers. The regime should also leave out flexibilities and exception measures for future deadlock and change.

2. **Arbitration Tribunal or Investment Court**

The ISDS reform also invites states to reconsider the nature and function of international investment arbitration. Arbitration, compared to litigation, is assumed to possess the advantages of the expedition, expertise and enforceability and reflect the fundamental need for freedom and autonomy in dispute resolution by private entities. ISDS derives its legitimacy in part from the parties giving consent to arbitration and appointing the arbitrators.[82] The strengths and advantages are still kept in most ISDS reform proposals, but states want more control of the adjudication system.

Within the EU, there is a trend of judicialisation of this dispute settlement mechanism in the place of conventional ISDS arbitration. In March 2018, the *Achmea* judgment[83] by the Court of Justice of the EU (CJEU) found that the investment dispute settlement mechanism established by the Netherland–Slovakia BIT is not capable of ensuring the proper application and full effectiveness of EU law. Later on, in its ruling of *Energoalians (Komstroy) v. Moldova,*[84] the CJEU confirmed its jurisdiction to interpret the ECT and all acts adopted by EU institutions, including international treaties. The EU thus proposed amending the definition of investment under the ECT as part of the overall 'modernisation' of the treaty.[85] Yet this modernisation must respect the constitutional arrangements and public policies of the states. Member State courts may decline to give effect to the *Achmea* judgment if the domestic court

[79] Keynes and Bown (2017).

[80] Magnuson (2010).

[81] European Commission, *The WTO Multi-party Interim Appeal Arrangement Gets Operational*(2020), *available at* https://trade.ec.europa.eu/doclib/press/index.cfm?id=2176.24 December 2021.

[82] Wälde (2006).

[83] Case C-741/19, Republic of Moldova v. Komstroy, 2021, ECLI:EU:C:2021:655.

[84] Energoalians TOB v. Republic of Moldova, UNCITRAL (2013).

[85] EU Text Proposal for the Modernisation of the Energy Charter Treaty (ECT), https://trade.ec.europa.eu/doclib/docs/2020/may/tradoc_158754.pdf, accessed 28 December 2021.

finds that CJEU exceeded the competence conferred on it by the EU Treaties to exercise its judicial functions in that case. There is criticism over the disproportionate CJEU judgment that violates Articles 5(1), 5(2) and 5(4) of the Treaty on European Union. The decision of the German Constitutional Tribunal (BVerfG) of 5 July 1967 held that the 'act of assent' to the founding treaties functions as the decisive 'order to give legal effect' to the European law. The BVerfG hinted at constitutional limitations on the transfer of public authority rights to the European Council in the context of the guarantee of fundamental rights of the German constitution. Similarly, the Czech Constitutional Court held that CJEU acted ultra in its judgment in *Landtová*[86] and gave Czech national law precedence over EU law.

Partly to avoid the conflicts of adjudication power on EU-related investment and strengthen the internal control of the EU in dispute resolution and investment governance, and partly to avoid the deficiency of the current ISDS regime, the EU proposed a MIC, in lieu of the ICSID tribunal for the settlement of investment disputes. This has been mentioned in the EU–Vietnam Trade and Investment Agreements (EVTIA) of June 2020, EU–Singapore Investment Protection Agreement (IPA) of January 2019, EU–Canada Comprehensive Economic and Trade Agreement (CETA) of 2016, and the European Commission proposal for Investment Protection and Resolution of Investment Disputes in the EU–US Transatlantic Trade and Investment Partnership (TTIP).[87] The CJEU has ruled on the compatibility of MIC with EU law,[88] and the EU Member States have agreed on the termination of BITs between them.[89] Institutionally modelled after the WTO dispute resolution system,[90] the MIC intends to be a permanent international institution. It combines elements of investment arbitration with judicial features, such as tenured judges, transparent proceedings and open hearings, appeals against a decision, third-party interventions and enforcement of the decisions.[91]

Underlying the establishment of MIC is a series of interactions between political economy and legal arrangements. The EU has built up a legal system with more considerable control while taking advantage of existing international institutions. EU investment agreements stated that both ICSID and UNCITRAL arbitration rules

[86] Marie Landtová v. Ceská správa socialního zabezpecen C-399/09. https://curia.europa.eu/juris/liste.jsf?language=en&num=C-399/09, accessed 28 December 2021.

[87] Markus Krajewski and Rhea Tamara Hoffmann, The European Commission's Proposal for Investment Protection in TTIP (2017). http://library.fes.de/pdf-files/bueros/bruessel/12662.pdf, accessed 24 December 2021.

[88] CJEU Opinion 1/17 of the Court, 30 April 2019. http://curia.europa.eu/juris/document/document.jsf?text=&docid=213502&pageIndex=0&doclang=EN&mode=lst&dir=&occ=first&part=1&cid=4976548, accessed 28 December 2021.

[89] Agreement for the Termination of Bilateral Investment Treaties Between the Member States of the European Union dated May 29, 2020. https://eur-lex.europa.eu/legal-content/EN/TXT/?uri=CELEX%3A22020A0529%2801%29, accessed 28 December 2021.

[90] Kho et al. (2017).

[91] Simoes (2020).

are applicable,[92] which renders the procedural rules familiar to investors and follows with the enforcement of awards under the ICSID Convention and the New York Convention.[93] Awards are binding between the disputing parties in respect of the claim. Signatories to the EU investment agreements must recognise the final award and enforce any pecuniary obligation within its territory as if it were a final judgment of a domestic court. The application of the New York Convention is feasible. In case the MIC awards are incompatible with Article 25, Article 53(1), Article 54(1), and Article 67 of the ICSID Convention, the EU and its trading parties may modify the ICSID Convention under Article 41(1)(b) of the Vienna Convention. Still, the annulment procedure will not apply to MIC proceedings because the EU investment agreements, *as lex specialis*, prevail over the ICSID Convention as *lex generalis*.

A crucial aspect that affects the legitimacy of a dispute settlement decision is the selection of adjudicators. In the current ISDS regime, arbitrators are appointed by the parties. In the investment court of the EU, cases shall be adjudicated by three tribunal members with third-country nationals presiding over such tribunals.[94] The three members appointed by the president of the tribunal will be random and unpredictable, affording equal opportunities to all members of the tribunal to serve.[95] This is contrary to the traditional ISDS, where the disputing parties are free to select their arbitrators,[96] subject to the condition that they should not be nationals of disputing parties.[97] Members of the tribunal will be paid by monthly retainers and must conform to specific standards of independence. The newly-reached EU–Singapore IPA offered a more detailed structure of the tribunal. The six members of the tribunal shall be appointed by both parties (two nominated by EU, two nominated by Singapore, and two jointly nominated by both parties), with an eight-year term that could be renewed.[98] Long-term appointments and secured tenure will enhance the independence of adjudicators by eliminating the incentives of reappointments. Hence, it could dispel any suspicions by removing the adjudicators from the adjudicative marketplace and positioning them as participants in a public institution.

Despite the tenured judges, there are concerns that the MIC may give foreign investors privileged access to dispute resolution, enabling them to bypass national courts and deter public policies. A regionally-established court system in the name of consistency, legitimacy and transparency may risk the impartiality of judgment and influence from politics, which adds to the uncertainty and partiality of decisions. Moreover, the location of the forum and institutional management of adjudicators are likely to affect the decision-making process and results. Solving these problems

[92] CETA. Article 8.23.2, EU–Singapore IPA, Article 3.6.1, EU–Vietnam IPA, Article 3.33.2, EU–Mexico GA, Article 7.2.

[93] CETA. Article 8.41.5, EU–Singapore IPA, Article 3.22.5, EU–Vietnam IPA, Article 3.57.7, EU–Mexico GA, Article 31.5.

[94] CETA, Article 8.27(6); EU–Singapore IPA, Article 3.9(7).

[95] CETA, Article 8.27(7).

[96] UNCITRAL Arbitration Rules, Article 9.

[97] ICSID Convention, Articles 38 & 39.

[98] EU–Singapore IPA, Article 3.9(4)(5).

largely depends on the negotiation between states. The EU has to shape political-economic consensus from its Member States and trading partners to carry on the MIC operations.

Since arbitrator selection requires capability, professionalism and democracy, it can be easier for the EU and its trading partners to agree on substantive protection standards, arbitral procedures, rules of arbitrator selection and references to domestic laws. By the time the current ISDS regimes are established, states could have no clear answer to the ambiguity and bifurcation of treaty interpretations. As states and reformers try to align these inconsistencies, states should take a chance to clarify emergent specific questions, as demonstrated by the reform notes of the UNCITRAL Working Group[99] or in what scenarios a different standard can be applied. For instance, clarifications are needed regarding whether a mere breach of the legitimate expectations of an investor could constitute a breach of the fair and equitable treatment standard and, if so, whether these expectations must be grounded on a specific commitment on the part of the host state or can arise from general legislation. States should try to provide specific, predictable and equal treatment of investments and ensure the judiciary power granted to the arbitral tribunals. States could also take the chance to strengthen human rights, labour and environmental protection in the investment treaty, to reshape the scope of legitimate expectations held by the investors.

As the EU seeks support in the international community, it may push forward a trend of fusion between traditional arbitration, which features efficiency and tenured adjudicator litigation granting more uncertainty in terms of adjudicator selection and substantial rules. Even though tenured judges may reduce the partiality and inconsistency of arbitral decisions, there is fundamental divergence in the power arrangements and policy considerations of states. In this regard, it is unlikely that neither an investment court nor a reverse to domestic court-dominated resolution could replace the status and advantages of the current ISDS regime. It is more imperative to clarify the source of legitimacy of the regime. This legitimacy further determines how much control states or a union can have in establishing such a venue, shaping its decisions and guaranteeing equal opportunities for all parties. Ultimately, so long as the founders of the forum are willing to devote money and efforts to support the institution, the various dispute settlement forums can exist in parallel. The investment court and arbitration tribunals of the EU can serve as a substitute to each other in the multi-polarisation trend. This can even be a good thing if investors can choose where to sue the government so that competition between dispute resolution mechanisms (including litigation, arbitration, mediation and conciliation) can promote fairer judgment or decisions. Institutions granting inefficient and partial judgments will be automatically eliminated by the forum 'market'.

[99] UNCITRAL Working Group III, Possible Reform of Investor-State Dispute Settlement (ISDS)—Consistency and Related Matters, U.N. Doc. A/CN.9/WG.III/WP.153.

B. Towards Legitimate Consistency

Some standard techniques can enhance its legitimacy, irrespective of the forum. Bifurcations and divergence are solvable so long as the common sense in dispute resolution (key concepts and provisions) are gradually shaped in various ways.

1. Interpretation Guidance and Notes

At a time of policy transition, and for the governance of the FDI, which is essentially heterogeneous and decentralised, soft law can have a superior effect to hard law. Because the former gives the state more flexibility to adapt to new rules and mitigate representational deficits in the design of cross-border dispute settlement norms.[100] Moreover, in this decentralised system of investment treaties and arbitral awards, it would be of immense help if some international organisations or entities could contribute some centralised efforts to align the diversity and guide the system practice towards some common standards, in similar ways taken by the World Bank and the International Monetary Fund.

The ICSID Convention committee and UNCITRAL working group may issue case guidance and treaty interpretation notes for the panels and potential arbitrators as a top-down approach. Case guidance can be seen as a fusion trend between case law and treaties. China has adopted the guiding cases system to align the court rulings on controversial legal issues in domestic legal systems.[101] Although these guiding cases are not legally binding as precedents, they reflect policy orientations and clarify legal uncertainties in specific contexts. Similarly, while guiding arbitral awards are not legally binding, they will provide an aligned reference for arbitrators to decide on the case. Guiding cases need to be updated every few months or years to remain current with the overall legal and social environment. These centralised institutions could also offer guidance on applying customary international law in ISDS arbitration.

Regarding the bottom-up efforts, forming consensus on jurisdiction and protection standards requires arbitral practice and common knowledge. These two components are similar to the essential elements of customary international law – state practice and *opinion Juris*. In particular, the decentralised nature of ISDS (given the diversity of FDI and social policies) requires even more time and effort to shape such a sense of legal obligation. Some of the common views among states and investors have been founded in implicit or explicit ways.

United Nations Conference on Trade and Development noted in a recent study that there is an increasing convergence regarding the standard of compensation included in BITs, with most of them incorporating the Hull standard.[102] The Organisation for Economic Cooperation and Development Report even concluded the standard as part of customary international law.[103]

---

[100] Ali (2021).

[101] Jia (2016).

[102] Subedi (2008).

[103] OECD, Indirect Expropriation, p. 2. https://www.oecd.org/daf/inv/internationalinvestmentagreements/37781493.pdf, accessed 14 December 2021.

The ICSID Committee may organise treaty parties to issue interpretation notes of key concepts and provisions. Since international investment arbitration is founded on the consent of the state, solutions to these problems ultimately go back to clearer and more precise agreements given by the parties, either through the specification of critical terms, exceptions and reservations in the treaty (CETA annexes, exclusions to the chapter, joint declarations and reservations from future measures) or through travaux préparatoires and interpretive notes to assist interpretation (NAFTA Note of Interpretation). The 'second-generation' investment treaties have made much progress on the clarity and specification of the treaty standards than their first-generation counterparts.[104] New treaties and interpretations can further reduce ambiguity. Existing criticism against inconsistencies offers a road map for the reflection of states on the conflicts between intended policy objectives and actual outcomes and decisions upon the balance of different priorities. States can also establish a committee to build up control over the interpretation of the treaty and an open list of fair and equitable treatment standards. Although retroactive interpretation has been questioned as a sort of amendment to the treaty, it indeed contributes to a coherent approach to the protection standard.

In deciding specific protection standards, proportionality is a crucial standard. A sound appreciation of proportionality requires considering the inherently imbalanced conception of international investment agreements, the incoherence of the ISDS regime, and the ad hoc ISDS method in interpreting diverging and ambiguous norms.[105] The diversity and even complexity of investment arbitration should be increasingly understood and accepted by countries and investors, given the various functions and effects of FDI in different countries and their domestic governance structure. This also aligns with the notion of policing a risk society[106]—regulation is based on specific risks brought by the investor, the other side of the investment protection standards.

To remove other ambiguities with the application of BITs or FTAs, the state can publicise documents and other supplementary materials to specify the protection standards and clarify key concepts in the treaty. This clarification will serve as an essential reference for interpretation and application. Of course, both guiding cases and interpretation notes should remain evolving to adapt to future situations and policy changes.

2. **Appellate Body**

An appellate mechanism has been recommended to conduct substantive reviews of decisions, enhance treaty interpretation consistency, and improve consistency among arbitral awards without having to start the process over. The appeal body can be authorised to conduct a substantive review of decisions within some days of their issuance, correct substantial legal and factual errors, and uphold, modify or reverse

---

104 U.N. Doc. A/CN.9/935, para. 28.

105 De Brabandere and da Cruz (2020).

106 Ericson (1997).

the award of the initial tribunal. Illustrations of appellate review mechanisms can be found in certain investment treaties,[107] including the MIC proposal of the EU.[108] This would result in the current ISDS regime maintaining most of its basic features while complementing an appellate body to guarantee fairness and consistency.

The appellate body could also act as a controlling mechanism in reviewing the substantial heterogeneous standards of investment protection and the various textual expression of treaty provisions. This updating has been acknowledged in many new agreements. The EU–Japan Economic Partnership Agreement confirmed it would not affect the right of the government to regulate public policy objectives. In both the EU–Vietnam IPA and EU–Singapore IPA, the beginning chapters established the right to regulate within their territories to achieve legitimate policy objectives, such as public health, safety, environment, public morals and cultural diversity.[109] Even similar textual wording does not necessarily indicate the same policy meaning. Specific interpretation, then, depends on the interpretations given by the state or other supplementary materials.

Conclusion

International investment regimes are coordination results of the states based on their consensus and agreements. The formation of such a regime reflects a variety of motivations of the states, especially their political economy considerations in domestic and international contexts. The consensus and agreement previously reached are now challenged by the heterogeneity of foreign investment scenarios. The legitimacy crisis of the ISDS regime reflects some of the changes in the ideology of investment institutions, represented by the divergent political-economic concerns of the states, which have not been adequately addressed in previous ISDS practices. In this process, democracy and globalisation sometimes come into conflict due to domestic policy needs and global coordination pressures.

There is no single correct answer regarding how the ISDS regime can produce fair and legitimate results. In the efforts towards the rule of law and transparency in the ISDS regime, the rule of law does not necessarily mean unification. The ISDS regime should allow for diversity in national institutions and priorities.[110] Uniform global investment protection standards under the ICSID framework can be a general rule applied to all FDI. However, key concepts and provisions can have different meanings in different contexts. ‘Fair and equitable treatment of investment’ and the ‘investor’s legitimate expectation’ require a re-examination of the role and effect of

[107] US–Uruguay BIT, 4 November 2005, Annex E; Chile–US FTA, 6 June 2003, Article 10.19 (10) and Annex 10-H; the Dominican Republic–Central America Free Trade Agreement, 5 August 2004; CETA, Article 8.28.

[108] CETA, Article 8.28; EVTIA, Article 28, Article 29(2); EU–Singapore IPA, Article 3.19(3).

[109] EU–Vietnam IPA, Article 2.2(1).

[110] Shen and Li (2021).

the FDI in a specific social-economic system. Irrespective of the situation, rights and responsibilities should proportionately coexist with the same player.

States should embrace the complexity of the institutional investment design and find ways to restore it—build up mutual trust, promote cooperation, and manage differences in a balanced way. As the investment community demands certainty and predictability from unequivocal arbitration rules and investment treaties, legitimacy based on consensus can be achieved in various ways. Procedural transparency and impartial arbitrators are undoubtedly a necessary guarantee of a fair legal system. As far as the substantive protection standards are concerned, consensus formation needs centralised coordination and decentralised efforts. To align the norms and practices of investment arbitration, case guidance, interpretation notes and appellate review are suggested within the current ISDS regime. Although these documents and materials are not binding, they will help find consensus from previous arbitral practices while allowing countries to voice their opinions, learn from each other and shape new agreements.

References

Ala'I P (1998) Free trade or sustainable development: an analysis of the WTO Appellate Body's shift to a more balanced approach to trade liberalization. Am Univ Int Law Rev 14

Ali SF (2021) Forming transnational dispute settlement norms: soft law and the role of UNCITRAL's regional centre for Asia and the Pacific. Edward Elgar Publishing

Büthe T, Milner HV (2008) The politics of foreign direct investment into developing countries: increasing FDI through international trade agreements? Am J Polit Sci 52

Cave D (2021) China battles the world's biggest coal exporter, and coal is losing. The New York Times

Colen L et al (2016) Bilateral investment treaties and FDI: does the sector matter? World Dev 83

De Brabandere E, da Cruz PBM (2020) The role of proportionality in international investment law and arbitration: a system-specific perspective. Nord J Int Law 89

Dolzer R (2012) Perspectives for investment arbitration: consistency as a policy goal? Transnatl Disput Manag (TDM) 9

Duval A (2020) Time to go public? The need for transparency at the court of arbitration for sport. TMC Asser Institute for International & European Law-Asser Research Paper 7

Ehlermann C-D (2003) Experiences from the WTO Appellate Body. Tex Int Law J 38

Ehlermann C-D (2017) The workload of the WTO Appellate Body: problems and remedies. J Int Econ Law 20

Ericson RV (1997) Policing the risk society. In: Haggerty KD (Ed). Oxford University Press, p 48

Garcia-Mora MR (1949) The Calvo clause in Latin American constitutions and international law. Marquette Law Rev 33

Giorgetti C et al. (2020) Independence and impartiality of adjudicators in investment dispute settlement: assessing challenges and reform options. J World Invest & Trade 21

Habermas J (1989) The structural transformation of the public sphere: an inquiry into a category of bourgeois society. Polity Press

van Harten G (2010) Perceived bias in investment treaty arbitration. In: Waibel M (Ed) The backlash against investment arbitration: perceptions and reality

Van Harten G (2012) Arbitrator behaviour in asymmetrical adjudication: an empirical study of investment treaty arbitration. Osgoode Hall Law J 50

Henckels C (2016) Protecting regulatory autonomy through greater precision in investment treaties: the TPP, CETA, and TTIP. J Int Econ Law 19
Jackson JH (2000) The Jurisprudence of GATT & the WTO: insights on treaty law and economic relations. Cambridge University Press, p 7
Jia M (2016) Chinese common law? Guiding cases and judicial reform. Harv Law Rev 129
Johnson OT, Gimblett J (2011) From gunboats to BITs: the evolution of modern international investment law. Yearbook on International Investment Law & Policy 649
Kennedy D (2013) Law and the political economy of the world. Leiden J Int Law 26
Keynes S, Bown CP (2017) Holding the WTO Hostage, Trump Style, Trade Talks Podcast
Kho SS et al. (2017) The EU TTIP investment court proposal and the WTO dispute settlement system: comparing apples and oranges? ICSID Rev-Foreign Invest Law J 32
Kidane W (2017) The culture of international arbitration. Oxford University Press, p 145
Klett J (2016) National interest vs. foreign investment-protecting parties through ISDS. Tulane J Int Comp Law 25
Laborde G (2010) The case for host state claims in investment arbitration. J Int Disput Settl 1
Langford M et al. (2017) The revolving door in international investment arbitration. J Int Econ Law 20
Li Q, Resnick A (2003) Reversal of fortunes: democratic institutions and foreign direct investment inflows to developing countries. Int Organ 57
Magnuson WJ (2010) WTO jurisprudence and its critiques: the Appellate Body's anti-constitutional resistance. Harv Int Law J Online 51
Miles K (2013) The origins of international investment law: empire, environment, and the safeguarding of capital. Cambridge University Press, p 21
Neumayer E, Spess L (2005) Do bilateral investment treaties increase foreign direct investment to developing countries? World Dev 33
Newcombe A, Paradell L (2009) Law and practice of investment treaties, standards of treatment. Kluwer Law Int, p 12
Ortino F (2006) Treaty interpretation and the WTO Appellate Body report in US-Gambling: a critique. J Int Econ Law 9
Powell R (1999) In the shadow of power: states and strategies in international politics. Princeton University Press
Putnam RD (1988) Diplomacy and domestic politics: the logic of two-level games. Int Organ 42
Rutgers MR, Schreurs P (2006) The morality of value-and purpose-rationality: the Kantian roots of weber's foundational distinction. Adm Soc 38
Salacuse JW, Sullivan NP (2005) Do BITs really work: an evaluation of bilateral investment treaties and their grand bargain. Harv Int Law J 46
Shen W, Li S (2021) China's engagement in isds reform: text, practice, and political economy. China WTO Rev 7
Simoes FS (2020) Can investment dispute settlement ever be depoliticized? Cardozo Int Comp Law Rev 4
Subedi SP (20008) International investment law: reconciling policy and principle. Hart Publication, pp 142–143
Valentini L (2014) No global demos, no global democracy? a systematization and critique. Perspect Polit 12
Vandevelde KJ (2005) A brief history of international investment agreements. UC Davis J Int Law Policy 12
Vidigal G (2020) A really big button that doesn't do anything? The anti-NME clause in US trade agreements between law and geoeconomics. J Int Econ Law 23
Wälde T (2006) Investment arbitration and sustainable development: good intentions—or effective results? Int Environ AgreemS: Polit, Law Econ 6
Walker VR (1998) Keeping the WTO from becoming the world trans-science organization: scientific uncertainty, science policy, and factfinding in the growth hormones dispute. Cornell Int Law J 31

Weber M (1978) Economy and society: an outline of interpretive sociology. University of California Press, p 4
Young OR (1991) Political leadership and regime formation: on the development of institutions in international society. Int Organ 45
Yu PK (2017) Crossfertilizing ISDS with TRIPS. Loyola Univ Chic Law J 49

Chapter 6
The Elephant in the Room? Russia and the ISDS Reform

Dmitry K. Labin and Alena V. Soloveva

Introduction

The calls for reforming the investment treaty regime are neither novel nor entirely unexpected. The need for that reform has recently reached its pitiful nadir where the UNCITRAL[1] Working Group III gathered for its first meeting in Vienna back in November–December 2017 to discuss states' concerns about investor-state dispute settlement (ISDS). These discussions constitute one of the most remarkable occurrences in the field of investment treaty arbitration. Of still greater significance are concerns advanced by the delegates about consistency, predictability and correctness, costs and transparency, facts and perceptions, appointment of arbitrators, etc.

States' concerns about the reform have been repeatedly referred to in recent publications,[2] but international law scholars have not yet discussed Russia's stance in detail. Then, an attempt has been made to fill the gap in the literature by introducing the Russian position which contrasts with some other approaches, for instance, of Canada or the European Union. For this reason, our account requires that we discuss in closer detail several (most controversial) statements advanced by Russian delegates and substantiate them with doctrinal and practical evidence to shed light on the reasoning behind those statements.

This article seeks to analyse the issues of transparency and third-party participation in the arbitral proceedings, focusing on the amicus curiae mechanism. The authors will provide a broad overview of commercial arbitration in the context of investment arbitration and Russia's incrementalist position with respect to the ISDS reform as exhibited through the delegates' statements on the dichotomy of facts and

[1] United Nations Commission on International Trade Law.

[2] See, e.g., Arato (2018); Roberts (2018a); Roberts and Bouraoui (2018a, b, c, d); Grill (2017).

D. K. Labin (✉) · A. V. Soloveva
MGIMO University, 76 Prospekt Vernadskogo, Moscow 119454, Russia
e-mail: d.labin@inno.mgimo.ru

© The Author(s), under exclusive license to Springer Nature Singapore Pte Ltd. 2024

S. Wei (ed.), *International Investment Law at the Juncture*, International Law in Asia,
https://doi.org/10.1007/978-981-97-2183-2_6

perceptions, coherence and consistency, and appointment of arbitrators. The article also traces recent swift normative developments in investment policy of Russia, which demonstrates the country's unique perspective on ICSID membership.

Russia in the UNCITRAL Working Group III

Transparency

Delving into current debates surrounding the importance of transparency, the authors begin with a notion that Russia seems to be one of the states that is most sceptical and reluctant to make efforts aimed at a more multilateral and transparent system, viewing the criticisms of the current system as mainly overblown. Those who have not participated in the UNCITRAL Working Group III meetings as an Observer can benefit from the readily available audio recordings of the past meetings.[3] On a separate note, while Russia took a rather active position in the reform discussions during the 34th and 35th meetings, it remained surprisingly mute in the 36th meeting and only advanced some commentaries on the last day of the Working Group session.

In the course of discussing the nature of transparency in the context of investment arbitration, it is first necessary to highlight the rationale and key features of this concept which must be approached with due diligence and care. The values of confidentiality and transparency are often invoked in the theory and practice of investment treaty arbitration. In a general sense, the term "transparency" is not immediately associated with international law. Yet, it has gained popularity and "became a foundation of international law" in large part due to the active participation of public and non-governmental organisations (NGOs) in global governance.[4] Transparency is an evolving concept. Since the 2000s, it has received "increasing recognition in international dispute settlement processes."[5] The term "transparency" in international investment law connotes that "host states have an obligation to publish all of the legal rules, regulations and other statutory requirements affecting investors."[6]

The Working Group III undertook its expected consideration of transparency in ISDS. Throughout the deliberations, the importance of transparency in ISDS was actively underlined. There is no lack of major variation as transparency is regarded by many as a key element of the rule of law, access to justice as well as the legitimacy of the ISDS system.[7]

There are different ways to address the lack of transparency. As a very modest starting point, enhanced transparency in the current ISDS system may be achieved

---

[3] Audio Recordings, UNCITRAL, *available at* https://uncitral.un.org/en/audio.

[4] Bianchi (2013).

[5] Saravanan and Subramanian (2018).

[6] Dolzer and Schreuer (2008).

[7] UNCITRAL, Rep. of Working Group III (ISDS) on the work of its thirty-fourth session, pt. I, 12, U.N. Doc. A/CN.9/930/Rev.1 (Dec. 19, 2017).

through transparency in the appointment of arbitrators and their compensation.[8] A broader concept of transparency is indeed cross-cutting and relates to many aspects of the possible ISDS reform.

On this issue, Russia vividly commented that the key to the solution can be found in bilateral or multilateral investment treaties or in the relevant arbitral rules. Therefore, transparency shall be ensured by states in line with their geopolitical and regional needs. And this in turn is the main advantage of investment treaty arbitration. Furthermore, transparency is a multi-layered problem. On the one hand, there have been ever-increasing calls for enhanced transparency of arbitral proceedings. On the other hand, from a state perspective, most arbitral proceedings tend to involve sensitive information which may potentially concern national security. Likewise, investors may also possess information which they will not be happy to share with the general public. As a result, there is a fine line between transparency requirements and protection of the legitimate interests of disputing parties. Russian delegates expressed their genuine surprise when they learned that this aspect appeared unpopular with other delegates and had not been mentioned in the document A/CN.9/WG.III/WP.142 which served as a base for the Working Group III considerations of transparency in ISDS.

Russia made it to the top ten of the most frequent respondent States in 1987–2017 with the total number of known cases reaching 24. Of these, 18 cases represent arbitrations under the UNCITRAL Arbitration Rules.[9] Although a higher degree of transparency is considered to be a distinguishable feature of investor-state arbitration, the 1976 and 2010 editions of the UNCITRAL Arbitration Rules did not contain any specific provisions on transparency. Thus, if a state or investor were unwilling to publish documents connected with a dispute, it was almost impossible to do so.[10] For example, in *Cesare Galdabini v. Russian Federation*,[11] the award (in favour of Russia) was never published. Similarly, in *Luxtona v. Russia*[12] and *Oschadbank v. Russia*,[13] no information is available to the public to date. Incidentally, in the infamous *Yukos Universal v. Russia*,[14] some 25 documents including legal and expert opinions remain closed to the general public. In a more recent closely-watched UNCITRAL case,

---

[8] *Supra* note 7, at 13.

[9] *Investment Dispute Settlement Navigator*, UNCTAD, *available at* https://investmentpolicy.unctad.org/investment-dispute-settlement.

[10] United Nations Commission on International Trade Law Rules on Transparency in Treaty-based Investor-State Arbitration and Arbitration Rules (as revised in 2010, with new Article 1, paragraph 4, as adopted in 2013), Article 34(5) (Dec. 16, 2013), U.N. Doc. G.A. Res. 68/109.

[11] Cesare Galdabini SpA v. The Russian Federation, Award (May 1, 2011), *available at* https://www.italaw.com/cases/236.

[12] Luxtona Limited v. The Russian Federation, *available at* https://www.italaw.com/cases/6625.

[13] Oschadbank v. The Russian Federation, PCA Case Repository No. 2016-14, *available at* https://www.italaw.com/cases/7491.

[14] Yukos Universal Limited (Isle of Man) v. The Russian Federation, PCA Case Repository No. 2005-04/AA227, *available at* https://www.italaw.com/cases/1175.

Privatbank and Finilon v. Russia,[15] observers can only benefit from press releases by the Permanent Court of Arbitration (PCA).

Russia has underperformed as a home state of claimants with only 22 known cases submitted by Russian investors. Again, more than 50 percent of those cases represent arbitrations under the UNCITRAL Arbitration Rules. A further overview reveals that in 11 cases decisions are pending with the oldest case dating to 2007.[16] Of the remaining cases, three were discontinued and one was settled. By way of simple arithmetic, there are only seven cases where an actual decision has been rendered. And in three cases the awards have not been published. Surprisingly, some cases do not even disclose information about the tribunal composition.[17] In 2016, Russian investors became more active[18] initiating most disputes under the UNCITRAL Arbitration Rules with the only ICSID[19] claim filed by subsidiaries of a Russian corporation.[20]

The UNCITRAL Arbitration Rules were revised in 2010 and 2013. A number of provisions were updated in 2010 to improve procedural efficiency. The adoption of the UNCITRAL Rules on Transparency in Treaty-based Investor-State Arbitration (hereinafter Rules on Transparency) triggered an additional revision of the UNCITRAL Arbitration Rules in 2013, with a new Article 1(4) providing for the application of the Rules on Transparency which came into effect on April 1, 2014. The Rules on Transparency comprise procedural rules on transparency, public access to investment treaty arbitration, and a full disclosure of most documents to the public.

The Rules on Transparency have been incorporated in most investment treaties concluded since their entry into force. In addition, there is a brand-new transparency-dedicated legal instrument—the United Nations Convention on Transparency in Treaty-based Investor-State Arbitration (hereinafter Mauritius Convention), which was signed by twenty-two States and entered into force on October 18, 2017, after

---

[15] PJSC CB PrivatBank and Finance Company Finilon LLC v. Russian Federation, PCA Case Repository No. 2015-21, *available at* https://www.italaw.com/cases/3970.

[16] S. Paushok, CJSC Golden East Company and CJSC Vostokneftegaz Company v. The Government of Mongolia, ICSID Case No. ARB/98/4, Award on Jurisdiction and Liability, (Apr. 28, 2011), *available at* https://www.italaw.com/sites/default/files/case-documents/ita0622.pdf.

[17] Oleg Deripaska v. The Republic of Montenegro, PCA Case Repository No. 2017-07, *available at* https://www.italaw.com/cases/4785.

[18] See, e.g., Min. of Land and Property of the Republic of Tatarstan v. Ukraine (2016), *available at* https://investmentpolicy.unctad.org/investment-dispute-settlement/cases/763/tatarstan-v-ukraine; Roscosmos State Corporation for Space Activities, RKTs Progress, KBOM and TsENKI v. French Republic, Case No. 16/01314, *available at* https://www.italaw.com/cases/4422; Ms. Olga Ovchinnikova v. Kingdom of Sweden (2016), *available at* https://www.italaw.com/cases/4365.

[19] International Centre for Settlement of Investment Disputes.

[20] Emergofin B.V. and Velbay Holdings Ltd. v. Ukraine, ICSID Case No. ARB/16/35, *available at* https://www.italaw.com/cases/4430. In this case, two subsidiaries of the Russian aluminium producer Rusal, Emergofin BV and Velbay Holdings, incorporated in the Netherlands and Cyprus respectively, filed a request for ICSID arbitration against Ukraine under Article 9 of the Netherlands-Ukraine BIT.

having been ratified by three States.[21] Incidentally, Russia is not even a signatory to the Mauritius Convention. This examination is especially valuable given that in 2016 the Government of the Russian Federation enacted the Regulation on Entering into International Treaties on the Encouragement and Mutual Protection of Investments (Regulation 2016),[22] which replaced the 2001 Russian Model Bilateral Investment Treaty (BIT) and contains non-binding guidelines for drafting and negotiating future investment protection treaties. Importantly, the 2016 Regulation specifies that any new investment treaty should expressly exclude the UNCITRAL Rules on Transparency and establish a duty of confidentiality with respect to any information about the dispute. This "concept of privacy and confidentiality originates primarily from the foundational underpinnings of international commercial arbitration, but it has also to a considerable extent been translated into the investment context."[23] This explains the rationale for Russia's visible reluctance to support concern about enhanced transparency in the ISDS system.

Amicus Curiae

Amicus briefs are an ancient legal instrument, originating in Roman law and gradually taking over the common law tradition and civil law jurisdictions.[24] Recent decades have seen a significant increase in the number of legal dispute settlement mechanisms, which has opened the door for NGOs to participate as "friends of the court" (amicus is a "friend of the court"). Such participation has been visible, in particular, in international investment arbitration.[25] Initially, only NGOs have submitted their amicus briefs in investment arbitration. This practice has lately shifted to include home states, international communities, and even individuals as amici curiae.[26] However, despite these interesting developments, "direct NGO participation in international courts and tribunals generally remains relatively limited so that their participation remains essentially a matter of domestic litigation."[27] The concept of amicus curiae is accepted in common law and even some civil law jurisdictions.[28] On the domestic level, amicus intervention has frequently involved a range of participants, including individuals and foreign governments.[29] Amicus participation ordinarily takes the

[21] So far, five States have ratified the Convention including Cameroon, Canada, Gambia, Mauritius, and Switzerland.

[22] Regulation on Entering into International Treaties on the Encouragement and Mutual Protection of Investments (No. 992 Regulation of The Russian Federation, Sept. 30, 2016).

[23] See generally Buys (2003).

[24] For a more substantial analysis, see Kochevar (2013).

[25] De Brabandere (2011).

[26] Saravanan and Subramanian (2016).

[27] Vierucci (2008).

[28] Bartholomeusz (2005).

[29] *Id.*

form of written submissions,[30] but oral hearings may also be arranged.[31] Therefore, the purpose and form of amicus briefs have not been stable across time and jurisdictions. In the US, for example, amicus briefs have shifted "from a source of neutral information to a flexible tactical instrument available to litigants and third parties."[32]

Investment arbitration tribunals initially refused to allow third-party participation.[33] In *Aguas del Tunari S.A. v. The Republic of Bolivia* (known as the Bechtel case)[34] the tribunal denied citizens and environmental groups standing at the arbitration due to the parties' unwillingness to consent to their participation. In recent years, however, there has been an "undeniable shift in investor-State arbitration toward greater tolerance of limited third-party participation, perhaps in response to continuing public pressure and criticism."[35]

The rapid rise to prominence of international investment arbitration has been accompanied by "mounting public concern about the system's legitimacy and accountability."[36] Commentators and civil society groups have called for increased public involvement in investment arbitration to incorporate broader policy considerations and add transparency.[37] In a similar vein, transparency is closely associated with amicus curiae which includes "measures such as the publication of information on proceedings, documents and awards, as well as attendance at and broadcasting of hearings."[38] In this sense, acceptance of receiving amicus curiae briefs in international investment law is commonly perceived as "a ground-breaking development and without a doubt paves the way to enhanced transparency in these proceedings."[39]

In the fifteen years since amicus briefs were first admitted in investor-state arbitrations, they have emerged as the principal means through which NGOs have been able to participate formally in arbitration proceedings. Russia's criticism has initially focussed on the alleged impact that home states may exert on decision-making in favour of foreign investors via NGOs as amici curiae. This in turn may lead to politicisation of the entire process.

There may be some ground for Russia's exhibition of frustration. It has generally been accepted that the main function of amicus curiae submissions is to assist the tribunal in its work "by offering expertise and arguments different from those

---

30 *Id.*

31 Levine (2011).

32 Krislov (1963).

33 *Supra* note 31, at 208.

34 Aguas del Tunari, S.A. v. Republic of Bolivia, ICSID Case No. ARB/02/3, Decision on Respondent's Objections to Jurisdiction (Oct. 21, 2005), *available at* https://www.italaw.com/sites/default/files/case-documents/italaw10957_0.pdf.

35 *Supra* note 31, at 208.

36 *Id.* at 200.

37 *Id.* See also Choudhury (2008); Newcombe and Lemaire (2001).

38 Lamb et al. (2017).

39 *Supra* note 25, at 112.

of the disputing parties."[40] Investment tribunals have been flexibly accepted that "third-party submissions could in fact contain useful information."[41] It should be emphasised that NGO participation through amicus curiae briefs is merely an "indirect form of participation, which perhaps does not warrant such profound apprehension."[42] Logically, the participation cannot be equated with that as a party to the disputes.[43] Hence, those states who are a party to a dispute remain "the masters of the dispute."[44] In a nutshell, amicus curiae briefs can actually be considered as very much equivalent to publicly available information (which is consistent with the treatment of amicus curiae briefs by the International Court of Justice).[45]

A quick example should illustrate the problem explicitly invoked by Russia. In February 2016 the tribunal in Eli Lilly made decisions on nine applications to file amicus briefs submitted by a total of twenty-five parties.[46] These parties included NGOs, individuals and industry associations. The six briefs that were eventually accepted focussed on the legality of certain Canadian patent laws. Canada, as a respondent State in the dispute, complained that the claimant was a member of two industry associations that had applied to file amicus briefs.[47] On a more technical level, the tribunal found that a disputing party's membership in an amicus curiae does not mean a lack of independence of the amicus per se. Instead, such membership should be viewed "in relation to the tribunal's consideration of the extent to which the amicus brief would assist the tribunal in determining a factual or legal issue related to the arbitration by bringing fresh perspective, knowledge or insight."[48] The tribunal proceeded to admit the briefs of the two amici.

The participation of NGOs in ISDS has been noticeable principally in cases involving matters of public interest, namely "in cases relating to the environment and water in their connection with trade and foreign investment."[49] In that sense, NGO participation is not necessarily to the benefit of the tribunal, but rather to the benefit of a greater "public interest," since the participation "increases the legitimacy, transparency and openness of international investment arbitration and international economic dispute settlement."[50]

---

[40] See Suez, Sociedad General de Aguas de Barcelona, S.A. and Vivendi Universal, S.A. v. Argentine Republic, ICSID Case No. ARB/03/19, Order in response to a Petition for Participation as Amicus Curiae, 13 (May 19, 2005).

[41] *Supra* note 25, at 106.

[42] *Id.* at 110.

[43] *Id.* at 106.

[44] *Id.* at 111.

[45] *Id.*

[46] Eli Lilly and Company v. The Government of Canada, ICSID Case No. UNCT/14/2, Procedural Order No. 4 (Feb. 23, 2016).

[47] Eli Lilly and Company v. The Government of Canada, ICSID Case No. UNCT/14/2, Respondent's Observations on Non-Disputing Party Applications (Feb. 19, 2016).

[48] *Supra* note 38, at 82–3.

[49] *Supra* note 40. See also Biwater Gauff (Tanzania) Ltd. v. United Republic of Tanzania, ICSID Case No. ARB/05/22, Award (July 24, 2008).

[50] *Supra* note 25, at 102.

The involvement of NGOs as amici in international proceedings has been sharply contested. Debate concerning the proper role of NGOs in international investment arbitrations has been "particularly intense."[51] Supporters claim that amicus activity by NGOs helps remedy deficits of participation and legitimacy at the international level.[52] Keeping such benefits in mind, some commentators have cited amicus activity as "a component of evolving global administrative law norms."[53] Opponents (including many developing countries) argue that amicus participation by NGOs gives these organisations too much influence and "unfairly benefits developed countries."[54] To the extent that common law correlates with economic development,[55] the common law origins of amicus activity also map onto this dispute. One commentator has stated that "the introduction of amici participation into investment arbitration may be seen as representing a victory of common law over civil law and of the developed world over the developing world."[56]

Linked to these concerns, it is indeed "difficult to measure directly the influence of amicus briefs on the determinations of tribunals."[57] As might be expected, no tribunal has expressly stated the amount of influence (or lack thereof) that an amicus brief has had on the tribunal's reasoning[58] which makes it difficult to assess the validity of Russia's concerns about NGO participation in ISDS. However, it is possible to draw some cautious conclusions based on other factors, such as how often, where and in what ways a tribunal refers to an amicus brief in an award.

Investment tribunals have elaborated three approaches to the contributory value of amicus briefs. First, some commentators conclude that amici have had little influence on tribunals. For instance, in relation to amicus briefs on human rights

---

[51] Bjorklund (2009).

[52] Esty (2006). (identifying *amicus* briefs at the WTO as "a new avenue for participation").

[53] *Id.* See also Stewart and Badin (2011). ("The Appellate Body's embrace of amicus briefs reflects the adoption of global administrative law to boost organizational legitimacy...").

[54] See, e.g., Dispute Settlement Body Special Session, Taiwan, Penghu, Kinmen & Matsu—DOHA Mandated Review of the Dispute Settlement Understanding (DSU), WTO Doc. TN/DS/W/25, at 2 (Nov. 27, 2002). ("To allow unsolicited amicus curiae submissions... would create a situation where those Members with the least social resources could be put at a disadvantage."); Dispute Settlement Body Special Session, Cuba, Honduras, India, Malaysia, Pakistan, Sri Lanka, Tanzania & Zimbabwe—Negotiations on the Dispute Settlement Understanding, WTO Doc. TN/DS/W/18, at 4 (Oct. 7, 2002) ("If . . . nongovernmental entities were allowed to influence the process and outcome of disputes, it would severely erode the Member governments' authority and ability to participate effectively in the dispute settlement process."); Statement by Uruguay at the General Council, Decision by the Appellate Body Concerning Amicus Curiae Briefs, WTO Doc. WT/GC/38 at 3 (Dec. 4, 2000). (arguing that acceptance of amicus briefs inappropriately altered the dispute settlement mechanism and limited the rights of parties to a dispute).

[55] This controversial correlation is known as the "legal origins thesis." See, e.g., Curran (2009). ("The legal origins thesis … contrasts countries with common and civil law origins, correlating common law origins with … greater economic well-being.").

[56] *Supra* note 51, at 1293.

[57] *Supra* note 38, at 85.

[58] *Id.*

issues submitted between 2011[59] and 2012,[60] previous scholarship has suggested that "tribunals have been much more selective when referring to amicus briefs in their substantive reasoning," but sometimes they did not observably employ even detailed and well-founded arguments, and sometimes explicitly ignored them.[61]

Second, other commentators conclude that tribunals have been influenced to some degree by amicus briefs, but with no express reference in their awards. Support for this view may be derived from tribunals' comments on the utility of a brief. For example, in Biwater Gauff,[62] the tribunal found the amici's observations useful. The case in which amicus briefs have been most influential is *Philip Morris*.[63] The ICSID tribunal referred throughout its award to submissions from the World Health Organization and the Pan-American Health Organization to support its findings on the merits of the case.[64] However, the amici's submissions were mainly factual and focussed on the efficacy of certain policies on public health issues, rather than legal arguments. This indicates that "amicus interventions are more likely to be influential where they focus on matters falling outside of the expertise of the tribunal (or the expertise of the disputing parties)."[65]

Finally, an alternative view is that tribunals "only permit influence where there is something special either about the points made or the amicus itself."[66] This view may explain the greater degree of attention tribunals seem to have accorded to the European Council in cases involving intra-EU BITs since the EC is distinguishable from traditional amici (NGOs) in its role as the "expert, administrator, enforcer and a maker of, EU law."[67] However, greater attention does not necessarily mean greater success, and tribunals have rarely taken EC points into consideration.[68]

Amidst the increasing acceptance of amicus curiae in the Investor-State Dispute Settlement (ISDS), there is a notable countervailing concern about the potential effects such an approach may have on proceedings, including increased costs and delays in proceedings. This is demonstrated by tribunals' exercise of their broad

---

[59] Methanex Corp. v. U.S.A., Decision of the Tribunal on Petitions from Third Persons to Intervene as "Amici Curiae" (Jan. 15, 2001), *available at* https://www.italaw.com/sites/default/files/case-documents/ita0517_0.pdf. (The NGOs eventually submitted amicus briefs on the basis of the NAFTA FTC Statement—Final Award of the Tribunal on Jurisdiction and Merits, 3 August 2005, pp. 26–30, pt. II, ch. C).

[60] Pac Rim Cayman LLC v. The Republic of El Salvador, ICSID Case No. ARB/09/12, Award (Oct. 14, 2016).

[61] *Supra* note 38, at 85.

[62] Biwater Gauff (Tanzania) Ltd., *supra* note 50.

[63] Philip Morris Brands Sàrl, Philip Morris Products S.A. and Abal Hermanos S.A. v. Oriental Republic of Uruguay, ICSID Case No. ARB/10/7, Award (July 8, 2016).

[64] *Id.* at pp. 389–410.

[65] *Supra* note 38, at 87.

[66] *Id.* at 86.

[67] *Id.*

[68] See, e.g., Electrabel S.A. v. Republic of Hungary, ICSID Case No. ARB/07/19, Award (Nov. 25, 2015); Ioan Micula, Viorel Micula, S.C. European Food S.A, S.C. Starmill S.R.L. and S.C. Multipack S.R.L. v. Romania [I], ICSID Case No. ARB/05/20, Final Award (Dec. 11, 2013).

procedural authority to reject applications for lateness, circumscribe the length and content of briefs, and reserve the right to impose costs upon amici. Despite these concerns, certain tribunals, treaty drafters and authors of arbitral rules are not averse to having more amicus briefs per se.

However, a question remains about the frequent categorisation of amicus participation as a transparency measure which may not always be entirely appropriate. This participation itself can often be a "one-way affair"[69] where a brief is filed without the amicus learning anything new about the case. Thus, there are also disadvantages to being an amicus.[70] Unlike parties, amici cannot control the direction of a dispute or case management; they are not generally served case documents and cannot offer evidence, examine witnesses or cross-examine them.[71]

This conundrum has practical relevance since objections to amicus participation, such as inefficiency, are sometimes viewed as applicable to transparency in general. Another interesting issue is whether transparency measures in investment arbitration might spill over into international commercial arbitration. The transparency debate "certainly is not new to commercial arbitration."[72] However, transparency has not gained the same amount of traction in this sphere since commercial arbitration is predominantly "a matter between private parties and therefore should not be subject to public scrutiny."[73] Although a comprehensive discussion is beyond the scope of this article, this is certainly something to watch "given the apparent present appetite for institutional and legislative reform."[74]

Holistic Approach to Procedural Reform

Each element has its advantages and disadvantages. And in order to accurately appreciate the significance of ISDS, both sides of the coin shall be equally respected and inspected. Otherwise, it would appear that the whole system of ISDS is painted only with dark shades which in turn produces a perverted landscape with rather sad scenery. Reality of course is more complex and nuanced. To underscore the importance of a balanced and holistic approach to procedural reform, Russia urged the Secretariat to request comments from the major arbitration centres in London, Stockholm, Singapore, and Hong Kong. Incidentally, the Secretariat responded that discussions had been conducted only with those heavily involved in ISDS (including the ICSID and the PCA), but not with commercial arbitration centres. Yet, Russia mentioned commercial arbitration because these centres administer a significant

[69] *Supra* note 38, at 91.

[70] Shelton (1994).

[71] Id.

[72] Rogers (2006).

[73] Hope (2016).

[74] *Supra* note 38, at 91.

number of arbitrations, and their experience would thus bring significant value given their status as most preferred arbitral institutions.[75]

Historically, the rise of investment treaty arbitration attracted not only those active in the field, but also practitioners "who did not have a background in public international law, but in international commercial arbitration"[76] largely because applicable procedural law was "either the same as that applicable to commercial arbitrations, as in the case of investment arbitrations under UNCITRAL Arbitration Rules, the Arbitration Rules of the Arbitration Institute of the Stockholm Chamber of Commerce (SCC Rules), or the Rules of the International Chamber of Commerce (ICC Rules), or modelled on commercial arbitration procedure, as in the case of ICSID arbitrations."[77]

Accordingly, international investment law is more characterised by a division between those from private commercial law and arbitration, and those from public international law and inter-state dispute settlement.[78] This naturally results in a "veritable culture clash"[79] that can be traced in the ongoing reform discussions. Private commercial and public international lawyers are known to have different perspectives on the function of dispute resolution. Whereas public international lawyers "embed international investment law firmly in general international law, commercial arbitration lawyers see investment treaty arbitration as a subset of international (commercial) arbitration."[80]

As this discussion suggests, "investment arbitral proceedings frequently rely on the same procedural rules that govern commercial arbitration, and contain certain privacy and confidentiality rights."[81] Thus, the UNCITRAL Arbitration Rules, which are frequently used in investment arbitration disputes, restrict the publication of any awards without the parties' consent.[82] In this regard, there are also similar confidentiality rights in the "investment-specific ICSID regime."[83] For instance, the ICSID Convention prohibits publication of the award without the consent of the parties.[84] As such, institutional rules have traditionally provided disputing parties with the

[75] For details, see 2018 International Arbitration Survey: The Evolution of International Arbitration conducted by the School of International Arbitration, Queen Mary University of London (QMUL) in partnership with White & Case LLP; White & Case, 2018 International Arbitration Survey: The Evolution of International Arbitration (May 9, 2018), http://www.arbitration.qmul.ac.uk/media/arbitration/docs/2018-International-Arbitration-Survey-report.pdf.

[76] Schill (2001).

[77] *Id.*

[78] Weiler (2001).

[79] *Supra* note 76, at 888.

[80] Legum (2005). See also Bjorklund (2007).

[81] Mistelis (2005).

[82] UNCITRAL Arbitration Rules Article 32(5), U.N. G.A. Res. A/65/465 (Dec. 6, 2010).

[83] *Supra* note 31, at 204.

[84] Convention on the Settlement of Investment Disputes between States and Nationals of Other States Article 48(5), Oct. 14, 1966, 575 U.N.T.S. 159 (hereinafter the "ICSID Convention").

advantage of "fashioning the investment arbitration proceedings to preserve privacy and confidentiality."[85]

Certainly, the classification into public international law and commercial arbitration approaches is "no more than a blueprint or archetype."[86] Yet, education, professional background, and practical experience will inevitably facilitate a certain mind-set that is in line with either public international law or commercial arbitration archetype.[87] This is visible, for example, in the different sources arbitrators with a commercial arbitration background and those with a public international lawyer's background make reference to in the awards,[88] in the chosen reasoning and preferred methods of interpretations,[89] and in their respective understanding of the role of arbitrators and dispute settlement.[90]

What we now understand to be Russia's resistance to accept any modifications of investment treaty reform stems from the scholarly-backed preference for private international law over public international law. Russia's tendency to favour commercial arbitration originates from a lifelong characterisation of international investment law as a form of private international law rather than public international law which explains Russia's reluctance to join the movement toward more public international law measures.[91] The existing system is built predominantly on international commercial arbitration, which has traditionally rejected transparency as an essential ingredient of dispute settlement. Hence, Russia's resistance which discords with the American, European, and Canadian approaches to the UNCITRAL reforms is largely due to an expressly manifested need for "greater legitimacy and public participation in international investment arbitration, as distinct from commercial arbitration."[92]

Russia's Dogmatic Camp

It is now axiomatic that there are three main dogmatic camps based on their approaches toward the ISDS reform: incrementalists, systemic reformers, and paradigm shifters.[93] Some commentators have opined that Russia belongs to the incrementalist group which views the criticisms of the current system as unfairly

[85] *Supra* note 31, at 204.

[86] *Supra* note 76, at 889.

[87] *Id.*

[88] Tribunals presided over by public international lawyers, *e.g.*, appear to make reference more frequently to decisions by the ICJ or the PCIJ than tribunals presided over by commercial arbitrators. See *supra* note 76, at 889.

[89] Wälde (2009).

[90] Schill (2010).

[91] For details, see Labin and Soloveva (2018).

[92] Recording: UN Comm'n. on Int'l Trade Law, 34th Sess. (Nov. 27–Dec. 1, 2017), *available at* http://www.uncitral.org/uncitral/audio/meetings.jsp.

[93] Roberts (2018b).

exaggerated and argues that "investor-state arbitration remains the best option available."[94] Hence, they favour retaining the existing dispute resolution system with only modest reforms that would redress specific concerns.

It can undoubtedly be noted that Russia has taken a remarkable pro-investor-state arbitration position consistent with incrementalism. Another issue to consider in evaluating Russia's commitment to the incrementalist camp concerns its attempts to challenge the severity of current ISDS problems such as inconsistency. Thus, Russian delegates have insisted that inconsistency is an advantage of the system rather than a disadvantage which helps ensure regional interests and political relations between countries. The delegates expressly argued in favour of the existing ISDS system with only targeted reforms addressing specific concerns modestly. In doing so, Russia is keeping true to its incrementalist approach and conceptualisation of the international investment system as a form of private international law.

In the international investment agreements (IIAs) signed in recent years, countries have implemented a large number of ISDS reform elements. Nearly all IIAs concluded in 2018 contain at least one, and most contain several, mapped ISDS reform elements. Against this background, within the Commonwealth of Independent States (CIS), no major ISDS policy shifts have occurred.[95] To illustrate, the Eurasian Investment Agreement 2008, signed by Belarus, Kazakhstan, Kyrgyzstan, Russia and Tajikistan, does not contain ISDS reform elements or procedural improvements.[96]

Incrementalists tend to question the severity of the existing system's problems by suggesting, for instance, that "the concerns about inconsistent decisions are a natural and positive consequence of the bilateral nature of investment treaties"[97] (thus, Russia argued that it is "an advantage of the system and not a disadvantage"[98]). In the following discussion, three related concerns, individually or in combination, have been offered to explain Russia's incrementalist position showcased in the reform discussions. Incidentally, Russia has never commented substantially on the establishment of a multilateral investment court.

Facts v. Perceptions

Russia's position *vis-à-vis* perceptions requires an evidence-based approach. The UNCITRAL is tasked primarily with improving international trade law rather than working with public opinion. Perhaps, if there are indeed problems with the perceptions of the current ISDS system, there are doubts as to its objectivity and efficiency. But the issue of perceptions is a subjective one. While perceptions should be taken

---

94 *Id.*

95 IIA Issues Note—Issue 1, *Reforming Investment Dispute Settlement: A Stocktaking* UNCTAD (Mar. 2019), *available at* https://unctad.org/en/PublicationsLibrary/diaepcbinf2019d3_en.pdf.

96 *Id.*

97 *Supra* note 93, at 415.

98 Roberts and Bouraoui (2018b).

into consideration, there is no need to overemphasise their importance. If, in a particular state, an investment agreement with a stipulated arbitration mechanism has been publicly criticised, that government is advised to explain to the general public the rationale for the criticised agreement. It does not necessarily imply that the international community must reshape the existing system, which could also be perceived negatively by that general public. Global concerns require global solutions. However, there is no persuasive reason to design global solutions to a local concern.

Most concerns would benefit when supported with facts, i.e. some verifiable data proving that a particular concern is a product of a particular system. A review of current trends reveals that there is, at present, no formalised or predictable process to address the interplay of these issues. Although this approach should be adopted with caution, it appears to represent an appropriate balance between addressing negative perceptions and facts, thereby enhancing the systemic legitimacy of ISDS.

Consistency and Predictability

Russian delegates have described the current system as piecemeal emphazing the need to streamline the application of standards in a practical context. The system is not uniform and even fragmentary. IIAs are an agreement between so that the divergence in terms of the content of such agreements is natural. But it appears that this is not a problem of the system as a whole, or arbitration as a dispute settlement mechanism. As such, this problem is intrinsic to the application of various standards. For instance, there may be issues with respect to the qualification and expertise of the arbitrators appointed by parties. In this regard, this is essentially a problem of those arbitrators, rather than the system.

Inconsistency is both a weak and strong point of the ISDS system. An additional reason supporting this statement is that the absence of a universal system helps better accommodate states' regional interests. Each agreement is a result of a negotiation process which includes political questions, trade system concerns, and distinct elements of national legal systems. Therefore, the ability to design the customised content of an agreement is a disadvantage, but an advantage of the system. Rule-making may be "haphazard, messy, and uneven, depending on what is needed and what is feasible in a given constellation of interests and forces."[99] These rationales for divergence play out in different combinations and to differing degrees with respect to states' regional ambitions.

Highlighting the importance of a practical solution to inconsistency, Russia has underscored the general nature of the arguments of the delegates because one particular arbitration relates to one particular treaty applicable to particular states, but not to the whole system.[100] Therefore, it is a huge misperception of reality to claim

---

99 Sauvant (2016).

100 Recording: UN Comm'n. on Int'l Trade Law, 35th Sess. (Apr. 23–27, 2018), *available at* http://www.uncitral.org/uncitral/audio/meetings.jsp.

that different decisions are being rendered in different corners of the world. Russian delegates argue that it is hardly feasible to arrange a uniform and unified system since IIAs are different per se. Consistency, therefore, shall be ensured in a practical context, which is a problem for a particular agreement and particular arbitrators, rather than the overall system.

Arbitrator Appointments

Throughout the reform discussions Russia has repeatedly emphasised the need to gather opinions from commercial arbitration centres in relation to the appointment of arbitrators as this will make the reform discussions comprehensive and integrated. Russian delegates believe that it is wrong to say that a system where parties assume the responsibility to appoint arbitrators, does not ensure impartiality and independence. The problem does not lie in the appointment mechanism but guaranteed compliance by arbitrators with the requirements.[101]

Perhaps even more surprising than the frequency of such arguments is that the appointment of arbitrators became the only concern which gained Russia's attention in the 36th meeting in Vienna. Generally speaking, Russia shared the general concern about compliance with the standards of independence and impartiality of arbitrators, but questioned the need for a code of ethics for arbitrators. Also, Russia asked for statistical data which would prove that arbitrators decide in favour of an appointing party.[102] This is a significant issue in its own right. A commonly-held belief has been that investment arbitrators, in an effort to please both parties and to win repeat appointments, often issue compromise decisions that will to some extent satisfy each party.[103] Another frequently-held belief maintains that investment arbitrators are usually biased against the respondent State and are more inclined to decide in favour of investors.[104] However, occasional studies[105] tend to reject both of these common beliefs: investment arbitrators usually issue an unbiased decision based on the evidence in each case as they strive to be fair and impartial in their decisions because they place a high value on their reputations.[106]

The best explanation to the serious attention Russia appears to give to the appointment of arbitrators in ISDS is simple legitimacy. The right to choose and appoint an arbitrator is what distinctly positions arbitration within dispute settlement mechanisms including any national court system. This right is inherent to the legitimacy

[101] *Supra* note 92; *supra* note 100.

[102] UN Comm'n. on Int'l Trade Law, 36th Sess. (Oct. 29–Nov. 2, 2018), *available at* http://www.uncitral.org/uncitral/audio/meetings.jsp.

[103] Blythe (2013).

[104] Alvarez (2008) (reviewing Gus van Harten, Investment Treaty Arbitration and Public Law (2007)).

[105] Kapeliuk (2010).

[106] *Supra* note 103, at 278.

of an arbitral award. Thus, Russia views the potential reform of the appointment mechanism in this connection as irrational and unreasonable.

Will Russia Ever Go to ICSID?

The approach to international arbitration taken by Russia—the most economically and politically influential CIS member state—has been in a state of flux in recent years.[107] Furthermore, the behaviour of Russia with respect to ratification demonstrates an unstable relationship with international regulatory framework. To illustrate, Russia ratified the New York Convention[108] in 1960 and is a signatory to the Kiev Convention.[109] Russia signed the ICSID Convention in 1992, but has not ratified it yet. Furthermore, while Russia is ignorant of the ICSID Convention, little mention (if any) is made about the exact origins of such ignorance. Likewise, although Russia signed the Energy Charter Treaty (ECT)[110] in 1994, it withdrew from the Treaty in 2009 via an effective termination of the provisional application, stating its intent not to become an ECT Contracting Party.[111] Arguably, this is a smart strategic move as the withdrawal triggered certain legal implications in the arbitration practice. Most notably, in *Yukos Universal Limited v. Russia*, the PCA award was revoked essentially because the ECT had not been ratified by the signatories. This meant that Russia was not bound by it. However, from 1994 to 2009, Russia applied the Treaty provisionally, albeit the application was fairly limited. Thus, notwithstanding its economic and political influence, "Russia has not developed as a major international arbitration jurisdiction."[112]

One avenue, which Russia may rely on to develop as a major international arbitration jurisdiction is the ratification of the ICSID Convention. Nothing in the text of the ICSID Convention can be interpreted so as to put a State in a deliberately vulnerable position. Among other things, Article 25(4) provides an opportunity for a State at the time of ratification to specify "the class or classes of disputes" which could be submitted to the jurisdiction of the ICSID. This means that when joining the ICSID Convention Russia can choose at its own discretion and in its best national interests to narrow down the list of arbitrable disputes administered by ICSID. It is, however, a topic for a separate discussion whether such an opportunity can be used wisely, as may be questioned after the arbitration law reform in Russia which

[107] Finizio and Beale (2014).

[108] United Nations Convention on the Recognition and Enforcement of Foreign Arbitral Awards (June 10, 1958), U.N. Doc. E/CONF.26/8Rev.1.

[109] Kiev Convention on Settling Disputes Related to Commercial Activities (Mar. 20, 1992), *available at* http://cisarbitration.com/wp-content/uploads/2017/02/Kiev-Convention-on-Settling-Disputes-Related-to-Commercial-Activities-russian.pdf.

[110] Energy Charter Treaty (December 17, 1994), I-36116 https://treaties.un.org/Pages/UNTSOnline.aspx?id=2&clang=_en

[111] For details, see Mironova (2014).

[112] *Supra* note 107, at 21.

introduced in September 2016 a license regime for arbitration institutions willing to permanently arbitrate in Russia.[113] As part of *travaux préparatoires*, in early 2014, the Russian Ministry of Justice proposed draft legislation designed "to make Russia a more attractive jurisdiction for international dispute resolution."[114] Yet, this draft legislation has been heavily criticised for, among other things, "failing to sufficiently narrow the scope of non-arbitrable disputes in Russia."[115]

Some mention should also be made of Article 26 which allows a State to require the exhaustion of local remedies as a condition of its consent to arbitration under the ICSID Convention. This provision adds another layer of confidence for a State unwilling to submit exclusively to an international arbitral institution, despite the fact that the ICSID arbitral awards are commonly recognised as "more easily enforceable and predictable compared with other international tribunals."[116] For this reason alone, it is hard to conclude that the ICSID Convention can in any way jeopardise the position of a joining State. On the other hand, the ratification of the ICSID Convention could be problematic from the viewpoint of not being able to annul an award on the ground of public policy exception because the ICSID Convention does not include public policy exceptions to enforce an award.[117] Elaborating on these propositions, so far Russia has not enforced a single arbitral award issued against it by an international investment tribunal.

The ICSID Convention has consistently attracted attention from major developed capital-exporting countries and developing capital-importing countries, with the most recent valuable addition to the ICSID system being Mexico.[118] Not only does this reinforce the numerical and geographical expansion of the ICSID membership, but also indicates the truly adequate nature of the ICSID Convention. Furthermore, no political aspect, such as a potential constraint to state sovereignty, is a demotivating barrier in this context.

The motivations for the disinterest in the ratification of the ICSID Convention are somewhat unclear in light of recent developments in investment treaty policy of Russia. Back in 2001 the Government of the Russian Federation adopted the Russian

---

[113] Federal Law On Arbitration Proceedings (Arbitration Courts) in the Russian Federation (No. 382-FZ, Dec. 29, 2015) (Russia); Federal Law On Amendments to Certain Legislative Acts of the Russian Federation and Repeal of Article 6.1(3) of the Federal Law on Self-Regulating Organization in Connection with the Adoption of the Federal Law On Arbitration Proceedings (Arbitration Courts) in the Russian Federation (No. 409-FZ, Dec. 29, 2015).

[114] *Supra* note 107, at 21.

[115] *Id.*

[116] Wenjing (2017).

[117] ICSID Convention, Articles 50–52.

[118] Mexico signed the International Centre for Settlement of Investment Disputes (ICSID) Convention last January 11, 2018. Upon the Senate's approval of the Convention, Mexico's president published the instrument in Mexico's Public Gazette (Diario Oficial de la Federación) and submitted the ratification instrument to ICSID on July 27, 2018. As a result, based on Article 68(2) of the ICSID Convention, this instrument formally came into force for Mexico on August 26, 2018. With Mexico, there are now 162 signatory states of the ICSID Convention, and 154 members.

Model BIT.[119] Basically, it reiterates the common refrain of the replaced Model BIT of 1992.[120] Yet, there were some novelties with respect to the dispute resolution mechanism. For instance, it introduced a landmark provision which recommended ICSID as an arbitral institution. Seemingly, this indicated a reviving interest in the ICSID membership, or a fragile willingness to start co-operation with ICSID. In practice, this means that foreign investors may have access to ICSID arbitration via the ICSID Additional Facility Rules.[121] Here, it is explicitly allowed by investment treaties with those countries that have not ratified the ICSID Convention. Ironically, Russia, which is not a party to the ICSID Convention, agreed to use the ICSID Additional Facility Rules to resolve disputes by virtue of regional conventions.[122]

The BITs between Russia and China, Japan, Singapore, UAE, and more recently, Cambodia expressly provide that investors may submit disputes for ICSID arbitration. If so, can foreign investors from these countries submit disputes with Russia to ICSID? A simple answer is yes. These BITs provide that if the ICSID Convention is effective in both countries, investors may submit disputes to ICSID pursuant to the ICSID Convention; if it is not effective in either country, investors may choose to apply the ICSID Additional Facility Rules.[123] It should be noted, however, that the ICSID Additional Facility Rules arbitration is not as enforceable as ICSID arbitration pursuant to the ICSID Convention, but "their awards are still more credible with more predictable results than other international investment arbitral awards."[124] Unlike the ICSID awards, "awards rendered under the ICSID Additional Facility Rules are subject to the supervision of a national court, and their enforcement is covered by the New York Convention."[125]

The new 2016 Regulation introduces a more stringent approach to some of the key provisions in a Russian Model BIT. The 2016 Regulation does not specify which international arbitration rules are to be included in new investment treaties. In the meantime, it explicitly encourages selection of the UNCITRAL Arbitration Rules where a dispute is submitted to an ad hoc arbitration.[126] These introductions mean that Russia might be willing to negotiate BITs which are more in line with the exact level of protection readily available to foreign investors in Russia. Consequently, investors could benefit from more certain protections than they currently have.

---

[119] Decree of the Government of the Russian Federation on Entering into International Treaties on the Encouragement and Mutual Protection of Investments between the Government of the Russian Federation and the Governments of Foreign States (Collection of Russian Federation Legislation, June 18, 2001, No. 25. at 2578).

[120] Decree of the Government of the Russian Federation No. 395 (June 11, 1992)

[121] Adopted on Sept. 27, 1978.

[122] See, e.g., CIS (Moscow) Convention for the Protection of Investors' Rights 1997; EurAsEc Convention for the Promotion and Mutual Protection of Investments 2008; Treaty on the Eurasian Economic Union 2014.

[123] China-Russian Federation BIT 2006, Article 9(1)(b).

[124] *Supra* note 116.

[125] Kryvoi (2018).

[126] Addendum 2 to the Regulation 2016, Article 53.

A common narrative assumes that access to ICSID arbitration is appealing to foreign investors and constitutes a motivating factor when planning investment paths. At present, there is no official position by Russia's authorities as to the ratification of the ICSID Convention. Whether or not Russia will ratify the ICSID Convention in the future, choosing a BIT that agrees on ICSID arbitration is good for protecting investors' interests.[127] Naturally, a treaty-based recourse to arbitration under the ICSID Additional Facility Rules does not provide new guarantees to investors with respect to investment treaty arbitration. However, this ICSID-bound mechanism is still a welcoming shift in position. Russia seems to be flirting with the idea of becoming a full-time member of ICSID at some point which cultivates the perfect environment for the ICSID community to provoke negotiations with Russia on ICSID membership. In the long run, it takes two to tango.

Conclusion

Russia is a significant state in the UNCITRAL Working Group III and any slight shifts in its approach in the UNCITRAL reforms are closely watched. During the previous 34th and 35th meetings, Russia was very opposed to multilateral reform efforts and consistently downplayed the need for public law measures such as transparency and multilateral investment courts. Yet, the 36th meeting in Vienna in October–November 2018 saw Russia less vocal and even silent on issues such as inconsistency. Whether Russia's position has softened or not, it is the right time to provide an analytical framework for understanding Russia's position in these reform dynamics.

Russia has an important voice in discussions, representing a major variation to the reform proponents. As one commentator noted, the bigger question is whether some of the states "that are less keen on a multilateral solution such as a multilateral investment court, will propose working on other options, such as a range of incremental reforms like developing a code of conduct or putting together a series of "best practices" on issues like multiple proceedings, non-disputing party submissions and frivolous claims."[128] We conclude that Russia has not submitted any such proposals to date. Improving the regime requires great effort, a considerable amount of time, and even more patience. As the preceding discussion highlights, there are a number of competing considerations that need to be taken into account in determining whether, and to what extent, multilateral solutions should be implemented in the ISDS reform. Above all, improvements in the ISDS regime need to be in the interest of governments, both in their status as home and host states, and other key stakeholders, to give it the legitimacy and robustness that every international regime requires to be viable.

---

[127] *Supra* note 116.

[128] Roberts (2018a).

It would seem that discussing a reform within different dogmatic camps is like the men, in the old Buddhist parable,[129] asked to identify what animal is in a dark room. Each of them was allowed to touch only one part of an elephant. As accurate as each of the men may be in their individual study of a particular part, it is unlikely they will discover the true nature of the animal unless they compare notes and communicate.

To avoid this problem and more accurately gauge the true nature of the ISDS reform, the Working Group III delegates should communicate their reform proposals as to the desired directions of a single reform or a suite of reforms. The broader implication of this discussion is that the current approach to the ISDS reform, which is largely chaotic and uncoordinated, is not satisfactory to capture the range of issues that are involved. This article has studied Russia's stance in the UNCITRAL Working Group III to push back on the misperception that Russia is opposed to reform as such, and it has reveals doctrinal implications about its behaviour.

Finally, by adding ICSID considerations, this article aims not to issue a final statement or make projections (which is always hard and not always reliable) about Russia's approach toward the ratification of the ICSID Convention, but rather to spark a renewed, more nuanced discussion of Russia's foreign investment policy and national and international actors that shape it.

References

Alvarez J (2008) Recent book on international law: book review. Am J Int'l L

Arato J (2018) A watershed moment for ISDS reform. International Economic Law and Policy Blog (Nov. 4, 2018). Available at https://worldtradelaw.typepad.com/ielpblog/2018/11/a-watershed-moment-for-isds-reform.html#_edn1

Bartholomeusz L (2005) The Amicus Curiae before international courts and tribunals. Non-St. Actors Int'l L 5:211

Bianchi A (2013) On power and illusion: the concept of transparency. In: Bianchi A, Peters A (eds) International law in transparency in international law, vol 1

Bjorklund A (2007) Private rights and public international law: why competition among international economic law tribunals is not working. Hastings L J 59:251

Bjorklund A (2009) The emerging civilization of investment arbitration. Penn St L Rev 113(4):1290–1294

Blythe S (2013) The advantages of investor-state arbitration as a dispute resolution mechanism in Bilateral investment treaties. Int'l Law 47:278

Bruce Goldstein E (2010) Encyclopedia of perception, vol 492. SAGE Publications

Buys C (2009) The tensions between confidentiality and transparency in international arbitration. Am Rev Int'l Arb 14:121

Choudhury B (2008) Recapturing public power: is investment arbitration's engagement of the public interest contributing to the democratic deficit? Vand J Transnat'l L 41:775

Curran V (2009) Comparative law and the legal origins thesis: "[N]on scholae sed vitae discimus. Am J Comp L 57(4):865

de Brabandere E (2011) NGOs and the "Public Interest": the legality and rationale of Amicus Curiae interventions in international economic and investment disputes. Chi J Int'l L 12:86–87 & 94 (2011)

[129] See Blind men and an elephant. Bruce Goldstein (2010).

Dolzer R, Schreuer C (2008) Principles of international investment law, vol 133
Esty D (2006) Good governance at the supranational scale: globalizing administrative law. Yale L J 115:1546
Finizio S, Beale K (2014) Russian arbitration reforms. Repatriating Russian disputes. Comm Disp Res 5:21
Grill A (2017) Mind the label: loyalists and reformists and ISDS. Kluwer Arbitration Blog (29 Dec 2017). Available at http://arbitrationblog.kluwerarbitration.com/2017/12/29/uncitral-isds-working-group-vienna-11-12-2017
Hope J (2016) Transparency in international arbitration, commercial dispute resolution, commercial dispute resolution (May 11, 2016). Available at https://www.cdr-news.com/categories/expert-views/6376-transparency-in-international-arbitration
Kapeliuk D (2010) The repeat appointment factor: exploring decision patterns of elite investment arbitrators. Cornell L Rev 96:89–90
Kochevar S (2013) Amici Curiae in civil law jurisdictions. Yale L J 122:1653
Krislov S (1963) The Amicus Curiae brief: from friendship to advocacy. Yale L J 72:704
Kryvoi Y (2018) Ratification of arbitration-related conventions by CIS states: global and regional framework. CIS Arb F. Available at http://www.cisarbitration.com/2018/05/18/ratification-of-arbitration-related-conventions-by-cis-states-global-and-regional-framework/
Labin D, Soloveva A (2018) International investment law as international law: Russian and western approaches. AJIL Unbound 112:202
Lamb S et al (2017) Recent developments in the law and practice of Amicus Briefs in investor-state arbitration. Ind J Arb L 5(2):90
Legum B (2005) Investment treaty arbitration's contribution to international commercial arbitration. Disp Res J 60:73
Levine E (2011) Amicus Curiae in international investment arbitration. Berkeley J Int'l L 29:208
Mironova I (2014) Russia and the energy charter treaty. International Energy Charter, 7 Aug 2014. Available at https://energycharter.org/what-we-do/knowledge-centre/occasional-papers/russia-and-the-energy-charter-treaty
Mistelis L (2005) Confidentiality and third-party participation: UPS v. Canada and Methanex Corp. v. USA. In: International investment law and arbitration, vol 169. Cameron
Newcombe A, Lemaire A (2001) Should Amici Curiae participate in investment treaty arbitrations? Vindobona J Int'l Comm L Arb 5:22
Roberts A, Bouraoui Z (2018a) UNCITRAL and ISDS reforms: what are states' concerns? EJIL: TALK! (June 5, 2018). Available at https://www.ejiltalk.org/uncitral-and-isds-reforms-what-are-states-concerns
Roberts A, Bouraoui Z (2018b) UNCITRAL and ISDS reforms: concerns about consistency, predictability and correctness. EJIL: TALK! (June 5, 2018). Available at https://www.ejiltalk.org/uncitral-and-isds-reforms-concerns-about-consistency-predictability-and-correctness
Roberts A, Bouraoui Z (2018c) UNCITRAL and ISDS reforms: concerns about arbitral appointments, incentives and legitimacy. EJIL: TALK! (June 6, 2018). Available at https://www.ejiltalk.org/uncitral-and-isds-reforms-concerns-about-arbitral-appointments-incentives-and-legitimacy
Roberts A, Bouraoui Z (2018d) UNCITRAL and ISDS reforms: concerns about costs, transparency, third party funding and counterclaims. EJIL: TALK! (June 6, 2018). Available at https://www.ejiltalk.org/uncitral-and-isds-reforms-concerns-about-costs-transparency-third-party-funding-and-counterclaims
Roberts A (2018) UNCITRAL and ISDS reforms: moving to reform options… the process. EJIL: TALK! (Nov. 7, 2018). Available at https://www.ejiltalk.org/uncitral-and-isds-reforms-moving-to-reform-options-the-process/#more-16626
Roberts A (2018b) Incremental, systemic, and paradigmatic reform of investor-state arbitration. Am J Int'l L 112(3):410
Rogers C (2006) Transparency in international commercial arbitration. U Kan L Rev 54:1301

Saravanan A, Subramanian SR (2016) The participation of Amicus Curiae in investment treaty arbitration. J Civil Legal Serv 5:4
Saravanan A, Subramanian S (2018) Transparency and confidentiality requirements in investment treaty arbitration. Brics L J 5(4):115
Sauvant K (2016) Lessons from the negotiations of the United Nations code of conduct on transnational corporations and related instruments. In: Lim C (ed) Alternative visions of the international law on foreign investment: essays in honour of Muthucumaraswamy Sornarajah, vol 192
Schill S (2001) W(h)ither fragmentation? On the literature and sociology of international investment law. Eur J Int'l L 22:887
Schill S (2010) Crafting the international economic order: the public function of investment treaty arbitration and its significance for the role of the arbitrator. Leiden J Int'l L 23:401
Shelton D (1994) The participation of nongovernmental organizations in international judicial proceedings. Am J Int'l L 88(4):612
Stewart R, Badin M (2011) The world trade organization: multiple dimensions of global administrative law. Int'l J Const L 9:582
Vierucci L (2008) NGOs before international courts and tribunals. In: Dupuy P, Vierucci L (eds) NGOs in international law: efficiency in flexibility? p 160
Wälde T (2009) Interpreting investment treaties: experiences and examples. In: International investment law for the 21st century—essays in honour of Christoph Schreuer, vol 724. Oxford University Press
Weiler J (2001) The rule of lawyers and the ethos of diplomats. J World Trade 35(2):194–197
Wenjing T (2017) Investing in Russia? Lessons learnt from the Yukos and Sanum cases. Lexology China L Insight 24 Mar 2017. Available at https://www.lexology.com/library/detail.aspx?g=bfbafe0f-1486-429f-99a9-cedf908adaaa

Dmitry K. Labin Professor of International Law at MGIMO University—Moscow, Russia; Editorial board member of the Moscow Journal of International Law, J.D. in International Private and Public Law (MGIMO), Ph.D (Institute for State and Law of the Russian Academy of Sciences), Doctor of Laws (Institute for State and Law of the Russian Academy of Sciences).

Alena V. Soloveva Ph.D. Candidate at MGIMO University—Moscow, Russia; Associate at an international law firm Kennedys (Moscow, Russia), B.A. (MGIMO), LL.M. (UCL)

Chapter 7
Two Bites at the Same Apple?: 'Derivative' ISDS Proceedings in the Revised Korea-US FTA

Jaemin Lee

KORUS Amendment and the Investment Chapter

The Republic of Korea ("Korea") and the United States of America ("US") concluded a Free Trade Agreement ("FTA") on March 15, 2012.[1] Among many features contained in the FTA, investment arbitration (Investor-State Dispute Settlement: "ISDS") proceedings set forth in Chapter 11 of the agreement turned out to be one of the stickiest and most controversial issues.[2] Since then, many observers have been closely watching how the ISDS mechanism in the Korea-US FTA ("KORUS")[3] is

---

[1] Office of the United States Trade Representative (USTR), *US—Korea Free Trade Agreement*, *available at* https://ustr.gov/trade-agreements/free-trade-agreements/korus-fta (last visited on Mar. 24, 2024).

[2] In many countries, the investment arbitration mechanism has become one of the most important issues in any BIT discussion and negotiation. See UNCITRAL, *Report of Working Group III (Investor-State Dispute Settlement Reform) on the work of its thirty-fourth session (Vienna, Nov. 27– Dec. 1, 2017)*, A/CN.9/930/Add.1/Rev.1, 51st session (Jun. 25–Jul. 13, 2018). This mechanism began to draw global attention starting from late 1990s. See Jackson et al. (2000).

[3] The full text of the Korea-US FTA is *available at* http://www.fta.go.kr/us/doc/1/ (last visited on Mar. 24, 2024).

This article was published by the Journal of East Asia and International Law, vol. 12, Issue 1 on May 30, 2019, and is now reproduced with the permission of the journal.

J. Lee (✉)
School of Law, Seoul National University, Seoul, South Korea
e-mail: jaemin@snu.ac.kr

© The Author(s), under exclusive license to Springer Nature Singapore Pte Ltd. 2024

S. Wei (ed.), *International Investment Law at the Juncture*, International Law in Asia,
https://doi.org/10.1007/978-981-97-2183-2_7

applied and implemented in practice. The level of interest and concern has further ratcheted up with the advent of the first ISDS proceeding initiated under the KORUS in 2018.[4]

In September 2017, at the request of the Trump Administration of the US, the two countries initiated negotiations to amend the KORUS.[5] Agreed in March 2018, the amended KORUS was signed in September 2018. After completing the two countries' domestic procedures, the amended KORUS went into effect on January 1, 2019.[6] Major areas so amended are (i) enhanced US access to the Korean automobile market[7]; (ii) improvement of procedures to verify countries of origin under the KORUS[8]; (iii) changes of Korea's pharmaceutical product pricing policies[9]; (iv) enhanced procedural due process in US trade remedy investigations against Korean exports[10]; and, most importantly, (v) updates of the investment chapter.[11]

In terms of legal complexity and systemic implication, the fifth agenda—revision of the investment chapter—stood out from the pack. Year-long negotiations to amend the investment chapter received a significant amount of attention both in Korea and the US. There are two reasons for this heightened attention. First of all, ISDS reform has suddenly become a hot topic in the global community at present.[12] As such, how Korea and the US agree to amend their FTA investment chapter prompted keen

---

[4] Since 2012, seven cases have been submitted for ISDS proceedings against the government of the Republic of Korea under various IIAs (as of Mar. 16 2019). Three of them are filed by US investors under the KORUS. The three proceedings were all raised in 2018. They are *Elliott Associates, L.P. v. Republic of Korea*; *Mason Capital L.P. and Mason Management LLC v. Republic of Korea* (PCA Case No. 2018–55); and *Jin Hae Seo v. Republic of Korea.* See United Nations Conference on Trade and Development ("UNCTAD"), *Investment Dispute Navigator, Korea, Republic of—As Respondent, available at* https://investmentpolicyhub.unctad.org/ISDS/CountryCases/111?partyRole=2 (last visited on Mar. 24, 2024).

[5] USTR, *Statement on the Conclusion of US-Korea (KORUS) FTA Meetings in Seoul*, (Jan. 2 2018), *available at* https://ustr.gov/about-us/policy-offices/press-office/fact-sheets/2018/january/statement-conclusion-us-korea-korus-0; For an overview of the renegotiation see Congressional Research Service, *US South Korea (KORUS) FTA,* (Dec. 28, 2018), *available at* https://fas.org/sgp/crs/row/IF10733.pdf (last visited on Mar. 24, 2024).

[6] Ministry of Trade, Industry and Energy, *Korea's National Assembly Ratifies Revised KORUS FTA,* (7 December 2018), *available at* http://english.motie.go.kr/en/pc/pressreleases/bbs/bbsView.do?bbs_cd_n=2&bbs_seq_n=685 (last visited on Mar. 24, 2024).

[7] See The Office of the United States Trade Representative, *Fact Sheet on US-Korea Free Trade Agreement Outcomes,* (Sept. 2018), *available at* https://ustr.gov/about-us/policy-offices/press-office/fact-sheets/2018/september/fact-sheet-us-korea-free-trade (last visited on Mar. 24, 2024).

[8] See *Id.*

[9] *Id.*

[10] See *Protocol between the Government of the Republic of Korea and the Government of the United States of America Amending the Free Trade Agreement between the Republic of Korea and the United States of America*, signed in New York on Sep. 24, 2018, para 3, *available at* https://ustr.gov/sites/default/files/files/agreements/FTA/KORUS/KORUS%20Protocol%20Amending%20Agreement%20-%20Signed.pdf (last visited on Mar. 24, 2024).

[11] See *Id.* at para. 4.

[12] See Chap. 2 of this article.

attention from other countries trying to "test the water." Secondly, because the investment chapter was the most controversial topic during the negotiation of the original KORUS in 2006–2007, how the chapter was to be amended this time naturally drew the attention of the watchers and the general public of the two countries.[13]

More than anything else, the ongoing global discussion on the ISDS reform significantly affected the bilateral KORUS amendment negotiation. Both Korea and the US have been actively participating in the global ISDS reform discussion. Apparently, the two countries must have felt compelled to reflect recent developments in the amended KORUS investment chapter.[14] This meant that the two countries also had to make a difficult decision as to which reform topic to include and which to leave out for now, since the level of consensus among the international community varies from topic to topic. As a result, only those issues with relatively clearer global support found their way into the amended KORUS investment chapter.

Newly added wordings and provisions have certainly modernized the original text of the investment chapter of the KORUS and clarified the meaning of some key provisions. They are (i) clarification of the meaning of the Fair and Equitable Treatment ("FET") provision[15]; (ii) clarification of the meaning of the Most Favored Nation ("MFN") treatment[16]; (iii) clarification of the meaning of the National Treatment ("NT")[17]; (iv) regulation of frivolous claims of investors[18]; and (v) suppression of parallel or multiple proceedings by related investors.[19] Among these, items (i), (ii), and (iii) address substantive norms, while (iv) and (v) target ISDS proceedings in a way that protects host state governments in potentially 'abusive' ISDS proceedings. All in all, the items included in the amendment represent an evolution and development of international investment norms, both substantively and procedurally, so as to ensure a more balanced legal system codified in International Investment Agreements ("IIAs").[20]

That said, it seems that the amended KORUS still contains a critical loophole. Despite the addition of new provisions and further clarification, a 'back door' arguably still remains open for 'multiple, subsequent or parallel' ISDS proceedings to be initiated essentially by the same investor against the same measure. This article calls this situation a 'derivative' ISDS proceeding. The term "multiple, subsequent or parallel" proceedings is frequently used at the moment in the ISDS reform context, but it apparently covers a broad range of situations where simply a series of proceedings are constituted either simultaneously or consecutively against a host

[13] Cho (2017); Schott (2017).

[14] For the amended text, *see Protocol between the Government of the Republic of Korea and the Government of the United States of America Amending the Free Trade Agreement between the Republic of Korea and the United States of America,* para. 4.

[15] *Id.* at para 4, sub-para (d).

[16] *Id.* at para 4, sub-para (a).

[17] *Id.* at para 4, sub-para (a).

[18] *Id.* at para 4, sub-para (l).

[19] *Id.* at para 4, sub-para (i).

[20] The term IIAs refer to both Bilateral Investment Treaties ("BITs") and investment chapters of FTAs.

state government. It should be noted that some of these simultaneous or consecutive proceedings are permitted under the IIAs, mainly because of the fragmented nature of IIAs. Therefore, the problem here lies in the fundamental nature of IIAs' fragmentation, with more than 3,300 IIAs globally. The cure for this problem is necessary and has been explored, but lies beyond the control of any one or two states. On the contrary, *certain* 'multiple, subsequent or parallel' proceedings arguably constitute abuse of process or illegitimate expansion of a treaty provision in a way that has not been envisaged by drafters or in a way that even goes against the basic design of the IIA at issue.

This article focuses on the latter category of 'multiple, subsequent or parallel' proceedings. To distinguish the latter from the former, the term 'derivative' proceeding is used in this article to describe the latter situation. This term is chosen to convey the meaning that the simultaneous or consecutive proceedings are in fact 'derived' from the initial, original ISDS proceedings. It implies that the same (or related) investor constitutes yet another ISDS proceeding against the same (or virtually identical) governmental measure, in contravention of the original intent of the contracting parties. In short, the investor is attempting to have a second bite at the same apple.

To clarify, this is not the fault of the negotiators from Korea or the US. If anything, derivative proceedings have not been on the list of ISDS reforms in a clear manner. The current ISDS reform debates, while identifying many important concerns and suggesting alternatives to address those concerns, have apparently failed to address this very issue upfront. The current ISDS reform debates do include the topic of "cost and duration," one of whose sub-categories relates to a situation of multiple, subsequent or parallel proceedings against the same governmental measure. Current discussion of "cost and duration," however, does not include a situation where multiple, subsequent, or parallel proceedings are raised by essentially the same investor against essentially the same measure—a situation that is called "derivative" proceedings in this article. As such, broadly treated regulation of multiple proceedings may let this abusive tactic remain unregulated. The KORUS amended investment chapter showcases this phenomenon.

This article is composed of four parts including Introduction and Conclusion. Section 2 discusses derivative ISDS proceedings in the general architecture of the current ISDS reform discussions. Section 3 then looks into the provisions of the KORUS relating to this issue, followed by legal analyses of the provisions, where still remaining loopholes for and possibilities of derivative proceedings are explained.

Derivative ISDS Proceedings in the ISDS Reform Discussion

The present ISDS reform discussion in the global community was kick-started by the proposal of the European Union ("EU") in September 2015.[21] The EU proposal criticized the current IIAs and their ISDS system, which suggested a new scheme to overhaul the present framework in a significant manner, including, most notably, the creation of a new standing international court to resolve investment disputes.[22]

It is agreed that investment disputes tend to touch upon issues of public concern. In the words of Cecilia Malmström, the EU Commissioner for Trade: "There is a fundamental and widespread lack of trust by the public in the fairness and impartiality of the old ISDS model. This has significantly affected the public's acceptance of ISDS and of companies bringing such cases."[23] The ISDS system's 'asymmetric structure,' wherein only a foreign investor can initiate an action, is another source that further deepens public concern.[24] The concern is again amplified because it is an ad hoc arbitration, as opposed to an ordinary international adjudication that is used to resolve these sensitive disputes.[25] Sometimes inconsistent and incorrect decisions,[26] a direct outcome of the fragmentation of international investment law and the absence of multilateral regime,[27] render the entire mechanism vulnerable to continuing criticism. In that respect, concerns over the ISDS mechanism are not just confined to capital importing developing countries, but have gradually expanded to capital exporting developed countries.[28]

Against this backdrop, in late 2017, the United Nations Commission on International Trade Law ("UNCITRAL") began a project to deliberate over possible ISDS reforms.[29] While other fora such as the International Center for the Settlement of

---

[21] See Malmström (2015).

[22] See generally European Union (2019); European Commission (2015); Woods (2016).

[23] See Malmström (2015).

[24] *See* Garcia et al. (2018).

[25] Compare Koskenniemi (2017).

[26] See UNCITRAL, *Report of Working Group III (Investor-State Dispute Settlement Reform) on the work of its thirty-fourth session (Vienna, Nov. 27–Dec. 1, 2017)*, A/CN.9/930/Add.1/Rev.1, 51st session (Jun. 25–Jul. 13, 2018), paras. 26–30; Note by the Secretariat, Possible Reform of Investor-State Dispute Settlement (ISDS): Consistency and Related Matters (2018) (ISDS Reform Note), A/CN.9/WG.III/WP.150, para. 4. Compare *SGS v. Pakistan* award para. 170 (finding that the umbrella clause provision 'was *not* meant to project a substantive obligation like those set out in Articles 3 to 7' of the Switzerland-Pakistan BIT) (emphasis in original) with Switzerland Note on Switzerland-Pakistan BIT ('the Swiss authorities are alarmed about the very narrow interpretation' of the applicable umbrella clause by the *SGS v. Pakistan* tribunal) and *SGS v Philippines*, ICSID Case No. ARB/02/6, Decision of the Tribunal on Objections to Jurisdiction (Jan. 29, 2004) paras. 120, 125 (reasons offered by *SGS v Pakistan* tribunal in support of its 'highly restrictive interpretation' of an umbrella clause provision were 'unconvincing').

[27] Pauwelyn (2014).

[28] Nottage (2017); Hamamoto (2015).

[29] UNCITRAL, Working Group III, *Investor-State Dispute Settlement Reform*, available at https://uncitral.un.org/en/working-group/3/investor-State State.html (last visited on Mar. 24, 2024). This initiative follows the publication of a paper by the UNCITRAL Secretariat, *Possible Reform of*

Investment Disputes ("ICSID") and the Organisation of Economic Co-operation and Development ("OECD") are also actively looking into the issue of ISDS reform, the UNCITRAL has been the most active and comprehensive venue for the discussion so far.

Identified Concerns and Suggested Course of Action

The UNCITRAL discussions have offered the states opportunities to register their concerns over the present ISDS mechanism and to propose various ideas to reform it. The discussions have been taking place at Working Group III, one of the six working groups of the UNCITRAL. States' concerns as expressed during the UNCITAL meetings are (i) inconsistency in arbitral decisions; (ii) limited mechanisms to ensure the correctness of arbitral decisions; (iii) lack of predictability; (iv) appointment of arbitrators by parties; (v) the impact of party-appointment on the impartiality and independence of arbitrators; (vi) lack of transparency; and (vii) increasing duration and cost of the procedure.[30]

The identified concerns and possible alternatives to address such concerns are listed in the table attached as an annex to this article. As the discussions are still going on at the UNCITRAL as of this writing, it is still too early to offer definitive conclusions on these issues in the attached table. Nonetheless, the table offers an overview of the current concerns and emerging ideas to counter them.

Some issues in the attached table relate to a structural flaw in the system. Other issues concern the perception of the general public toward the ISDS proceedings. Even if only perception is involved, it still matters. To borrow the famous words of a Chief Justice of the English Courts in this regard: "Justice should not only be done, but should manifestly and undoubtedly be seen to be done."[31] The statement applies to ISDS proceedings with equal force. Should justice not be seen to be done in the eyes of the general public, it is itself a problem.

Generally speaking, the current UNCITRAL discussion looks to a successful cousin in the international economic law, the World Trade Organization ("WTO") and its dispute settlement body. Despite the surge of global protectionism and the lack of its leadership as the hub of multilateralism, the WTO is regarded as offering a far more elaborated and systematic structure in terms of a global legal system. The WTO also tried to strike a balance between the two competing objectives: a government's right to regulate and treaty obligations.[32] Regardless of the current setbacks of the WTO, the dispute settlement mechanism and the role of its Appellate Body may

---

Investor- State Dispute Settlement (ISDS), 34th session (Sept. 18, 2017) UN Doc A/CN.9/WG.III/WP.142.

[30] See UNCITRAL, *Possible future work in the field of dispute settlement: Reforms of investor-State dispute settlement (ISDS)*, A/CN.9/917, 50th session (Jul. 3–21, 2017), paras. 11–12.

[31] Lord Chief Justice G. Hewart in *R v Sussex Justices, Ex Parte McCarty* [1924] 1 KB 256.

[32] Wagner (2014).

shed helpful light on the present discussion of ISDS reforms. As such, the WTO's experience, both good and bad, is being relied upon by countries for guidance in the ISDS reform discussion.

Cost and Duration

In practice, "cost and duration" is a real concern for states participating in ISDS proceedings. Strong consensus has been formed to introduce a new system where litigation costs can be reduced and the length of the proceedings shortened. "Cost and duration" gets more serious attention because ISDS disputes deal with sovereign states' authority to regulate.[33] Obviously, the problem of cost and duration raises a particular concern for developing states that have difficulty in defending themselves against foreign investors.[34]

Firstly, litigation cost is a huge concern for a state.[35] A 2017 study illustrates the financial burden for parties participating in ISDS proceedings. According to the study, an average claimant-investor assumes a total litigation cost of USD 6,019,000, while an average respondent-state faces a total litigation cost of USD 4,855,000. In addition to these party costs, the organization and administration of an average arbitration tribunal requires additional cost of USD 933,000.[36] So, taken together, the total average cost for an ISDS proceeding stands at USD 11,807,000.[37] As a respondent state is supposed to take up a half of the tribunal cost, a state usually looks at a total spending of USD 5,321,500 on average, which is arguably a significant financial burden for the state. Undeniably, the burden becomes more acute for a developing state. It should be also borne in mind that this is just the cost for one proceeding: in the case of multiple proceedings, the cost increases proportionately.

A surge of the cost has led to yet another new phenomenon of third-party funding, i.e., a financing method in which an outside private entity agrees to finance an ISDS proceeding for an investor in anticipation of remuneration once the investor prevails in the proceedings.[38] This funding scheme certainly helps destitute investors finance their ISDS litigation and ensure their access to justice.[39] At the same time, third party

---

[33] Roberts (2013).

[34] Riesenberg (2011) *et seq.* See also UNCTAD, *Reform of Investor-State Dispute Settlement: In Search of a Roadmap,* International Investment Agreement Issues Note, No. 2 (Jun. 2013) at 4.

[35] See Gaukrodger and Gordon (2012).

[36] Hodgson and Campbell (2017).

[37] *Id.*

[38] See Nieuwveld and Sahani (2017); Henriques (2017).

[39] Goeler (2016); Henriques, *supra* note 38, at 127–128.

funding may also bring into question the very integrity of an ISDS proceeding by commercializing ISDS claims.[40]

Secondly, duration of a case is also a major practical concern for a state. One recent study found that the average duration of ICSID ISDS proceedings is calculated as 3.75 years, or 1,370 days (with median of 1,266 days).[41] For the UNCITRAL ISDS proceedings, the average duration stands at 3.96 years, or 1,446 days (with median of 1,246 days).[42] In 2011, the Arbitration Institute of the Stockholm Chamber of Commerce ("SCC") reported the average length of an investment case under its rules as 21 months.[43] The average four-year duration for the ICSID and UNCITRAL proceedings, which take up a majority of ISDS proceedings, means that governmental agencies and officials of a respondent state should be involved in and follow up an ISDS proceeding for a lengthy period of time. This obviously causes a significant logistical burden for the state.

The issue of the increasing cost and duration should be put into perspective. That is, the entire caseload continues to expand.[44] The number of known treaty-based ISDS disputes reached 855 by the end of 2017 including 65 cases initiated in that year.[45] In total as many as 109 states out of the 193 UN members have been drawn to the proceedings as respondents so far. In this context, 'multiple, subsequent or parallel' ISDS proceedings are causing a serious concern for states. The workload and financial burden would simply multiply if a state had to defend itself in many litigation proceedings at the same time or in sequence. It is true that multiple proceedings are sometimes inevitable because of the fragmented nature of the international investment law composed of more than 3,300 IIAs globally. Granted, many different investors could initiate multiple ISDS proceedings against the same host state government for the same government measure based on their respective IIAs. Likewise, it is legally and logistically possible for an investor to initiate multiple ISDS proceedings under multiple IIAs simultaneously against the same governmental measure of a respondent state, unless there is a provision explicitly prohibiting such a scheme. Not surprisingly, the respondent state would face a higher burden and increased pressure in a multiple proceeding scenario than an ordinary, single-case

[40] Stoyanov and Owcarzek (2015). For an overview of some notable conferences dedicated to the issue see Seidel (2013); Darwazeh and Leleu (2016); Goeler, *supra* note 39, at 87–88; Nieuwveld & Sahani, *supra* note 38, at 16.

[41] Jeffery Commission, *How long is too long to wait for an award,* Global Arbitration Review, (Feb. 18, 2016); *How Much Does an ICSID Arbitration Cost? A Snapshot of the Last Five Years, Kluwer Arbitration Blog,* (Feb. 29, 2016); and *The Duration and Costs of ICSID and UNCITRAL Investment Treaty Arbitrations, Funding in Focus Report Three,* (Vannin Capital, Jul. 2016), *available at* https://www.vannin.com/downloads/funding-in-focus-three.pdf (last visited on Mar. 24, 2024) The study is based on an analysis of 138 ICSD arbitration between 2011 and 2015.

[42] *Id.*

[43] SCC Statistics (2011), p. 4, *available at* https://sccinstitute.com/statistics/statistics-2008-2016/ (last visited on Mar. 24, 2024).

[44] Roberts (2013).

[45] UNCTAD, *Investment Dispute Settlement Navigator, available at* http://investmentpolicyhub.unctad.org/ISDS (last visited on Mar. 24, 2024).

ISDS scenario. Financial and logistical burden would increase substantially in such circumstances. Therefore, it is critical to contemplate and introduce a system where the number of (unnecessary or illegitimate) disputes can be regulated or suppressed.

As "cost and duration" is one of the main concerns of the states as regards the ISDS system,[46] it is critical that future IIAs contain provisions that can help reduce the cost and duration of the proceedings. Many options are being contemplated in this regard. Early dismissal of frivolous claims, consolidation of related claims, creation of a legal advisory center, awarding legal fees and expenses for successful host states, and restriction of multiple, subsequent or parallel proceedings are such examples. These are vehicles that can help drive down the overall cost and duration of litigation from the perspective of a host state.[47] Some of these suggestions are now being accepted and implemented in recent IIAs.[48]

Thus, addressing multiple, subsequent or parallel ISDS proceedings is an important challenge for states within the context of "cost and duration." Identifying and regulating such circumstances have become one of the key topics in the ISDS reform discussion and IIA negotiations at the moment. The original KORUS[49] and the amended KORUS[50] contain provisions to that effect as well. These provisions in KORUS and other IIAs help regulate multiple, subsequent or parallel proceedings. But, critically, they fail to fully identify and regulate the situation of 'derivative' proceedings.

Derivative Proceedings

The current discussions at the UNCITRAL regards the issue of "cost and duration" as one of the core items of the ISDS reform, in which the regulation of multiple, subsequent or parallel proceedings constitutes a key sub-item. Multiple, subsequent or parallel proceedings are not taking up the bulk of the ISDS proceedings yet, but they are turning out to be a real threat for a respondent state. *Ampal-American and others v. Egypt*[51] offers an example in this regard, where four parallel ISDS proceedings went ahead with essentially the same factual matrix, the same witnesses

[46] See UNCITRAL, *Possible reform of investor-State dispute settlement (ISDS)*, A/CN.9/WG.III/WP.149, 37th session (Sept. 5, 2018), at 4.

[47] It should be noted that "cost and duration" is also an important consideration factor for an investor. Claimant investors usually purport to reduce the overall time for a proceeding by opposing 'bifurcation' so as to expedite the proceeding. They also consider finding sources of financing from third party funding mechanisms that reduce their financial burden during the proceeding.

[48] See, e.g., KORUS (Amended) Articles 11.20.8, 11.25, 11.26.2.

[49] See KORUS Article 11.18, para 2.

[50] See KORUS Article 11.18, para 2.

[51] *Ampal-American Israel Corp., EGI-Fund (08–10) Investors LLC, EGI-Series Investments LLC, BSS-EMG Investors LLC and, BSS-EMG Investors LLC and David Fischer v. Arab Republic of Egypt* (ICSID Case No. ARB/12/11), Division on Jurisdiction, 1 February 2016, *available at* https://www.italaw.com/cases/1926 (last visited on Mar. 24, 2024); UNCTAD, "Investor-State Dispute

and identical claims. The current intensity and frequency of ISDS proceedings highly indicate the likelihood of similar occurrences in the future. So, the approach taken in the current ISDS reform discussion is all the more appropriate.

In the present discussion, however, what is omitted is a situation where an investor purports to abuse the process, by repeating or duplicating ISDS proceedings against the same governmental measure.[52] Increasingly, states are faced with such proceedings. Consider *CME Czech Republic (The Netherlands) v. Czech Republic*[53] and *Lauder v. Czech Republic*,[54] where the two cases had essentially the same facts: the latter involving Lauder himself submitting a claim to arbitration against the Czech Republic under the US-Czech Republic BIT, while the former involved Lauder's Dutch subsidiary submitting a claim to arbitration under the Netherlands-Czech Republic BIT. Similar undertakings also took place in *Orascom v. Algeria*.[55] They involve essentially the same investor against the same governmental measure. Although in a slightly different context, advance planning of ISDS proceedings using subsidiaries or affiliated entities located in multiple jurisdictions was also observed, and in fact presented as a contentious issue in *Philip Morris v. Australia*,[56] *Phoenix Action Ltd v Czech Republic*,[57] *Pac Rim v El Salvador*,[58] and *Aguas del Tunari v. Bolivia*.[59] Critics pinpoint the problem,[60] with structural advantages for multinational corporations being underscored.[61]

If the IIAs at issue do not contain provisions to prohibit these options and planning, it would be hard to close the avenue. On the other hand, if there is a provision in an IIA to that effect (i.e., to close such an avenue), and yet the provision is not tight or clear enough to prevent an investor from utilizing such a loophole, that would be a different story. The UNCITRAL discussions, and others for that matter, have not yet identified or taken up this issue, which would leave the host states in a vulnerable

Settlements: Review of Developments in 2016", International Investment Agreements Issues Note (May, 2017), at 10.

52 See UNCITRAL, *Possible reform of investor-State dispute settlement (ISDS)*, A/CN.9/WG.III/WP.149, 37th session (Oct. 29–Nov. 2, 2018).

53 UNCITRAL, Award (Mar. 14, 2003).

54 UNCITRAL, Award (Sept. 3, 2001).

55 *Orascom TMT Investments S.a.r.l. v. People's Democratic Republic of Algeria* (ICSID Case No. ARB/12/35), Award, May 31, 2017, *available at* https://www.italaw.com/cases/2040 (last visited on Mar. 24, 2024); UNCTAD (2018) (discussing three arbitrations under different investment treaties by different companies controlled by the same shareholder).

56 *Philip Morris Asia Limited v. The Commonwealth of Australia*, UNCITRAL, PCA Case No. 2012–12, *available at* https://www.italaw.com/cases/851 (last visited on Mar. 24, 2024).

57 *Phoenix Action, Ltd v Czech Republic*, ICSID Case No ARB/06/5, Award (Apr. 15, 2009), *available at* https://www.italaw.com/cases/850 (last visited on Mar. 24, 2024).

58 *Pac Rim Cayman LLC, v Republic of El Salvador*, ICSID Case No ARB/09/12, Decision on the Respondent's Jurisdictional Objections (Jun. 1, 2012), *available at* https://www.italaw.com/cases/783 (last visited on Mar. 24, 2024).

59 Agua del Tunari, S.A. v. Republic of Bolivia, ICSID Case No., ARB/02/3, *available at* https://www.italaw.com/cases/57 (last visited on Mar. 24, 2024).

60 Wehland (2016); Valasek and Dumberry (2011).

61 Maupin (2014); Puig (2015); Klett (2016).

situation even with a (loosely worded) provision regulating multiple, subsequent or parallel proceedings. This problem has not received adequate attention yet. The reason may be that the discussion on "cost and duration" still remains in the early stage, so that states have not had time to contemplate all aspects of the issue.

The original and amended KORUS include provisions to identify and regulate such multiple, subsequent or parallel proceedings by the same investor against the same government measure. In other words, derivative proceedings are marked up in the bilateral FTA. This is a reflection of the intention of the contracting parties to regulate such derivative proceedings. In that respect, the KORUS sets forth an updated version of text in this area. That said, however, the wording of the provisions of the KORUS still leaves open a possibility for an investor to still attempt to circumvent the provisions and pursue derivative proceedings. Clearer provisions and tighter regulation would have closed out this back-door avenue, as intended by negotiators of the two countries.

KORUS Provisions and Legal Issues

Prompted by the increasing concerns over the ISDS mechanism generally and the possibility of multiple, subsequent or parallel proceedings specifically, the KORUS contains provisions to address the problems. The original KORUS included provisions for this purpose, while the 2018 amended KORUS introduced further stipulation in that regard. The fortification notwithstanding, an avenue for derivative proceedings still remains unclosed.

Provisions in the Original KORUS

Multiple, subsequent or parallel proceedings were a major source of concern early on in the context of the KORUS investment chapter. As such, the original KORUS contained various provisions to address the problem. For instance, the KORUS contains a standard consolidation clause in Article 11.25.[62] This is a legal wherewithal to collapse concurrent ISDS proceedings where common legal and/or factual issues are involved.[63] Obviously, a respondent state stands to benefit from such streamlined

---

[62] The article provides, in pertinent part, the following:

Article 11.25: Consolidation

1. Where two or more claims have been submitted separately to arbitration under Article 11.16.1 and the claims have a question of law or fact in common and arise out of the same events or circumstances, any disputing party may seek a consolidation order in accordance with the agreement of all the disputing parties...

3. Unless the Secretary-General finds within 30 days after receiving a request ...that the request is manifestly unfounded, a tribunal shall be established under this Article.

[63] See Id.

and converged proceedings in terms of efficiency and simplicity. These concurrent ISDS proceedings being contemplated in consolidation provisions, however, involve *different* investors against the same or similar government measures of a host state. In other words, it covers 'multiple' proceedings but not 'derivative' proceedings.

Likewise, the imposition of time limits within which to bring ISDS claims is another way to address the problem of multiple, subsequent or parallel proceedings. Article 11.18 of the KORUS stipulates this scheme.[64] Under the provision, a claim should be brought to an ISDS proceeding within three years from an investor's knowledge of violation.[65] Multiple, subsequent or parallel proceedings will be suppressed to some extent due to this de facto statute of limitation.

A coordination provision also helps address the problem.[66] This is a provision which recommends that plural arbitration tribunals covering related issues coordinate among themselves. The KORUS has provisions to this effect in Articles 11.25.6 and 11.25.10. Albeit indirectly, these provisions also help states respond to multiple proceedings arising from the same events or occurrences. They foster efficiency of the related proceedings and deter potential abuse of process by investor-claimants.

Most notably, the original KORUS introduced a provision that stipulates a "fork in the road" in an ISDS proceeding. This provision was explained during the original negotiation period of 2006–2007 as one of the critical safeguards for a host state's government attempting to avoid or reduce multiple proceedings.[67] More specifically, Article 11.18 of the KORUS provides that a 'waiver' of other legal proceedings should be given by a claimant as a specific 'condition' to submit any claim to an ISDS proceeding under the agreement. Article 11.18 (Conditions and Limitations on Consent of Each Party) provides in pertinent part:

> [...]
>
> 2. No claim may be submitted to arbitration under this Section unless: (a) the claimant consents in writing to arbitration in accordance with the procedures set out in this Agreement; and
>
> (b) the notice of arbitration is accompanied,
>
> (i) for claims submitted to arbitration under Article 11.16.1(a), by the claimant's written waiver, and

---

[64] The article provides:

Article 11.18: Conditions and Limitations on Consent of Each Party

1. No claim may be submitted to arbitration under this Section if more than three years have elapsed from the date the claimant first acquired, or should have first acquired, knowledge of the breach alleged under Article 11.16.1 and knowledge that the claimant (for claims brought under Article 11.16.1(a)) or the enterprise (for claims brought under Article 11.16.1(b)) has incurred loss or damage

[65] See *Id.*

[66] The EU-Vietnam FTA contains an interesting provision addressing the coordination between the settlement of an investor-State dispute under the permanent tribunal and a concurrent submission of a claim to State-to-State dispute settlement. *See* Article 8.8 (providing that where claims "concerning the same treatment" are brought before the two fora, a division of the tribunal constituted to hear the investor-State dispute shall "take into account proceedings pursuant to [the FTA's section on State-to-State settlement]" and "[t]o this end, it may also, if it considers necessary, stay its proceedings").

[67] Shin and Chung (2015).

> (ii) for claims submitted to arbitration under Article 11.16.1(b), by the claimant's and the enterprise's written waivers of any right to initiate or continue before any administrative tribunal or court under the law of either Party, *or other dispute settlement procedures, any proceeding with respect to any measure alleged to constitute a breach referred to in Article 11.16.*
>
> […] [Emphasis added]

Article 11.18 dictates that a claimant make a choice, at the time of the initiation of an ISDS proceeding, between a domestic court or tribunal of a host state and an ISDS path.[68] Once a decision is made, the investor cannot move backwards or change its decision. At the same time, the claimant-investor also promises to forego its right to proceed to "other dispute settlement procedures … with respect to [the] measure" being alleged to be in violation under Article 11.16.[69] The term "other dispute settlement procedures" here plausibly includes other ISDS proceedings. In short, a foreign investor is precluded to proceed to any other ISDS proceeding once s/he initiates one under the KORUS. Thus, a strong "fork in the road" is stipulated in this provision. It should be noted, however, that the operating terms here are 'investor' and 'measure.' In other words, this waiver or attached condition applies to the same investor against the same measure. Assuming (either technically or legally) different investors come in against different measures, the strong "fork in the road" provision above may not be able to achieve its basic objective, even if the investors or the measures are to be regarded as virtually the same.

Provisions in the Amended KORUS

The 2018 amended KORUS makes a new attempt to further tighten the loose end of provisions relating to multiple, subsequent or parallel proceedings. Finally noting that, despite all the safeguards in the KORUS, *affiliated* entities are still able to file multiple, subsequent or parallel proceedings after an ISDS proceeding is initiated by a covered investor, Korea and the US agreed to include a new provision in the agreement. Article 11.18.4 of the KORUS thus provides:

> 4. (a) An investor of a Party may not initiate or continue a claim under this Section if a claim involving *the same measure or measures* alleged to constitute a breach under Article 11.16 and *arising from the same events or circumstances* is initiated or continued pursuant to an agreement between the respondent and a non-Party by:
>
> (i) a person of a non-Party that owns or controls, directly or indirectly, the investor of a Party; or
>
> (ii) a person of a non-Party that is owned or controlled, directly or indirectly, by the investor of a Party.
>
> (b) Notwithstanding subparagraph (a), the claim may proceed if the respondent agrees that the claim may proceed, or if the investor of a Party and the person of a non-Party agree

[68] See KORUS Article 11.18, para 2.

[69] *Id.*

> to consolidate the claims under the respective agreements before a tribunal constituted under this Section. [Emphasis added]

The entire provision above is a new addition from the 2018 amendment. Basically, this provision prohibits a covered investor from resorting to an ISDS proceeding under the KORUS if one of its affiliated entities has initiated an ISDS proceeding under a different IIA or if such an ISDS proceeding remains pending. This provision has been touted as one of the critical updates of the amendment.[70] Indeed, this provision is supposed to fill a crucial loophole concerning derivative proceedings. Advance or subsequent planning using subsidiaries or affiliated entities is now to be regulated. On its surface, this provision offers a strong regulation. If an ISDS proceeding is ever initiated or continued under any other IIA, a Korean or US investor may not initiate or continue an ISDS proceeding under the KORUS. In other words, a prior initiation or subsequent initiation under other IIAs during the pendency of an ISDS proceeding under KORUS will lead to the termination of the KORUS proceeding due to the lack of jurisdiction by the KORUS ISDS tribunal.

This is an important addition. By way of comparison, this provision is not found in the *Agreement between the United States of America, the United Mexican States, and Canada* ("USMCA"), a successor to the North American Free Trade Agreement ("NAFTA"), signed by the three countries on November 30, 2018,[71] although it was negotiated by the US roughly within the same timeframe with the KORUS.[72] The above provision is an important stride in the right direction. And yet, this provision is still premised on the assumption of the existence of 'the same measure' and of the identification of 'control,' subjects that arguably lend themselves to different meanings and interpretations.

Legal Issues Relating to Derivative Proceedings

In essence, paragraphs 2 and 4 of Article 11.18 of the KORUS, taken together, set forth detailed rules to regulate and avoid derivative proceedings where an investor purports to have a second or third bite at the same apple through the ISDS mechanism. With a provision in the original investment chapter[73] and another one added in the 2018 amendment,[74] there seems to be an (erroneous and complacent) understanding that the current scheme restricting parallel proceedings is enough to counter the identified problems of derivative proceedings. In fact, the two provisions of Article 11.18 still contain critical ambiguities.

---

[70] Schott and Jung (2018), *Policy Brief 18–22,* at 5.

[71] The full text of the USMCA is *available at* https://ustr.gov/trade-agreements/free-trade-agreements/united-states-mexico-canada-agreement/agreement-between (last visited on Mar. 24, 2024).

[72] See USMCA, Chapter 22.

[73] See KORUS Article 11.18, para 2.

[74] See KORUS Article 11.18, para 4.

Both provisions aim to identify and deter derivative proceedings by prohibiting the same investor-claimant from pursuing duplicate ISDS proceedings for the same governmental measure. This scheme, however, is likely to be defeated because the current text of KORUS, along with most other IIAs for that matter, does not clearly circumscribe the meaning of (i) entities affiliated with an investor and (ii) challengeable governmental measures. Ambiguities left unattended have arguably opened a loophole of which an investor could attempt to take advantage. In other words, in essence, even under the amended KORUS an investor can initiate derivative proceedings against the same measure, either by wearing the cloak of an ostensibly different investor or by coming up with a different measure by adjusting the scope of what is essentially the same government measure. To the extent that avoiding derivative proceedings is of the utmost concern for a respondent state under the KORUS, it is imperative that these loopholes be filled appropriately through future clarification.

1. The Amorphous Concept of a "Measure"

Both paragraphs 2 and 4 of Article 11.18 are based on an assumption that the same measure is implicated. The term used in paragraph 2, sub-paragraph (b), item (ii) of Article 11.18 reads "with respect to any measure alleged to constitute a breach referred to in Article 11.16."[75] In contemplation, "measure … referred to in Article 11.16" here means the measure being challenged under the present ISDS proceeding. In other words, what is being waived by an investor in accordance with paragraph 2 is the right to litigate a case regarding the same measure that is now being brought to the present ISDS proceeding. Future proceedings against the 'same measure' is then forfeited by dint of the waiver. Thus, if a measure to be challenged in future ISDS proceedings is not the same as the one being challenged at present, the foreign investor is still arguably free to initiate and continue the challenge through a prospective ISDS proceeding in the future. Given the fact that a governmental 'measure' is broadly defined, covering both action and inaction of a government agency that affects the interest of a foreign investor,[76] an investor may try to break down a dispute into different measures through planning in advance.[77] One batch of a dispute can be raised first in an ISDS proceeding, and afterwards a remaining batch can be taken to another ISDS proceeding either simultaneously or successively. This would defeat the very objective of paragraph 2 of Article 11.18. Stated differently, the perception that there will always be a single measure in the entire universe of a particular investment dispute is not always accurate. It may be too naive an assumption.

Suppose that a dispute between an investor and a host government contains three different governmental measures such as tax measure, licensing measure, and environmental regulation measure adopted roughly around the same time when the relationship between the investor and the government went sour. Suppose, furthermore,

[75] KORUS Article 11.18, para 2, sub-paragraph (b), item (ii).

[76] Johnson et al. (2015).

[77] In the KORUS Investment Chapter, there is no provision that stipulates that entire measures involving the same investor at issue arising from the same circumstances should be brought to an ISDS proceeding in a single stroke.

that a foreign investor has raised two measures in an investment dispute with respect to the dispute at issue at an ISDS proceeding. If the investor raises a remaining third measure for the first time in a separate, future ISDS proceeding, either concurrently or subsequently, should it be considered the 'same measure' within the meaning of paragraphs 2 and 4 (in which case such an attempt will be rejected by a tribunal) or a different measure? In other words, even if the underlying circumstances leading to the dispute are the same it is still possible that different sets of measures exist or co-exist. Current provisions in Article 11.18 are not detailed and sufficient enough to deal with these delicate situations. If so, the purported objective of identifying and rejecting derivative proceedings may not be realized as easily as is intended by the drafters.

More importantly, derivative proceeding provisions are distinct from consolidation provisions. Indeed, consolidation provisions also play an important role in ISDS proceedings, but they serve different purposes. They purport to address a situation where *bona fide* different investors are challenging the same government measure.[78] Examples would include regulatory measures affecting a number of different investors at the same time. As the challenged measure is the same, efficiency would dictate related cases be consolidated and reviewed together.[79] Again, the critical element here is the existence of 'different' investors.[80] These different investors are entitled, in the first place, to pursue their own respective ISDS proceedings under applicable IIAs.[81] At the request of parties, related proceedings can be consolidated to be reviewed by a single arbitral tribunal.[82] This is merely an attempt to enhance efficiency and facilitate simultaneous resolution of a dispute.[83]

On the other hand, derivative proceedings imply abuse of process. They envisage a situation where essentially the same investor challenges the same governmental measure twice or three times.[84] If the basic underlying idea is for an investor to have a single bite at the apple, such proceedings would render the idea futile. Doing so would almost constitute an illegitimate circumvention of the related provisions. The problem of the current IIAs is that various 'multiple, subsequent or parallel proceeding' provisions are not formulated so as to achieve the intended objectives, which is, at least, to identify and eliminate 'derivative' proceedings. As much as derivative proceeding provisions aim to deal with abuse of process, they stand to be distinguished from consolidation provisions which is mainly about efficiency. In short, consolidation provisions would not be able to address the problem of derivative proceedings either.

2. The Indeterminate Nature of "Control"

---

[78] See KORUS Article 11.25.

[79] See *Id.*

[80] *Id.*

[81] *Id.*

[82] *Id.*

[83] See generally Kaufmann-Kohler et al. (2016).

[84] See KORUS Article 11.18, para 4.

In the same vein, the newly added provision includes the critical term 'control' in determining the existence of the same investor.[85] Article 11.18, paragraph 4 stipulates "control or ownership" to assess the closeness or proximity of affiliation between the investor in a prior ISDS proceeding and the one in a subsequent ISDS proceeding.[86] Between the two, the term 'ownership' is relatively easy to determine: the ownership or holdings by an investor *vis-à-vis* the other can be objectively investigated and confirmed. But the term 'control' is arguably more malleable and flexible, requiring a case-by-case examination taking into account the totality of circumstances. The existence or the absence of control is a contentious source of disputes in many international litigation. Mere reference to control could thus invite controversies and ensuing disputes in the actual application.

Critically, it does not seem clear what "control" means for the purpose of this provision. Multinational corporations own shares in various entities globally in various forms and quantities. They maintain a variety of arrangements for joint ventures and common undertakings. Identifying control from these webs of networks would be a difficult, if not entirely impossible, task. Given the importance of this provision, it is noteworthy that a definition or explanation of control is absent in the provision or in the chapter. Depending upon how control is understood, the scope of the new provision could oscillate between any two points widely apart—probably a source of another concern and dispute.

3. Suggestions for Future Clarification

In retrospect, clearer wording should have been adopted in both the negotiations of the original KORUS and the recently amended one. For instance, at the end of paragraph 2 of Article 11.18, now ending with "breach referred to in Article 11.16", the following wording could be inserted right after "in Article 11.16" in order to clarify: "whether or not it is raised in the present proceeding to the extent it arises from the same dispute under the totality of circumstances." Arguably, the new addition would make clear that any measure, whether it is being raised in the present ISDS proceeding or saved, knowingly or unknowingly, for future proceedings, is to be precluded from any future ISDS proceeding if the measure is considered to be part of the universe of the dispute that has triggered the investment dispute in the first place. The absence of such clarification in the present text has apparently left the door open for an investor to pursue 'derivative' proceedings in the future.

Likewise, the newly added paragraph 4 in Article 11.18 contains a similar problem. Certainly, paragraph 4 attempts to completments by regulating situations prior to the application of paragraph 2 and contains the wording: "a claim involving the same measure or measures alleged to constitute a breach under Article 11.16 and *arising from the same events or circumstances*." (emphasis added) So, presumably, a more tightened approach is being taken here, as not only the same measure but also the same events or circumstances are attached as a condition. The meaning of these "same events or circumstances", however, is not entirely clear. It is possible that a measure

[85] See *Id.*

[86] *Id.*

or measures stemming from the same events or circumstances have led to a 'dispute' between the investor and the host state. It is also possible, however, that a measure or measures stemming from many different events or circumstances have led to a dispute at hand. A more proper wording, therefore, would be "dispute" as opposed to "event" or "circumstance." In light of this, a more accurate and safer insertion would read, to be added right after "under Article 11.16" of the present text, "to the extent it arises from the same dispute under the totality of circumstances, whether or not it is raised in the present proceeding,...".

As can be seen in other agreements, more detailed guidelines would be necessary for the proper and effective application of the provisions in the future. By way of reference, similar attempts have been made in the renamed Comprehensive and Progressive Agreement for Trans-Pacific Partnership ("CPTPP"), [87] which entered into force on December 30, 2018, and USMCA although in a slightly different context.[88] The two agreements, while defining a State-Owned Enterprise ("SOEs") as "an enterprise that is principally engaged in commercial activities" and "is owned or controlled by the state," provides more detailed legal guidelines to determine "control" in the context of free trade agreements.[89] Those attempts and resulting implications can be borrowed for future clarification and elaboration of the above provisions in the KORUS.

These clarifications and elaborations do not necessarily require a further amendment of the agreement. The KORUS establishes a Joint Committee in accordance with Article 22.2, which is co-chaired by the United States Trade Representative and the Minister for Trade of Korea.[90] Critically, the Joint Committee is authorized to issue an interpretation of the provisions in the investment chapter that will 'bind' reviewing investment tribunals.[91] Thus, if and when the two countries agree, the Joint Committee is able to issue an interpretation of related provisions of the

---

[87] *Comprehensive and Progressive Agreement for Trans-Pacific Partnership Texts*, N.Z. FOREIGN AFF. & TRADE, available at https://mfat.govt.nz/en/free-trade-agreements/free-trade-agreements-in-force/ (last visited Mar. 24, 2024) *Who Needs America?*, THE ECONOMIST, Nov. 16, 2017, *available at* https://www.economist.com/news/finance-and-economics/21731428-eleven-countries-resurrect-trans-pacific-partnership-who-needs-america (last visited on Mar. 24, 2024).; Donnan (2017); Mulgan (2017).

[88] United States-Mexico-Canada Agreement, USTR, *available at* https://ustr.gov/trade-agreements/free-trade-agreements/united-states-mexico-canada-agreement (last visited on Mar. 24, 2024); Frankel (2018).

[89] See CPTPP Article 17.1, which provides:

For the purposes of this Chapter: ... state-owned enterprise means an enterprise that is principally engaged in commercial activities in which a Party: (a) directly owns more than 50 per cent of the share capital; (b) controls, through ownership interests, the exercise of more than 50 per cent of the voting rights; or (c) holds the power to appoint a majority of members of the board of directors or any other equivalent management body.

USMCA contains essentially the same provision in Article 22.1.

[90] See KORUS Article 22.2, paragraph 1.

[91] See KORUS Article 11.22.3, which provides:

3. A decision of the Joint Committee declaring its interpretation of a provision of this Agreement under Article 22.2.3(d) (Joint Committee) shall be binding on a tribunal, and any decision or award issued by a tribunal must be consistent with that decision.

KORUS so as to identify and deter derivative proceedings. Indeed, a missing part cannot be newly created because 'creation' is not an area of 'interpretation.' However, vague terms can be clarified and loose wording can be elaborated, a situation which would arguably fall under the realm of interpretation, which may help address the prospective problem of derivative proceedings.

Conclusion

The 2018 amendment of the KORUS is a hybrid outcome of many different factors. Needless to say, the Trump Administration's unilateralism on the trade front played an important role. It is also unusual, though not entirely unprecedented, for a treaty just five years old to be subject to an amendment negotiation. The overall score sheet is evaluated as largely reflecting the concerns and interests of the US, most notably with respect to the contentious auto trade.

That said, the amendment has made an important stride in the investment chapter of the KORUS. The two countries made efforts to incorporate new developments in the international community regarding the reform of the ISDS mechanism. The amendment introduced several components where strong global consensus has been confirmed thus far. The best example is a new provision to regulate multiple, subsequent or parallel ISDS proceedings involving the same measure of a respondent state. Such a phenomenon arises in the case of multinational corporations that have a plethora of IIA choices due to a number of subsidiaries and affiliated entities in many different countries. These multiple, subsequent or parallel proceedings exert a significant legal and logistical burden on a respondent state that is forced to defend a series of proceedings simultaneously or consecutively. This realization has prompted the global community to include this topic as one of the key items in the currently ongoing ISDS reform discussions. The 2018 KORUS amendment incorporated this very issue in the investment chapter, which is regarded as an important update for the chapter.

At the same time, the new provisions in the chapter contain inherent limitations. They do not fully address a situation where different measures arising from the same dispute are involved. Given that the definition of a governmental measure is quite broad and flexible, a measure can be broken down into sub-measures or plural measures can be collapsed into a mega-measure, even if they are emanating from the same dispute between an investor and a host state. This means that the new provisions will not be able to fully prevent multiple, subsequent or parallel proceedings, arguably falling under an umbrella of the same dispute, from taking place. As a matter of fact, more detailed wording and elaborations would have been needed to achieve the intended objective of the drafters. Future tribunals may attempt to interpret the provisions in a tighter fashion, but there is no guarantee at this point. If anything, future Joint Committee decisions or additional amendment, when proper opportunities arise, will be able to face the problem and find a solution.

Likewise, the new introduction does not touch upon a more fundamental issue. Forum shopping creates a lopsided playing field in favor of investor- claimants. Forum shopping does not take place just within the IIAs. It also takes place horizontally, crisscrossing the boundary of international investment law, international trade law and possibly other sectors of public international law. Once a decision to choose an ISDS proceeding is made, it should foreclose other avenues to proceed to dispute settlement proceedings under other branches of international law. This part is not yet clear either under the current IIAs or the amended KORUS. It all depends upon how the term "measure" or "dispute" is understood or interpreted.

As the current global discussion has the potential to bring a significant change to the ISDS regime, it is not unthinkable that the two countries will have to meet again to incorporate further updates into the KORUS investment chapter in several years' time. In addition, Korea and the US will face amendments of other IIAs once the future course of the ISDS regime is mapped out as a result of the current discussion in various forums of the global community. These opportunities and experiences will enable Korea and the US to consider inserting new forms of wording and clarifying existing ones in the KORUS to address the increasingly contentious issue of multiple, subsequent or parallel ISDS proceedings.

Annex: ISDS Reform: Concerns, Options and Impacts[92]

Reform options for various concerns	Possible implications on the system
Common concern: inconsistency and lack of predictability	
Option: enhancing states' control over IIAs	• Introduces new mechanisms for IIA interpretation • Strengthens and generalizes existing mechanisms for IIA interpretation
Option: strengthening state-state framework	• Strengthens the role of states regarding their own IIAs • Develops pre-dispute consultation mechanism between states
Option: appellate mechanism to review awards and decisions of arbitral tribunals or investment courts	• Introduces an appellate review mechanism(s): either a stand-alone appellate body or respective appellate mechanisms for IIAs • Affects provisions in ICSID Convention & New York Convention

(continued)

[92] Table summarized and compiled by the author based on UNCITRAL document concerning the ISDS reform (United Nations Commission on International Trade Law, Working Group III (Investor-State Dispute Settlement Reform), Thirty-sixth Session, *Possible Reform of Investor-State Dispute Settlement (ISDS), Note by the Secretariat*, A/CN.9/WG.III/WP.149 (Sept. 5, 2018), at Annex).

(continued)

Reform options for various concerns	Possible implications on the system
Option: international investment court	• Needs to consider specifics such as functioning, composition, instruments, funding and judge selection of a new court • Needs to consider co-existence with the present ISDS regime or regional investment courts
Option: guidance to arbitral tribunals for such issues as consolidation, information exchange, stay of proceedings, preliminary rulings, etc	• Develops new legal standards and includes them in IIAs • Addresses abuse of process, judicial economy, and cost • Affects arbitral institutions, their rules, practices and role
Common concern: arbitrators/decision-makers	
Option: development of a code of conduct for arbitrators, decision makers, counsel and experts	• Introduces a new legal standard, enforcement mechanism and soft law to supplement and harmonize with existing ones • Requires changes in IIAs and rules and codes of arbitral institutions
Option: development of rules and procedures to strengthen existing challenge mechanisms	• Introduces a new legal standard and soft law guidance to strengthen and harmonize with the existing ones • Affects arbitral institution's practice and rules and domestic legislation
Options: enhances diversification of arbitrators and decision makers	• Establishes a new framework (either IIA, soft law, guidance or arbitration rules) to ensure participation of arbitrators, judges and decision makers with diverse backgrounds
Common concern: cost and duration	
Option: dispute prevention	• Develops good practices and institutional information • Addresses excessive financial burden on respondent States and SMEs
Option: promotion of dispute settlement methods other than arbitration	• Introduces and facilitates non-binding dispute settlement mechanism such as mediation or ombudsman
Option: expedited procedures for smaller claims and non-complex cases	• Develops rules and practice for expedited proceedings minding due process concerns • Amends IIAs and arbitration rules
Option: establishment of advisory centers	• Forms a convention-based entity that provide support to developing states and SMEs, similar to ACWL of the WTO • Considers logistics about funding, formulation, recruits, etc
Option: regulation of third-party funding (TPF)	• Introduces rules in IIAs & arbitration rules to regulate TPF • Causes impact (positive & negative) on the overall ISDS proceedings

(continued)

(continued)

Reform options for various concerns	Possible implications on the system
Option: replacement of ad hoc arbitrators by full-time judges	• Contemplates a permanent mechanism or body with full-time judges • Explores a new conventions or instruments to establish a standing body which may help reduce the overall litigation cost and time
Option: streamlined procedure and cost management	• Introduces stricter timelines and compliance mechanisms • Formulates an effective cost management system in IIAs and rules
Option: an effective early dismissal mechanism	• Ensures states to avoid unnecessary litigation and related costs • Amends IIAs and arbitration rules to reflect the objectives
Option: allocation of cost and security for costs	• Develops principles and rules to offer guidance to tribunals in allocating costs and ordering security for costs • Amends IIAs and arbitration rules to reflect these changes

References

Cho K (2017) Investor-state dispute system called “toxic provision” in KORUS FTA, Hankyoreh. Available at http://english.hani.co.kr/arti/english_edition/e_business/824008.html. Last visited on 16 Mar 2019

Darwazeh N, Leleu A (2016) Disclosure and security for costs or how to address imbalances created by third party funding. J Investment Arbitration 33: 125, 127–129

Donnan S (2017) Long live the TPP—pacific trade pact survives largely intact. Financial Times. Available at https://www.ft.com/content/c5cdd3aa-c82d-11e7-ab18-7a9fb7d6163e. Last visited on 16 Mar 2019

European Commission (2015) Commission proposes new investment court system for TTIP and other EU trade and investment negotiations. Press Release. Available at http://trade.ec.europa.eu/doclib/press/index.cfm?id=1364. Last visited on 16 Mar 2019

European Union (2019) Proposal for the reform of the ISDS mechanism for working group III discussion. Available at www.uncitral.org. Last visited on 16 Mar 2019

Frankel J (2018) Trump hasn’t improved on NAFTA—but at least he hasn’t blown up trade. The Guardian. Available at https://www.theguardian.com/business/2018/oct/09/donald-trump-nafta-trade-usmca. Last visited on 16 Mar 2019

Garcia F, Cho HJ, Santosuosso T, Scarlett R, Thrasher R (2019) The case against third-party funding in ISDS: executive summary, (Boston College Law School—PUC University of Chile, working group on trade & investment law reform, third-party funding task force 2018). Available at https://lawdigitalcommons.bc.edu/lsfp/1126/. Last visited on 16 Mar 2019

Gaukrodger D, Gordon K (2012) Investor-state dispute settlement: a scoping paper for the investment policy community. OECD working papers on international investment 2012/03 19. OECD Publishing

Goeler J (2016) Third party funding in international arbitration and its impact on procedure. Kluwer Law International, pp 82–83

Hamamoto S (2015) Recent anti-ISDS discourse in the Japanese diet: a dressed-up but glaring hypocrisy. J World Investment Trade 931
Henriques D (2017) Third-party funding: a protected investment? Spain Arbitration Rev 30:100, 115
Hodgson M, Campbell A (2017) Damages and costs in investment treaty arbitration revisited. Allen & Overy. Available at http://www.allenovery.com/SiteCollectionDocuments/14-12-17_Damages_and_costs_in_investment_treaty_arbitration_revisited_pdf. Last visited on 16 Mar 2019
Jackson J, Bronckers M, Quick R (2000) New directions in international economic law: essays in honour of John H. Jackso. Kluwer Law International, pp 392–393
Johnson L, Sachs L, Sachs J (2015) Investor-state dispute settlement, public interest and US domestic law. Columbia Center on Sustainable Investment (CCSI) Policy Paper, p 2. Available at http://ccsi.columbia.edu/files/2015/05/Investor-State-Dispute-Settlement-Public-Interest-and-US-Domestic-Law-FINAL-May-19-8.pdf. Last visited on 16 Mar 2019
Kaufmann-Kohler G, Chazournes L, Bonnin V, Mbengue M (2016) Consolidation of proceedings in investment arbitration: how can multiple proceedings arising from the same or related situations be handled efficiently. ICSID Rev For Investment Law J 21:59–125
Klett J (2016) National interest vs. foreign investment—protecting parties through ISDS. Tulane J Int Comp Law 25:228–229
Koskenniemi M (2017) It's not the cases, it's the system. J World Investment Trade 18: 343–352
Malmström C (2015) Proposing an investment court system. Available at http://ec.europa.eu/commission/2014-2019/malmstrom/blog/proposing-investment-court-system_en. Last visited on 16 Mar 2019
Maupin J (2014) Public and private in international investment law: an integrated systems approach. Va J Int Law 24:380
Mulgan A (2017) Japan's rush to conclude TPP-11. The Diplomat. Available at https://thediplomat.com/2017/11/japans-rush-to-conclude-tpp-11. Last visited on 16 Mar 2019
Nieuwveld L, Sahani V (2017) Third party funding in international arbitration (1), 2nd edn. Kluwer Law International
Nottage L (2017) Investor-state arbitration policy and practice in Australia. In: de Mestral A (ed) Second thoughts: investor-state arbitration between developed democracies. Centre for International Governance Innovation
Pauwelyn J (2014) At the edge of chaos? Foreign investment law as a complex adaptive system, how it emerged and how it can be reformed. ICSID Rev 29:372
Puig S (2015) The merging of international trade and investment law. Berkeley J Int Law 36–38
Riesenberg D (2017) Fee shifting in investor-state arbitration: doctrine and policy justifying application of the English rule. Duke L J 60:977–1013, 107
Roberts A (2013) Clash of paradigms: actors and analogies shaping the investment treaty system. Am J Int Law 107(1):45–94, 58–63
Schott J, Jung E (2018) KORUS amendments: minor adjustments fixed what trump called "Horrible Trade Deal". Peterson Institute for International Economics
Schott J (2017) Returning the KORUS FTA. Peterson Institute for International Economics. https://piie.com/blogs/trade-investment-policy-watch/retuning-korus-fta. Last visited on 16 Mar 2019
Seidel S (2013) Third-party investing in international arbitration claims. In: Cremades B, Dimolitsa A (eds) Third party funding in international arbitration, vol 18. ICC Publication No 752E
Shin H-T, Chung LK-H (2015) Korea's experience with international investment agreements and investor-state dispute settlement. J World Investment Trade 16:976
Stoyanov M, Owcarzek O (2015) Third-party funding in international arbitration: is it time for some soft law rules? BCDR Int Arbitration Rev 1(2):171
UNCTAD (2018) Investor-state dispute settlement: review of developments in 2017. International Investment Agreements Issues Note, p 11
Valasek M, Dumberry P (2011) Development in the legal standing of stockholders and holding corporations in 26:1 ISDS. ICSID Rev-For Investment Law J 60–61

Wagner M (2014) Regulatory space in international trade law and international investment law. U Pa J Int'l L 36(1):1–87

Wehland H (2016) The regulation of parallel proceedings in investor-state disputes. ICSID Rev 31(3):579–580

Woods L (2016) Fit for purposes? The EU's investment court system. Kluwer Arbitration Blog. Available at http://kluwerarbitrationblog.com/2016/03/23/to-be-decided/. Last visited on 16 Mar 2019

Chapter 8
Investor-State Mediation in a China-EU Bilateral Investment Treaty: Talking About Being in the Right Place at the Right Time

Chunlei Zhao

Introduction

In the field of international investment, the current Investor-State dispute settlement (hereinafter "ISDS") system[1] is largely dominated by adversarial rule-based arbitration, often preceded by power based negotiation, and supplemented by rule-based conciliation and interest-based mediation. In the past decades, however, focus has been squarely on arbitration,[2] while much less attention has been paid to the other available mechanisms.

In an on-going project, when there is a dispute between an investor and the host State, resolving the dispute is critical, but restoring the relationship and ensuring

[1] The phrase "Investor-State dispute settlement (ISDS) system" used in this paper refers to a comprehensive system composed of different mechanisms, such as negotiation, mediation, conciliation, and arbitration.

[2] This has promoted a strong backlash and various corresponding efforts to improve the situation. Criticism was made and measures were taken by different subjects (such as States, international institutions, scholars, and practitioners) on various issues (such as amicus curiae, transparency, and appeal mechanisms). Taking transparency as an example: To realize greater transparency in investment arbitration which had been held behind closed doors, there were efforts made by international institutions, such as the issuance of UNCITRAL Rules on Transparency in Treaty-based Investor-State Arbitration in 2014; by States, such as the EU's proposal of an investment court system characterized by transparency reflected in EU-Canada Comprehensive Economic and Trade Agreement (finally updated in 2016); and by academics, such as Stephan Schill, Transparency as a Global Norm in International Investment Law, Kluwer Arbitration Blog, 15 September 2014 (http://kluwerarbitrationblog.com/2014/09/15/transparency-as-a-global-norm-in-international-investment-law/) (accessed 4 December 2017).

C. Zhao (✉)
School of Law Mingli Building, Tsinghua University, Haidian District, Beijing 100084, China
e-mail: chunlei_zhao@mail.tsinghua.edu.cn

© The Author(s), under exclusive license to Springer Nature Singapore Pte Ltd. 2024

S. Wei (ed.), *International Investment Law at the Juncture*, International Law in Asia,
https://doi.org/10.1007/978-981-97-2183-2_8

continued operation of the investment project are of paramount importance. As was pointed out by the arbitral tribunal in *Achmea BV v Slovakia*, a black and white solution to a legal decision in which one side wins and the other side loses may not be the optimum outcome in every case.[3] So, when negotiations fail, rather than resorting to adversarial-based arbitration, a dispute settlement mechanism (hereinafter "DSM") that encourages creative and amicable solutions, based on the parties' interests, would contribute to that desired on-going cooperative relationship better than arbitration, which often acts to polarize the parties. In fact, a research study conducted by Roberto Echandi suggested that both investors and host States alike would benefit from settling their investment disputes short of adversarial proceedings, using means such as arbitration and litigation.[4]

Mediation, on the other hand, is not conceived as adversarial and, in recent years, it has been increasingly recognized for investment dispute resolution. Correspondingly, incipient measures have been taken to promote the use of Investor-State mediation. China and the EU, which are negotiating a China-EU Bilateral Investment Treaty (hereinafter "China-EU BIT"), have expressed clear intentions of developing mediation as one of the mechanisms to resolve Investor-State disputes. If successful, the prospective China-EU BIT, with its developed DSMs, such as mediation, can be a model for other treaties.

As such, this paper proposes that this is the right time and the prospective China-EU BIT is the right place to examine more in depth a carefully designed Investor-State mediation mechanism. In order to do so, this paper is divided into six sections. This introduction is Sect. "Introduction". Next, Sect. "Mediation—Valuable to ISDS and Indispensable to the ISDS System" analyses why mediation is valuable to ISDS and should be built into an ISDS system. Section "Recent Promotion of Investor-State Mediation by States and International Institutions" looks at the *status quo*, with special attention paid to recent developments in Investor-State mediation, including in international investment agreements (hereinafter "IIAs"),[5] and international institutions' promotion efforts. Section "Recognition of Mediation for Investment Dispute Resolution by China and the EU" focuses on the increasing use of mediation for ISDS, particularly by China and the EU. Then, Sect. "The Design of Investor-State Mediation in a China-EU BIT" offers some reflections on crucial but thorny issues regarding Investor-State mediation in the context of a China-EU BIT. The final Sect. "Conclusion" summarizes and concludes.

---

[3] In this case, at the end of a hearing, the tribunal observed that the aims of both sides seemed to be approximately aligned, and a legal decision was not the optimum outcome. Thus, it recommended the parties to seek out somebody acting as a mediator or reconciliatory to settle the dispute. See Achmea BV v. Slovakia, Final award, PCA Case No 2008-13 (7 December 2012), 14–15.

[4] Echandi (2013).

[5] In this paper, the phrase "international investment agreement (IIA)" is used in a broad sense, which refers to an agreement on investment concluded by States, no matter it is in the form of an independent treaty or part of a comprehensive economic agreement in a bilateral or multilateral context.

Mediation—Valuable to ISDS and Indispensable to the ISDS System

A DSM serves to resolve disputes, so the needs of disputing parties should weigh much in the evaluation of it. At the same time, a DSM usually exists in a dispute settlement system comprised of various DSMs that are expected to functionally supplement each other. As such, this section analyses Investor-State mediation from two perspectives: its value to ISDS and its function in an ISDS system.

A Valuable Dispute Settlement Mechanism to ISDS

An Investor-State dispute refers to a dispute over investment between an investor and its host State, the basis of which can be a contract between disputing parties or an IIA between the investor's home State and the host State. During the dispute settlement process, besides resolving the present dispute, continuing the involved investment project after dispute resolution is very often expected, but at risk.[6] The often-expressed desire of disputing parties for settling the dispute in a swift and cost-effective way and preserving the long-term link between the investor and the host State was particularly reviewed by the State Mediation Subcommittee on the occasion of an IBA annual meeting.[7] In addition, investment disputes are likely to be complex, involving both legal and non-legal issues, which requires thorough consideration of various elements. Therefore, solutions based on parties' interests, instead of lying strictly inside legal remedies, should be preferred.

In this regard, mediation has the potential to offer a viable option.[8] Generally speaking, mediation is defined as a confidential, informal, structured and voluntary mechanism, where disputes are resolved in an amicable and cost-effective process with the assistance from a third party.[9] It encourages parties to be forward-looking, and normally extra-legal interests are included in the discussion to permit the development of "integrative solutions".[10] In this way, mediation creates additional value by restructuring parties' relationship to make it as profitable as possible.[11] In addition, although mediation is mainly interest-based pursuant to parties' needs, it can

[6] It was pointed out that in fact, many investors who commenced Investor-State arbitration preferred to remain active participants in the host State market. See Jean E. Kalick, Mediation of Investor-State Disputes: Revisiting the Prospects, Kluwer Arbitration Blog, 2013 (http://kluwerarbitrationblog.com/2013/06/14/mediation-of-investor-state-disputes-revisiting-the-prospects/) (accessed 4 December 2017).

[7] Legum et al. (2013).

[8] Ali (2015); Ali and Repousis (2016–2017).

[9] Bradley (2010); Davidson (2012).

[10] Menkel-Meadow et al. (2010).

[11] Wälde (2006).

also be rule-based according to applicable laws, which creates flexibility when there is such a need.[12]

In brief, mediation can foster parties' understandings, reconcile their interests, repair the damaged relationship and contribute to further cooperation. By providing parties a process to "build upon consensual solutions that respect legitimate policy considerations and preserve on-going cooperative relationships",[13] mediation can add extra value to ISDS.[14]

An Indispensable Component of an ISDS System

There are several mechanisms of investment dispute resolution: arbitration and mediation, as mentioned, but also negotiation and conciliation.[15] Mediation is a necessary supplement to other DSMs for building a comprehensive architecture of an ISDS system. Its unique function cannot be substituted by arbitration, negotiation, conciliation or State-State mediation.

First of all, mediation and arbitration normally have distinct purposes, and hence distinct moralities—the morality of mediation lies in "optimum settlement", but that of arbitration is in "a decision according to the law of the contract".[16] In addition, in comparison with adversarial arbitration, the amicable environment in mediation is more suitable for restoring the relationship between disputing parties by encouraging investors and States to develop trust, or at least reduce distrust.[17] Particularly, recent decades have witnessed a public-minded revolution of Investor-State arbitration, making it more confrontational, more transparent, and more akin to litigation. As a result, aggressive positions are openly entrenched, and the final result can be unsatisfying, even to a winning party.[18] In short, mediation is more suitable for satisfying the need of interest-based solutions.

---

[12] Interest-based mediation and rule-based mediation are used to describe the mediators' function in the substantive aspect of dispute resolution—suggesting a resolution according to parties' interests or making an assessment of parties' positions based on the applicable law. See Schonewille and Lack (2014).

[13] Coe (2007).

[14] Welsh and Schneider (2013).

[15] Not all of these DSMs are included in an ISDS system under an IIA. For example, under the North American Free Trade Agreement (NAFTA), mediation is not provided for ISDS. See NAFTA (entered into force on 1 January 1994), Chapter 11.

[16] Fuller (1962).

[17] Bottini and Lavista (2010); Salacuse (2007); Esme Shirlow, The Rising Interest in the Mediation of Investment Treaty Disputes, and Scope for Increasing Interaction between Mediation and Arbitration, Kluwer Arbitration Blog, 2016 (http://kluwerarbitrationblog.com/2016/09/29/the-rising-interest-in-the-mediation-of-investment-treaty-disputes-and-scope-for-increasing-interaction-between-mediation-and-arbitration/) (accessed 4 December 2017).

[18] For example, in the case Metalclad v. Mexico (Metalclad Corporation v. The United Mexican States, ICSIID Case No. ARB(AF)/97/1 (19 May 1997)), after winning a $17 million USD arbitral award against Mexico, the Chief Executive Officer of Metalclad expressed regret at having resorted

Secondly, negotiation, which resembles mediation regarding its amicable feature, is less structured and, thus, the procedural predictability is lower. Also, without the assistance of a neutral third party, the communication between disputing parties in negotiation is liable to be affected by their power asymmetries. In this regard, mediators can help ameliorate the unpleasant influence of the imbalance and let parties "be realistic about their options" in a more organized process.[19]

Thirdly, conciliation is quite similar to mediation, but not identical. Traditionally, conciliation implies a rule-based process with a high level of institutionalization, while mediation implies a facilitative one with little institutional management.[20] The Investor-State conciliation in practice is represented by ICSID conciliation proceedings,[21] which is a lengthy and arbitration-like framework.[22] Among the scant eight concluded ICSID conciliation cases,[23] at least two of them lasted for about three years and appear to have taken the form of hard-fought trials.[24] In addition, although the ICSID Conciliation Rules do not contain any provision stipulating or indicating evaluating the merits of a dispute on a legal basis, as shown by a statement made by Lord Wilberforce as the conciliator in an ICSID conciliation case, the role of a conciliator was conceived as "to examine the contentions raised by the parties, to clarify the issues, and to endeavor to evaluate their respective merits and the likelihood of their being accepted, or rejected, in Arbitration or Court proceedings".[25]

---

to this mechanism by noting that despite "winning" the case, "the arbitration had been so dissatisfying that [he] wished the company had relied on other options to resolve the dispute". See Timothy Gracious, Investor-State Mediation/Conciliation in India, 2015 (www.mediate.com/articles/TimothyG3.cfm#) (accessed 4 December 2017). See also: Franck (2007); Jr Jack J. Coe, above n.13, 8–9.

[19] Nancy Welsh and Andrea Kupfer Schneider, above n.14, 82–83.

[20] Robert B. Davidson, above n.9, 521; Esme Shirlow, above n.17. For more discussion on the distinction between mediation and conciliation, see Lack (2011); Lack and Bogacz (2012).

[21] These proceedings were held under the auspices of the World Bank by applying ICSID Conciliation Rules or ICSID Conciliation (Additional Facility) Rules.

[22] Nitschke (2014); Shahla F. Ali and Odysseas G. Repousis, above n.8, 237. The ICSID conciliation procedures are similar to arbitration in many aspects, while admittedly with two key differences: first, conciliation procedures are more informal, less expensive and, potentially, less time-consuming; second, no binding award is rendered. See Nurick and Schnably (1986).

[23] ICSID, The Icsid Caseload–Statistics (Issue 2017-1), 2017, (https://icsid.worldbank.org/en/Documents/resources/ICSID%2OWeb%20Stats%202017-1%20(English)%20Final.pdf) (accessed 4 December 2017).

[24] These two cases are: RSM Production Corporation v. Republic of Cameroon, ICSID Case No. CONC/1/1 (This case was registered on 6 December 2011 and the Commission rendered its Report on 11 June 2013), and Republic of Equatorial Guinea v. CMS Energy Corporation and others, ICSID Case No. CONC(AF)/12/2 (This case was registered on 29 June 2012 and the Sole Conciliator rendered its Report on 12 May 2015). Based on the published procedural details, these two conciliation cases went through proceedings similar to arbitration, such as parties submitting several rounds of written statements, conciliators issuing procedural orders and participants having hearings, which were quite adversarial and tit-for-tat. Since not all information of these eight cases has been published, except for these two there may be more cases held in similar process.

[25] Lester Nurick and Stephen J. Schnably, above n.22, 348.

This was similar to that of an arbitral tribunal.[26] Therefore, it is understandable that parties were reluctant to opt for ICSID conciliation, "a process that was perceived to simply prolong (or prevent) the production of a binding legal document".[27]

Last but not least, Investor-State mediation cannot be replaced by mediation in the context of State-State dispute resolution either. In other words, one possible alternative to dispute resolution between the actual investor and the host State, is State-State dispute resolution, wherein the investor's home State steps in to handle the dispute on behalf of the investor. However, this alternative is hard to be realized. On the one hand, it is clear that not very often can complaints from a private investor motivate its home State to initiate mediation with another State; even when such mediation is available, it would still be "the most responsive in the investment treaty context" to engage the investors directly in discussion and decision-making.[28] On the other hand, ISDS was in fact designed to minimize home State's intervention in investment disputes,[29] and there are good reasons that investors may actually wish to avoid diplomatic protections.[30]

It is not argued that mediation is always better than other DSMs,[31] but a valuable option. Promoting mediation and offering other mechanisms is not contradictory and can be realized at the same time. For example, mediation is scheduled to precede adjudication[32] in the "cooling-off" process as a complementary alternative or a compulsory step, or provided as available at any point during the whole dispute resolution process alongside other DSMs.[33] Even if a complete settlement is not achieved, mediation may narrow issues for later adjudication or open lines of communication for subsequent negotiations.

[26] This echoes that the qualifications set forth for ICSID conciliators are largely the same qualities required of ICSID arbitrators, except that for ICSID arbitrators, "[c]ompetence in the field of law shall be of particular importance". See Convention on the Settlement of Investment Disputes between States and Nationals of Other States (enforced on 14 October 1966), Articles 14(1) and 31(2).

[27] Stevens and Love (2010).

[28] Nancy Welsh and Andrea Kupfer Schneider, above n.14, 132.

[29] Kishoiyian (1994).

[30] United Nations Conference on Trade and Development, Investor-State Disputes: Prevention and Alternatives to Arbitration, UNCTAD/DIAE/IA/2009/11, 2010, 6–7, (http://unctad.org/en/docs/diaeia200911_en.pdf) (accessed 4 December 2017).

[31] For example, where disputing parties do not have the intention of reaching a settlement or continuing cooperation, other DSMs, such as Investor-State arbitration, are in a better position to resolve the dispute.

[32] Such adjudication process can be investment arbitration or litigation in the investment court system proposed by the EU. For easy reference, "adjudication" will be used in the same way in the following discussion. Regarding the EU's proposal of the investment court system, see EU-Vietnam FTA (agreed text as of January 2016), Chapter 8 Section 3 Sub-section 4; CETA (provisionally entered into force on 21 September 2017), Articles 8.22–8.43.

[33] It was argued that offering mediation, conciliation, and arbitration alongside each other may, in fact, be the most effective way to achieve sustainable investment dispute settlement and economic development. See Frauke Nitschke, above n.22, 132.

Recent Promotion of Investor-State Mediation by States and International Institutions

Because of the generally confidential nature of mediation, published information on the existing Investor-State mediation cases is very scarce and often limited to its occurrence without further details.[34] Despite this, it still can be inferred that, compared to arbitration, the real use of mediation has been much less.[35]

Probably sparked by the rise in the number of Investor-State disputes and the drawbacks of investment arbitration, growing interest in Investor-State mediation is becoming particularly clear in recent years. This is mainly reflected in two aspects: reference by States in their IIAs, and promotion from international institutions, typical examples of which are introduced and analysed in this section, in order to have a taste of how Investor-State mediation has been perceived in deals among States and by international institutions.

Reference to Investor-State Mediation in IIAs

The integration of mediation into an ISDS system is becoming more frequently reflected in IIAs. The incorporation is often quite simple, while more detailed mediation rules can be found in some lately concluded IIAs.

Simple Reference

The Trans-Pacific Partnership Agreement (TPP), which was signed among 12 States on 4 February 2016,[36] sets out a provision for Investor-State mediation. In "Section B: Investor-State Dispute Settlement", Article 9.18 "Consultation and Negotiation" stipulates:

---

[34] For instance, a recent disclosed Investor-State mediation happened between a French company and the Philippines under the France-Philippines BIT (1994). This case was filed under the IBA Rules for Investor-State Mediation (2012), with the assistance of the ICC-ADR Centre. It was brought by Systra SA and its local subsidiary Systra Philippines Inc., arising out of allegedly long overdue invoices for services and work performed on metro and rail projects. Other information about this case has not entered into public view. See Investment Arbitration Reporter, In an apparent first, investor and host-state agree to try mediation under IBA Rules to resolve an investment treaty dispute, 2016, (www.iareporter.com/articles/in-an-apparent-first-investor-and-host-state-agree-to-try-mediation-under-iba-rules-to-resolve-an-investment-treaty-dispute/) (accessed 4 December 2017).

[35] Nancy Welsh and Andrea Kupfer Schneider, above n.14, 144.

[36] A final agreement of TPP was drafted on 5 October 2015, made public on 5 November 2015, and signed on 4 February 2016. After the US's withdraw in January 2017, the other 11 TPP countries (Australia, Brunei Darussalam, Canada, Chile, Japan, Malaysia, Mexico, New Zealand, Peru, Singapore, and Vietnam) agreed in May 2017 to revive the deal without the US's participation. Currently, this agreement is not in force.

> In the event of an investment dispute, the claimant and the respondent should initially seek to resolve the dispute through consultation and negotiation, which may include the use of *non-binding, third party procedures*, such as good offices, conciliation or *mediation* (emphasis added).

Here, only the possibility of using mediation as a "non-binding, third party" DSM is mentioned. No further guidance is provided.

In another recently concluded and widely discussed agreement, the EU-Canada Comprehensive Economic and Trade Agreement (CETA), Investor-State mediation was also included.[37] Article 8.20 provides:

1. The disputing parties may *at any time agree to have recourse to mediation.*
2. Recourse to mediation is *without prejudice to the legal position or rights of either disputing party* under this Chapter and is governed by the rules agreed to by the disputing parties including, if available, the rules for mediation adopted by the Committee on Services and Investment pursuant to Article 8.44.3(c).
3. The *mediator* is appointed by agreement of the disputing parties. The disputing parties may also request that the Secretary-General of ICSID appoint the mediator.
4. The disputing parties shall endeavour to reach a resolution of the dispute *within 60 days* from the appointment of the mediator.
5. If the disputing parties agree to have recourse to mediation, *Articles 8.19.6 and 8.19.8 shall not apply* from the date on which the disputing parties agreed to have recourse to mediation to the date on which either disputing party decides to terminate the mediation. A decision by a disputing party to terminate the mediation shall be transmitted by way of a letter to the mediator and the other disputing party (emphasis added).

Compared to TPP, it is clear that CETA offers more guidance on some key issues, such as temporal availability of mediation, appointment of mediator and time limits, although such guidance is still limited and not specific. At the same time, a Code of Conduct for Mediators is provided in an Annex to CETA.[38]

Reference with Comprehensive Procedural Rules

Besides a general reference to mediation and Codes of Conduct for Mediators,[39] a separate comprehensive set of rules of Investor-State mediation is provided in each of the EU's other two recently concluded agreements, the EU-Vietnam Free Trade Agreement (hereinafter "EU-Vietnam FTA") and the EU-Singapore Free Trade

---

[37] CETA was concluded on 29 February 2016, the provisional application of which started from 21 September 2017. See International Centre for Trade and Sustainable Development, EU, Canada Confirm CETA Provisional Application Date, 2017 (www.ictsd.org/bridges-news/bridges/news/eu-canada-confirm-ceta-provisional-application-date,) (accessed 4 December 2017).

[38] CETA (provisionally entered into force on 21 September 2017), Annex 29-B.

[39] EU-Vietnam FTA (agreed text as of January 2016), Chapter 8-Chapter II Section 3 Annex II; EU-Singapore FTA (authentic text as of May 2015), Annex 9-F.

Agreement (hereinafter "EU-Singapore FTA").[40] These two sets of Investor-State mediation rules are nearly identical, both covering the issues of objective and scope of mediation, initiation of the procedure, selection of the mediator, rules of the mediation procedure, implementation of a mutually agreed solution, time limits, costs, etc. Under these rules, mediation is constructed as a voluntary and structured process, and much room is left to party autonomy and mediators with regard to detailed procedural arrangements.[41]

One issue that deserves particular attention is that such freedom excludes mediators conducting rule-based mediation. For example, in the EU-Vietnam FTA, it is stated:

> The mediator *may offer advice and propose a solution* for the consideration of the disputing parties which may accept or reject the proposed solution or may agree on a different solution. However, the mediator *shall not advise or give comments on the consistency of the measure at issue with this Agreement* (emphasis added).[42]

Promotion of Investor-State Mediation from International Institutions

International institutions have taken various efforts to promote the use of mediation for ISDS, which are represented by adopting bespoke mediation rules, issuing guides and establishing centers for using Investor-State mediation, and providing professional training for potential mediators.

Adopting Bespoke Mediation Rules

A number of international institutions have adopted bespoke rules for mediation, such as the International Chamber of Commerce Mediation Rules (2014) and the Mediation Rules of the Arbitration Institute of the Stockholm Chamber of Commerce (2014). Although investment mediation is not excluded from their scopes of application, most of these rules were designed to target commercial dispute resolution.

Going along this trend, there is a noticeable innovation: in 2012, the International Bar Association (IBA) adopted its IBA Rules for Investor-State Mediation (2012),

[40] EU-Vietnam FTA (agreed text as of January 2016), Chapter 8-Chapter II Section 3 Annex I; EU-Singapore FTA (authentic text as of May 2015), Annex 9-E.

[41] EU-Vietnam FTA (agreed text as of January 2016), Chapter 8-Chapter II Section 3 Annex I, Article 4.2; EU-Singapore FTA (authentic text as of May 2015), Annex 9-E, Article 4.2.

[42] EU-Vietnam FTA (agreed text as of January 2016), Chapter 8-Chapter II Section 3 Annex I, Article 4.3. This echoes the relevant provision in the EU-Singapore FTA, see EU-Singapore FTA (authentic text as of May 2015), Annex 9-E, Article 4.3.

providing detailed and practical guidelines for the conduct of Investor-State Mediation.[43] Compared to the ICSID Conciliation Rules, the application of this set of rules is not restricted to "legal disputes arising directly out of an investment", but encompasses "investment-related differences or disputes". At the same time, specialties of ISDS have been taken into account in procedural arrangements. A typical example is the issue of transparency. Under this set of rules, deviating from the normal confidential feature of mediation, only privacy is provided,[44] and the area to which confidentiality obligation shall not extend is explicitly stipulated, which includes the existence of mediation and the terms of a settlement agreement.[45] Additionally, there are innovative designs for facilitating using mediation, such as co-mediators and mediation management conference.[46]

This action taken by the IBA demonstrates "the existence of an appetite for mediation as a new process choice" and represents "an extremely important first step toward legitimizing investor-state mediation".[47]

Other Institutional Efforts on Promotion

Besides adopting bespoke rules of mediation, international institutions have also taken other efforts to promote Investor-State mediation. For example, on 19 July 2016, the Energy Charter Conference endorsed a Guide on Investment Mediation, recognizing Investor-State mediation as "a helpful, voluntary instrument to facilitate the amicable resolution of investment disputes".[48] This Guide was formed as an "explanatory document", explaining basic issues in the mediation process, possible roles of the Energy Charter Secretariat and other institutions, as well as various

---

[43] As shown in its name, this set of rules specifically serve mediation to resolve disputes between investors and States. It was drafted by a subcommittee of the IBA's mediation group, comprising members of the IBA mediation and arbitration committees, present and former officials of country governments, members of the secretariats of the ICC, ICSID, the PCA and the SCC, academics, and in-house counsel for major investors. See Herbert Smith Freehills LLP, International Bar Association Launches Investor-State Mediation Rules, 2012 (http://hsfnotes.com/adr/2012/10/23/international-bar-association-launches-investor-state-mediation-rules/) (accessed 4 December 2017).

[44] IBA Rules for Investor-State Mediation (2012), Article 10.1.

[45] Ibid, Article 10.3.

[46] Ibid, Articles 4.1 and 9. For comments on these innovations, See Munir Maniruzzaman, A Rethink of Investor-State Dispute Settlement, 2013 (http://kluwerarbitrationblog.com/2013/05/30/a-rethink-of-investor-state-dispute-settlement/) (accessed 4 December 2017); Herbert Smith Freehills LLP, above n.43; Barton Legum, Anna Joubin-Bret and Inna Manassyan, above n.7, 269.

[47] Nancy Welsh and Andrea Kupfer Schneider, above n.14, 84.

[48] International Energy Charter, Guide on Investment Mediation, CCDEC 2016 12 INV, 2016 (www.energycharter.org/fileadmin/DocumentsMedia/CCDECS/2016/CCDEC201612.pdf) (accessed 4 December 2017). The Guide was prepared with the support of the International Mediation Institute (IMI), the International Centre for Settlement of Investment Disputes (ICSID), the Arbitration Institute of the Stockholm Chamber of Commerce (SCC), the International Court of Arbitration of the International Chamber of Commerce (ICC), the United Nations Commission on International Trade Law (UNCITRAL) and the Permanent Court of Arbitration (PCA).

available mediation or conciliation rules. It aims at encouraging investors and States to actively consider using mediation for resolving any dispute amicably.

Another example is the establishment of the Dispute Resolution and Negotiation Centre by the Secretariat of the Energy Community in October 2016.[49] This Centre focusses on negotiating and mediating Investor-State energy disputes at an early stage. Considering the unique skills required for qualified Investor-State mediators, the Energy Community is also forming a panel of mediators with recognized competence to provide assistance to this Centre.[50] Similarly, the Investor-State Mediation Task Force of the International Mediation Institute developed a comprehensive set of competency criteria for Investor-State mediators, aiming at creating a pool of qualified professionals from which parties can choose with confidence.[51]

Recognition of Mediation for Investment Dispute Resolution by China and the EU

China and the EU are two of the biggest players in the field of international investment. In the past four years, the foreign direct investment inflows and outflows of China and of the EU were among the top five in the world.[52] Under the blossoming of IIAs in the world, China and the EU have also made concerted efforts to negotiate a China-EU BIT, which was formally launched at the 16th EU-China Summit of 21 November 2013.[53] This BIT will replace the 26 existing BITs between China and 27 individual EU Member States with one single comprehensive investment agreement.[54] Once

[49] The Energy Community, Energy Community Secretariat establishes Dispute Resolution and Negotiation Centre, 2016 (www.energy-community.org/news/Energy-Community-News/2016/10/25.html) (accessed 4 December 2017).

[50] The Energy Community, Call for expression of interest: Creating a panel of mediators, 2017 (www.energy-community.org/news/Energy-Community-News/2017/01/18.html) (accessed 4 December 2017).

[51] International Mediation Institute, IMI Competency Criteria for Investor-State Mediators, 2016 (https://imimediation.org/private/downloads/RTdBTV1oyxkSpTLKtlLV5w/IMI_IS_Med_Competency_Criteria_19_Sept_2016.pdf) (accessed 4 December 2017).

[52] UNCTAD, World Investment Report 2017, UNCTAD/WIR/2017, 2017 (http://unctad.org/en/PublicationsLibrary/wir2017_en.pdf) (accessed 4 December 2017); UNCTAD, World Investment Report 2015, UNCTAD/WIR/2015, 2015 (http://unctad.org/en/PublicationsLibrary/wir2015_en.pdf) (accessed 4 December 2017).

[53] European Commission, EU and China Begin Investment Talks, 2014 (http://europa.eu/rapid/press-release_IP-14-33_en.htm) (accessed 4 December 2017). The negotiations for a China-EU BIT officially started in January 2014.

[54] Up to now, there have been 12 rounds of negotiations. The 12th round of negotiations took place in Brussels during the week of 26 September 2016. See Directorate-General for Trade European Commission, Note to File: EU-China Investment Agreement: Report of the 12th Round of negotiations, 2016 (http://trade.ec.europa.eu/doclib/docs/2016/october/tradoc_155061.pdf) (accessed 4 December 2017).

concluded, this investment deal, including the ISDS system contained therein, will undoubtedly be influential.

Against the background of an increasing awareness of mediation as a valuable alternative to ISDS, particularly, both China and the EU have shown their intention of increasing the use of mediation for investment dispute resolution. Supporting evidence comes from each side's approach at the international as well as internal levels. The legal systems of these two parties not only prove their preferences but also indicate the elements that probably affect investors' attitudes towards mediation therefrom.[55]

China's Preference for Mediation

China presented its interest in using Investor-State mediation by incorporating this DSM into the latest China Model BIT (2010) and some IIAs. China's fourth Model BIT, which was drafted in 2010, expressly pointed out the possibility of going through mediation to resolve Investor-State disputes.[56] Article 13 "Settlement of Disputes Between Investors and One Contracting Party" provides:

> Any legal dispute between an investor of one Contracting Party and the other Contracting Party in connecting with an investment in the territory of the other Contracting Party shall, as far as possible, be settled amicably through negotiations between the parties to the dispute, *which includes mediation* (emphasis added).

Similar references to Investor-State mediation also exist in China's concluded IIAs. The most recent example is the Bilateral Agreement for the Promotion and Protection of Investments between the Government of the Republic of Colombia and the Government of the People's Republic of China (2013).[57] In this agreement,

---

[55] Regarding the real use of an Investor-State mediation mechanism, it is equally important, if not more, that mediation is a familiar and possibly functional option to investors, which is expected to be affected by the role of mediation in the legal systems of investors' home States.

[56] This Model BIT has not been officially published, but the content can be reached through an academic article. The discussion here is based on the disclosed information in this article. See Xiantao Wen 温先涛, Discussion on "China Model Bilateral Investment Treaty" (draft) (1)《中国投资保护协定范本》(草案) 论稿 (一), 18(4) Guo Ji Jing Ji Fa Xue Kan 国际经济法学刊 (2011), 169–204; Xiantao Wen 温先涛, Discussion on "China Model Bilateral Investment Treaty" (draft)(2)《中国投资保护协定范本》(草案) 论稿 (二), 19(1) Guo Ji Jing Ji Fa Xue Kan 国际经济法学刊 (2011), 132–161; Xiantao Wen 温先涛, Discussion on "China Model Bilateral Investment Treaty" (draft)(3)《中国投资保护协定范本》(草案) 论稿 (三), 19(2) Guo Ji Jing Ji Fa Xue Kan 国际经济法学刊 (2011), 57–90.

[57] It is noticeable that the promotion of using Investor-State mediation is more comprehensively reflected in a new agreement on investment arrangement between mainland China and Hong Kong, which was just concluded on 28 June 2017 under the framework established by the Mainland China and Hong Kong Closer Economic Partnership Arrangement (CEPA). In this agreement, for disputes between investors from mainland China that invest in Hong Kong and Hong Kong investors that invest in mainland China, mediation takes a dominant position in the whole dispute resolution system created thereunder (three out of six DSMs are in nature mediation). Although considering

Article 9.3 states that, for settlement of disputes between one contracting party and an investor of the other contracting party,

> Nothing in this Article shall be construed as to prevent the parties of a dispute from referring their dispute, by mutual agreement, *to ad hoc or institutional mediation* or conciliation *before or during the arbitral proceeding* (emphasis added).[58]

Like the language in TPP Article 9.18, which was discussed in Sect. "Simple Reference", *supra*, only a simple reference without any practical guidance is provided in either China's model BIT (2010) or any of its concluded IIAs, as shown in the IIA between China and Columbia.

In China's domestic legal system, as far as foreign investment is concerned, mediation plays a significant role in dispute resolution, where both independent and mixed mediation mechanisms are available. Specifically, for disputes between investors and relevant authorities, independent mediation hosted by a branch of the State Administration of Industry and Commerce can be resorted to.[59] If that is not selected by parties or it fails for any reason, mediation still structurally exists in other DSMs, including administrative reconsideration,[60] arbitration,[61] as well as litigation,[62] which extends the possible use of mediation to a large extent.

In addition, since 2006, a mechanism particularly designed for foreign investment dispute resolution, "complaints coordination", has been promulgated.[63] This DSM was further prescribed in the recently published draft Foreign Investment Law of

---

the relationship between mainland China and Hong Kong, it is hard to use this agreement as a concrete reference to infer China's attitude in its prospective IIAs with other States, it still heralds a potentially greater use of Investor-State mediation by mainland China. See Mainland China and Hong Kong Closer Economic Partnership Arrangement Investment Agreement《内地与香港关于建立更紧密经贸关系的安排》投资协议 (2017), Articles 19.1 and 20.1.

[58] Bilateral Agreement for the Promotion and Protection of Investments between the Government of the Republic of Colombia and the Government of the People's Republic of China (signed on 22 November 2008, entered into force on 2 July 2013), Article 9.3.

[59] Administration of Administrative Mediation of Contract Dispute by the State Administration for Industry and Commerce of the People's Republic of China (enforced on 3 November 1997), Article 6.

[60] Administrative reconsideration applies to the situation where a citizen, legal person or any other organization considers that his or its lawful rights and interests have been infringed upon by a specific administrative act and applies for administrative reconsideration to an administrative organ. Mediation can be conducted during the administrative reconsideration process. See Administrative Reconsideration Law of the People's Republic of China (enforced on 1 October 1999, as amended on 27 August 2009), Articles 2, 50, and 51.

[61] This kind of mediation is realized through conducting mediation during the arbitration process whenever there is consent from parties. See Arbitration Law of the People's Republic of China (enforced on 1 September 1995, as amended on 27 August 2009), Article 51.

[62] During litigation, mediation can be referred to in three stages: before case registration, after case registration but before a hearing, and during or after a hearing but before the issuance of the final judgment. See Civil Procedure Law of the People's Republic of China (enforced on 9 April 1991, as amended on 31 August 2012), Articles 122, 133 and 142.

[63] In 2006, the Ministry of Commerce of China promulgated a set of interim measures on complaints coordination dealing with complaints from foreign-invested enterprises, according to which foreign-invested enterprises or foreign investors which deem that their legitimate rights or interests have

China as one of the available DSMs for foreign investors to resolve disputes.[64] In nature, this is a quasi-mediation process, where complaints from foreign investors are dealt with by relevant organs as third parties through reflecting the real situation, setting forth suggestions, opinions or claims, or transferring it to local complaint acceptance organs or relevant departments, towards reaching a settlement amicably.[65]

The EU's Exploration of Mediation

As introduced in Sect. "Reference to Investor-State Mediation in IIAs", *supra*, the EU's intention of incorporating mediation into ISDS has been clearly and concretely shown in each of its recently concluded IIAs, including the EU-Singapore FTA, the EU-Vietnam FTA and CETA. Considering such consistency in these agreements, it is expected that similar practice will be adopted in the EU's proposals for other prospective IIAs in the near future.[66]

The EU has also promoted the use of mediation internally. A typical example is the "Directive 2008/52/EC of the European Parliament and of the Council of 21 May 2008 on certain aspects of mediation in civil and commercial matters" to facilitate access to alternative dispute resolution and to promote the amicable settlement of disputes.[67] Although there is no clear evidence showing mediation is the EU's particularly preferred DSM for investment, this is a reflection of the EU's increasing awareness of mediation as a means of improving access to justice.[68]

---

been infringed by an administrative authority may file a complaint with the complaint acceptance authority for coordination or settlement. See Interim Measures of the Ministry of Commerce of the People's Republic of China for the Work Relating to the Complaints of Foreign-funded Enterprises (enforced on 1 December 2006), Article 2.

64 Draft Foreign Investment Law (released on 19 January 2015), Article 118. More guidance on using complaints coordination is also provided in this draft. See ibid., Chapter 8.

65 Ibid, Articles 2 and 11. See also: Guiguo (2011).

66 Since Investor-State mediation does not involve the issue of depriving jurisdictions of Member States over investment cases, it should be less problematic in terms of the Court of Justice of the European Union (CJEU)'s Opinion 2/15. See CJEU Opinion 2/15 of the Court (Full Court), 16 May 2017. In this Opinion, upon the request of the European Commission regarding the EU's competence in entering into comprehensive economic agreements in the context of the EU-Singapore FTA, the CJEU found that the EU did not have exclusive competence over ISDS provisions, since a choice between bringing a dispute before a court of a Member State and submitting it to arbitration had the effect of removing the case from the jurisdiction of a Member State.

67 Directive 2008/52/EC of the European Parliament and of the Council of 21 May 2008 on certain aspects of mediation in civil and commercial matters, OJ L 136, 24 May 2008.

68 Green Paper on alternative dispute resolution in civil and commercial law, COM(2002) 196 final, 19 April 2002, 5, 9–10 (http://eur-lex.europa.eu/legal-content/EN/ALL/?uri=CELEX:52002DC0196) (accessed 4 December 2017). See also: Mª Pía Calderón Cuadrado and José Luis Iglesias Buhigues, Mediation as an "alternative" to jurisdiction: Directive 2008/52, in: European Civil Procedure (Thomson Reuters, 2011), 249–250. To follow up the implementation of this Directive on Mediation and guarantee its real effect, some projects have also been initiated. See e.g. Policy Department C: Citizens' Rights and Constitutional Affairs Directorate-General

It can be said that mediation as a valuable mechanism for ISDS has received increasing emphases by both China and the EU. Particularly, regarding investment dispute resolution between these two parties, a public consultation conducted by the European Commission on "The future investment relationship between the EU and China" within the EU Member States showed that the EU investors took arbitration as a last resort, fearing that it would deteriorate their relationship with the Chinese Government.[69] Based on this, a functional Investor-State mediation mechanism in the prospective China-EU BIT would possibly be more than welcome by the EU investors for resolving disputes with China.

The Design of Investor-State Mediation in a China-EU BIT

There has been no released information regarding the negotiations on the ISDS system in the prospective China-EU BIT, but it is reasonable to predict that both sides' recognition of mediation for ISDS does not necessarily mean that it would be easy for them to reach an agreement on the design of Investor-State mediation. Besides the issues that can be inferred from their distinctive existing practices, considering both sides' intention to promote a greater use of mediation, more innovative designs, and thus more uncertainties, can be expected.

Four crucial but controversial issues may stand in the way of the negotiations on an Investor-State mediation mechanism in a China-EU BIT: voluntariness, mediation styles, transparency and enforcement of settlement agreements. These issues are explored below, all with a mind to figuring out potential solutions that are palatable to contracting parties, attractive to potential users and functional to ISDS. At the same time, the discussion in this section could provide inspirations to other States and investors as well.

Voluntariness

A preliminary question is the voluntariness of initiating Investor-State mediation: should this DSM be set as a compulsory stop on the way to adjudication or a voluntary one? Arguments exist supporting each side. On the one hand, to increase the possibility of amicable settlement, robust mediation engagement is preferred. Namely,

for Internal Policies, "Rebooting" the Mediation Directive: Assessing the Limited Impact of its Implementation and Proposing Measures to Increase the Number of Mediations in the EU, PE 493.042, 2014 (www.europarl.europa.eu/RegData/etudes/etudes/join/2014/493042/IPOL-JURI_ET(2014)493042_EN.pdf) (accessed 4 December 2017).

[69] Director General for Trade European Commission, Summary of contributions to the European Commission's public consultation on "The future investment relationship between the EU and China", 2011, 4 and 10 (http://trade.ec.europa.eu/doclib/docs/2011/december/tradoc_148394.pdf) (accessed 4 December 2017).

mediation is argued to be made compulsory accompanied by a minimum time period, so as to push disputing parties to make a try. On the other hand, voluntariness is one of the fundamental features of mediation. Even if a disputing party can terminate participation at a certain point, compulsory initiation prolongs the dispute resolution process anyhow. On this issue, both China's and the EU's existing practices support voluntariness.[70]

For a China-EU BIT, adhering to the voluntariness of mediation is supposed to be the suitable choice, but some procedural adjustment can be made to realize a greater use of Investor-State mediation. As pointed out by an IBA subcommittee, the use of Investor-State mediation was largely affected by a lack of awareness by parties and practitioners.[71] Therefore, it is suggested that under the prospective China-EU BIT, if it is not chosen spontaneously, mediation should be presented to disputing parties at the beginning of the adjudication process. Such "coercion" can be productive, considering that it ensures parties' clear understanding and concrete consideration of Investor-State mediation.

Any party who rejects mediation can then choose to opt out but must demonstrate why mediation would be duplicative of earlier efforts, unlikely to be productive, or might even cause harm.[72] This arrangement can promote the use of Investor-State mediation without prejudicing party autonomy. When the dispute is not suitable for mediation, compared to compulsory mediation, it minimizes the time waste.

Mediation Styles

As mentioned in Sect. "A Valuable Dispute Settlement Mechanism to ISDS", *supra*, mediation can be interest-based or rule-based. Although interest-based mediation is arguably preferable to ISDS, rule-based mediation may also have its value, especially when disputing parties prefer it.

In terms of the EU's existing practice on this issue, as introduced in Sect. "Reference with Comprehensive Procedural Rules", *supra*, mediators are explicitly prevented from giving advice or comments on the consistency of the measure at issue with the applicable IIA.[73] This means only interest-based mediation is allowed.

On the side of China, it is hard to tell its perception of the appropriate type of Investor-State mediation, because no concrete procedural rule is available in China's

[70] For China, voluntariness is provided for all kinds of mediation, such as mediation held by the people's courts. See Civil Procedure Law of the People's Republic of China (enforced on 9 April 1991, as amended on 31 August 2012), Articles 9 and 93. For the EU, see Directive 2008/52/EC of the European Parliament and of the Council of 21 May 2008 on certain aspects of mediation in civil and commercial matters, OJ L 136, 24 May 2008, Article 3(a).

[71] Herbert Smith Freehills LLP, above n.43; Barton Legum, Anna Joubin-Bret and Inna Manassyan, above n.7, 266.

[72] McAdoo and Welsh (2004).

[73] EU-Vietnam FTA (agreed text as of January 2016), Chapter 8-Chapter II Section 3 Annex I, Article 4.3; EU-Singapore FTA (authentic text as of May 2015), Annex 9-E, Article 4.3.

concluded IIAs or its model BITs. Neither do legislations give useful clues to tell the mediation style held in China's domestic legal system. With regard to practice, the dominant style was described as evaluative and right-based.[74] It was also argued that in a sense, Chinese mediation synthesizes the Western concepts of mediation, arbitration, and litigation.[75]

Under such a situation, a combined model, taking interest-based mediation as the default type and rule-based mediation as a supplement, is recommended for a China-EU BIT.[76] In other words, non-evaluative mediation based on parties' interests is the normal practice. When disputing parties reach a different agreement, it is possible to transfer to an evaluative rule-based type. Besides taking into account disputing parties' preferences in each case, such combination ensures mediation as an interest-based process to a large extent, which is beneficial to trust-building and information exchange between parties. It also gives necessary freedom to mediators to customize the style as the process goes on.[77] In fact, it was argued that mediation is "most likely to be helpful when it includes both legal analysis and probing for interests".[78] Particularly in sophisticated mediation, disputing parties are likely to prefer a type of mediation that can uncover their extralegal interests as well as discuss applicable laws and litigation realities.[79]

This combined model is suggested to be explicitly prescribed in the prospective China-EU BIT, so as to give disputing parties clear information, increase predictability of the process, and decrease undue influence from elements such as the backgrounds of participants of the dispute resolution process.[80]

Other detailed procedural arrangements, such as whether to caucus or not and time management, can be left to disputing parties and mediators to decide case by case, but these agreements should always be clearly specified at the beginning.[81] In order to realize this, a checklist which lists key procedural issues and describes

---

[74] Chan (2016). In this doctoral thesis, the author explored the features of mediation in China's contemporary legal system based on a doctrinal analysis and an empirical legal research.

[75] Clarke (1997).

[76] A similar arrangement was argued by Nancy Welsh and Andrea Kupfer Schneider for Investor-State mediation in general. Specifically, the authors suggested that the process should begin in a facilitative manner. Discussion of relevant legal norms and evaluations by the mediator is supposed to be permitted at a later stage. See Nancy Welsh and Andrea Kupfer Schneider, above n.14, 71.

[77] Mediators can make a proposal for changing the mediation style, if he deems the change is appropriate at any point during the process. For example, a mediator may start with an interest-based approach, then propose to transit to a rule-based style for finally reaching a settlement agreement.

[78] Nancy Welsh and Andrea Kupfer Schneider, above n.14, 114.

[79] Welsh and Schneider (2012).

[80] The existence of different sorts of legal-cultural idiosyncrasies counsels that rules should clarify the models that may be used if mediation is added to the investment context. See Timothy Martin (2011).

[81] ON procedural arrangements of international mediation, "difficulties could easily be addressed by providing clear guidelines and definitions on mutually identified parameter", which would "at least inform disputants of differences and how they may have an impact on the process or the outcome to their dispute". See Manon Schonewille and Jeremy Lack, above n.12, 21.

possible choices or offers some guidelines—which parties are free to choose from—can be attached to the provided mediation rules. In this regard, a reference to the IBA Investor-Mediation Rules can be another option, subject to the provisions in the prospective China-EU BIT and disputing parties' other agreements. The overarching guiding principle here should be making the Investor-State mediation process useable by a wide range of end-users through ensuring flexibility, predictability and legitimacy.

Transparency

Transparency has been extensively discussed and increasingly realized in Investor-State arbitration, the underlying reasons for which include the involvement of public interest, the requirement for the accountability of the host State's government,[82] and the criticism of not resulting in precedent or "jurisprudential growth" incurred by confidentiality.[83] These factors still exist in mediation. However, different from arbitration, confidentiality is one of the core advantages of mediation. It creates a desirable environment for parties to freely renegotiate, without the fear of their positions being disclosed, being used against it in future dispute resolution proceedings, or having other negative effects. Consequently, mediators can gather necessary information to help parties reach satisfying settlement. If transparency was required, parties would probably reconsider the approach and be more cautious about their interaction. As a result, the possibility of ending the dispute with a settlement agreement is likely to be largely reduced.

Under the EU's Investor-State mediation mechanisms in its concluded IIAs, the final result of mediation is available to the public.[84] Such a deviation from confidentiality can cause concerns from China and Chinese investors. Various reasons contribute to such an inference. First of all, mediation is prescribed as confidential in Chinese mediation rules, only subject to parties' agreement otherwise.[85] More

[82] Horodyski (2016).

[83] Note: Mediation of Investor-State Conflicts, 127 Harvard Law Review (2014), 2556.

[84] For example, in the EU-Singapore FTA, it is provided that "[m]utually agreed solutions shall be made publicly available. However, the version disclosed to the public may not contain any information that a disputing party has designated as confidential [...] All steps of the procedure, including any advice or proposed solution, shall be confidential. However, any disputing party may disclose to the public that mediation is taking place". See EU-Singapore FTA (authentic text as of May 2015), Annex 9-E, Articles 4.6 and 6.3. This is similar to the relevant provision in the IBA Rules for Investor-State Mediation. See IBA Rules for Investor-State Mediation (2012), Article 10.3.

[85] See e.g. China Council for the Promotion of International Trade (CCPIT)/China Chamber of International Commerce (CCOIC), CCPIT/CCOIC Mediation Rules (enforced on 1 May 2012), Article 22.

importantly, the general preference for mediation is affected by the fact that its confidential feature is in line with the Chinese tradition of "no litigation".[86] Specifically, disputes are expected to be avoided and resolving a dispute transparently is regarded as similar to washing the dirty linen in public, which causes discomfort to disputing parties. Thus, if confidentiality is missing, mediation's attractiveness would be largely diminished.

Although it seems that under the general international background of advocating transparency, China has changed its attitude towards transparency in Investor-State arbitration from rejection to acceptance,[87] mediation is another story. There is no sign showing the surge in the transparency of ISDS exists in China, and there is no international pressure supporting transparency in Investor-State mediation. Furthermore, considering mediation is taken by China as the DSM with Chinese characteristics that it does well,[88] the prospect of accepting a practice that deviates from one of the fundamental features of Chinese mediation looks bleak. It deserves special attention that the newly published Arbitration Rules of the China International Economic and Trade Arbitration Commission for International Investment Disputes (2017) create the possibility of holding Investor-State mediation during arbitration and it is clearly stated that such mediation shall be confidential.[89] Therefore, it is reasonable to expect that transparency for Investor-State mediation, which is distinct from its existing understanding and practice, would be hard for China to accept; even if that is accepted in the prospective China-EU BIT, it is likely to become a big hurdle in its use by China or Chinese investors in the future.

Under such a situation, for a China-EU BIT, confidentiality is proposed to be respected as a rule, but an exception can be created for party autonomy. Namely, parties can disclose the existence of mediation, main aspects of their settlement agreement, or other details of the process, if they reach corresponding agreements.[90] Thus, the confidential nature of mediation is largely kept, and the possibility of other arrangements is not excluded. In addition, considering the fact that transparency would very likely exist in adjudication, which is another part of an ISDS system, from the perspective of keeping systematic comprehensiveness, maintaining mediation's confidentiality as the default rule should be preferred.

---

86 Zhang (2014).

87 Malanczuk (2015).

88 For instance, the combination of mediation and arbitraiton as "Med-Arb" is deemed as one of its key advantages by China International Economic and Trade Arbitration Commission (CIETAC). See China International Economic and Trade Arbitration Commission (CIETAC), Why CIETAC 为何选择CIETAC (http://www.cietac.org.cn/index.php?m=Page&a=index&id=117) (accessed 4 December 2017).

89 Arbitration Rules of the China International Economic and Trade Arbitration Commission for International Investment Disputes (enforced on 1 October 2017), Article 43(2).

90 There have been several examples of non-confidential public sector resource mediation, which demonstrated the possibility of transparency to various extents in Investor-State mediation cases. See e.g. McGovern (2006).

Enforcement of Settlement Agreements

Enforcement of settlement agreements is another issue that may let mediation face skepticism as a way of resolving Investor-State disputes. Successful mediation leads to a new agreement between disputing parties, the realization of which is not guaranteed since they are not readily enforceable as arbitral awards which benefit from the enforcement regimes under the Convention on the Settlement of Investment Disputes between States and Nationals of Other States (ICSID Convention) or the 1958 Convention on the Recognition and Enforcement of Foreign Arbitral Awards (New York Convention). As a result, mediation may simply prolong the dispute resolution process without any reliable result. Although resolving a dispute through mediation implies the expectation of a high possibility of voluntary conformity, disputing parties probably prefer to have certain guarantee of compliance.

Neither China nor the EU explicitly dealt with this issue in their existing IIAs. Relevant provisions only stressed that "each disputing party shall endeavor to take the measures necessary to implement the mutually agreed solution within the agreed timeframe" and "[t]he implementing disputing party shall inform the other disputing party in writing of any steps or measures taken to implement the mutually agreed solution".[91] While internally both sides have created mechanisms to confer enforceability to agreements resulting from mediation,[92] such domestic arrangements are hard to transfer to the international level.

Lessons may be drawn from commercial arbitration, so mediation in the investment context may prove similar: if a settlement agreement is reached through mediation, disputing parties can refer to arbitration, asking an arbitral tribunal to incorporate the settlement in the form of an award by consent.[93] In this way, the enforceability of a final award under the ICSID Convention or New York Convention is attracted. A similar approach can be adopted in the context of the investment court system proposed by the EU. Namely, settlement can be incorporated into the decision-making stage; thus the realization of settlement agreements is guaranteed by the enforcement system therein.[94]

[91] EU-Vietnam FTA (agreed text as of January 2016), Chapter 8-Chapter II Section 3 Annex I, Articles 5.1 and 5.2. See also: EU-Singapore FTA (authentic text as of May 2015), Annex 9-E, Articles 5.1 and 5.2.

[92] Regarding the EU, see Directive 2008/52/EC of the European Parliament and of the Council of 21 May 2008 on certain aspects of mediation in civil and commercial matters, OJ L 136, 24 May 2008, Article 6. In terms of China's legal system, there are different ways to add an enforcement effect to a settlement agreement from mediation. For example, parties may make an application to the competent people's court to confirm their settlement agreement. See Civil Procedure Law of the People's Republic of China (enforced on 9 April 1991, as amended on 31 August 2012), Article 26.

[93] In fact, at least in 15 ICSID cases, the arbitral tribunals were asked to incorporate parties' settlement in the form of a consent award. See Jean E. Kalick, above n.6.

[94] It is noticeable that this does not deal with the unneglectable weakness of the EU's investment court system that its judgments may not be enforced in the States who are not subject to this system. For more analysis on this point, see Just Published: Analysis of EU's "Investment Court System",

It is worth noting that UNCITRAL recently made progress towards the development of the Convention on the Enforcement of Mediated Settlements (CEMS). This was initially proposed in July 2014, aiming at establishing provisions on the enforceability of international commercial settlement agreements reached through mediation.[95] Based on that, similar developments can be expected to address the issue of enforceability of settlement agreements resulting from Investor-State mediation, or to apply the one for commercial mediation in the field of international investment.

Conclusion

Mediation can help resolve disputes amicably based on parties' interests. It is particularly a valuable dispute settlement mechanism (DSM) in the context of Investor-State dispute settlement (ISDS), when there is a need for restoring the relationship and ensuring further cooperation between disputing parties. In the context of the current ISDS system, which is basically dominated by rule-based DSMs, there is an increasing awareness of mediation's potential value to ISDS. The recent practices of China and the EU are examples. Considering the prospective BIT that is being negotiated by these two parties, it is suitable, practicable and beneficial to incorporate a carefully designed Investor-State mediation mechanism, and the time is now ripe for both sides to seriously consider this.

With regard to the design of Investor-State mediation in a China-EU BIT, four issues deserve particular attention. Firstly, the basic principle of voluntariness should be adhered to. Based on that, if disputing parties do not choose mediation spontaneously, it should be presented at the beginning of the adjudication process to let them learn about and seriously consider the use of this DSM. Secondly, interest-based mediation is suggested to be prescribed as the default type, subject to parties' agreements otherwise. Regarding other procedural arrangements, parties can choose to adopt any set of bespoke mediation rules or use the checklist that is suggested to be attached to this prospective BIT. Relevant agreements are recommended to be explicitly reached between parties or decided by mediators at the beginning. Thirdly, it is better to keep confidentiality as a fundamental feature of the Investor-State mediation process, unless parties reach a different agreement. Finally, in terms of enforcement of settlement agreements, a possible solution is incorporating such agreements into the decision-making stage of adjudication to trigger the enforcement system thereunder.

Stockholm Chamber of Commerce ISDS Blog, 2016 (http://isdsblog.com/2016/10/27/just-published-analysis-of-eus-investment-court-system/) (accessed 4 December 2017).

[95] Report of the United Nations Commission on International Trade Law, Forty-Seventh Session (July 7–18, 2014), UN Doc A/69/17, 2014, 124 (https://documents-dds-ny.un.org/doc/UNDOC/GEN/V14/053/54/PDF/V1405354.pdf?OpenElement) (accessed 4 December 2017). See also Laila El Shentenawi, A New York Convention for Mediation May be Coming Soon, 28 August 2015 (www.tamimi.com/en/magazine/law-update/section-11/section-13/a-new-york-convention-for-mediation-may-be-coming-soon.html) (accessed 4 December 2017).

In brief, the prospective China-EU BIT is a valuable chance to promote the use of Investor-State mediation: the automatic presentation at the beginning of other DSMs will remind disputing parties of the availability and function of Investor-State mediation; detailed illustration of the process in the prospective treaty can make this DSM practicable to potential users; and the innovative designs create the possibility of curing the inherent features that put mediation at a disadvantage. A properly designed Investor-State mediation mechanism will most likely contribute to successful ISDS under a China-EU BIT, and provide useful inspirations to others. This DSM in the prospective China-EU BIT is expected to motivate the significant integration of mediation into the fabric of the investment treaty context, and head forwards to build a more comprehensive ISDS system, composing power-based, rule-based as well as interest-based DSMs.

References

Ali SF, Repousis OG (2016–2017) Investor-state mediation and the rise of transparency in international investment law: opportunity or threat? Denver J Int Law Policy 45:235

Ali SF (2015) Prospects of utilizing investor-state mediation and UNCITRAL rules on transparency for polycentric environmental disaster-related disputes: the case of vattenfall v. Germany. In: Ramaswamy MP, Ribeiro J (eds) Trade development through harmonization of commercial law. New Zealand Association for Comparative Law, p 137

Bottini G, Lavista V (2010) Conciliation and BITs. In: Rovine AW (ed) Contemporary issues in international arbitration and mediation: the fordham papers 2009. Martinus Nijhoff Publishers, pp 359 and 365

Bradley AS (2010) Integration matters: rethinking the architecture of international dispute resolution, Univ Pa J Int Law 32:23

Chan PCH (2016) The position of mediation in contemporary chinese civil justice: a proceduralist perspective, to obtain the doctoral degree. Maastricht University, p 224

Clarke DC (1997) Dispute resolution in China. In: Lee TV (ed) Contract, guanxi, and dispute resolution in China. Garland Publishing, pp 369–422

Coe JJ (2007) Toward a complementary use of conciliation in investor-state disputes—a preliminary sketch. Transnatl Disput Manag 12:8–9

Davidson RB (2012) Initiating an international mediation. In: Chernick R, Kolkey DM, Neal BR (eds) Practitioner's handbook on international arbitration and mediation, 3rd ed, Juris Publishing, p 479

Echandi R (2013) Complementing investor-state dispute resolution: a conceptual framework for investor-state conflict management. In: Echandi R, Sauvé P (eds) Prospects in international investment law and policy: world trade forum. Cambridge University Press, p 270

Franck SD (2007) Integrating investment treaty conflict and dispute systems design. Minn Law Rev 92:266

Fuller LL (1962) Collective bargaining and the arbitrator. In: Kahn ML (ed) Collective bargaining and the arbitrator's role: proceedings of the fifteenth annual meeting of national academy of arbitrators (Bureau of National Affairs Inc., pp 29–30

Guiguo W (2011) Chinese mechanisms for resolving investor-state disputes. Jindal J Int Aff 1:211

Horodyski D (2016) Democratic deficit of investment arbitration in the view of rules on transparency and mauritius convention on transparency. US-China Law Rev 13:166–167

Kishoiyian B (1994) The utility of bilateral investment treaties in the formulation of customary international law. Northwest J Int Law Bus 14:330

Lack J, Bogacz F (2012) The neurophysiology of ADR and process design: a new approach to conflict prevention and resolution? Cardozo J Confl Resolut 4:33–80
Lack J (2011) Appropriate dispute resolution (ADR): the spectrum of hybrid techniques available to the parties. In: Ingen-Housz A (ed) ADR in business, practice and issues across countries and cultures. Kluwer Law International, pp 339–379
Legum B, Joubin-Bret A, Manassyan I (2013) Rules for investor–state mediation: draft prepared by the International Bar Association State Mediation Subcommittee. In: Echandi R, Sauvé P (eds) Prospects in international investment law and policy—world trade forum. Cambridge University Press, pp 265–266
Malanczuk P (2015) China and the emerging standard of transparency in investor-state dispute settlement (ISDS). N Z Assoc Comp Law 19:91–93
McAdoo B, Welsh NA (2004) Court-connected general civil ADR programs: aiming for institutionalization, efficient resolution, and the experience of justice. In: Stienstra D, Yates S (eds) ADR handbook for judges. American Bar Association, pp 16–17
McGovern F (2006) Mediation of the snake river basin. Ida Law Rev 42:548–553
Menkel-Meadow CJ et al (2010) Dispute resolution: beyond the adversary model, pp 270–296
Nitschke F (2014) The IBA's investor–state mediation rules and the ICSID dispute settlement framework. ICSID Rev 29:113–114
Nurick L, Schnably SJ (1986) The first ICSID conciliation: tesoro petroleum corporation v. trinidad and tobago ICSID Rev 1:342
Salacuse JW (2007) Is there a better way? Alternative methods of treaty-based, investor-state dispute resolution. Fordham Int Law J 31:155
Schonewille M, Lack J (2014) Mediation in the European union and abroad: 60 states divided by a common word? In: Schonewille M, Schonewille F (eds) The variegated landscape of mediation: a comparative study of mediation regulation and practices in europe and the world . Eleven International Publishing, pp 25–35
Stevens M, Love B (2010) Investor-state mediation: observations on the role of institutions. In: Rovine AW (ed) Contemporary issues in international arbitration and mediation: the fordham papers 2009. Martinus Nijhoff Publishers, p 411
Timothy Martin A (2011) International mediation: an evolving market. In: Rovine AW (ed) Contemporary issues in international arbitration and mediation: the fordham papers 2010. Martinus Nijhoff Publishers, p 415
Welsh N, Schneider AK (2012) Becoming "Investor-State Mediation". Penn State J Law Int Aff 1(1):94
Welsh N, Schneider AK (2013) The thoughtful integration of mediation into bilateral investment treaty arbitration. Harv Negot Law Rev 18:116–117
Wälde TW (2006) Efficient management of transnational disputes: mutual gain by mediation or joint loss in litigation. Arbitr Int 22:206
Zhang J (2014) The tradition and modern transition of Chinese law, pp 429–456. Springer

Chunlei Zhao Assistant researcher of the Institute of International Dispute Settlement at Tsinghua University. This paper was orignially published in Chinese Journal of International Law, Volume 17, Issue 1, March 2018, Pages 111–135.

Chapter 9
China and the Investment Treaty Regime: Rule Taker or Rule Maker?

Sheng Zhang

The year of 2018 marks the 40th anniversary of China's opening-up policy, which gives us a great opportunity to review China's developments and contributions in the area of international investment treaty regime. Since its first bilateral investment treaty (BIT) with Sweden in 1982, China has signed BITs with more than 130 countries. Indeed, China's practice in international investment law is also a microcosm of China's participation in general international law. When signing BITs, China mainly follows the template or style as set by western countries. Yet with the development of China's economic growth, China is more willing to establish its own approach toward the investment treaties. The Belt and Road Initiative (BRI), and the BITs negotiations separately with the US and the EU, reveals China's proactive approach to participate in the global economic governance. The experience in dealing with the cases filed with foreign investors against China also enables China to review its BIT policy. In a time of anti-globalisation, China's more open and liberal attitude toward foreign investment not only helps to restore foreign investors' confidence, but also to maintain the stability of the international investment law regime.

Against this background, this chapter will present a stocktaking of China's practice in international investment law. Apart from the conclusion, it contains four parts: part I attempts to describe the path of development of China's FDI policy and BITs practice; Part II focuses on China's practice in international investment arbitration by delving into the reasons for why there have been only a few cases against China. Part III compares China's BITs practice with those of the EU and the US, addressing to what extent China maintains some basic positions. Part IV discusses China's

This chapter was first published in the book "The Asian Turn in Foreign Investment". See Sheng Zhang, China and the Investment Treaty Regime: Rule Taker or Rule Maker?, in Mahdev Mohan and Chester Brown (eds.), The Asian Turn in Foreign Investment, Cambridge University Press, 2021.

S. Zhang (✉)
28 Xian Ning West Road, Xian, China
e-mail: sheng-zhang@xjtu.edu.cn

© The Author(s), under exclusive license to Springer Nature Singapore Pte Ltd. 2024

S. Wei (ed.), *International Investment Law at the Juncture*, International Law in Asia,
https://doi.org/10.1007/978-981-97-2183-2_9

proactive approach in particular with the implementation of the BRI. Based on such discussions, this chapter tries to reveal that approach of utilitarianism and flexibility in China's BITs negotiations. Yet, China is not simply copying the EU's or the US's treaty text, but will be basing on their own political system and economic reality to make the necessary adjustments. It also maintains some basic positions to incorporate the concept of sovereignty and the identity of a developing country.

The Evolving Approach of China's FDI Policy and the BITs Practice

China launched its BIT programme in ced in 1978, the BIT programme was intended to attract FDI to fuel economic growth. Earlier Chinese BITs mainly targeted developed countries. By 1986, China had already signed BITs with many European States. Yet, the initial BITs were very conservative, and reflected China's traditional scepticism toward international law.[1] Most BITs do not grant foreign investors national treatment or provide them with a limited national treatment subject to domestic laws. Meanwhile, China insisted that only disputes about the amount of compensation could be submitted to international arbitration.

The 1990s witnessed a surge of foreign investment in China. To better accommodate the benefits of FDI and further stimulate the flow of FDI, China started to make adjustments to its economic system, abandoning the planned economy and accepting 'the market economy' in the form of the 'socialist market economy'. The constitutional status of these changes was established in 1993 through amendments to the Constitution.[2] At the international level, in line with further economic reform and the 'opening-up' policy, China signed the ICSID Convention on 9 February 1990 and ratified it on 7 January 1993.[3]

A more liberal approach has been applied to foreign investment since 1998. The unprecedented amount of FDI and the intensified competition for FDI with Latin American and Eastern European states pushed China into updating its BIT programme. At the same time, China's rapid economic growth, in particular the increase in foreign exchange reserves, created the need for an outward direct investment strategy.[4] In 1998, the 'going abroad' strategy was introduced; the aim was to explore international markets and take advantage of foreign resources to strengthen the development and potential of the Chinese economy. This strategy was officially stated in the Outline of the Tenth Five-Year Plan (FYP) for the National Economy and Social Development in 2001.[5] Another factor in these changes was China's accession to the World Trade Organisation (WTO) in 2001. Unlike the first stage of BITs,

---

[1] Schill (2007). See also Wang (2001–2002).

[2] Gallagher and Shan (2009), pp. 7–8.

[3] Gallagher and Shan (2009), p. 38.

[4] Shan et al. (2012), pp. 120–144.

[5] Rongji (2001).

which was characterised by the need to attract FDI and emphasised capital import, the investment policy during this period has been based on both the import and export of capital, with an emphasis on the protection of outward direct investment. Since the 1998 China-Barbados BIT, which is the first treaty to accommodate these changes in polices, most Chinese BITs have included full national treatment and access of all investor-state disputes to international arbitration.

However, most of the liberal BITs remain focused solely on investment protection and are silent on sustainable development issues. There are three factors influencing this focus. First, since 1998, apart from renegotiating BITs with European States, China has mainly signed BITs with developing countries from Asia, Africa, and Latin America. These BITs, like other BITs between developing countries, show few deviations from the European-style BITs.[6] Indeed, the traditional European-style BITs still play a dominant role in world BITs.[7] Secondly, China's BIT strategy continued to be based on economic considerations, particularly the need for inbound FDI to power rapid economic growth.[8] At the same time, the implementation of the 'going abroad' policies meant that China needed to facilitate and protect the interests of China's overseas enterprises. Thirdly, from a theoretical perspective, the restrictions implied in the clause 'in accordance with the domestic laws and regulations', which was common in Chinese BITs, entitled the host state to impose regulatory measures.

This approach has changed in recent years, in particular since 2008 when China adopted a more balanced type of investment treaty, with a recalibration of the substantive provisions.[9] A notable development is the introduction of the concept of sustainable development. In actual fact, it was developments in China's internal policies that lead China's investment treaties to embrace the concept of sustainable development. Since 2006, China shifted its emphasis from the quantity of FDI to the quality of FDI. This change was clearly demonstrated in the 11th FYP on Foreign Capital Utilisation, where China asserted it would propel the fundamental conversion from 'being quantity oriented' to 'being quality oriented' and focus more on sustainable development, which is further supported by the introduction of a 'scientific outlook on development'.[10] By pursuing a 'People-orientated, comprehensive, co-ordinated

[6] UNCTAD (2005). It is also observed that the dynamic of BITs between more developed Southern country versus the lesser-developed Southern mirrors that of the BITs between developed countries and developing countries and, therefore the North–South European template is used. Further, such template could avail the Southern countries to negotiate the specialist legal instruments given that they have traditionally had limited capacity and knowledge. See Malik (2010).

[7] For instance, an observation of the examples of BITs concluded in 2010 and 2011 reveals that several countries continued to adopt such traditional approach. See Schill and Jacob (2013).

[8] Indeed, behind the high rate of growth, there was a severe environmental degradation. However, among the leadership and the public, development was primarily regarded as economic growth, while damage to the environment or natural resources was perceived as 'growing pain' and unavoidable costs for economic development. See Xue (2012), p. 172.

[9] Berger (2015), pp. 843–868 at 843.

[10] The 11th Five-Year Plan on the Utilization of Foreign Investments, published by the State Development and Reform Commission (SDRC) on 6 November 2006. English version is

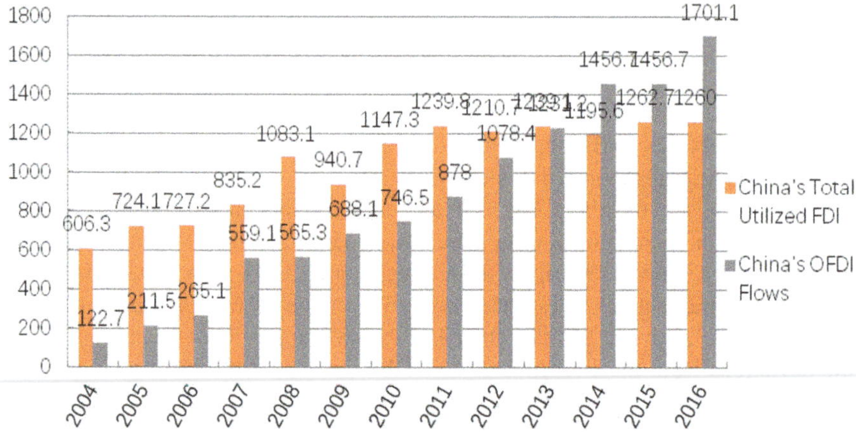

Chart 9.1 China's FDI and OFDI from 2004–2016 (Unit: 100 Million US dollars). *Source* MOFCOM

and sustainable development', the 'scientific outlook on development' is similar to or even broader than the concept of sustainable development.[11]

China's BIT entered into a new phase in 2013, when China and the US agreed to negotiate an investment treaty based on pre-establishment national treatment and negative list.[12] Such a move was regarded as the beginning of an emerging Chinese BIT 4.0.[13] It is a result of a combination of economical and political factors. Economically, as revealed in Chart 9.1, with the steady increase of the outward direct investment, China has been a net capital exporting country since 2014. It is unsurprising that China would play a more proactive role to provide sufficient support of the outward FDI. Politically, when domestic reform enters a deep water zone, a push from external forces would be necessary to ensure that the internal reform proceeds smoothly. As opening up and reform have been launched as integral parts of the same initiative, a breakthrough in the investment treaty practice would lead to deeper reform. The negative list approach, in particular, requires a reform of state governance, which need further streamline for the administration and 'cancel all administrative approval procedures for economic activities under the effective regulation of the market mechanism.'[14]

available at www.fdi.gov.cn/pub/FDI_EN/Laws/GeneralLawsandRegulations/MinisterialRulings/t20061220_68109.jsp. In line with this new FDI policy, China also made steady efforts to reform the domestic laws to eliminate the preferential treatment enjoyed by foreign investment. For details, please see Shan et al. (2012), pp. 129–138.

[11] Xue (2012), pp. 192–193.

[12] MOFCOM (2013).

[13] Shan and Chen (2016), pp. 223–254.

[14] CPC (2014).

In parallel with BITs, China is also proactive in FTA negotiations. Currently, China has concluded 15 FTAs covering 23 countries or regions.[15] FTAs are deemed by China as a new platform for further opening up and speeding up domestic growth, as well as an effective approach to integrating into the global economy. FTAs also help to strengthen China's economic cooperation with other economies. China's early FTAs were confined to trade affairs,[16] but more recent ones provide wider coverage in goods, services, investment, and most of them explicitly consider the concept of sustainable development. Furthermore, FTAs normally include a broader understanding of environmental protection than the BITs.[17]

China's Practice in International Investment Dispute Settlement

Although China signed a great number of investment treaties, China's exposure to international investment arbitration remains rare. This seems a bit surprising as China continues to be a source of increasing FDI. Behind this lies a series of legal and cultural reasons.

First, as mentioned above, almost all the Chinese BITs signed before 1998 only allow disputes concerning the amount of compensation for expropriation to be submitted to international investment arbitration. This narrower offer of consent to arbitration prevents China from being sued frequently in investment arbitration. It should be pointed out that such a position may not be solid as it seems. In the cases of *Tza Yap Shum v. Peru* and *Sanum v. Laos*, both the tribunals held that the word 'involving' in the phase 'involving the amount of compensation for expropriation' in the 1994 China-Peru BIT and the 1993 China-Laos BIT was broad enough to cover claims of expropriation.[18] However, while the wording supports claims of expropriation, it would not cover other claims, such as those regarding fair and equitable treatment or full protection and security, as held by the tribunal of *Tza Yap*

[15] China FTA Network, http://fta.mofcom.gov.cn/english/index.shtml.

[16] Such as the Closer Economic Partnership Agreements concluded in 2001 with Hong Kong and Macau and the FTA with Chile in 2005.

[17] Hepburn et al. (2007).

[18] *Señor Tza Yap Shum v. The Republic of Peru*, ICSID Case No. ARB/07/6, Decision on Jurisdiction and Competence, 19 June 2009, para. 188. *Sanum Investments Limited v. Lao People's Democratic Republic*, UNCITRAL, PCA Case No. 2013–13, Award on Jurisdiction, 13 December 2013, para. 342. Some may also argue that the Most Favoured Nation (MFN) clause in the BITs would be applied to broaden the scope of consent of arbitration, as held by the tribunal of *RosInvest v. Russia*. By referring to the MFN provision of the UK-Russia BIT and relying on a more extensive dispute settlement provision in the Denmark-UK BIT, the tribunal held that the investors from UK could submit a claim over expropriation to arbitration, while the basic treaty only allowed for arbitration over claims involving the amount of compensation for expropriation. See *RosInvestCo UK Ltd. v. The Russian Federation*, SCC Case No. V079/2005, Award on Jurisdiction, October 2007, para. 139.

Shum v. Peru.[19] Further, uncertainty still exists in case law. A Swedish appeal court, for instance, rejected a broad interpretation when interpreting a similarly narrowly worded treaty provision in the Spain-Russia BIT. Article 10 of the Spain-Russia BIT only allows arbitration for disputes relating to the amount or method of payment of the compensation for expropriation. The Court of Appeal concluded that the arbitral tribunal's jurisdiction under the treaty did not cover a review as to whether expropriation occurred or not.[20]

Secondly, most of the Chinese BITs obligate foreign investors to go through the appropriate domestic administrative review process before seeking international arbitration. Even in BITs where China agreed to grant investors full access to international investment arbitration, China has continued to insist on such an obligation. For instance, in the Protocol of the 2003 China-Germany BIT, to Article 9 of the investor-state dispute settlement, it provides that:

> With respect to investments in the People's Republic of China an investor of the Federal Republic of Germany may submit a dispute for arbitration under the following conditions only:
>
> (a) the investor has referred the issue to an administrative review procedure according to Chinese law,
>
> (b) the dispute still exists three months after he has brought the issue to the review procedure, and
>
> (c) in case the issue has been brought to a Chinese court, it can be withdrawn by the investor according to Chinese law.

Under such an obligation, foreign investors cannot immediately commence investment arbitration. Indeed, there have been cases between foreign investors and Chinese local governments that were settled through administrative remedies.[21]

Thirdly, the legal regime relating to the recognition and enforcement of investment arbitral awards also discourages foreign investors to seek international investment arbitration. When acceding to the New York Convention on the Recognition and Enforcement of Foreign Arbitral Awards (New York Convention), the Chinese government made a commercial reservation that China would apply the New York Convention only to differences arising out of legal relationships which are considered as commercial under Chinese national law.[22] Subsequently, the People's Republic of China issued the Notice on the Implementation of the New York Convention, which clearly excluded arbitral awards in relation to international investment disputes

[19] *Tza Yap Shum v. The Republic of Peru*, ICSID Case No. ARB/07/6, Decision on Jurisdiction and Competence, 19 June 2009, para. 216.

[20] SVEA Court of Appeal, Judgment, 18 January 2016, available at www.italaw.com/sites/default/files/case-documents/italaw7714_8.pdf.

[21] For details, please see Gallagher and Shan (2009), pp. 371–376.

[22] New York Arbitration Convention, Contracting States, www.newyorkconvention.org/countries.

from the list of awards that could be recognised and enforced in China.[23] Such a commercial reservation does not apply to an arbitral award rendered by an ICSID arbitral tribunal in accordance with the ICSID Convention, as Article 54 creates a system of self-execution. However, China has not enacted any specific legislation to comply with the recognition and enforcement obligations under the ICSID Convention, creating uncertainty regarding China's compliance with these obligations.[24] Meanwhile, given that Article 54(3) provides that the 'execution of the award shall be governed by the laws concerning the execution of judgment in force in the State in whose territories such execution is sought'; the execution against the property of a State would be a problem in China. China continues to insist on the principles of absolute sovereign immunity. This would also prevent the local courts from attaching the assets of a State to execute an ICSID award.[25]

Finally, in a country where the traditional culture prefers an amicable settlement of disputes, arbitration or litigation would be regarded as serious challenges to harmony and good relationships.[26] In most Asian countries, law and contracts are subordinated to evolving circumstances and relational values. Contracts are seen more as a beginning of a good relationship than is a conclusion of a deal.[27] Particularly in China, there has been a longstanding tradition of a dislike of litigation. As of now, Confucianism, which attaches significance to harmony, still maintains a great degree of cultural influence over Chinese society.[28] In light of this culture, investment arbitration may be considered as jeopardising the good relationship between the foreign investors and the host governments, which may eventually lead to a phasing out of foreign investment in China.

As of September 2017, China has been involved in only three ICSID cases, one filed by a Malaysian investor in 2011, one filed by a South Korean investor in 2014, and the third one filed by a German investor in 2017. These three cases will be analysed as follows:

1. ***Ekran v. China***[29]

This was the first ICISD case against China. This case, which was filed by a Malaysian investor in 2011, arose out of a dispute concerning the rights under a lease over 900 hectares of land in one Chinese local province held by Ekran Berhad's (Ekran's) local subsidiary. Ekran claimed that the local government revoked its subsidiary's rights to the leasehold land due to a failure to develop the land as required under local

[23] People's Supreme Court of China, Notice of the Supreme People's Court on Implementing the Convention on the Recognition and Enforcement of Foreign Arbitral Awards Acceded to by China, No. 5 (1987) of the Supreme People's Court, 4 October 1987.

[24] Ku (2013).

[25] Wang (2011), pp. 204–233 at 228.

[26] Wang (2011), p. 222.

[27] Hwang (2005), pp. 410–411.

[28] Wang (2011), pp. 222–224.

[29] *Ekran Berhad v. People's Republic of China*, ICSID Case No. ARB/11/15.

regulations. This case was settled even before the tribunal was constituted.[30] While further details remain unknown to the public, one thing is for sure: China normally takes a cautious approach toward international disputes. This may explain why the first ICSID case against China ended up in a settlement rather than arbitration.

2. ***Ansung Housing v. China***[31]

Ansung Housing (Ansung) is a South Korean investor that invested in a golf course and condominium development project in the Jiangsu province. By alleging that the various arbitrary and illegal actions and omissions of the local government had deprived it of use and enjoyment of its investment, Ansung brought an ICSID claim against China on 4 November 2014. With respect to the dispute settlement, Article 9 of the 2007 China-South Korea BIT provides that:

1. For the purposes of this Article, an investment dispute is a dispute between one Contracting Party and an investor of the other Contracting Party that has incurred loss or damage by reason of, or arising out of, an alleged breach of this Agreement with respect to an investment of an investor of that other Contracting Party.
2. In the event of an investment dispute, the investment dispute shall, if possible, be settled by consultation or negotiation. If it is not so settled, the investor may submit the investment dispute for resolution under one of the following alternatives:

   (a) a competent court of the state where the investment was made;
   (b) international arbitration after four months from the date the dispute has been raised for consultation by either party.

3. In case of international arbitration, the dispute shall be submitted, at the option of the investor, to:

   (a) International Center for Settlement of Investment Disputes (ICSID) under the Convention on the Settlement of Disputes between States and Nationals of Other States, done at Washington on March 18, 1965;or.
   (b) an ad hoc arbitration tribunal established under UNCITRAL Arbitration Rules or any other arbitration rules agreed upon by both parties;

……

4. Notwithstanding the provisions of paragraph 3 of this Article, an investor may not make a claim pursuant to paragraph 3 of this Article if more than three years have elapsed from the date on which the investor first acquired, or should have first acquired, knowledge that the investor had incurred loss or damage.

The temporal limitation period as established in paragraph 7 of Article 9 was the central debate in this case. China filed an objection under Rule 41(5) of the ICSID

[30] Qi (2012).

[31] *Ansung Housing Co., Ltd. v. People's Republic of China*, ICSID Case No. ARB/14/25.

Arbitration Rules, asserting that Ansung's claim was 'manifestly without legal merit'. China claimed that Ansung instituted the arbitration more than three years after it first acquired knowledge that it had incurred loss or damage and the MFN clause in the 2007 China-South Korea BIT could not save Ansung's untimely claim.[32] China argued that Article 9(7) of the 2007 China-South Korea BIT, as provided above, addressed knowledge of the *fact* that there had been a loss, but not knowledge of the *quantum* lost.[33] Ansung necessarily knew of the fact that it had incurred loss on some date prior to the disposal of its investment in October 2011. Given that the case was registered by ICSID only on 4 November 2014, China therefore asserted that Ansung did not follow Article 9(7) of the treaty, which rendered the claim time-barred.[34] The tribunal agreed that the facts revealed that Ansung first acquired or should have first acquired knowledge that it had incurred loss or damage before October 2011.[35] In the tribunal's view, 'Ansung's actual sale of its shares on December 17, 2011 marked the date on which it could *finalize* or *liquidate* its damage, not the *first* date on which it had to know it was incurring damage'.[36] With respect to the *dies ad quem* for the applicable temporal limitation period, the tribunal argued that the plain language in Article 9(7) of the 2007 China-South Korea BIT pointed to the date on which the investor deposited its request for ICSID arbitration, which was the date of 7 October 2014 electronically and the date of 8 October 2014 physically. Either date is more than three years after the *Dies a Quo*.[37] The tribunal therefore concluded that the three-year limitation period had elapsed and the claim was time-barred.[38]

The tribunal further considered that whether the MFN clause in the 2007 China-South Korea BIT could save Ansung's claim from being time-barred. Article 3 of the 2007 China-South Korea BIT provides:

5. Each Contracting Party shall in its territory accord to investors of the other Contracting Party and to their investments and activities associated with such investments by the investors of the other Contracting Party treatment no less favourable than that accorded in like circumstances to the investors and investments and associated activities by the investors of any third State(hereinafter referred to as 'most-favoured-nation treatment') with respect to investments and business activities, including the admission of investment.

[32] *Ansung Housing Co., Ltd. v. People's Republic of China*, ICSID Case No. ARB/14/25, Award, 9 March 2017, para. 56.

[33] *Ansung Housing Co., Ltd. v. People's Republic of China*, ICSID Case No. ARB/14/25, Award, 9 March 2017, para. 76.

[34] *Ansung Housing Co., Ltd. v. People's Republic of China*, ICSID Case No. ARB/14/25, Award, 9 March 2017, para. 85.

[35] *Ansung Housing Co., Ltd. v. People's Republic of China*, ICSID Case No. ARB/14/25, Award, 9 March 2017, para. 114.

[36] *Ansung Housing Co., Ltd. v. People's Republic of China*, ICSID Case No. ARB/14/25, Award, 9 March 2017, para. 110.

[37] *Ansung Housing Co., Ltd. v. People's Republic of China*, ICSID Case No. ARB/14/25, Award, 9 March 2017, para. 115.

[38] *Ansung Housing Co., Ltd. v. People's Republic of China*, ICSID Case No. ARB/14/25, Award, 9 March 2017, para. 122.

……

6. Treatment accorded to investors of one Contracting Party within the territory of the other Contracting Party with respect to access to the courts of justice and administrative tribunals and authorities both in pursuit and in defence of their rights shall not be less favourable than that accorded to investors of the latter Contracting Party or to investors of any third State.

Ansung argued that the term 'treatment' and 'investment activities' in Article 3(3) of the treaty should be interpreted to cover dispute settlement procedures. Yet China contested that a contextual interpretation of Article 3(5) of the treaty demonstrated that Article 3(3) is unrelated to dispute settlement.[39] By referring to Article 3(5), the tribunal concluded that a plain reading of Article 3 does not extend to MFN treatment for a State's consent to arbitrate with investors and, in particular, not to the three-year period in Article 9(7) of the treaty.[40] Article 3(5) only offers MFN protection in relation to an investor's remedies through domestic avenues, while such express reference to international dispute resolution is conspicuously absent in Article 3(3).[41]

As a result, the tribunal determined that China established its Rule 41(5) objection 'clearly and obviously, with relative ease and despatch'.[42] The tribunal therefore found Ansung's claim to be manifestly without legal merit.[43]

3. ***Hela Schwarz v. China***[44]

On 21 June 2017, ICSID registered the third case against China. It was brought by a German investor in accordance with the 2003 China-Germany BIT. As of now, the tribunal has yet to be constituted and little is known about the case. The claimant, Hela Schwarz GmbH (Hela Schwarz), is a German-owned spice and food additive manufacturer, and it had invested in the city of Jinan since 1996.[45]

Considering that China is proactive in the international investment treaty regime, and with foreign investors becoming increasingly aware of the protection under the BITs, it is not unlikely that more cases will be brought against China in the future. China's participation in the ICSID cases also illustrates that China's attitude toward international investment arbitration is developing toward greater acceptance and engagement.[46] More cases could be expected, in particular if the China-US BIT and the China-EU BIT are successfully concluded.

---

[39] *Ansung Housing Co., Ltd. v. People's Republic of China*, ICSID Case No. ARB/14/25, Award, 9 March 2017, paras. 127–8.

[40] *Ansung Housing Co., Ltd. v. People's Republic of China*, ICSID Case No. ARB/14/25, Award, 9 March 2017, para. 138.

[41] *Ansung Housing Co., Ltd. v. People's Republic of China*, ICSID Case No. ARB/14/25, Award, 9 March 2017, para. 139.

[42] *Ansung Housing Co., Ltd. v. People's Republic of China*, ICSID Case No. ARB/14/25, Award, 9 March 2017, para. 142.

[43] *Ansung Housing Co., Ltd. v. People's Republic of China*, ICSID Case No. ARB/14/25, Award, 9 March 2017, para. 143.

[44] Hela Schwarz GmbH v. People's Republic of China, ICSID Case No. No. ARB/17/19.

[45] Peterson and Williams (2017).

[46] Moynihan (2017).

Rule Taker or Rule Maker?

In contrast to the uncompromising position taken by the US, China maintains a great flexibility in its BITs negotiations.[47] Such an approach, termed as utilitarianism or pragmatism,[48] could explain why China mainly follows the prototype of the states it is negotiating with. As observed by Axel Berger, China normally chooses the partner country's BIT template as the starting point, and only when such a BIT template does not exist or the partner country fails to put forward the template, China would propose its own model to facilitate the negotiations.[49] Since most of the Chinese BITs signed in the 1980s were between China and the European states, it is easier to understand why most of the BITs signed by China adopt the European style, focusing mainly on investment protection.[50] All three versions of the Chinese model BIT also resemble the European style BITs. Given that the European style BIT is simply drafted, it is more manageable and makes it much easier to push negotiations forward, in particular when there is a tight agenda and the negotiators lack sufficient expertise in the earlier stages.[51] However, the European style BITs may fall short in addressing the non-economic concerns, such as the environment, labour, and national security. Hence, there is an increasing Americanisation of investment treaties, as the American BITs, represented by the NAFTA, are much more comprehensive, featuring broad coverage and a balanced regime.

With the fast development of its economy, in particular the development of outward-flow of FDI, China has developed from a mere capital-importing country to a country with a mixed status of being a top country of both capital-importing and capital-exporting. Meanwhile, the shift of tension on global BIT regime has been developing from the 'north–south divide' to the 'private–public debate'.[52] Against this background, China considers pursuing a partially "NAFTA" inspired investment policy, and there seems to be a shift from the European investment treaty model to the American one in China's recent IAAs, in particular since the 2008 China-New Zealand FTA.

Yet, in its BIT practice, China does not mechanically imitate the European states or the US. A closer look at the treaty texts reveals China still maintains a degree of flexibility to accommodate its political system and economic reality.

First, China still attaches significance to the concept of sovereignty. The principle of sovereignty was the foundation of China's relations with the international community, and it was the source of China's other principles. China's persistent

---

[47] See Kong (1998), pp. 105–136, 110 and Berger (2015), p. 866.

[48] As pointed out by Professor Kenneth Vandevelde, the US mainly proposed to negotiate the BITs largely based on its model BIT, and it was extremely reluctant from the beginning to compromise on any but a few of the BIT provisions. If such proposal was not accepted, there would be no BIT with that state. See Vandevelde (2009).

[49] Berger (2015), pp. 865–866.

[50] Li (2014).

[51] Chi (2017).

[52] Shan (2007).

stand has its roots in the miserable and humiliating experience of foreign oppression and invasion since the Opium War in 1840s.[53] Such a position also affects China's attitude toward international investment disputes, featuring a hesitant embrace of international investment arbitration. Given that jurisdiction of domestic courts is also one manifestation of sovereignty, some BITs, such as the BIT with Sri Lanka, also requires the legality of any measure of expropriation to be reviewed by the competent domestic court in the manner prescribed by the domestic law.[54]

Based on the principle of sovereignty and the 'Five Principles of Peaceful Co-existence', China further developed 'three guiding principles' of international economic co-operation and exchange: the principle of sovereignty; equality and mutual benefit; and reference to international practice.[55] These guiding principles have been expressly referenced in China's BITs practice. Most of the BITs concluded between 1988 and 1993 include a reference to the principles of mutual respect for sovereignty and equality and mutual benefit in their preambles. These BITs are mainly signed with Asian countries and former Soviet Union countries. Some of the BITs with developed countries also have such preambular wordings, such as the 1988 China-Australia BIT and the 1992 China-Spain BIT. While direct reference to the principle of mutual respect for sovereignty is omitted in most of the BITs concluded after 1993, this does not render the concept of sovereignty unimportant. The principle of equality and mutual benefit remains to be seen, and the recent China-Tanzania BIT witnessed a return of this novel concept, as it emphasises the principle of respecting economic sovereignty in the preamble. This reveals that China mainly considers BITs as an instrument of economics and it should hence bear the essence of the depoliticisation. It could also explain why China refused to put the issue of human rights on the table during the negotiations, such as during the FTA talk with Australia.[56]

Secondly, BITs negotiations should accommodate the political system and economic reality.[57] As mentioned by Li Shishi, China maintains that BITs should be based on the political independence and economic self-determination of Contracting States.[58] Before China's Constitution was revised to make the development of a socialist market economy one of the fundamental policy goals in 1993, China maintained a planned economy, in which state ownership, collective ownership and individual ownership co-existed. Given that it was quite different from the market economy, it was impossible for China to grant foreign investors national treatment.[59] Only when the role of the market was changed from the edge to the centre of economic development, national treatment becomes a common reference in Chinese BITs.

---

[53] Indeed, Judge Wang Tieya described China has been 'a most enthusiastic champion' for the principle of sovereignty. See Wang (1990).

[54] Article 6(2) of the 1986 China-Sri Lanka BIT.

[55] Kong (1998), p. 109.

[56] Petrovic and Grunberg (2017).

[57] Shan and Chen (2016), pp. 248–250.

[58] Li (1988) p. 164.

[59] Li (1988), p. 167.

In spite of its fast economic growth, China still sees itself as a developing country. This perspective enables China to adhere to some different approaches from the developed countries. For instance, China used to stand firmly with other developing countries to fight against the 'Hull Formula' of 'adequate, effective and prompt compensation' with respect to the standard of expropriation. While changes have been made in the recent BITs to gradually conform to the practice of the US, China is still hesitant to refer directly to the 'Hull Formula'. Meanwhile, China does not accept that the 'Hull Formula' reflects the customary international law concerning the obligation of States with respect to expropriation.[60] The general approach is expropriation should be made against compensation, yet there is no uniform standard of compensation. Indeed, the standard of compensation is one subject to be discussed during the BITs negotiations.[61] It should also be noted that the 'Hull Formula' is not adopted by the International Law Commission in the 'Responsibility of States for Internationally Wrongful Acts' (2001), which only provides that 'the compensation shall cover any financially assessable damage including loss of profits insofar as it is established'.

China's identity as a developing country also makes it better placed to consider the different levels of developments of the Contracting States in its investment treaties negotiations, such as the Regional Comprehensive Economic Partnership (RCEP) negotiations, which directly refers to special and different treatment. Under such a principle, the RCEP negotiations should take into consideration the different levels of development of the participating countries, and the RCEP will include appropriate forms of flexibility in drafting specific provisions.[62] This principle has already been incorporated in the preamble of the China-Association of Southeast Asian Nations (ASEAN) Agreement on Investment.[63]

The political system and the economic reality also affect China's position on the State Owned Enterprises (SOEs). Although the share of SOEs in China's outward foreign direct investment (OFDI) is decreasing in recent years, SOEs still play a dominant role in China's OFDI. By the end of 2015, SOEs has taken a share of 50.4% in China's non-financial outward FDI stock.[64] It would be impossible for Chinese BITs not to offer protection to SOEs.[65] When defining 'enterprise' as a covered investor, Article 1(2) of the 2013 China-Tanzania BIT provides that it means:

any entity, including companies, firms, associations, partnerships and other organizations, incorporated or constituted under the law and regulations of either Contracting Party and that have their seat and substantial business activities in that

[60] See Annex B of the 2012 US Model BIT.

[61] Sornarajah (2010), p. 209.

[62] Guiding Principles and Objectives for negotiating the Regional Comprehensive Economic Partnership, available at https://dfat.gov.au/trade/agreements/rcep/Documents/guiding-principles-rcep.pdf.

[63] China FTA Network, Agreement on Investment of the Framework Agreement on Comprehensive Economic Co-operation between China and ASEAN, http://fta.mofcom.gov.cn/dongmeng_phase2/annex/touzixieyi_en.pdf.

[64] MOFCOM (2016), p. 110.

[65] Shan and Chen (2016), pp. 249–250.

Contracting Party, irrespective of whether it is owned or controlled by a private person or the government.

Similar wording can also be found in the recent FTAs, such as Article 1(f) of the 2009 FTA between China and the ASEAN. In practice, as held by the tribunal in the case of *Beijing Urban v. Yemen,* China's publicly funded and wholly state-owned enterprises, could file investment arbitration with ICSID.[66] There is no doubt that Chinese SOEs should follow the rules of the host states, but they should also be entitled to the same protection as private investors as long as they are not acting as an agent for the government or performing government functions.

Thirdly, China's BIT practice is also shaped by the reflection on investment treaties by the international society, and in such a process China is seeking a different approach. As discussed in part II, China is only involved in a handful of investment arbitration disputes as a respondent. But as mentioned by Ms Li Yongjie, the Deputy Director-general of the Treaty and Law of MOFCOM, China needs to consider the global and domestic factors when considering a new generation of investment treaties, and the global context lies in the recent practice to improve the BITs by drawing on lessons from the ISDS practice.[67] The 2012 China-Canada BIT illustrates parties having greater control over ISDS. According to Article 20(2) of the China-Canada BIT, when a dispute arises out of a prudential measure, the investor-state tribunal cannot not decide whether and to what extent the defence of prudential measures is a valid defence, and it shall first seek the joint decision of the financial services authorities of the Contracting States. If such joint decision fails, a state to state arbitral tribunal should be established, and the holdings of the state to state arbitral tribunal shall be binding on the investor-state tribunal. In this respect, it seems that China is exploring a different approach from the US or Canada, as according to the Canadian or American model BITs, if the financial service authorities fail to reach a joint decision, the investor-state tribunal established could still proceed to reach a decision.[68] China's position, in actual fact, demonstrates the re-emergence of state to state dispute settlement, which represents a development toward a new third era of the investment treaty regime, featuring a co-existence of state to state arbitration and investor-state arbitration.[69] In recent treaty practice, such as the 2012 China-Canada BIT, 2015 China-South Korea FTA, and 2015 China-Australia FTA, China has already considered exploring the consensus-building approach between the Contracting States to interpret the meaning and scope of the treaty, and limiting the scope of disputes subject to the ISDS.

---

66 *Beijing Urban Construction Group Co. Ltd. v. Republic of Yemen,* ICSID Case No. ARB/14/30, Decision on Jurisdiction, 31 May 2017, paras. 40–1.

67 Li (2014), p. 173.

68 Article 17 of the 2004 Canadian Model BIT, and Article 20 of the 2012 US Model BIT.

69 Roberts (2014).

China's Role in Future International Investment Law

The international investment treaty regime has manifested, to some extent, China's growing confidence in adopting international rules and making its contribution. As an emerging power in international law, China is still discovering the best approaches to establish its soft power. Some have argued that China has failed to 'provide the world with ideological contribution that fundamentally challenges the triumph of liberal ideology in the wake of the end of the Cold War'.[70] However, recent years have already shown a more proactive China in the IIA developments.

The BRI, which was first proposed by Chinese president Xi Jinping in 2013, has gone beyond Asia to cover countries from all continents. While still in the early age of its implementation, it has been greeted with excitement globally and has been incorporated by the United Nations in its resolution. The UN Resolution, titled 'The Situation in Afghanistan', urged further efforts to strengthen the process of regional economic cooperation through BITs and other regional development efforts.[71]

As the BRI mainly covers emerging countries, the political, social, and economic climate of these countries will have essential bearings on the success of the investment under the BRI, including infrastructure investment that needs a higher volume of capital. However, the current dispute settlement mechanism is not well posited to solve the investment disputes. A closer look at the investment agreements between China and the countries of the BRI reveals that these treaties do not accord sufficient investment protection, nor do they sufficiently address the states' right to regulate.[72] In particular, there exists a large degree of divergence in the provisions of the ISDS in these investment agreements. No consistent approach could be found in areas of arbitral institutions and rules, the pre-conditions for submitting a claim, and the enforcement of arbitral awards.[73] Hence, a well set out dispute resolution mechanism would be imperative to minimise the potential risks. China could voice its contributions to build a consistent, predictable, and balanced system to effectively solve investment disputes.[74] Steps have been taken by China to facilitate the dispute settlement in the context of the BRI. On 16 June 2015, China's People's Supreme Court issued the "Several Opinions of the Supreme People's Court Concerning Judicial Services and Safeguards Provided by the People's Courts for the "Belt and Road" Construction"[75] to provide effective services and to guarantee the smooth

[70] Fidler (2005).

[71] United Nations (2016).

[72] See Dai (2017).

[73] Shu (2017). As mentioned by the UNCTAD, it is the time to move to a new phase of the reform of international investment agreement by modernizing the existing stock of old-generation treaties. See UNCTAD (2017a).

[74] Shu (2017), p. 106.

[75] The People's Supreme Court of The People's Republic of China, Opinions of the Supreme People's Court on people's courts providing judicial services and guarantees for the construction of the Belt and Road Initiative (in Chinese), 7 July 2015, available at, www.court.gov.cn/zixun-xiangqing-14900.html.

construction of the BRI. It was pointed out, in particular, that "Chinese courts should further expand the channels for international judicial exchange, closely watch the progress of the Asian Investment Bank and the construction of the Silk Road Fund, study in-depth the development trends of international law especially in finance, trade, investments, and maritime issues, and actively take part in and promote the formulation of relevant international rules."[76] In September 2017, the China International Economic and Trade Arbitration Commission (CIETAC) adopted the CIETAC Investment Arbitration Rules.[77] This is the first time that a Chinese arbitral institution adopted a set of rules specially designed for the settlement of international investment disputes. By referring to the practice in international investment arbitration, the CIETAC Investment Arbitration Rules include provisions on transparency[78] and third party funding.[79] This set of rules also incorporates some culture specific features, including the principle of good faith (*chengshi xinyong*)[80] and the combination of conciliation and arbitration.[81]

Meanwhile, under the active promotion of China, the Group of Twenty (G20) has reached a multilateral consensus on investment matters. The G20 Guiding Principles for Global Investment Policymaking, which was endorsed the by the G20 leaders at the Hangzhou Summit in September 2016, lays out the first global framework of multilateral rules governing international investment. These guiding principles feature the concrete efforts of G20 countries to push forward the development of international investment treaty regime toward multilateralism. Although these guiding principles are non-binding, they could serve as guiding instrument for updating domestic FDI policies and negotiating BITs.[82]

In addition, the ongoing negotiations of the China-US BIT and the China-EU BIT have great implications on the global investment regime. BITs between the largest developing country, and the world's largest developed country and the largest economy would not only incorporate the reflections by these countries on the ISDS, but also set up a model for other countries to refer to when considering improving their BITs. It should also be noted that during these negotiations, China would not purely imitate the text proposed by the EU and the US. Instead, with its BITs experience, China will naturally bring its interests on the table during the negotiations.[83] For instance, reports of the China-EU BIT negotiations, demonstrate that China did not follow the proposal by the European Commission and there are divided opinions

[76] The People's Supreme Court of The People's Republic of China, Opinions of the Supreme People's Court on people's courts providing judicial services and guarantees for the construction of the Belt and Road Initiative (in Chinese), 7 July 2015, para.15, available at, www.court.gov.cn/zixun-xiangqing-14900.html.

[77] CIETAC (2017).

[78] See for instance, Article 44 "Third Party Written Submission" and Article 55 "Publication" of the CIETAC Investment Arbitration Rules.

[79] Article 27 "Third Party Funding" of the CIETAC Investment Arbitration Rules.

[80] Article 6 "Good Faith" of the CIETAC Investment Arbitration Rules.

[81] Article 43 "Combination of Conciliation with Arbitration" of the CIETAC Arbitration Rules.

[82] UNCTAD (2017b).

[83] Zhang (2014).

in some areas.[84] With respect to ISDS, it seems that China is trying to maintain a balanced position between two ends separately held by the EU and the US. While the EU is vigorously pursuing the establishment of the international investment court system to reform the current ISDS system, the US still considers arbitration as the priority method to solve investment disputes.[85] With the steady increase of China's OFDI, China may not be averse to international investment arbitration, which would also be essential to solve international investment disputes during the implementation of the BRI. Yet, this does not mean China would be loyal to the traditional mechanism. Recent treaty practice has revealed that China would like to maintain a more restrictive scope of application for arbitration and maintain greater control over the investment arbitration, such as the establishment of the carve-out, the use of the alternative dispute resolution, the introduction of joint interpretation by the Contracting Sates, the increasing use of the state to state dispute settlement,[86] and the appeal mechanism.[87]

Conclusion

Within 30 years of development since implementing its opening-up policy, China's practice in international investment law has developed from being peripheral to the centre of focus. It has also helped to promote the transformation of related domestic law. Indeed, such development is just a microcosm of China's active role in the international law-making process in all fields. In its process to integrate in the global system, China is also trying to find an approach that does not blindly follow the path of the developed countries, but incorporates its identity as a developing country and its political economy. In the case of the rise of the protectionism and the anti-globalisation, China's implementation of the BRI would help to continue to build a more liberal and open world. The ongoing negotiations of the RCEP, the China-US BIT and the China-EU BIT would promote the global investment treaty regime to grow a more balanced direction and serve as the template for the reform of the investor-state dispute settlement, in particular when the United Nations Commission on International Trade Law is considering the reforms of this dispute settlement mechanism.[88]

---

[84] European Commission, EU-China Investment Agreement: Report of the 13th Round, 15 June 2017, available at http://trade.ec.europa.eu/doclib/docs/2017/june/tradoc_155625.pdf.

[85] According to Michael Froman, US Trade Representative in the Transatlantic Trade and Investment Partnership (TTIP) negotiations, the US is wary of the investment court system and he said 'It's not obvious to me why you would want to give companies a second bite of the apple.' See Krista Hughes and Philip Blenkinsop, US Wary of EU Proposal for Investment Court in Trade Pact, Reuters, 30 October 2015, available at www.reuters.com/article/us-trade-ttip/u-s-wary-of-eu-proposal-for-investment-court-in-trade-pact-idUSKCN0SN2LH20151029.

[86] See, for instance, Section 3 of the 2012 China-Canada BIT.

[87] See, for instance, Article 23, Chapter 9 of the 2015 China-Australia FTA.

[88] For details, please see UNCITRAL (2017).

References

Berger A (2015) Hesitant embrace: China's recent approach to international investment rule-making. J World Invest Trade 16(3)

Chi M (2017) From Europeanization toward Americanization: the shift of China's dichotomic investment treaty-making strategy. Can Foreign Policy J 23(2):158–170, 164

CIETAC (2017) CIETAC investment arbitration rules (for trial use) (in Chinese), 26 September 2017. www.cietac.org/Uploads/201709/59c8d60367bb5.pdf

CPC (2014) Decision of the CCCPC on some major issues concerning comprehensively deepening the reform, China.org.cn, 17 January 2014. www.china.org.cn/chinese/2014-01/17/content_31226494_4.htm

Dai AC (2017) The international investment agreement network under the "One Belt One Road" initiative'. Trans Disput Manag 14(3). www.transnational-dispute-management.com/article.asp?key=2474

Fidler DP (2005) The Asian century: implications for international law. Singapore year book of international law, vol 9, pp 19–35

Gallagher N, Shan W (2009) Chinese investment treaties: policies and practice. Oxford University Press, Oxford

Hepburn J et al (2007) Sustainable development in regional trade and investment agreements: policy innovations in Asia? Legal Working Paper, Centre for International Sustainable Development Law, p 40

Hwang M (2005) Why is there still resistance to arbitration in Asia. In: Aksen G, Briner R (eds) Global reflections on international law, commerce and dispute resolution: liber amicorum in honour of Robert Briner, International Chamber of Commerce, pp 410–411

Ku J (2013) The enforcement of ICSID awards in the People's Republic of China. Contemp Asian Arbitr J 6(1):31–48

Kong Q (1998) Bilateral investment treaties: the Chinese approach and practice. In: Asian Yearbook of international law, vol 8

Li S (1988) Bilateral investment promotion and protection agreements: practice of the People's Republic of China. In: de Waart PJIM, Peter P, Denters EMG (eds) Int Law Dev Martinus Nijhoff Publisher, London

Li Y (2014) Factors to be considered for China's future investment treaties. In: Shan W, Su J (eds) China and international investment law: twenty years of ICSID membership. Brill, Leiden

Malik M (2010) South-South bilateral investment treaties: the same old story?, In: IV annual forum for developing country investment negotiators background paper, New Delhi, October 27–29, 2010. www.iisd.org/pdf/2011/dci_2010_south_bits.pdf

MOFCOM (2013) MOFCOM spokesman Shen Danyang comments on China and US to promote energetically negotiations on bilateral investment agreement, July 16, 2013, http://english.mofcom.gov.cn/article/newsrelease/policyreleasing/201307/20130700200566.shtml

MOFCOM (2016) 2015 statistical bulletin of China's outward foreign direct investment. China Statistics Press, p 110

Moynihan H (2017) China's evolving approach to international dispute settlement. Chatham House

Petrovic J, Grunberg B (2017) Intersecting trade, politics and human rights: the negotiation phase of the Australia-China free trade agreement. J World Trade 51(1):67–104

Peterson LE, Williams Z (2017) Asia round-up: China and Vietnam face new BIT claims-by Hela Schwarz GmbH and Trinh Vinh Binh respectively-as proceedings against Korea and Indonesia move forward. Investment Arbitration Reporter, 22 June 2017

Qi T (2012) How exactly does China consent to investor-state arbitration: on the first ICSID case against China. Contemp Asia Arbitr J 5(2):265–291

Roberts A (2014) State-to-state investment treaty arbitration: a hybrid theory of interdependent rights and shared interpretive authority. Harv Int Law J 55(1):1–70

Rongji Z (2001) Report on the outline of the tenth five-year plan for national economic and social development, 5 March 2001, www.gov.cn/english/official/2005-07/29/content_18334.htm

Schill S (2007) Tearing down the great wall: the new generation investment treaties of the People's Republic of China. Cardozo J Int Comp Law 15:73 at 82
Schill S, Jacob M (2013) Trends in international investment agreements, 2011–2012: the increasing complexity of international investment law. In: Sauvant K (ed) Yearbook on international investment law & policy 2011–2012. Oxford University Press, Oxford, p 155
Shan W (2007) From "North-South Divide" to private-public debate: revival of the Calvo doctrine and the changing landscape in international investment law. Northwest J Int Law Bus 27(3):631–664, 664
Shan W, Chen H (2016) China-US BIT negotiation and the emerging Chinese BIT 4.0? In: Lim CL (ed) Alternative visions of the international law on foreign investment. Cambridge University Press, Cambridge
Shan W, Gallagher N, Zhang S (2012) National treatment for foreign investment in China: a changing landscape. ICSID Rev 27(1):120–144 at 123
Shu Z (2017) China's approach in drafting the investor-state arbitration clause: a review from the "Belt and Road" Regions' perspective. Chin J Comp Law 5(1):79–109, 98
Sornarajah M (2010) The international law on foreign investment, 3rd edn. Cambridge University Press, Cambridge, p 209
UNCITRAL (2017) Possible future work in the field of dispute settlement: reforms of investor - State dispute settlement (ISDS), A/CN.9/917. United Nations Publications, New York. https://documents-dds-ny.un.org/doc/UNDOC/GEN/V17/023/69/PDF/V1702369.pdf?OpenElement
UNCTAD (2005) South-South cooperation in international investment arrangements, UNCTAD series on international investment policies and development. United Nations Publications, New York and Geneva, p 31
UNCTAD (2017a) Phase 2 of IIA reform: modernizing the existing stock of old-generation treaties, IIA Issue Note, Issue 2. United Nations Publications, New York and Geneva, p 1
UNCTAD (2017b) World investment report 2017: investment and the digital economy. United Nations Publications, New York and Geneva, pp 118–119
United Nations (2016) General assembly adopts resolution supporting Afghanistan's efforts, as Speakers Vow to Help Conflict-affected Nation Achieve Untapped Potential, 17 November 2016, www.un.org/press/en/2016/ga11858.doc.htm
Vandevelde K (2009) US international investment agreements. Oxford University Press, Oxford, p 32
Wang T (1990) International law in China: historical and contemporary perspective. Recueil des Cours II (Collected Courses) 221: 203, 252–253
Wang G (2011) Chinese mechanisms for resolving investor-state disputes. Jindal J Int Aff 1(1):204–233 at 228
Wang J (2001–2002) China and the universal human rights standards. Syracuse J Int Law Commer 29:135–158 at 146
Xue H (2012) Chinese contemporary perspectives on international law: history, culture and international law. Hague Academy of International Law. Brill, Leiden
Zhang S (2014) The China-United States BIT negotiations: a Chinese perspective. Columbia FDI Perspectives, No. 112, 6 January 2014

Chapter 10
Investing in Macao—New Opportunities and Challenges Under the New Macao Financial Regulations

Cheng Hang Leong

Introduction

Unique Microeconomic Entity

China's Macao, as a microeconomic entity, exhibits distinctive characteristics in its economic and financial development.

Confronted with the objective reality of a relatively small-scaled economy, limited financial depth, and a somewhat concentrated industry structure, the key focus for Macao's banking industry lies in effectively harnessing both the unique advantages of an open economic system and the China-Portugal platform. This entails shrewdly leveraging the diverse policy measures provided by the central government to support Macao's development.

Since the handover more two decades ago, Macao has enjoyed a fast-paced economic growth paired with a remarkable transformation in its economic and social landscape. The total economic output has experienced an extraordinary growth, skyrocketing from 51.9 billion Macau patacas in the year of Macao's return in 1999 to 434.7 billion Macau patacas[1] before the outbreak of the pandemic (by the end of 2019), representing an increase of over eightfold. Furthermore, Macao consistently maintains a leading global position in terms of per capita GDP.

Benefiting from the rapid expansion of Macao's economy and the accelerating pace of China's mainland opening up, the financial sector in Macao has attained notable achievements. With the banking industry at its core, Macao's financial sector

[1] The data is sourced from the Statistics and Census Service of Macao.

C. H. Leong (✉)
Senior Instructor, Programme Coordinator of Bachelor of Law (Conducted in Chinese and Portuguese), Programme Coordinator of Bachelor of Law in Chinese Language, Faculty of Law, University of Macau, Avenida da Universidade, Taipa, Macau, China
e-mail: chleong@um.edu.mo

© The Author(s), under exclusive license to Springer Nature Singapore Pte Ltd. 2024

S. Wei (ed.), *International Investment Law at the Juncture*, International Law in Asia,
https://doi.org/10.1007/978-981-97-2183-2_10

has demonstrated robust and rapid development since the handover which deserves nothing but unfettered plaudits.

Literature Review

No worthwhile literature review can possibly forsake—let alone relinquish—the axiom according to which Financial Law boasts a close connection with Law and Economics. The rationale behind such assertion is as clear as straightforward: the social consequences—or social costs[2]—of Financial Law must be seen through the lens of Law and Economics. Financial law deals with financial legal issues, which, in turn, have a humongous impact on a given economy. No further words need to be uttered as to depict that Financial Law and Law and Economics are tightly interlocked.[3] Put otherwise, the latter is deeply woven into the fabric of the former. However, Financial Law is not amenable to be thoroughly grasped decoupled from, nor detached from, a fine-grained attention to the economic consequences[4] prompted by the godly financial transactions that occur in a daily basis in a given jurisdiction. Macau is no exception in this regard.

Financial Law boils down to striking a delicate balance between the social costs and the social advantages arising out a profusion of financial transactions[5] occurred in a given[6] jurisdiction.[7] Put it bluntly, Financial Law must gauge the extent to which the financial regulations that govern a vast assortment of issues are either functional or shoddy in a given jurisdiction.[8] Hence the overriding importance of a fine-grained cost–benefit analysis[9] that undergirds—must undergird—the enactment of financial regulations on a given jurisdiction.

[2] Coase (1961); Posner (1998); Calabresi (1961), passim. But see: Dworkin (1980). Social costs derive from social norms. Social norms produce three effects: (1) expression, (2) deterrence, and (3) internalization. Cooter (2000).

[3] But see: Summers (2000), (arguing that law is autonomous from economics though).

[4] Becker (1968), passim.

[5] Pasquale (2015).

[6] Just think of the batch of unlawful financial transactions related with money laundering that take place daily in a given jurisdiction. In Brazilian doctrine: Cardoso (2015) e passim; Bottini (2019). In Portuguese doctrine: Hugo Luz dos Santos, Programas de *Compliance* e Inteligência Artificial: consequências ao nível da *Law and Economics*, do Direito Penal, do Processo Penal e da *Behavioral Law and Economics*, Braga, NovaCausa Edições Jurídicas, 2024.

[7] Jensen and Meckling (1976).

[8] Agrawal et al. (2022), passim.

[9] See: Sunstein (2014a): passim; Bayefsky (2014); Cass R. Sunstein, *Valuing Life: Humanizing the Regulatory State*, (2014): 8 ff.; Gordon (2014); Sunstein (2014b); Adler and Posner (2006); Miles and Sunstein (2008); Coates (2015); Posner and Glen Weyl (2015).

Whilst both China's banking system[10] and Macau's banking system[11] have been previously pored over, there is still a perceived dearth of academic research as far as the investment legal landscape in Macau is concerned. Especially from the standpoint of the bundle of advantages that arise from the enactment of robust and comprehensive financial regulations to such jurisdiction. This paper plugs such a perceived gap by providing a brief (thumbnail sketch) overview on the matrix of Macau's legal framework in that regard while offering insightful inputs on the areas that require further improvement.

The Significance of Macao's Financial Advancement

Developing a modern financial industry serves as a primary driver for achieving a well-balanced and diversified economy in Macao.

The "Outline Development Plan for the Guangdong-Hong Kong-Macao Greater Bay Area" explicitly sets out the vision to transform Macao into a world-class hub for tourism and leisure, as well as a prominent service platform for trade cooperation between China and Portuguese-speaking countries. Emphasizing the promotion of moderate economic diversification, it aims to establish Macao as a vibrant center for cultural exchange and collaboration, where Chinese culture takes the lead while embracing diverse cultural influences. Moreover, the Macao SAR Government has explicitly outlined a strategic approach to moderate diversification in its 2023 Policy Address, with a focus on optimizing the industrial structure.[12] Within this framework, the modern financial industry has been identified as one of the four key priority sectors.

Over a protracted span of time, Macao's economy has been traditionally underpinned by four key pillars: the exportations to overseas, tourism and gaming industry, construction and real estate industry, and financial and insurance industry. However, the scope of Macao's financial sector development has progressively expanded, accompanied by a shift in perception.

In November 2015, the Macao SAR Government formally set forth the objective of "developing distinctive financial industries by leveraging Macao's strengths" in the "2016 Policy Address for the Fiscal Year."[13] This marked a significant milestone in recognizing the importance of aligning Macao's unique advantages with the development of specialized financial sectors.

In 2016, the strategic objective of "developing distinctive financial industries" was officially incorporated into Macao's "Five-Year Development Plan." Subsequently,

---

[10] Shen (2020).

[11] Hang (2020).

[12] See Macao Special Administrative Region Government's, "Policy Address for the Fiscal Year 2023" November 2022, p. 25.

[13] See Macao Special Administrative Region Government's, "Policy Address for the Fiscal Year 2016" November 2015, p. 60.

in December 2017, the Monetary Authority of Macao and the China Banking Regulatory Commission signed a Memorandum of Cooperation on the Development of Macao's Distinctive Financial Sector. This marked a significant milestone in fostering collaboration and synergy between the two entities.

Furthermore, in February 2019, the Central Committee and the State Council of China issued the comprehensive "Outline Development Plan for the Guangdong-Hong Kong-Macao Greater Bay Area." This plan explicitly underscored the support for Macao's development of specialized financial services, with a sharper focus on leasing and other distinctive financial sectors.

Building upon this momentum, the Central Committee and the State Council of China issued the "Overall Plan for the Construction of the Hengqin Guangdong-Macao Deep Cooperation Zone" in September 2021. This plan further emphasized the imperative of developing the modern financial industry, reinforcing the strategic significance of Macao's financial sector in the region.

Consequently, the Macao SAR Government, in its policy spanning from 2020 to 2023, consistently emphasized the pivotal role of the "modern financial industry." Notably, the government expanded the scope of Macao's modern financial industry to encompass diverse areas such as bond markets, wealth management, financial leasing, RMB clearing, private equity funds, and green finance. Within this framework, the government accorded priority attention to the bond market and wealth management, recognizing their potential to leverage Macao's unique status and competitive advantages.

To facilitate the development of Macao's modern financial industry and establish a robust legal framework, the Macao SAR Government diligently revised the "Legal Framework of the Financial System." This comprehensive revision, which was meticulously conducted, culminated in the passage of the law as subsidiary legislation by the Macao Legislative Assembly on July 31, 2023. The revised legislation officially came into force on November 1, signifying a significant step towards creating an enabling environment for the growth and success of Macao's financial industry.

By undertaking these strategic initiatives and legal reforms, Macao aims to create a truly distinctive and internationally recognized financial center. The Macao SAR Government remains committed to providing ample space and support for the future development of Macao's financial industry, ensuring its continued growth and contribution to the broader economic landscape.

In parallel, the Monetary Authority of Macao has made significant strides in recent years by establishing crucial financial infrastructure projects. These include the implementation of the "Macao Central Securities Depository System"[14] for the bond market, the development of the "Fast Payment System," and the establishment

[14] Macao Central Securities Depository and Clearing Limited (MCSD), also known as CENTRAL DE DEPÓSITO E LIQUIDAÇÃO DE VALORES MOBILIÁRIOS DE MACAU SOCIEDADE UNIPESSOAL LIMITADA, is a wholly owned subsidiary established by the Monetary Authority of Macao. MCSD commenced its external operations in December 2021 and currently focuses on providing services such as securities registration, clearing, settlement, custody, and other related services.

of real-time payment and settlement systems for Macao Pataca, Renminbi, and Hong Kong Dollar.

Despite its relatively late start and the nascent stage of its emerging financial sectors, Macao's financial industry exhibits remarkable flexibility and resilience. With ongoing improvements in financial legislation and regulations, as well as the fostering and expansion of the financial talent pool, Macao has witnessed the orderly upgrading of its infrastructure systems. Additionally, the gradual establishment of new types of financial institutions has contributed to the diversification and enrichment of the local financial landscape. As a living testament to these advancements, the financial industry has emerged as the second-largest sector in Macao.

Current Status of Macao's Financial Investment Development

Continuous Expansion of the Financial Industry Scale

The financial industry in Macao has undergone remarkable development over the past few decades, emerging as a vital pillar of the local economy. The Macao financial market has witnessed a substantial expansion in scale, accompanied by a steady growth in the number of financial institutions. Moreover, the sector has experienced a diversification of financial services, offering robust support to both the economic advancement and financial stability of Macao.

According to statistical data, the financial industry in 2021 attracted significant foreign direct investment, ranking second only to the gaming industry with an influx of nearly 15 billion RMB. During the same year, foreign capital in the financial sector yielded profits of 16 billion RMB,[15] presenting a stark contrast to the losses incurred by the gaming industry. With its robust foundation, the modern financial industry in Macao holds immense potential for further development if it continues to exert efforts and seize key opportunities.

The Macao SAR Government, in its "Policy Address for the Fiscal Year 2023," explicitly emphasizes the pragmatic advancement of the modern financial industry. Leveraging Macao's unique status and distinctive advantages, the government will prioritize the development of the bond market, wealth management, financial leasing, RMB clearing, private equity funds, and green finance. It aims to enhance the investment and financing ecosystem, elevate the standards of modern financial services, and establish an outward-facing financial services platform that connects with the global market and supports the new "dual circulation" development pattern, particularly the Sino-Portuguese financial service platform. Furthermore, efforts will be made

[15] See "2021 Direct Investment Statistics" published by the Statistics and Census Service of Macao SAR, available on the website of the Government Information Bureau of the Macao SAR at https://www.gcs.gov.mo/detail/zh-hant/N22KUiKaKS, Last accessed on December 23, 2023.

to advance the construction of the RMB clearing center for Portuguese-speaking countries.

At present, the number of licensed financial institutions in Macao stands at 98, marking a significant increase of 35 institutions since 1999. This expansion has introduced a diverse range of financial entities to the local market, engaging in activities such as electronic payments, financial leasing, investment fund management, investment banking, and financial asset trading. These institutions have contributed to the growth and dynamism of Macao's financial sector.[16]

The bond market in Macao has experienced progressive development since 2019. As of June 2023, a cumulative total of 298 bonds have been issued or listed in Macao, amounting to an impressive value of 488.5 billion Macao Patacas. These bonds represent a diverse array of categories, including sovereign bonds, local government bonds, corporate bonds, green bonds, financial bonds, and capital supplement bonds. In 2021, the Guangdong-Hong Kong-Macao Greater Bay Area jointly introduced the "Cross-border Wealth Management Connect," facilitating seamless individual cross-border investments for residents in the Greater Bay Area. As of June 2023, Macao banks have successfully opened 17,100 accounts for Greater Bay Area residents, recording an aggregate of 7,700 transactions, with 12% of these transactions linked to the Shenzhen-Hong Kong Cooperation Zone. In addition to local capital, Macao's banking industry is comprised of branches from various countries and regions, including Mainland China, Portugal, Hong Kong SAR, the United Kingdom, the United States, and Singapore, reflecting its highly internationalized nature. As of the end of June 2023, Macao banks' international assets have reached an impressive total of 2.12 trillion Macao Patacas, accounting for 84.7% of the banking system's overall assets.[17]

Presently, the financial industry has emerged as the second-largest sector in Macao, with the Monetary Authority of Macao (AMCM) actively enhancing the financial infrastructure to foster an improved market environment and attract diverse categories of financial institutions to establish their operations in Macao. In recent years, over a dozen institutions engaged in cutting-edge activities such as electronic payments, financial leasing, investment fund management, investment banking, and financial asset trading have been enticed to set up their presence in Macao. The advent of these novel institutions has not only brought forth fresh business models but also infused newfound vigor into the robust growth of Macao's financial industry. Thus enhancing the soft and hard infrastructure of the bond market, engaging with international central securities depositories (ICSD), timely introducing related products and value-added services, expanding the international investor base, and promptly

[16] See "Monetary Authority of Macao: 'Optimizing the Financial Market Environment to Unleash Growth Potential with a Balanced Approach of Diversification'" published on the website of the Government of the Macao Special Administrative Region of the People's Republic of China, available at https://www.gov.mo/zh-hant/news/1005118/, Last accessed on December 21, 2023.

[17] See "Monetary Authority of Macao: 'Optimizing the Financial Market Environment to Unleash Growth Potential with a Balanced Approach of Diversification'" published on the website of the Government of the Macao Special Administrative Region of the People's Republic of China, available at https://www.gov.mo/zh-hant/news/1005118/, Last accessed on December 21, 2023.

implementing supportive policies to encourage bond issuance in Macao; thus accelerating the development of the Securities Law and its accompanying regulations; thus improving the regulatory framework for private equity funds and fostering the growth of the private equity fund industry.

Through concerted efforts between the central government and the financial industry, the bond market in Macao has experienced steady growth, accompanied by an increasing variety of bond offerings. As of October 2022, there were 136 outstanding bonds issued or listed in Macao, encompassing diverse types such as corporate bonds, financial bonds, and green bonds, with a total outstanding value of 344.8 billion Macao Patacas.[18]

The Ministry of Finance of the People's Republic of China has once again undertaken the issuance of 3 billion Chinese Yuan government bonds in Macao in 2023, following their successful issuance in 2019. Additionally, they have extended their support by facilitating the issuance of 2 billion Chinese Yuan offshore local government bonds in Macao by Guangdong Province, building upon their previous issuance in 2021.[19] Both bonds were registered and held in custody within the "Central Securities Depository System (CSD)" of Macao, representing the inaugural utilization of the CSD for the registration and custody of sovereign bonds and local government bonds since its introduction at the end of 2022.

Macao Central Securities Depository Settlement Co., Ltd. (MCSD), the entity responsible for operating the CSD, has obtained approval to become a member of the International Securities Services Association (ISSA) and has become a member institution of the Society for Worldwide Interbank Financial Telecommunication (SWIFT) in 2022. Moving forward, MCSD will actively pursue collaborations with international central securities depositories to enhance liquidity in the Macao bond market.

The Macao "Securities Act" and "Legal System of the Financial System," which encompass regulations relevant to the bond market, have been implemented. Currently, there are ongoing revisions to the "Guidelines for the Issuance and Trading Transfer of Corporate Bonds" and the "Guidelines for Underwriting and Custody Services of Corporate Bonds." Additionally, research is being conducted to introduce subsidy policies aimed at promoting bond issuance in Macao, thereby enhancing the appeal of the Macao bond market.

[18] See "Macao's Financial Industry Soars as the Second Largest Sector, Accounting for 15.4% of GDP," published on the Hong Kong-Macao channel of People's Daily Online. Retrieved from http://hm.people.com.cn/n1/2022/1120/c42272-32570255.html, Last accessed: December 17, 2023.

[19] See "Macao's Financial Industry Soars as the Second Largest Sector, Accounting for 15.4% of GDP," published on the Hong Kong-Macao channel of People's Daily Online. Retrieved from http://hm.people.com.cn/n1/2022/1120/c42272-32570255.html, Last accessed: December 17, 2023.

Legislative Support for the Development of the Financial Industry

The Chinese government attaches great importance on the development of the financial industry in Macao and has accordingly implemented a wide range of favorable policies to encourage financial institutions to establish branch offices in Macao and expand their business operations. Furthermore, the government has strengthened regulatory measures for the Macao financial market, enhancing its stability and transparency, thereby creating a conducive environment for the growth of the financial sector in Macao.

In support of the development of new financial formats, the Macao SAR government has successfully revised and enacted five financial laws, including the "Legal System of Financial Leasing Companies," "Legal System of Insurance Business," "Trust Law," as well as the "Legal System of Currency Issuance" effective from September 1, 2023, and the "Legal System of the Financial System" effective from November 1, 2023. Currently, simultaneous efforts are being made to formulate/revise three additional financial laws, namely the "Law on Insurance Intermediary Business," "Regulation on the Establishment and Operation of Investment Funds and Investment Fund Management Companies," and the "Securities Law."

The total assets of the Macao financial industry have expanded from 217.62 billion Macau patacas before the pandemic to 291.19 billion Macau patacas as of the end of the first quarter of 2023.[20] As the market environment continues to improve and considering the opportunities presented by collaborative development with the Greater Bay Area, the financial industry in Macao is poised to unlock its tremendous growth potential under market-driven dynamics. This will further facilitate the moderate diversification of the Macao economy, promoting its sustainable and multifaceted development.

[20] See Macau Monetary Authority: "Optimizing the Financial Market Environment to Unleash Growth Potential in the context of the '1 + 4 Moderate Diversification' Strategy." Retrieved from the official website of the Macau Special Administrative Region Government of the People's Republic of China at https://www.gov.mo/zh-hant/news/1005118/, Last accessed on December 21, 2023.

The Advancement of Macao's Financial System

The Introduction of Banks with Limited Business Operations as a New Banking Category

Financial License

The recently revised "Legal System of the Financial System" in Macao officially came into effect on November 1, 2023, thus marking a significant milestone for the local financial industry. During the revision process, legislators carefully considered the development of the Macao financial market, incorporating feedback and recommendations from the banking industry, as well as adhering to internationally recognized standards and best practices. This includes the core principles of effective banking supervision established by the Basel Committee on Banking Supervision, alongside financial regulatory frameworks from other countries or regions closely associated with the financial activities of the Macao Special Administrative Region or sharing similar legal systems.[21]

One crucial provision in the recently revised "Legal System of the Financial System" is the significant optimization of the financial institution licensing regime. This includes the introduction of a new category of license known as the "Restricted Business Bank" license. This strategic move aims to bolster the flexibility of the existing system and create ample space for the future development of new financial business models.

The "Restricted Business Bank" license encompasses a range of institutions, including wholesale banks, retail banks, investment banks, and similar entities. Prior to the enactment of this legislation, the banking license framework in Macao was solely built around a single universal bank license. However, it was recognized that smaller banks with limited business operations do not necessarily require the full spectrum of banking privileges. By incorporating the "Restricted Business Bank" license, the legislation effectively mitigates the risk of mismatches between the actual business scope and the type of bank license held, thereby ensuring a more adaptable framework that aligns with future industry developments.

In response to the dynamic landscape of modern financial formats, the Macao SAR government is actively fostering an environment that attracts a diverse array of innovative financial institutions and diverse banking models to establish a presence in Macao. Consequently, this new legislation not only provides clarity on the permissible operations of "Restricted Business Banks" but also enhances the overall flexibility of Macao's banking licensing regime.

[21] See Legislative Assembly of Macau: "Statement of Reasons for the Financial System Legal Framework," Opinion Paper No. 4/VII/2023 of the Second Standing Committee of the Legislative Assembly of Macau, p. 2.

Establishment of Temporary Licensing Regime

The newly revised "Legal System of the Financial System" establishes a temporary licensing regime for fintech projects, creating a regulatory sandbox for eligible research companies or academic institutions to experiment with fintech initiatives in a controlled-risk environment, even without obtaining a formal license. This provides a space for financial innovation and establishes a field for trial and error.

A regulatory sandbox is a typical approach to regulate fintech, allowing qualified entities to test fintech projects in a controlled-risk environment without holding a financial license. It provides a real market environment for testing innovative financial products, services, and business models, with regulatory measures that are more tolerant and prudent compared to those outside the sandbox. This approach helps reduce the time and potential costs associated with bringing innovative concepts to the market.

Regarding the recent controversial financial innovation platform, DGT Macao Financial Assets Exchange Co., Ltd. (referred to as "DGT Macao Exchange"), the platform engages in the issuance, registration, custody, and settlement of innovative financial products. Through "daily revenue sharing contracts" signed with qualified small and medium-sized enterprises (SMEs), the platform converts the rights to share revenue during the contract period into "daily revenue sharing certificates" and lists these certificates for trading, allowing regulated financial institutions, both local and overseas, to participate in investments. The investment funds are intended to support the operational development of small and medium-sized enterprises.

The Macao government adheres to a "risk-based" regulatory principle and conducts regular monitoring of the operations and management of DGT Macao Exchange. This includes requiring the platform to utilize digital technology to monitor the revenue data of SMEs' physical stores, implementing control measures to ensure the accuracy and integrity of the relevant data. Adequate investor protection measures are in place, ensuring comprehensive disclosure of financial product information, such as key features, terms, conditions, and associated risks. Moreover, measures are taken to ensure that the revenue sharing is deposited into investors' accounts on time. System security, data protection, and business continuity management are prioritized. Effective internal control measures are implemented to ensure clear segregation of responsibilities in business, transactions, and settlement processes.

The revised "Legal System of the Financial System" places particular emphasis on the convergence of finance and technology, the synergy between finance and innovative operations, and the optimization of financial business activities and regulatory frameworks. The introduction of the "Temporary License for Financial Innovation" is expected to propel significant advancements in Macao's financial industry. However, it should be noted that Restricted Business Banks must adhere to the company capital requirements outlined within the respective license. Drawing upon relevant regulations governing Restricted Business Banks in other jurisdictions, Macao explicitly specifies that the minimum capital requirement for Restricted Business Banks shall not be less than MOP 100 million.[22]

The revised "Legal System of the Financial System" emphasizes the convergence of finance and technology, the synergy between finance and innovative operations, and the optimization of financial business activities and regulatory frameworks. The introduction of the "Temporary License for Financial Innovation" is seen as a significant driver for substantive advancements in Macao's financial industry.

The temporary licensing regime provides eligible research companies or academic institutions with the opportunity to experiment with fintech projects without the need for a formal license. This regulatory sandbox allows the testing of innovative financial products, services, and business models in a controlled environment with more tolerant yet prudent regulatory measures. This approach reduces the time and potential costs associated with bringing innovative concepts to the market.

However, Restricted Business Banks are required to comply with the company capital requirements specified within their relevant licenses. Drawing upon regulations governing Restricted Business Banks in other jurisdictions, Macao explicitly sets the minimum capital requirement for Restricted Business Banks at no less than MOP 100 million. This requirement ensures that these banks have sufficient financial strength to fulfill their business responsibilities effectively.

Streamlining the Public Issuance of Bonds

The Macao SAR government has identified the modern financial industry as a key driver for diversified industrial development, with the bond market being one of its crucial projects. In line with this, the recently revised "Legal System of the Financial System" aims to optimize and streamline the process of public bond issuance. This transition from an "approval-based" system to a more efficient "registration-based" system is expected to enhance the issuance process and increase the appeal of the Macao bond market for investors.

To support the development of the bond market, the Monetary Authority of Macao (AMCM) has undertaken various initiatives. One such initiative is the establishment of the Central Securities Depository (CSD), which was launched on December 15, 2021. Ongoing efforts are being made to further enhance the system, aligning it with international standards and best practices. The adoption of the SWIFT messaging system and integration with international clearing and settlement requirements will facilitate the participation of international institutions in Macao's primary and secondary bond markets.

In February 2023, Macao introduced qualified bond repurchase operations, allowing local banks to optimize their liquidity management through repurchase transactions involving government bonds, local bonds, and policy bank bonds issued in Macao. This measure aims to encourage industry participation in the bond market's

[22] Article 25, Paragraph 2 of Law No. 13/2023, titled "Legal Framework for the Financial System".

investment and financing activities. Additionally, the Macao government is planning feasible schemes to subsidize bond issuance costs, aiming to attract high-quality issuers to participate in Macao's bond market. Efforts will also be made to attract reputable issuers such as the Ministry of Finance, local governments, and policy banks to continue issuing bonds in Macao.

In December 2023, Industrial and Commercial Bank of China (Macau) Limited successfully issued a 2 billion Macau Pataca two-year bond in the Macao market. This marked the first public issuance of bonds in Macao after the implementation of the registration-based system under the 13/2023 regulation of the "Legal System of the Financial System."

Promoting Cross-Border Financial Planning

China's establishment of the "dual circulation" development pattern and the gradual increase in the internationalization of the Renminbi (RMB) present new development opportunities for Macao to integrate into the national development agenda. Macao possesses unique advantages in bond development, including extensive international connections, a low tax rate system, currency convertibility, free movement of capital, and a highly open financial system. As Macao's financial infrastructure continues to improve and its legal and regulatory framework becomes more refined, the role of Macao's financial market in connecting with the mainland and the world will be further highlighted.

In its 2016 Policy Address, the Macao SAR government first proposed the concept of developing a distinctive financial industry, with wealth management identified as one of the three key areas of focus. The launch of the "Cross-border Wealth Management Pilot Scheme for the Guangdong-Hong Kong-Macao Greater Bay Area" in October 2021 exemplifies innovative collaboration among the three regions, facilitating cross-border personal investments for Greater Bay Area residents and promoting interconnectedness within the financial markets of the Bay Area. This initiative also provides new impetus for the development of wealth management services in Macao.

In 2023, Macao plans to optimize the Wealth Management Connect, and it is expected that the optimized implementation rules will be jointly issued and implemented by the three regions in the near future, thereby promoting the development of wealth management services in Macao.

The optimization of the Wealth Management Connect focuses on five key aspects. Firstly, it aims to optimize investor access conditions, enabling a larger number of residents from the Greater Bay Area to participate in the pilot scheme. Secondly, it seeks to expand the range of participating institutions by including qualified securities companies as participants, thereby offering investment products and related services to individual customers in both the "Southbound" and "Northbound" directions. Thirdly, there is a plan to broaden the scope of eligible investment products for "Southbound" and "Northbound" investors, better accommodating the diverse investment needs of Greater Bay Area residents. Fourthly, it aims to appropriately increase the investment quota for individual investors. Lastly, further improvements will be made to marketing and sales arrangements, guiding financial institutions to provide high-quality financial services to residents of the Greater Bay Area.

Macao is also collaborating with the Hengqin Guangdong-Macao In-depth Cooperation Zone ("Hengqin Cooperation Zone") in developing fund businesses. In coordination with the Financial Development Bureau of the Hengqin Cooperation Zone, simplified licensing procedures have been arranged for eligible Hengqin Cooperation Zone private fund management companies seeking to conduct business in Macao. Several fund management companies have already applied for licenses in Macao through the recommended mechanism of the Financial Development Bureau of the Hengqin Cooperation Zone.

In 2022, Macao enacted the "Trust Law," establishing the trust system in the Macao SAR. This significant breakthrough in Macao's legal framework provides a favorable long-term foundation for wealth management services, enabling Macao's financial institutions to develop competitive wealth management products and attract more overseas customers, especially high net worth individuals, for asset management in Macao.

Expansion of Financing Lease Regulations

Macao stands as one of the most promising investment destinations globally. The enactment of Law No. 6/2019, titled "Legal Framework for Financing Lease Companies," has significantly relaxed the regulations governing our financing lease market. This legislation introduces the concept of subsidiary financing lease project companies and provides clear definitions for both financing lease companies and financing lease project subsidiaries in Article 2 of Law No. 6/2019.

In accordance with these definitions, financing lease companies are now recognized as financial institutions engaged in financing lease activities, no longer classified as credit institutions. They remain subject to financial regulation; however, the regulatory requirements are comparatively more lenient than those imposed on credit institutions. Financing lease project subsidiaries, on the other hand, are wholly owned financial institutions held by banks or financing lease companies licensed to operate within the Macao Special Administrative Region. Their primary function is to solely manage and oversee individual financing lease projects, and they are subject to financial regulation as well.

Under Article 6 of the "Legal Framework for Financing Lease Companies," financing lease companies have the flexibility to establish themselves as either limited liability companies or joint-stock companies. Furthermore, Article 7 of the law reduces the minimum capital requirement for financing lease companies from MOP 30 million to MOP 10 million.

The legislation also appropriately streamlines the administrative requirements imposed on the regulatory authority overseeing financing lease companies. As per

Article 14 of the "Legal Framework for Financing Lease Companies," the administrative authority is now comprised of a single member, who must be a resident of the Macao Special Administrative Region. This provision grants companies' greater operational freedom while simultaneously preventing them from being mere "shell companies."

In conclusion, the enactment of Law No. 6/2019, the "Legal Framework for Financing Lease Companies," has expanded Macao's financing lease market and created a favorable business environment for industry development. By introducing the framework for subsidiary financing lease project companies, providing clear definitions, and reducing regulatory burdens and capital thresholds, Macao aims to attract a diverse range of financing lease businesses, fostering further growth within the sector. This legislation strikes a balance between granting operational flexibility and ensuring regulatory compliance, positioning Macao as an appealing destination for financing lease enterprises worldwide.

Macao's Financial Position in the Guangdong-Hong Kong-Macao Greater Bay Area

Overview of Economic Integration in the Guangdong-Hong Kong-Macao Greater Bay Area

The various sectors in Macao understand the mainland China plays a vital role in providing long-term stability and development for the financial industry in Macao. Since the 18th National Congress of the Communist Party of China, the Party Central Committee led by Comrade Xi Jinping has been dedicated to promoting the long-term prosperity, stability, and integration of Macao into the national development framework. A series of documents issued by the Party Central Committee and the State Council have explicitly expressed support for expanding the business opportunities of Hong Kong and Macao financial institutions in the mainland, fostering better and faster connectivity, cooperation, and development between the mainland and the Hong Kong-Macao region.

In recent years, Macao has consistently capitalized on its distinct advantages in outward orientation and openness, actively engaging in collaborations within the Pan Pearl River Delta region, and enhancing cross-border regional integration. The Macao SAR Government highlighted in its 2023 Policy Address the active participation in Pan Pearl River Delta cooperation and the encouragement extended to local governments and qualified enterprises in the Pan Pearl River Delta provinces and regions to raise funds through the Macao bond market.[23] Simultaneously, cooperation between Macao and mainland China is continuously extending to cities such

[23] Government of the Macau Special Administrative Region of the People's Republic of China: "Policy Address for the Fiscal Year 2023," November 2022, p. 40.

as Beijing, Shanghai, and Zhejiang, significantly expanding the scope for regional integration and development.

The banking industry in Macao showcases a prominent outward-oriented nature and maintains close ties with mainland China and Hong Kong, naturally fostering the drive and essence required for promoting cross-border regional integration. According to data disclosed by the Macao government, as of the end of September 2023, the total value of international assets held by Macao banks reached MOP 2,040.4 billion (USD 253 billion). Among these assets, external holdings experienced a quarterly decline of 4.3% to MOP 1,480.5 billion, while local foreign currency assets decreased by 3.2% to MOP 559.8 billion. Notably, non-bank loans from external sources, which form a significant portion of international assets, witnessed a decline of 7.7%, amounting to MOP 575.9 billion.[24]

To complement the national strategy of high-level external engagement, Macao's banking institutions, including Macao International Bank, Tai Fung Bank, and Banco Nacional Ultramarino, are strategically aligning their development plans to effectively expand their presence in the mainland market. This proactive approach is aimed at facilitating the rapid formation of a new framework for openness in China while consistently representing the voice of Macao throughout the ongoing process of promoting a two-pronged strategy for internal and external openness in China.

The Role of Macao in the Greater Bay Area Financial Landscape

Macao as a Trading and Service Platform Between China and Portuguese-Speaking Countries

Macao, known as a "bridgehead" for China's external opening-up, serves as a vital gateway connecting the mainland to the international stage and acts as a convergence point within the new development paradigm of "dual circulation."[25] It not only enjoys the advantages of being a free port with unrestricted capital flows, no foreign exchange controls, a simplified tax system, and low tax rates[26] but also holds a distinctive position as a platform for trade and cooperation between China and Portuguese-speaking countries.

Clearly, Macao will undertake a significant mission in the establishment of the new development paradigm under the framework of China's "dual circulation" strategy.

---

[24] See Monetary Authority of Macau, "Macau International Banking Business Statistics for September 2023," retrieved from the official website of the Macau Special Administrative Region Government at https://www.gov.mo/zh-hans/news/726482/, Last accessed on December 22, 2023.

[25] See Chen Guanghan, Li Xiaoying, "World-class Economic Zone: Research on the Construction of the Guangdong-Hong Kong-Macao Greater Bay Area," China Publishing Group, 2022 edition, p. 7.

[26] See Fung Pong In, "Macau Economy in the Period of Transition: Twenty Years of Evolution and Development," Joint Publishing (Hong Kong) Co., Ltd., Macau Foundation, 2019 edition, p. 297.

The banking industry in Macao must adapt to the current landscape, identify its role and positioning, and seize the opportunities that arise accordingly.

Macao should effectively utilize its advantageous position as a platform bridging China and Portuguese-speaking countries and proactively engage in the Belt and Road Initiative.[27] Chairman Xi Jinping has repeatedly emphasized the special status and role of Macao in the Belt and Road Initiative, outlining a long-term plan for Macao's involvement in the initiative. Since 2015, various documents, including the "Vision and Actions on Jointly Building Silk Road Economic Belt and 21st-Century Maritime Silk Road" and the "Arrangements to Support Macao's Comprehensive Participation and Contribution to the Belt and Road Initiative," have explicitly expressed support for Macao's participation in the initiative. Furthermore, the Macao SAR government has consistently highlighted its involvement in the Belt and Road Initiative as an important aspect of its governance reports for eight consecutive years, and it has incorporated participation in the initiative as a key element of its five-year development strategy.

Through years of dedicated efforts, Macao has achieved a significant progress in the construction of the China-Portuguese platform. Since October 2003, the Forum for Economic and Trade Cooperation between China and Portuguese-Speaking Countries (Macao) has been held consecutively, with the establishment of institutions such as the "China-Portuguese Forum (Macao) Training Center," the China-Portuguese Cooperation Development Fund, initiated in 2013, officially relocated its headquarters to Macao in June 2017, thus solidifying Macao's position in the cooperative efforts.[28]

Promoting the internationalization of the Renminbi (RMB) and facilitating RMB settlement with Portuguese-speaking countries constitute a significant mission bestowed upon Macao by the central government. In May 2019, Portugal became the first Eurozone nation to issue Panda bonds in China,[29] marking a noteworthy milestone in Sino-Portuguese financial collaboration. Looking ahead, the banking sector in Macao can forge partnerships with various stakeholders, providing essential capital market services such as bond issuance and listing for an array of Sino-Portuguese cooperative ventures and enterprises operating within Portuguese-speaking countries and regions.

Moreover, Portuguese-speaking countries and regions are geographically dispersed across multiple continents, including Europe, the Americas, Africa, and Asia. Boasting a combined population of nearly 300 million and abundant reserves of oil, natural gas, and minerals, these nations have witnessed a shift in their economic and trade cooperation with China from traditional commodity trading to encompass

---

[27] See Li Lue, Law Kam Yee, "Macau and the Belt and Road Initiative," China Publishing Group (Hong Kong) Co., Ltd., 2019 edition, p. 4.

[28] See Li Lue, Law Kam Yee, "Macau and the Belt and Road Initiative," China Publishing Group (Hong Kong) Co., Ltd., 2019 edition, p. 10.

[29] See Xinhua News, "Portugal Becomes the First Eurozone Country to Issue Panda Bonds," published on China Financial Information Network, available at https://www.cnfin.com/rmb-xh08/a/20190531/1838404.shtml, Last accessed on December 23, 2023.

broader domains such as processing trade, capacity cooperation, and the development of infrastructure and industrial parks. In the foreseeable future, Macao holds the potential to emerge as a crucial investment and financing platform between China and Portuguese-speaking countries, facilitated by avenues such as the bond market and RMB settlement.

Looking ahead, Macao's future in the global landscape appears promising. As a vital hub bridging China and Portuguese-speaking countries, Macao is poised to play an increasingly significant role in promoting economic cooperation and cultural exchange within these regions.

With its unique advantages as a free port and a platform for international trade, Macao is well-positioned to contribute to the Belt and Road Initiative. The continued development and enhancement of infrastructure, such as transportation networks and logistics facilities, will further strengthen Macao's connectivity and facilitate seamless trade flows between China and Portuguese-speaking countries.

Furthermore, Macao's expertise in the financial sector, particularly in RMB internationalization and capital market services, can propel it into a prominent investment and financing platform. As the Renminbi gains more traction globally, Macao's role in facilitating RMB settlement and promoting financial cooperation with Portuguese-speaking countries is expected to expand, fostering greater financial integration and growth.

In addition to economic prospects, Macao's rich cultural heritage and vibrant tourism industry will continue to attract visitors from around the world. The fusion of Chinese and Portuguese cultures, coupled with Macao's historical sites, entertainment offerings, and renowned culinary scene, will ensure its status as a top destination for tourists seeking a unique and immersive experience.

Overall, Macao's future is bright, with ample opportunities for economic, cultural, and social development. By leveraging its strategic location, fostering international partnerships, and capitalizing on its existing strengths, Macao is poised to thrive as a dynamic global player in the years to come.

Facilitating Financial Connectivity

To further drive financial openness and innovation, deepen financial cooperation between mainland China and Hong Kong/Macao, and provide substantial financial support for the development of the Guangdong-Hong Kong-Macao Greater Bay Area, the People's Bank of China, China Banking and Insurance Regulatory Commission, China Securities Regulatory Commission, and State Administration of Foreign Exchange jointly issued the "Opinions on Financial Support for the Construction of the Guangdong-Hong Kong-Macao Greater Bay Area" on May 15, 2020. These opinions outline 26 specific measures across five key areas to bolster the Greater Bay Area's leading role in national economic development and its prominence in international integration.

The opinions encompass various aspects, including the facilitation of cross-border trade and investment in the Greater Bay Area, the expansion of financial industry openness, the promotion of financial market and infrastructure connectivity, the enhancement of financial service innovation, and the effective management of cross-border financial risks.

Furthermore, the opinions emphasize the steady progress in the internationalization of the Renminbi (RMB) and the exploration of an adaptable account management system and cross-border wealth management mechanisms tailored to the Greater Bay Area's development. These measures aim to support Hong Kong and Macao residents in accessing wealth management products offered by mainland banks, while also allowing residents of the Greater Bay Area's nine cities to invest in wealth management products offered by banks in Hong Kong and Macao.

Regarding banking and financial services, the opinions propose supporting eligible banks to expand their operations in the Greater Bay Area through various avenues, and welcome foreign banks to establish branches and subsidiaries within the region. In terms of cross-border investment activities, the opinions suggest implementing different fund pools and investment pilot programs, along with other measures to improve cross-border fund management and services in the insurance industry.

The People's Bank of China highlights that the promotion of the Greater Bay Area's construction is a significant strategic decision by the central government, with profound and far-reaching implications for fostering a new era of China's reform and opening.

Looking ahead, Macao's financial and legal system, which harmonizes well with the legal frameworks of Portuguese-speaking countries and the European continent, can serve as a catalyst for efficient connectivity of financial products between mainland China, Portuguese-speaking countries, and the European region. Local banks in Macao can leverage their role as a bridge in Sino-Portuguese cooperation platforms, strategically positioning themselves in Portuguese-speaking countries and cities along the Belt and Road Initiative. This will facilitate financial market connectivity between mainland China and Portuguese-speaking countries, providing targeted financial support for trade, infrastructure development, tourism, and cultural exchanges. Consequently, it will contribute to the overall cooperation and mutual development between China and Portuguese-speaking countries, while bolstering the Belt and Road Initiative.

Drawing inspiration from international experiences, Ireland's proximity to the London financial center has enabled it to become the world's largest aviation leasing financial hub, thanks to its unique positioning. Similarly, Luxembourg, a small European country sharing similarities with Macao, has emerged as the second-largest global investment fund center and the largest private banking hub in the Eurozone. Looking forward, Macao's modern financial industry, backed by the Chinese mainland and actively integrated into the national development framework, holds immense potential for growth. As a key participant and driving force in promoting Macao's moderate economic diversification, Macao must be proactive and seize opportunities for modern financial development. By leveraging its distinctive characteristics and advantages, Macao can define its role and positioning within the national development framework. It should continuously voice its opinions in the realm of finance, while contributing its financial insights and wisdom to the ongoing process of integrating the region and supporting the mutual growth of China and Portuguese-speaking countries.

In conclusion, the issuance of the "Opinions on Financial Support for the Construction of the Guangdong-Hong Kong-Macao Greater Bay Area" reflects the commitment to deepen financial cooperation and connectivity in the region. These opinions establish a comprehensive framework and specific measures to promote trade facilitation, financial market opening, infrastructure connectivity, financial innovation, and risk management. With Macao's compatible financial and legal systems, it can leverage its strengths to facilitate seamless financial product flow between mainland China, Portuguese-speaking countries, and the European region. Through active participation in the national development framework and seizing opportunities for modern financial development, Macao can play a pivotal role in promoting regional integration and contribute its financial expertise to support the mutual growth of China and Portuguese-speaking countries. This will foster a prosperous future characterized by enhanced financial connectivity and shared development.

Attractiveness to Investors

Similar Operating Model to European Financial Institutions

Macau operates with a similar model to European financial institutions, which makes it more familiar to foreign investors and enhances the convenience of conducting business investments. As a Sino-Portuguese platform, Macau's advantage lies in its proficiency in the Portuguese language, providing excellent opportunities for China's investments in Portuguese-speaking countries. Professor Chan Fong Chang from City University of Hong Kong's Business School suggests that Macau should focus on Spanish-speaking countries and further expand its outreach by leveraging the linguistic and cultural similarities[30] between Macau and Spanish-speaking nations.[31]

---

[30] This statement is overblown to say the least. Caution must be exercised accordingly. Spain is a western jurisdiction that praises individualism and the "glorification of the individual". On the opposite pole, Macau does not fall far behind its Confucian way of thinking that awards primacy to the might collective instead. The cultural differences between both jurisdictions are nothing but legion. The behemoth differences between individualism-laden jurisdictions and collectivism-fraught jurisdictions have been extensively studied in the field of anthropology and applied psychology. To name a few empirical studies: Sullivan et al. (1982), *passim*; Triandis (1989); Kolman et al. (2003); LeBaron 2003; Abramson (2009); dos Santos (2023a).

[31] See Macao Trade and Investment Promotion Institute, "Macao Prepares to Bridge the Financial Gap," published on the website of Macao Trade and Investment Promotion Institute, available at https://www.ipim.gov.mo/zh-hant/publication/issue-76-jun-2020/focus/macao-prepares-to-bridge-the-financial-gap/, Last accessed on December 20, 2023".

Renminbi Settlement Space and Recognition of Digital Currencies

Macau's potential as a renminbi settlement center can be observed through its trade volume, cultural connections, and financial ties. While offshore renminbi settlement centers in Hong Kong, London, and Singapore remain competitive, there is market development potential in Macau or other regions, such as facilitating business settlements for smaller-scale enterprises. Smaller enterprises, due to their relatively smaller business scale, require a convenient renminbi settlement center to expedite business efficiency. According to statistics from the Society for Worldwide Interbank Financial Telecommunication (SWIFT), approximately 40% of financial institutions worldwide handle renminbi settlement transactions. However, the global share of renminbi as a payment currency is less than 2%.

If the renminbi's asset value can be increased, for example, by issuing renminbi-denominated bonds, it will attract more business transactions using the renminbi. Especially for countries with a higher circulation rate of the renminbi compared to the US dollar and other foreign currencies, financial products denominated in renminbi would be popular financial derivatives in the market. Currently, countries adopt a conservative attitude towards taking a "do-or-die" approach. The overreliance on the US dollar has already caused damage to the economies of South America.

Currently, China has reached currency swap agreements with over 30 countries and regions, and some of the imported crude oil trade is conducted in renminbi. China expects the renminbi to be used more extensively, aligning with the country's development goals and increasing its influence in international trade and economic affairs.

Establishing a renminbi settlement center in Macau is an aspiration that lays the foundation for the rooted financial services industry in Macau. The decisive and robust policies of the Macau government rely on the strong support given by the motherland. Robby de Caluwé believes that allowing Mainland Chinese financial and insurance companies to list renminbi-denominated bonds in Macau also reflects the central government's support for developing Macau as a financial service platform.

Bonds from several state-owned enterprises have been listed on the Macau Financial Assets Exchange Co., Ltd. On March 18, 2023, a three billion US dollar bond issued by Beijing Capital Land Ltd. was successfully listed on the Macau Financial Assets Exchange Co., Ltd. The bond matures in 2023 with a coupon rate of 2.8%.

Once the Mainland Chinese development strategies are implemented, they will be driven by state-owned enterprises. Macau government can collaborate with the People's Bank of China to promote digital currencies and position Macau as a testing ground for digital currencies.

In May 2019, the Portuguese government issued debt securities denominated in renminbi for the first time, and the actual demand was three times higher than expected. Robby de Caluwé states that Portugal's success can serve as an encouragement for other Portuguese-speaking countries to follow suit, and Macau can also help them raise domestic funds.

The "Currency Issuance Legal Framework Law," which took effect on September 1, 2023, stipulates that the legal tender in the Macau Special Administrative Region consists of banknotes, coins, and digital currencies. The specific regulatory framework for digital currencies will be established by future special regulations, providing legal space for digital forms of currency.

Stable Social Situation

Macau enjoys a highly stable social environment,[32] which is a crucial asset. No entrepreneur wishes to invest in a place with an unstable political and economic environment. As a Special Administrative Region of China, Macau has its background advantages. Under the economic cooperation of the Belt and Road Initiative, Macau, a place where Eastern and Western cultures collide,[33] can serve as a bridge between China and Portuguese-speaking countries,[34] as well as a gateway to the Greater Bay Area.

Directions for the Forthcoming Future: Macau Needs to Address the Candent Issues Arising Out Omnipotent Artificial Intelligence in the Remit of Financial Law

Macau needs to embrace the pressing challenges posed by an ever-evolving artificial intelligence[35] that never ceases[36] to amaze.[37] Whilst Macau has made rapid strides in creating a legal framework aligned with the most advanced jurisdictions is somewhat lagging behind when it comes to addressing multitudinous issues posed a fast-paced smart regulatory technology.[38] To the extent that this data-driven world we live in[39] is currently undergoing a «transformation numérique»[40] Macau must keep abreast

[32] But see: Menkel-Meadow (2018) and passim (this lauded scholar notes, however, that inequality, social cleavages and lack of tolerance beset the globalized world).

[33] dos Santos (2023a).

[34] dos Santos (2023b), passim.

[35] See in French doctrine: Baller and Deffains (2018) (stating that Artificial Intelligence has catalyzed a slew of drastic changes with regard to lawyers´ functional activities).

[36] Re and Solow-Niederman (2019) and passim (broach the topic of a full-blown system powered by a both boundless and inscrutable artificial intelligence).

[37] Suzor (2019) (passim).

[38] Brownsword (2020).

[39] Wu (2019) and passim.

[40] In French doctrine: Deffains (2019) and passim.

with the newest developments of informational capitalism[41] or reputational damages may otherwise occur.[42]

Machine Learning Algorithms[43] are fully equipped to make informed investment decisions without any help of humans whatsoever.[44] A legal framework is in dire need of being created to shrewdly address this sizzling hot topic sooner rather than later.[45] But not just that though. Macau must also pay a keen attention to the challenges unlocked by *Financial Intelligent Automation*,[46] which is shaping up to put the fundamental tenets of Financial Law at odds.

Conversely, Financial Law pundits must realize that we are steadily heading towards a both chequered and variegated world against the backdrop of which a vast array of intelligences are to set to emerge.[47]

That is true, but truer still the *Capitalismo Immateriale*[48] (*Immaterial Capitalism*) brought to bear by an omnipotent Artificial Intelligence[49] will surely launch the protection of financial investors 'personal data[50] into a frenzy. For a simple reason: Macau's legal framework is woefully ill-prepared to deal with legal issues arising out the digital financial world which has been thrust upon us.

Last but not least, Macau must pay a keen attention to the challenges arising out the dichotomy between machine learning algorithms and economic justice[51] which, taken together, have every chance to play havoc with our ability to foretell the next meaningful step in the remit of Financial Law, which is seldom an auspicious omen.

Conclusion

Macau has made significant strides in aligning its financial regulations with the most advanced jurisdictions in the globalized world we currently live in. Macau has thus kept abreast with the newest legal developments in this regard.

---

41 Cohen (2019).

42 In German doctrine: Grunsky (2008), passim.

43 Géron (2019).

44 In Portuguese doctrine: dos Santos (2022a, b, c).

45 Not that just that though. The digital world we currently live is increasingly ebbing the window of privacy allotted to each and every one of us. Which will inevitably impact the quality of the investment decisions made by humans (v.g. an hyper surveilled human will be deprived from its best judgment to make informed decisions in the remit of Financial Law). This subject has been broached by the German doctrine—albeit from a point of view loosely related with Financial Law: Müller (2010).

46 Bornet et al. (2020).

47 Tegmark (2018).

48 See in Italian doctrine: Quintarelli (2019).

49 Grimm (2021) and passim.

50 Sivarajah et al. (2017) and passim.

51 Slaughter (2021).

Macau is the right place to invest, but challenges remain to be thoroughly addressed for the sake of the long-term stability of its financial environment.

Amongst which stands arguably the perceived concern that Macau's legal framework is woefully ill-prepared to deal with a slew of legal issues arising out omnipotent artificial intelligence that is set to put the fundamental tenets of Macau's legal framework at odds.

This paper has brought forth a vast array of on-point suggestions that aim to prevent that from happening. Local policymakers and lawmakers should take heed of those suggestions or a seismic shift in Macau's legal landscape may otherwise occur.

References

Abramson H (2009) Outward bound to other cultures: seven guidelines. Honeyman C, Coben J, De Palo G (eds) Rethinking negotiation teaching: innovations for context and culture. DRI Press, Saint Paul, Minnesota, pp 293–313

Adler M, Posner EA (2006) New foundations of cost-benefit analysis. Regul Gov 3:72

Agrawal A, Gans J, Goldfarb A, Machines P (2022) The simple economics of artificial intelligence, 2nd edn. Harvard Business Review Press, Massachusetts

Baller S, Deffains B (2018) Intelligence artificielle et devenir de la professions d'avocat; l'avenir est present. Revue pratique de la prospective et de innovation 1:14 and ff

Bayefsky R (2014) Dignity as a value in agency cost-benefit analysis. Yale Law J 123:1740

Becker G (1968) Crime and punishment: an economic approach. J Polit Econ 76

Bornet P, Barkin I, Wirtz J (2020) Intelligent automation: learn how to harness artificial intelligence to boost business and make out world more human, pp 1–432

Bottini PC (2019) Programas de compliance voltados à prevenção da lavagem de dinheiro. In: Badaró GH, Bottini PC (eds) Lavagem de dinheiro: aspectos penais e processuais penais: comentários à Lei 9.613/1998, com alterações da Lei 12.683/2012, 4ª edição revista, atualizada e ampliada. Thomson Reuters Brasil, São Paulo, pp 48–68

Brownsword R (2020) Law, technology and society: re-imagining the regulatory environment. Routledge, London, pp 1–361

Calabresi G (1961) Some thoughts on risk distribution and the law of torts. Yale Law J 70

Cardoso DM (2015) Criminal compliance naperspectiva da lei de lavagem de dinheiro. LiberArs, São Paulo, pp 124 e ss

Coase R (1961) The problem of social cost. J Law Econ 3:1–8

Cooter RD (2000) Three effects of social norms on law: expression, deterrence, and internalization. Or Law Rev 79(1):1–3

Coates JC IV (2015) Cost-benefit analysis of financial regulation: case studies and implications. Yale Law J 124:882–911

Cohen JE (2019) Between truth and power: the legal constructions of informational capitalism. Oxford University Press, Oxford, pp 1–376

Deffains B (2019) Le monde du droit face à la transformation numérique. Revue Française d'Études Constitutionnelles et Politiques 170:49 and ff

Dworkin R (1980) Why efficiency? A response to professors calabresi and posner. Hofstra Law Rev 8:563–590

Géron A (2019) Hands-on machine learning with Scikit-Learn, Keras, and TensorFlow: concepts, tools, and techniques to build intelligent systems. O'Reilly Media, Sebastopol, California, pp 1–856

Gordon J (2014) The empty call for cost-benefits analysis for financial regulators. J Leg Stud 43:351

Grimm PW (2021) Practical considerations for the admissibility of artificial intelligence evidence. Md Bar J 2(3):39 and ff
Grunsky W (2008) Aktuell Probleme zum Begriff des Vermögensschadens, 2. Auflage, München, C. H. Beck, München
Hang LC (2020) Macau banking law and financial institutions. In: Arner DW, Wan WY, Goodwin A, Shen W, Gibson E (eds) Research handbook on Asian financial law, Cheltenham, UK, Northampton, Massachusetts, USA, pp 315–335
Jensen M, Meckling W (1976) Theory of the firm: managerial behavior, agency costs and ownership structure. J Financ Econ 3(4):308–337
Kolman L, Nooderhaven NG, Hofstede G, Dienes E (2003) Cross-cultural differences in Central Europe. J Manag Psychol 18(1):76–88
LeBaron M (2003) Bridging cultural conflicts: a new approach for a changing world. Jossey-Bass, San Francisco
Menkel-Meadow C (2018) Why We can't "Just All Get Along: Dysfunction in the Polity and Conflict Resolution and What We Might do About It". J Disput Resolut 1(5):6 and ff
Miles TJ, Sunstein CR (2008) The real world of arbitrariness review. Univ Chic Law Rev 75:761
Müller H (2010) EuropäischeRechtssicherheit gegen Deutsches Sicherheitsrecht? Zur EGMR-Entscheidung in Sachen nachträgliche (Verlängerung der) Sicherungsverwahrung. Kritische Justiz 43(3):256–268
Pasquale F (2015) The black box society: the secret algorithms that control money and information. Harvard University Press, Cambridge, Massachusetts, pp 1–320
Posner EA, Glen Weyl E (2015) Cost-benefit analysis of financial regulations: response to criticisms. Yale Law J 124:246–265
Posner R (1998) Values and consequences: as an introduction to economic analysis of law. John M. Olin Law & Economics Working Paper, vol 53, pp 2 and ff
Quintarelli S (2019) Capitalismo Immateriale—Le tecnologie digitali ed il nuovo conflitto sociale, 7ª edizione. Bollati Boringhieri, Turin, pp 1–198
Re RM, Solow-Niederman A (2019) Developing artificially intelligent. StanfTechnol Law Rev 22:242 ff
dos Santos HL (2022a) Inteligência Artificial e Processo Penal. NovaCausa Edições Jurídicas, Braga, pp 1–256
dos Santos HL (2022b) Inteligência Artificial e Processo Civil na Era do Metaverse e dos Machine Learning Algorithms. NovaCausa Edições Jurídicas, Braga, pp 1–262
dos Santos HL (2022c) Inteligência Artificial (ChatGPT/AutoGPT/Robots-Advogados/Robots-Procuradores/Robots-Juízes) e Responsabilidade Penal das Pessoas Colectivas, NovaCausa Edições Jurídicas, Braga, pp 1–112
dos Santos HL (2023a) Towards a four-tiered model of mediation. Springer, Singapore, Beijing, Berlin, New York, pp 1–216
dos Santos HL (2023b) Expedited arbitration in the far-east (Macau), Wolters Kluwer
Shen W (2020) China's puzzling banking and shadow banking sectors after the global financial crisis. In: Arner DW, Wan WY, Goodwin A, Shen W, Gibson E (eds) Research handbook on Asian financial law, Cheltenham, UK, Northampton, Massachusetts, USA, pp 293–314
Sivarajah U et al (2017) Critical analysis of big data challenges and analytical methods. J Bus Res 70:263 and ff
Slaughter RK (2021) Algorithms and economic justice: a taxonomy of harms and a path forward for the federal trade commission. Yale J Law Technol 23:S1 and ff
Summers RS (2000) Economics and the autonomy of law, legal analysis and legal theory. In: Legal analysis and legal theory, Rechtstheorie, Beiheft 10, Dordrecht, Kluwer, pp 395–408
Sunstein CR (2014a) The real world of cost-benefits analysis: thirty-six questions (and almost as many answers). C Law Rev 114 (1)
Sunstein CR (2014b) The limits of quantification. Calif Law Rev 103:1369
Sullivan JL, Pierson J, Marcus GE (1982) Political tolerance and American democracy. University of Chicago Press, Chicago

Suzor NP (2019) Lawless: the secret rules that govern our digital lives. Cambridge University Press, Cambridge, United Kingdom, pp 1–218

Tegmark M (2018) Life 3.0: being human in the age of artificial intelligence. Knopf, New York, pp 1–384 (pp. 24 and ff)

Triandis HC (1989) Cross-cultural studies of individualism and collectivism. In: Nebraska symposium on motivation. University of Nebraska Press, Lincoln, pp 41–133

Wu T (2019) Will artificial intelligence eat the law? The rise of hybrid social-ordering systems. C Law Rev 119:2001 and ff

GPSR Compliance
The European Union's (EU) General Product Safety Regulation (GPSR) is a set of rules that requires consumer products to be safe and our obligations to ensure this.

If you have any concerns about our products, you can contact us on

ProductSafety@springernature.com

In case Publisher is established outside the EU, the EU authorized representative is:

Springer Nature Customer Service Center GmbH
Europaplatz 3
69115 Heidelberg, Germany

www.ingramcontent.com/pod-product-compliance
Ingram Content Group UK Ltd.
Pitfield, Milton Keynes, MK11 3LW, UK
UKHW022211051026
15624UKWH00001B/119
9789819721825